# An Alaskan Reader

*Books by* ERNEST GRUENING

THESE UNITED STATES (editor)
MEXICO AND ITS HERITAGE
THE PUBLIC PAYS, AND STILL PAYS
THE STATE OF ALASKA
THE BATTLE FOR ALASKA STATEHOOD
AN ALASKAN READER (editor)

# An Alaskan Reader
## 1867–1967

*Selected and edited by*

ERNEST GRUENING
U.S. SENATOR FROM ALASKA

Meredith Press  New York

F
904
G69

*First edition*

To Dorothy, my beloved wife,
devoted comrade through the years,
in joy and in sorrow

# ACKNOWLEDGMENTS

For arrangements with various authors or their representatives and publishers and for their courtesy in permitting the reprinting of copyrighted material, the following credits are gratefully given:

Chapters VII and XI of *Personal Exposures* by Rex Beach. Copyright 1940 by Rex Beach. Reprinted by permission of Harper & Row, Publishers.

From *Bering's Voyages: An Account of the Efforts of the Russians to Determine the Relations of Asia and America*, Volume 2, edited by Frederick A. Golder. American Geographical Society, Research Series No. 2, 1925. Reprinted by permission of American Geographical Society.

From *Look to the Wilderness* by W. Douglas Burden. Copyright © 1960 by W. Douglas Burden, with permission of Atlantic-Little, Brown and Company.

"The Proud Eskimo *Igloo*-Wife" from *Moonlight at Midday* by Sally Carrighar. Copyright © 1958 by Sally Carrighar. Reprinted by permission of Alfred A. Knopf, Inc.

From *Russian America* by Hector Chevigny. Copyright © 1965 by Hector Chevigny. Reprinted by permission of The Viking Press, Inc.

From *My Wilderness: The Pacific West* by William O. Douglas. Copyright © 1960 by William O. Douglas. Reprinted by permission of Doubleday & Company, Inc.

From *Ice Palace* by Edna Ferber. Copyright © 1958 by Edna Ferber.

From "The Last New Land" by Harmon R. Helmericks, *Alaska Sportsman*, November 1965. Reprinted by permission of the author and *Alaska Sportsman*.

"Change" by Charles J. Keim, *Alaska Review*, Fall 1964. Reprinted by permission of Charles J. Keim.

"The Rhyme of the Three Sealers" by Rudyard Kipling. Reprinted in Canada by permission of Mrs. George Bambridge and The Macmillan Company of Canada.

From *North to the Orient*, copyright 1935, 1963, by Anne Morrow Lindbergh. Reprinted by permission of Harcourt, Brace & World, Inc.

"Lost Face," "To Build a Fire," and "Too Much Gold" by Jack London, copyright 1910, copyright renewed 1938. Reprinted by permission of Irving Shepard.

"The Alaska Grizzly" by Harold McCracken, *Field & Stream*, 1941. Reprinted by permission of the author and *Field & Stream*.

From *Bezaubernde Wildnis* ("Enchanted Wilderness") by Hans Otto Meissner. Reprinted by permission of the author.

"Billy Mitchell in Alaska" by Brig. Gen. William Mitchell, *American Heritage*, February 1961. Reprinted by permission of Lucy Mitchell Gilpin.

From *History of U.S. Naval Operations in World War II*, Volume VII, *Aleutians, Gilberts and Marshalls*. Copyright 1951 by Samuel Eliot Morison. Reprinted by permission of the author and Atlantic-Little, Brown and Company, publishers.

From *Travels in Alaska* by John Muir. Reprinted by permission of Houghton Mifflin Company.

From "Beating the Arctic Bush" by Richard L. Neuberger, *Collier's Magazine*, April 17, 1948. Reprinted by permission of Maurine B. Neuberger.

From *My Life of High Adventure* by Grant H. Pearson with Philip Newill. Reprinted by permission of Prentice-Hall, Inc.

"The Trail of Ninety-eight" and "The Law of the Yukon" by Robert W. Service. Reprinted by permission of Dodd, Mead & Company, Inc., from *The Collected Poems of Robert Service*. Copyright 1916, 1921 by Dodd, Mead & Company, Inc. Reprinted in Canada from *The Collected Poems of Robert W. Service* by permission of the Ryerson Press, Toronto.

From *Ten Thousand Miles with a Dog Sled* by Hudson Stuck. Reprinted by permission of Charles Scribner's Sons.

" 'The Great One': The Story of Mount McKinley" from *High Conquest* by James Ramsey Ullman. Copyright 1941 by James Ramsey Ullman. Published by J. B. Lippincott Company.

From *Old Yukon: Tales—Trails—and Trials* by James Wickersham. Reprinted by permission of Washington Law Book Company.

"Day of Terror" by Forest H. Young, Jr., *Outdoor Life*, June 1957. Reprinted from *Outdoor Life*. Copyright © 1957.

From *Hall Young of Alaska: The Mushing Parson* by Samuel Hall Young. Reprinted by permission of Fleming H. Revell Company.

"The Nome Creek Ghost" by Darrill R. Kniffen, *Alaska Review*, Winter, 1965. Copyright © Alaska Methodist University. Reprinted by permission of the author and Alaska Methodist University.

# CONTENTS

# INTRODUCTION

THE physical facts concerning Alaska are impressive. Its area of 586,400 square miles makes it larger than the combined areas of the next three largest states, Texas, California, and Montana. An often-reproduced map of Alaska superimposed upon the older forty-eight states shows Alaska touching the Atlantic and Pacific Oceans, the Canadian and Mexican boundaries. So that, although only one fifth in area of what before Alaskan statehood were the forty-eight United States, Alaska is as wide and as deep as they. Its coastline of 26,000 miles is longer than their combined Atlantic, Gulf, and Pacific coastlines. It contains four time zones and would have five but for the international dateline being obligingly bent far westward to foreclose any part of Alaska being tomorrow—a day ahead of the rest of it. It will surprise many that Attu, Alaska's westernmost island, is farther west than Auckland, New Zealand. Alaska is thus America's farthest north and west, and also, since Alaska extends into the eastern hemisphere, America's farthest east! Its vertical dimensions are correspondingly striking; Mount McKinley's 20,300 feet make it the loftiest peak in North America, and ten other mountains are higher than those in any of the other states.

In contrast, Alaska's population is the smallest of any state. It was estimated at 250,000 in the mid-sixties, though growing, and it is the youngest, for the median age in 1966 was 23.3—seven years younger than in the rest of the nation. Of this population, perhaps one sixth is of aboriginal stock: Eskimos in the north and far west; Aleuts, an Eskimoid people who live along the Alaska Peninsula and Aleutian Island chain; and Indians, Athapaskan in the interior, and Tlingit, Haida, and Tsimpsian in the southeast. The other five sixths emigrated largely from the area of the forty-eight states; a few, directly from the Old World. In venturing to Alaska, they followed the oldest American trend—the westward quest for greater freedom and greater opportunity. These pioneers affectionately called Alaska "the last frontier," as indeed it has been, in America—both in time and in space. For the first significant trek to Alaska came only at the turn of the century, with the gold discoveries in the Klondike, then in the Tanana Valley and around Nome. Till then Alaska was a forgotten and abandoned province, vouchsafed not even the traditional appellation of Territory, but a mere District. The nation's greater concern for settling the West, Alaska's ill-founded repute as an unhabitable wasteland, and Federal neglect caused it to lie dormant till the close of the nineteenth century. When the gold fever subsided, downright governmental discrimination aggravated its previous neglect and Alaska stagnated for the twentieth century's first four decades. World War II and the belated recognition of Alaska's strategic position brought a rediscovery of Alaska by the American people. Alaskans' insistence on their previously totally lacking defenses and their increasing awareness of the unrelieved discriminations by a distant Federal government galvanized the drive for statehood. They deemed it an overdue fulfillment of the pledge in the Treaty of Cession that the inhabitants of the ceded territory would be admitted to the "enjoyment of all the rights, privileges and immunities of citizens of the United States."

A pro-statehood resolution was adopted and a referendum to ascertain Alaskans' views was provided by the 1945 legislature for the 1946 election. For the next eight years hearings were held in Washington, D.C., and in Alaska by the appropriate Senate and House committees. Their reports were unvaryingly favorable but action in both houses in the same Congress was not forthcoming, although public sentiment in the nation increasingly supported Alaska's aspiration for statehood.

Impatient at the delay, the 1955 Territorial legislature provided for a constitutional convention which would draw up a constitution for the hoped-for state. Elected by popular vote, fifty-five delegates assembled on the campus of the University of Alaska. In seventy-five days they drafted a document that political scientists declared was at least as good as, if not better than, any existing state constitution. The delegates approved a further proposal to be submitted to the voters: Should they, in advance of action by the Congress, elect two senators and a representative and send them to the national capital? This idea, brought to the convention by a public-spirited Louisianian named George H. Lehleitner, who believed deeply that Hawaii and Alaska should have statehood, had its genesis in earlier American history. In 1796 the people of the area lying west of North Carolina, vexed at the failure of the first three Congresses to grant them statehood, and contrasting this delay with Kentucky's admission in 1792, elected two senators and sent them to the national capital to lobby the Congress for statehood. They were successful. Tennessee became the sixteenth state. A similar procedure was adopted by six other states: Michigan in 1837, Iowa in 1846, California in 1850, Minnesota in 1858, Oregon in 1859, and Kansas in 1861. But nearly a century had elapsed since this bold procedure, and it had been all but forgotten. The Alaska Constitutional Convention approved placing such a proposal on the ballot when the voters would be asked to accept or reject the constitution. They approved both. So, under the Alaska-Tennessee Plan, as it was called, Alaskans elected two senators and a representative and sent them to Washington. While not accepted by the Congress in their assigned roles, they devoted the next two years to persuading their future colleagues to grant Alaska statehood. They succeeded. House and Senate enacted the necessary legislation in 1958, and President Eisenhower proclaimed Alaska's statehood on January 3, 1959.

Substantial obstacles had been overcome to achieve that long-awaited result. For the first time a noncontiguous area was admitted to the Union. But the action constituted a ringing reaffirmation of that most basic of American principles: Government by consent of the governed.

Alaska's diversity and unique past are reflected in the selections that follow. In prose and poetry they deal with episodes in its brief recorded history of two and a quarter centuries, with its people and some of their adventures, with its superlative natural heritage. It seems appropriate and timely that these varied fragments of a part of the great American epic be assembled as Alaska is celebrating in 1967 the centennial of its purchase, and as a prologue to a more challenging and significant future for the Forty-ninth State.

E. G.

# An Alaskan Reader

# 1

# THE DISCOVERY OF ALASKA

VITUS BERING'S voyages brought the first "discovery" of America from the West. Over two centuries ago the only inhabited portion of the earth that was undiscovered and unmapped was the northwest coast of North America, whose outlines on all previous maps disappeared north of Cape Mendocino in California. Prior to Peter the Great's commissioning of Bering's expeditions, it was unknown whether Asia and America were joined, or whether a subcontinental mass lay between them.

The two vessels for Bering's second expedition left Petropavlovsk on June 4, 1741. The *St. Peter*, commanded by Bering, and the *St. Paul*, commanded by Alexei Chirikov, became separated on June 20 and never again found each other. Chirikov's ship sighted land on July 15, the coast of one of the islands in the Alexander Archipelago—southeastern Alaska. On July 18 he sent a boat ashore in charge of a fleetmaster and ten armed men. It rounded a point and was not seen again. Assuming, after an anxious six-day wait, that the boat had been damaged, on July 24 the *St. Paul's* remaining boat was sent ashore with a carpenter and a caulker. On the next day, two boats, which were at first taken to be the *St. Paul's*, put out from the shore but proved to be manned by paddlers, not oarsmen, and hence were clearly those of natives. Shouts were exchanged and on the *St. Paul* handkerchiefs were waved in the hope of drawing the boats nearer. But they returned to shore and into the bay into which the *St. Paul's* two boats had

1

gone. Her second boat likewise failed to return. The sea had been calm and the conclusion reached was that their two crews had been killed. To this day their fate has remained a mystery. The place of this disaster has been identified as five miles west southwest of Lisianski Strait off Chichagof Island. The *St. Paul* was now short of water and had no more small boats. Reluctantly her officers ordered the return to Petropavlovsk, which the vessel reached on October 12.

The *St. Peter* sighted land on July 15. The sky had been overcast. Suddenly the clouds parted and the snowy cone of Mount St. Elias, rising over 18,000 feet from the sea, exposed itself to the gaze of the awestruck crew. On board was German-born Georg Steller, who had been attracted to what seemed the greater opportunities of St. Petersburg. He had studied medicine and botany and had achieved his heartfelt desire to accompany Bering's expedition as its naturalist. Steller had difficulties with his shipmates because of an understandable intellectual arrogance, a somewhat quarrelsome disposition, and a tendency, based on his superior intellect and education, to criticize and inject his counsels into affairs for which he had no direct responsibility. He was at first refused permission to land on Kayak Island, the *St. Peter*'s first landfall. Having overcome that obstacle, he was, however, denied the assistance to which he felt, properly, his mission entitled him, and his time for exploration there and at a subsequent landfall on Nagai Island were ruthlessly cut short. His frustrations were amply compensated for, however, after the wreck of the *St. Peter* on Bering Island, where he and the survivors of the crew spent the winter—and where Bering died of scurvy—before building a vessel from the wreckage of the *St. Peter* which carried them safely home to Petropavlovsk, where they had been given up for dead. During his nine months on Bering Island, despite physical hardships, Steller was able to put his knowledge and enterprise to good purpose, so that he was able, in his subsequently published great work, *De bestiis marinis,* to give the world its first account of four previously unknown marine mammals—the fur seal, the sea otter, the sea lion, and sea cow. The first two of these were to be of tremendous economic value and promptly brought about the eastward outpouring of Russian hunters and the consequent inclusion of Russian America in the Czar's dominions.

Steller also discovered and described in detail another animal which has become extinct, the spectacled cormorant, as well as that most gorgeously plumed and swiftest of the four varieties of eider ducks which bears his name. His scientific zeal caused him to dissect a four-ton female sea cow—in the circumstances doubtless an unparalleled anatomical research venture.

But there was even more in the way of achievement. In his scant hours on Kayak Island, he collected among ten different, to him "strange and unknown" birds—one deep blue and crested—a likeness of which he recalled having seen, before leaving St. Petersburg, in a book newly published in London on the birds and plants of the Carolinas.

"This bird proved to me that we were really in America," his journal records. It was a startling yet correct assumption. Bering's first voyage, concluded in 1731, passing northward through the straits that now bear his name and rounding East Cape, had proved that Asia and America were not joined. But whether the land to the east was America or a large island—a subcontinent—was still unascertained. Bering's last voyage ascertained it. But Steller was the first to jump at that conclusion—on the first occasion possible— and was thus the first to discover and identify America on an expedition from the west. Thus, he well merits historian F. A. Golder's estimate that "his discoveries in America and on Bering Island insure him eternal fame." Moreover, apart from the two ships' logs, his was the only account of Bering's historic voyage that has come down to us. So, the following extract from his journal, recording his hours on Kayak Island, which indeed signifies the discovery of Alaska, is of historic value and interest.

Bering's voyages and Steller's diary had the benefit of thorough research by American historians, geographers, and naturalists. They were published by the American Geographic Society in 1922–25 and were edited by F. A. Golder, with the collaboration of Leonhard Stejneger, naturalist and author of the definitive biography of Steller, Captain E. P. Bertholf, Commandant of the U.S. Coast Guard, and Dr. Alfred H. Brooks of the U.S. Geological

Survey. In the American Geographic Society's volumes there were
numerous footnotes by the collaborators, most of which have been
omitted here. Several are retained, including one dealing with
Stejneger's visit to Kayak Island in 1922, where he sought to
identify the landmarks to which Steller refers.

From · · ·

*Bering's Voyages: An Account of the Efforts of the Rus-*
*sians to Determine the Relation of Asia and America,*
edited by Frederick A. Golder

We saw land as early as July 15, but because I was the first
to announce it and because forsooth it was not so distinct that a
picture could be made of it, the announcement, as usual, was regarded as one of my peculiarities; yet on the following day, in
very clear weather, it came into view in the same place. The land
was here very much elevated; the mountains, observed extending
inland, were so lofty that we could see them quite plainly at sea at
a distance of sixteen Dutch miles. I cannot recall having seen
higher mountains anywhere in Siberia and Kamchatka. The coast
was everywhere much indented and therefore provided with numerous bays and inlets close to the mainland.

Once having determined to tell the truth and be impartial in all
things, I must not fail to mention one circumstance which perhaps
may not escape the notice of the high authorities but may receive
an interpretation different from the actual facts. . . . It can easily be
imagined how happy every one was when land was finally sighted;
nobody failed to congratulate the Captain Commander, whom the
glory for the discovery mostly concerned. He, however, received
it all not only very indifferently and without particular pleasure,
but in the presence of all he even shrugged his shoulders while
looking at the land. Had the Commander survived and had he intended to take any action against his officers because of their mis-
doings, they would have been ready to point to his conduct then as
evidence of his evil-minded disposition. But the good Captain
Commander was much superior to his officers in looking into the

future, and in the cabin he expressed himself to me and Mr. Plenisner as follows: "We think now we have accomplished everything, and many go about greatly inflated, but they do not consider where we have reached land, how far we are from home, and what may yet happen; who knows but that perhaps trade winds may arise, which may prevent us from returning? We do not know this country; nor are we provided with supplies for a wintering."

. . . Now that we were close to land it was great fun to listen to the conflicting expressions of great self-conceit and expectations of future reward and pathetic effusions. Some would at once make for the shore and search for a harbor. Others represented this as very dangerous. However, everybody acted for himself, and no one made any representations to the Captain Commander. Councils and commissions, that were so often called on shore in case of trivial matters, were neglected now when we had come to the most important business and the culmination of the ten years' Kamchatka Expedition, and it was quite plain that we had nothing in common and nothing to keep us united except that we were locked up together on the same ship.

Since after July 16 more noteworthy happenings occurred daily than during the six preceding weeks, I shall from now on continue my record according to what took place each day.

On the 17th, the wind being light, we gradually drew nearer the land. On Saturday, the 18th, we were so close to it towards evening, that we were enabled to view with the greatest pleasure the beautiful forests close down to the sea, as well as the great level ground in from the shore at the foot of the mountains. The beach itself was flat, level, and, as far as we could observe, sandy. We kept the mainland to the right and sailed northwesterly in order to get behind a high island [1] which consisted of a single mountain covered with spruce trees only. This had to be accomplished by continuous tacking, as the wind was contrary, the coming night being consumed with this.

On Sunday, the 19th, we were opposite the northwestern [2] end of the island, about two miles distant. This morning there arose again

[1] Kayak Island.
[2] Northeastern or southwestern?

a petty quarrel. We had already noticed the day before the channel between the mainland and the island, and the thought occurred at once to me that a notably large stream must be flowing from the land into the channel, the current of which could be observed two miles from shore while the difference in the water could be inferred partly from the floating matter and partly from the lesser salinity; it was consequently my opinion that an attempt could have been made to enter this channel,[3] where it would have been just as safe to anchor as, if not safer than, in the place under the lee of the island selected on the 20th. It might even have been possible to find a harbor for our ship, with its nine feet draught, in the mouth of the river, which was large enough and therefore probably also deep enough. But the retort I got was, had I been there before and made certain of it? Yet in uncertain things it is better to act on even the slightest indication than for no reason at all and only trusting to good luck.

The day was spent in tacking in order to get close to the island, to enter the large bay seen from the distance, and at the same time to come under the lee of the land. This was also accomplished, with the greatest apprehension, when on Monday the 20th we came to anchor among numerous islands. The outermost of these had to be named Cape St. Elias, because we dropped our anchor under the lee of it on St. Elias' day. For the officers were determined to have a cape on their chart notwithstanding the fact that it was plainly represented to them that an island cannot be called a cape,[4] but that only a noticeable projection of land into the sea in a certain direction can be so designated, the same meaning being conveyed by the Russian word *nos* (nose), while in the present case the island would represent nothing but a detached head or a detached nose.

Orderly management as well as the importance of the matter would now have demanded a harmonious consideration of what

[3] Steller's observation of physical phenomena was excellent, in thus deducing the presence of the river now called the Bering River and other glacial streams descending from Bering Glacier; the naval officers, however, were correct in their decision to sail around the southern end of Kayak Island, as the channel between it and the mainland, according to the modern chart of the region (U.S. Coast and Geodetic Survey Chart No. 8513), shoals to four feet before reaching the mouth of Bering River channel.

[4] The officers called the island St. Elias and its southern cape, Cape St. Elias. The cape is still so called.

ought to be done, how to utilize the time and opportunity to the best advantage, what to explore on shore and how to go about it; furthermore, whether, considering the season and the provisions as well as the distance, the following up of the coast should be continued at this late time of the year, or whether we should winter here, or, finally, try the straight way for home. However, all this was not considered worthy the calling of a council, but everyone kept silent and did as he pleased. Only on one point were all unanimous, viz. that we should take fresh water on board, so that I could not help saying that we had come only for the purpose of bringing American water to Asia. It was agreed, besides, that the small yawl should be used for the transportation of the water, while the larger one should be given to Master Khitrov with a sufficient crew and ammunition in order that he might explore the country, a task for which he possessed the best qualifications. I asked to be sent with Khitrov, since after all he himself did not know everything, but in spite of his making the same request permission was refused. At first an attempt was made to scare me with dreadful tales of murder, to which I answered that I had never been so womanish as to fear danger and that I could not guess why I should not be allowed to go ashore, especially since that was in the line of my principal work, my calling, and my duty and that it was my determination to serve the Crown to the best of my ability in the future, as I had done in the past; moreover, that, if for reprehensible reasons I were not given the permission, I would report this action in the terms it deserved. For this I was called a wild man, who would not let himself be held back from business even when treated to chocolate, which was just then being prepared. Seeing now that it was the intention to force me against my will to inexcusable neglect of my duty, I finally put all respect aside and prayed a particular prayer,[5] by which the Commander was at once mollified so as to let me go ashore with the water carriers, without any assistance whatever and with no other person but the cossack

[5] The meaning of this passage is scarcely doubtful. It is plain that Steller was very much wrought up by the refusal to let him go ashore, and a few lines above he had threatened to report the officers for their action. Lauridsen (*Vitus Bering*, Danish edition, p. 136; American edition, p. 151) therefore—and probably correctly—regards the "particular prayer" as a euphemism for an oath.

Thomas Lepekhin, whom I myself had brought with me. On my leaving the ship he again made a test as to how far I could distinguish between mockery and earnest, by causing the trumpets to be sounded after me, at which, without hesitation, I accepted the affair in the spirit in which it was ordered. By this time I saw only too clearly why he had wanted to persuade me to go along. I was to fulfill in my person one point of the instructions, in regard to which it would otherwise have been impossible to give an accounting, namely that which related to the investigation of the mineral resources by certain properly qualified persons. For eight years it had been forgotten to requisition them from Ekaterinburg,[6] and the assayer Hartepol, who was staying at Okhotsk, had been sent to Yakutsk in order to accompany Spanberg, so that at the departure he could not be taken along. Under the circumstances it was intended that I, though only in name, should confer upon the whole affair a greater distinction and at the same time fill the office of ship's doctor and physician in ordinary, since with an assistant surgeon it was considered that [the expedition] was too poorly supplied.

The events of the day consequently relate to four distinct parties: Half of the command, including all of the officers except the master [Khitrov], remained on board as watch busying themselves with hauling out the empty and stowing away the filled water casks. With another party I was sent off after water, to make watery observations, while others were out on a windy expedition.

As soon as I, with only the protection and assistance of my own cossack, had landed on the island [7] and realized how scant and

6 Ekaterinburg, in the Urals, was founded by Peter in 1723 and named in honor of the Empress. This city soon became an important mining center.

7 The landing place and other points of Steller's route were identified by me during a visit to Kayak Island on June 30, 1922. This visit was made as a side trip while I was a member of the party which accompanied the Assistant Secretary of Commerce on a voyage in the U.S. Coast Guard vessel *Mojave* to examine into the conditions of the fisheries and other industries of Alaska. From Cordova, at which port the *Mojave* had called, Katalla was reached by motor boat. From here another motor boat was used for the trip to the island. Six hours, from 6 P.M. to midnight, were spent on the island, during which the western shore was followed on foot northeastward for 2 statute miles from our landing place.

This landing place was chosen after inquiring of the owner of the boat, a local resident, where a ship wanting to take in water would be most likely to find it. He pointed out the mouth of a creek about 7 statute miles from the southern end of the

precious was the time at my disposal, I seized every opportunity
to accomplish as much as possible with the greatest possible dispatch. I struck out in the direction of the mainland in the hopes
of finding human beings and habitations. I had not gone more than
a verst along the beach before I ran across signs of people and
their doings. Under a tree I found an old piece of a log hollowed
out in the shape of a trough, in which, a couple of hours before,
the savages, for lack of pots and vessels, had cooked their meat
by means of red-hot stones, just as the Kamchadals did formerly.
The bones, some of them with bits of meat and showing signs of
having been roasted at the fire, were scattered about where the
eaters had been sitting. I could see plainly that these bones belonged to no sea animal, but to a land animal, and I thought myself justified in regarding them as reindeer bones,[8] though no such
animal was observed on the island but was probably brought there
from the mainland. There were also strewn about the remains of
yukola, or pieces of dried fish, which, as in Kamchatka, has to
serve the purpose of bread at all meals. There were also great
numbers of very large scallops over eight inches across, also blue
mussels similar to those found in Kamchatka and, no doubt, eaten
raw as the custom is there. In various shells, as on dishes, I found
sweet grass completely prepared in Kamchadal fashion, on which
water seemed to have been poured in order to extract the sweetness.
I discovered further, not far from the fireplace, beside the tree, on
which there still were the live coals, a wooden apparatus for making fire, of the same nature as those used in Kamchatka. The tinder,
however, which the Kamchadals make from a species of grass,
was here different, namely a species of fountain moss (*Alga fonti-
nalis*), which was bleached white by the sun and of which I have

---

island. On landing there we found a small stream of clear, cold water rushing out of
a dark wood of spruce. These conditions, together with the fact that there is no
other suitable watering place along this stretch of shore and that this point is about
6 versts, or 4 miles, from a hill descending abruptly into the sea, all of which closely
agrees with Steller's statements, makes it highly probable that the mouth of the
creek was the spot where Steller landed. With this point established, it was possible
to identify other points on Steller's route [Stejneger].

[8] Steller was probably correct in identifying the bones found as those of reindeer,
or caribou. The region is a typical caribou country. The species is probably *Rangifer
stonei Allen*, originally described from the Kenai Peninsula.

kept a sample to be forwarded. . . . From all this I think I may
conclude that the inhabitants of this American coast are of the
same origin as the Kamchadals, with whom they agree completely
in such peculiar customs and utensils, particularly the preparation
of the sweet grass, which have not been communicated even to the
Siberian natives nearest to Kamchatka, for instance the Tunguses
and Koryaks. But if this is so, then it may also be conjectured that
America extends farther westward and, opposite Kamchatka, is
much nearer in the north, since in view of such a great distance as
we traveled of at least 500 miles, it is not credible that the Kamchadals would have been able to get there in their miserable craft.

The chopped-down trees, as I came across them here and there,
were miscut with many dull blows in such a way that in all likelihood the cutting of trees must be done by these savages, as in
Kamchatka, with stone or bone axes similar to those used by the
Germans of old and known today as "thunderbolts."

After having made a brief examination of all this I pushed on
farther for about three versts, where I found a path leading into
the very thick and dark forest which skirted the shore closely. I
held a brief consultation with my cossack, who had a loaded gun,
besides a knife and ax, as to what we should do in case we met one
or more persons, and I commanded him to do nothing whatever
without my orders. I myself was only armed with a Yakut palma
(dagger) for the purpose of digging up rocks and plants. No sooner
had we taken this path than I noticed that the natives had tried to
cover it up but had been prevented by our quick approach and as a
results had made it only more conspicuous. We saw many trees
recently bared of bark and conjectured that they must have used
it for houses or *ambars* [9] and that these must be near by, since in
whatever direction we looked there was no lack of fine forests.
However, as the first trail broke up into a number of paths through
the forest, we explored some of them for a little distance into the
wood, and after half an hour we came to a spot covered with cut
grass. I pushed the grass aside at once and found underneath a
cover consisting of rocks; and when this was also removed we
came to some tree bark, which was laid on poles in an oblong

[9] Russian word meaning storehouses or sheds.

rectangle three fathoms in length and two in width. All this covered a cellar two fathoms deep in which were the following objects: (1) lukoshkas, or utensils made of bark, one and a half ells high, filled with smoked fish of a species of Kamchatkan salmon at Okhotsk called *nerka* in the Tungus language but in Kamchatka known by the common name *krasnaya ryba*.[10] It was so cleanly and well prepared that I have never seen it as good in Kamchatka, and it also was much superior in taste to the Kamchatkan; (2) a quantity of *sladkaya trava* [or sweet grass], from which liquor is distilled; (3) different kinds of plants, whose outer skin had been removed like hemp, which I took for nettles, which grow here in profusion and perhaps are used, as in Kamchatka, for making fish nets; (4) the dried inner bark from the larch or spruce tree done up in rolls and dried; the same is used as food in time of famine, not only in Kamchatka but all through Siberia and even in Russia as far as Khlynov and elsewhere on the Vyatka; (5) large bales of thongs made of seaweed which, by making a test, we found to be of uncommon strength and firmness.

Under these I found also some arrows in size greatly exceeding those in Kamchatka and approaching the arrows of the Tunguses and Tatars, scraped very smooth and painted black, so that one might well conjecture that the natives possessed iron instruments and knives.

In spite of my fear of being attacked in the cellar I continued my search but, discovering nothing more, took away with me, as proof, two bundles of fish, the arrows, a wooden implement for making fire, tinder, a bundle of thongs of seaweed, bark, and grass and sent them by my cossack to the place where the water was being taken on, with instructions to bring them to the Captain Commander; at the same time I asked once more for two or three men to help me further in my investigations of nature; I also had those on shore warned not to feel too secure but to be well on their guard. I then covered over the cellar as it had been and proceeded, now all alone, with my project of investigating the noteworthy features of the three kingdoms of nature until my cossack should

[10] *Krasnaya ryba* (red fish) is the usual name in Kamchatka for the red salmon (*Oncorhynchus nerka*).

return. However, when I had gone about six versts, I came to a
steep rock extending so far into the sea beyond the beach that it
was impossible to go farther.[11] I determined to climb the rock and
after much difficulty reached the top, where I discovered that the
east side was steep as a wall and that it was impossible to proceed
farther. I therefore turned south in the hope of getting to the other
side of the island in order to follow the beach there to the channel
and thus investigate my theory regarding the existence there of a
river and harbor. However, as I descended the mountain, which
was covered with a thick and dark forest, without finding any trace
of a path, I saw that I could not get through here. Considering at
the same time that it would be impossible for my cossack to find me,
also that I was too far away from the others in case something
should happen, and that it might be impossible for me to return
before nightfall, not to mention other dangers, which I should not
have feared had I had the least assistance of companions, I climbed
the mountain again and looked once more sorrowfully at the barrier to my investigations, with real regret over the action of those
who had in their hands the direction of such important matters, for
which nevertheless all of them had let themselves be rewarded with
money and honors.

When I was once more on the top of the mountain and turned my
eyes toward the mainland to take a good look at least at that
country on which I was not vouchsafed to employ my endeavors
more fruitfully, I noticed smoke some versts away ascending from
a charming hill covered with spruce forest, so that I could now
entertain the certain hope of meeting with people and learning

[11] This rock, later in the journal referred to as a mountain, was identified during
my 1922 visit as the hill about 250 to 300 feet high which is shown on the chart as
a bold projection from the western shore of the island in 59° 56′ N. and which
appears in the background of two of the photographs. Although I was not able to
approach its base nearer than a mile and a half, because of a comparatively recent
rock fall which made progress along the shore impossible at this point, the general
topographical relations and the agreement of distances with those given by Steller
made the identification practically certain.

This hill is without a name. It would seem eminently fitting that it should bear the
name of the naturalist who first set foot here on Alaskan soil, and it is herewith
proposed, as was previously done in regard to a similar feature on Bering Island
(*Deutsche Geogr. Blätter*, Bremen, Vol. 8, 1884, p. 226 and Pl. 5), that this piece of
classic ground in the history of American discovery be called "Steller's Hill"
[Stejneger].

from them the data I needed for a complete report. For that reason I returned in great haste and went back, loaded with my collections, to the place where I had landed. Through the men who were just ready to hurry back to the ship in the boat I informed the Captain Commander and asked him for the small yawl and a few men for a couple of hours. Dead tired, I made in the meantime descriptions on the beach of the rarer plants which I was afraid might wither and was delighted to be able to test out the excellent water for tea.

In an hour or so I received the patriotic and courteous reply that I should betake myself on board quickly or they would leave me ashore without waiting for me. . . . I reflected that God gives to each one the place and the opportunity to do that which he is ordered to do, so as to enable one to present one's services favorably to the highest authorities and after long waiting and untold expenses to the Empress [i.e. Government] work out one's destinies. However, as matters now stand, it is probable that at our departure we all saw Russia for the last time, since under the present circumstances it is impossible to expect the divine help on the return voyage, if wind and weather were to become as hostile [toward us] as we have been to the general object of the expedition and thereby to our own good fortune. . . . However, since there was now no time left for moralizing, only enough to scrape together as much as possible before our fleeing the country, and as evening was already nearing, I sent my cossack out to shoot some rare birds that I had noticed, while I once more started off to the westward, returning at sunset with various observations and collections. . . . Here I was given once more the strict command that, unless I came on board this time, no more notice would be taken of me. I consequently betook myself with what I had collected to the ship and there, to my great astonishment, was treated to chocolate. . . .

Although I did not need to trouble myself for the benefit of anybody except those who were capable of judging what I was doing, I nevertheless showed some of the objects and made known my ideas about various things, but only a single one of these was accepted. Namely, an iron kettle, a pound of tobacco, a Chinese pipe, and a piece of Chinese silk were sent to the cellar, but in return the latter was plundered to such an extent that, if we should come again to these parts, the natives would certainly run away even faster or they would show themselves as hostile as they themselves had been treated, especially if it should occur to them to eat or drink the tobacco, the correct use of which probably could be as little known to them as the pipe itself. . . . A couple of knives or hatchets, the use of which was quite obvious, would have aroused the interest of these savages much more. But to this it was objected that such presents might be regarded as a sign of hostility, as if the intention were to declare war. How much more likely was it, particularly if they attempted to use the tobacco in the wrong way, for them to conclude that we had intended to poison them! On the other hand, we learned later how gladly the savages had accepted a few knives from Captain Chirikov and how eager they were to have more.

I had been on the ship scarcely an hour when Khitrov with his party of about fifteen men also returned in the great boat and made the following report. He had discovered among the islands lying close to the mainland a harbor where one could anchor without any danger. Although he had seen no human beings on land, he had nevertheless come across a small dwelling built of wood, the walls of which were so smooth that it seemed as if they had been planed and in fact as if it had been done with cutting tools. Out of this building he brought with him various tangible tokens, for instance, a wooden vessel, such as is made in Russia of linden bark and used as a box; a stone which perhaps, for lack of something better, served as a whetstone, on which were seen streaks of copper,[12] as if the savages, like the ancient Siberian tribes, possessed cutting tools of copper; further a hollow ball of hard-burned

---

[12] The stone on which Steller thought he recognized some stains of copper was probably a whetstone which had been used on some copper implement. It is, however, possible that the whetstone originally contained pyrite or chalcopyrite, which Steller mistook for native copper. Some native copper was obtained by the coast natives by trade with the interior natives. This copper came from two localities, one at the head of the White River and the other in the Chitina basin, tributary to the Copper River. In 1899 I met a party of natives searching for native copper nuggets on Kletsandek Creek, tributary to the upper White River. They used caribou horns for digging in the gravel banks of the streams.

clay, about two inches in diameter, containing a pebble which I regarded as a toy for small children; and finally a paddle and the tail of a blackish gray fox.

These, then, are all our achievements and observations, and these not even from the mainland, on which none of us set foot, but only from an island which seemed to be three miles long and a half mile wide and the nearest to the mainland (which here forms a large bay studded with many islands) and separated from it by a channel less than half a mile wide. The only reason why we did not attempt to land on the mainland is a sluggish obstinacy and a dull fear of being attacked by a handful of unarmed and still more timid savages, from whom there was no reason to expect either friendship or hostility, and a cowardly homesickness which they probably thought might be excused, especially if those high in authority would pay no more attention to the testimony of the malcontents than did the commanding officers themselves. The time here spent in investigation bears an arithmetical ratio to the time used in fitting out: ten years the preparations for this great undertaking lasted, and ten hours were devoted to the work itself. Of the mainland we have a sketch on paper; of the country itself an imperfect idea, based upon what could be discovered on the island and upon conjectures.

What can be said from comparison and observations at a distance may be summed up about as follows: The American continent (on this side), as far as the climate is concerned, is notably better than that of the extreme northeastern part of Asia. For, although the land, wherever it faces the sea, whether we looked at it from near or far, consists of amazingly high mountains,[13] most of which had the peaks covered with perpetual snow, yet these mountains, in comparison with those of Asia, are of a much better nature and character. The Asiatic mountains are thoroughly broken up and long since deprived of their coherency, consequently too loose for the circulation of mineral gases and devoid of all inner heat, ac-

[13] Steller refers to the high mountains of the St. Elias region, which is the part of Alaska he had best opportunity to see. The mountains of the Alaska Peninsula and Aleutian Islands, which he had some glimpses of, have somewhat similar topography and vegetation to those of the Kamchatka Peninsula.

cordingly also without precious metals.[14] On the other hand the American mountains are solid; not naked rocks covered with moss but everywhere with good black soil, and therefore not, as are the former, barren, with stunted dwarf trees among the rocks, but densely covered to the highest peaks with the finest trees; also they are decked with short grass and herbs, some succulent, some drier, but not with moss, marsh vegetation, and water plants. The springs, of which I discovered so many, flow out of the valleys at the base of the mountains, and not as in Siberia everywhere among the rocks, often up to the summits and in stagnant hollows. The plants are about the same size and appearance whether found on the summit of the mountains or lower down, owing to the equally distributed interior heat and moisture. In Asia, on the other hand, the plants are often so different according to their station that one is tempted to make different species of the same plant if one is not mindful of this general difference, because a plant which in the valley is two ells high often on the mountains reappears scarcely half a foot high. . . . In America on the 60th parallel one sees most beautiful forests directly on the shore, while in latitude 51° in Kamchatka willow and alder bushes only begin 20 versts from the sea, birch woods not nearer than 30 to 40 versts, not to mention that no conifers are found there but are first seen 60 versts inland from the mouth of the Kamchatka River. In latitude 62° for instance from Anadyrsk on, no tree is to be met with for 300 or 400 versts inland. I therefore hold that continuous land must extend northwards from Cape St. Elias to about 70° or farther,[15] which by furnishing shelter against the north wind promotes the fertility of the coast, which moreover, towards the east, is protected by the mountains. On the other hand the Kamchatkan shores, particularly on the Sea of Penzhina, are directly exposed to the north winds; while the eastern side is somewhat better provided with trees, because of the protection of the Chukchi Promontory.[16]

[14] The student of the history of science will be interested in these and other obsolete views, such as that immediately below on the geothermal control of plant distribution, expressed by Steller in this summary of the physical geography of Kayak Island.

[15] It is of interest to note the remarkable accuracy of this deduction of Steller's.

[16] The climate of Kamchatka is somewhat colder than that of Alaska lying between the same parallels of latitude. Steller's theory that the geologic constitution of the mountains directly controls the distribution of vegetation is without merit. Kamchatka

... Owing to the milder temperature it also comes about that in America the fishes go up from the sea earlier than in Kamchatka. On July 20 we found there the fish supply already stored, while in Kamchatka this, the day of St. Elias, indicates the time only for the beginning of good fishing. That plants which only start to bloom in Kamchatka at this time already have mature seed here in America is only a partial argument, because in the northern regions the usually longer days and the sudden great heat and dryness contribute greatly to this result, as I had already observed in Yakutsk in 1740.

Whoever stops to consider how much one man, without assistance, can accomplish in ten hours on a small island will easily see that my failure to discover any minerals is not due to carelessness or laziness on my part. I confess freely that I observed nothing else than sand and gray rock.

Of fruit-bearing shrubs and plants I only met with a new and elsewhere unknown species of raspberry in great abundance, although not yet quite ripe. This fruit on account of its great size, shape, and delicious taste had well deserved that a few bushes of it should have been taken along in a box with soil and sent to St. Petersburg to be further propagated. It is not my fault that space for such was begrudged, since as a protester I myself took up too much space already.... Such well-known berries as the Chamaecerasi, red and black whortleberries, the scurvy berry, Empetrum, and such like were here as plentiful as in Kamchatka. The other plants collected by me in America I have recorded in a separate list.

The animals occurring there and supplying the natives with their meat for food and with their skins for clothing are, so far as I had opportunity to observe, hair seals, large and small sharks,[17]

---

lies within the region of permanent ground frost, which is not true of the Pacific littoral of Alaska. This to some extent influences the distribution of springs. The comparisons between the soil and vegetation of Kamchatka and the part of Alaska which he knew best are in general correct. The differences are largely due to differences of climate [Bertholf].

[17] The number of species of sharks known from Kamchatkan and Alaskan waters is not great. The large and small sharks seen by Steller may well have been the mackerel shark [*Lamna cornubica* (Gmelin)] and the dogfish [*Squalus sucklii* (Girard)], both common in the region [Stejneger].

whales, and plenty of sea otters, the excrements of which I found everywhere along the shore; from this circumstance it may also be concluded that the natives, because otherwise sufficiently provided with food, do not trouble themselves greatly about them, since otherwise these animals would not have come ashore, any more than they now do in Kamchatka, where there are so many people interested in their pelts. Of land animals, aside from what has been inferred above about the reindeer, I as well as others, saw at various times black and red foxes and did not find them particularly shy, perhaps because they are hunted but little. . . . Of birds I saw only two familiar species, the raven and the magpie; however, of strange and unknown ones I noted more than ten different kinds, all of which were easily distinguished from the European and Siberian [species] by their very particularly bright coloring. Good luck, thanks to my huntsman, placed in my hands a single specimen, of which I remember to have seen a likeness painted in lively colors and described in the newest account of the birds and plants of the Carolinas published in French and English, the name of the author of which, however, does not occur to me now.[18] This bird proved to me that we were really in America. I would have enclosed the drawing herewith, were it not that I had to leave it behind, as my return voyage had to be made on foot from Avacha to the Bolshaya River, and consequently it will have to be forwarded at some future time.

[18] The late lamented [Steller] refers to the work of the English traveler Catesby [Mark Catesby, *The Natural History of Carolina, Florida, and the Bahama Islands*, etc., 2 vols., London, 1731–43] and to Plate 15 in Vol. 1 of the English edition, on which the North American blue jay [*Cyanocitta cristata* (Linn.)] is figured, to which the bird observed by Steller, it is true, has considerable resemblance, but is a different species, as is sufficiently clear from Steller's description which will be published elsewhere. This bird, consequently, could give no proof as to America. But nobody, notwithstanding, will doubt that Steller really has been in America [Pallas].

Pallas is right with regard to Catesby, but singularly wrong in denying that Steller's bird furnished proof of its American origin. It was described by Gmelin, 1788, as *Corvus stelleri* and is a member of the same genus as our blue jay, which genus, *Cyanocitta*, is exclusively American, *Cyanocitta stelleri*, consequently, furnished conclusive proof that the expedition had reached America and vindicates Steller's excellent judgment. He must have had not only a wonderful memory to be able to remember Catesby's figure so well, but also a fine appreciation of zoogeographical relations to draw the above conclusion in 1741 [Stejneger].

# 𝒵

# *THE ERA OF*
# *ALEKSANDR BARANOV*

ALEKSANDR ANDREEVICH BARANOV (1746–1819) was the leading figure in the middle period of Russian occupation—the years 1790–1818—when he was the manager of the Russian-American Company and first governor of Russian America. In retrospect he looms up as the outstanding personality in the century and a quarter of Russia's American colony.

Frank A. Golder, the leading American authority of this period, summarizes him as follows:

> Baranof was a fur-trader rather than an empire builder. He worked for a company that demanded dividends and asked no questions as to means employed. He satisfied the company by exploiting the country and the natives. In this he was no worse than the average trader. He was superior to most of them, however, in that he succeeded against such odds. He had to depend on himself, on his fist and on his brain. This strenuous life began to tell on his health as he grew older. In 1809 he asked to be relieved, but it was not before 1858 that a successor appeared. Taken ill, he died at sea on his way back to Russia.

A partial explanation of Baranov's failing health may be found in the description of his habits in Chapter LVII of Washington Irving's *Astoria* which follows. Wilson Price Hunt, who was the commander of the Astoria overland expedition, was doubtless the chief source for Irving's not too favorable portrayal of Baranov.

From • • •

### Astoria, or, Anecdotes of an Enterprise Beyond the Rocky Mountains, by Washington Irving

It will be recollected, that the destination of the *Beaver*, when she sailed from Astoria on the 4th of August in 1812, was to proceed northwardly along the coast to Sheetka, or New Archangel, there to dispose of that part of her cargo intended for the supply of the Russian establishment at that place, and then to return to Astoria, where it was expected she would arrive in October.

New Archangel is situated in Norfolk Sound, lat. 57° 2′ N., long. 135° 50′ W. It was the head-quarters of the different colonies of the Russian Fur Company, and the common rendezvous of the American trading along the coast.

The *Beaver* met with nothing worthy of particular mention in her voyage, and arrived at New Archangel on the 19th of August. The place at that time was the residence of Count Baranhoff, the governor of the different colonies; a rough, rugged, hospitable, hard-drinking, old Russian; somewhat of a soldier, somewhat of a trader; above all, a boon companion of the old roystering school, with a strong cross of the bear.

Mr. Hunt found this hyperborean veteran ensconced in a fort which crested the whole of a high rocky promontory. It mounted one hundred guns, large and small, and was impregnable to Indian attack, unaided by artillery. Here the old governor lorded it over sixty Russians, who formed the corps of the trading establishment, besides an indefinite number of Indian hunters of the Kodiak tribe, who were continually coming and going, or lounging and loitering about the fort like so many hounds round a sportsman's hunting quarters. Though a loose liver among his guests, the governor was a strict disciplinarian among his men; keeping them in perfect subjection, and having seven on guard night and day.

Beside those immediate serfs and dependants just mentioned,

the old Russian potentate exerted a considerable sway over a numerous and irregular class of maritime traders, who looked to him for aid and munitions, and through whom he may be said to have, in some degree, extended his power along the whole northwest coast. These were American captains of vessels engaged in a particular department of the trade. One of these captains would come, in a manner, empty-handed to New Archangel. Here his ship would be furnished with about fifty canoes and a hundred Kodiak hunters, and fitted out with provisions, and everything necessary for hunting the sea-otter on the coast of California, where the Russians have another establishment. The ship would ply along the California coast from place to place, dropping parties of otter hunters in their canoes, furnishing them only with water, and leaving them to depend upon their own dexterity for a maintenance. When a sufficient cargo was collected, she would gather up her canoes and hunters, and return with them to Archangel; where the captain would render in the returns of his voyage, and receive one half of the skins for his share.

Over these coasting captains, as we have hinted, the veteran governor exerted some sort of sway, but it was of a peculiar and characteristic kind; it was the tyranny of the table. They were obliged to join him in his "prosnics" or carousals, and to drink "potations pottle deep." His carousals, too, were not of the most quiet kind, nor were his potations as mild as nectar. "He is continually," said Mr. Hunt, "giving entertainments by way of parade, and if you do not drink raw rum, and boiling punch as strong as sulphur, he will insult you as soon as he gets drunk, which is very shortly after sitting down to table."

As to any "temperance captain" who stood fast to his faith, and refused to give up his sobriety, he might go elsewhere for a market, for he stood no chance with the governor. Rarely, however, did any cold-water caitiff of the kind darken the door of old Baranhoff; the coasting captains knew too well his humor and their own interests; they joined in his revels, they drank, and sang, and whooped, and hiccuped, until they all got "half seas over," and then affairs went on swimmingly.

An awful warning to all "flinchers" occurred shortly before Mr.

Hunt's arrival. A young naval officer had recently been sent out by the emperor to take command of one of the company's vessels. The governor, as usual, had him at his "prosnics," and plied him with fiery potations. The young man stood on the defensive until the old count's ire was completely kindled; he carried his point, and made the greenhorn tipsy, willy nilly. In proportion as they grew fuddled they grew noisy, they quarrelled in their cups; the youngster paid old Baranhoff in his own coin by rating him soundly; in reward for which, when sober, he was taken the rounds of four pickets, and received seventy-nine lashes, taled out with Russian punctuality of punishment.

Such was the old grizzled bear with whom Mr. Hunt had to do business. How he managed to cope with his humor; whether he pledged himself in raw rum and blazing punch, and "clinked the can" with him as they made their bargains, does not appear upon record; we must infer, however, from his general observations on the absolute sway of this hard-drinking potentate, that he had to conform to the customs of his court, and that their business transactions presented a maudlin mixture of punch and peltry.

The greatest annoyance to Mr. Hunt, however, was the delay to which he was subjected, in disposing of the cargo of the ship, and getting the requisite returns. With all the governor's devotions to the bottle, he never obfuscated his faculties sufficiently to lose sight of his interest, and is represented by Mr. Hunt as keen, not to say crafty, at a bargain, as the most arrant water-drinker. A long time was expended negotiating with him, and by the time the bargain was concluded, the month of October had arrived. To add to the delay he was to be paid for his cargo in seal skins. Now it so happened that there was none of this kind of peltry at the fort of old Baranhoff. It was necessary, therefore, for Mr. Hunt to proceed to a seal-catching establishment, which the Russian company had at the island of St. Paul, in the Sea of Kamtschatka. He accordingly set sail on the 4th of October, after having spent forty-five days at New Archangel boosing and bargaining with its roystering commander, and right glad was he to escape from the clutches of "this old man of the sea."

Hector Chevigny, author of three popular as well as authoritative books on the Russian period in Alaska, writing over a century and a quarter later, gives a somewhat different picture of Baranov in a quotation from a Russian midshipman, Davidov, taken from Chevigny's book, *Lord of Alaska:*

> He [Baranov] is below average size, flaxen-haired, and thin. His face habitually wears an ingenuous expression which apparently has not been affected by either hardships or age, for he is already in his fifty-sixth year. He is reticent with strangers yet will argue with great warmth when he is interested.... He has lived for years among savage tribes, surrounded by continual danger, struggling against the innate depravity of the kind of Russian sent to this country, suffering endless privations and hardships—even hunger—unable to depend on a single man for the furtherance of his plans.... I have the feeling he would, in time, have found some means of establishing this huge enterprise all by himself, if he had been forced to.... He makes few acquaintances but stands firmly by his friends.... Complete disinterestedness is probably his chief characteristic. He is not eager to become wealthy and sends his gains to absent acquaintances in want....

# 3

## *A STORY OF RUSSIAN AMERICA*

JACK LONDON, known for his stories of the Gold Rush, wrote also of the Russian period. The following tale is a horrendous picture of the early Russian fur thieves and Indian reprisals.

### *Lost Face,* by Jack London

It was the end. Subienkow had traveled a long trail of bitterness and horror, homing like a dove for the capitals of Europe, and here, farther away than ever, in Russian America, the trail ceased. He sat in the snow, arms tied behind him, waiting the torture. He stared curiously before him at a huge Cossack, prone in the snow, moaning in his pain. The men had finished handling the giant and turned him over to the women. That they exceeded the fiendishness of the men the man's cries attested.

Subienkow looked on and shuddered. He was not afraid to die. He had carried his life too long in his hands, on that weary trail from Warsaw to Nulato, to shudder at mere dying. But he objected to the torture. It offended his soul. And this offense, in turn, was not due to the mere pain he must endure, but to the sorry spectacle the pain would make of him. He knew that he would pray, and beg, and entreat, even as Big Ivan and the others that had gone before. This would not be nice. To pass out bravely and cleanly, with a smile and a jest—ah, that would have been the way. But to lose control, to have his soul upset by the pangs of the flesh, to screech and gibber like an ape, to become the veriest beast—ah, that was what was so terrible.

There had been no chance to escape. From the beginning, when he dreamed the fiery dream of Poland's independence, he had become a puppet in the hands of fate. From the beginning, at Warsaw, at St. Petersburg, in the Siberian mines, in Kamchatka, on the crazy boats of the fur thieves, fate had been driving him to this end. Without doubt, in the foundations of the world was graved this end for him—for him, who was so fine and sensitive, whose nerves scarcely sheltered under his skin, who was a dreamer and a poet and an artist. Before he was dreamed of, it had been determined that the quivering bundle of sensitiveness that constituted him should be doomed to live in raw and howling savagery, and to die in this far land of night, in this dark place beyond the last boundaries of the world.

He sighed. So that thing before him was Big Ivan—Big Ivan the giant, the man without nerves, the man of iron, the Cossack turned freebooter of the seas, who was as phlegmatic as an ox, with a nervous system so low that what was pain to ordinary men was scarcely a tickle to him. Well, well, trust these Nulato Indians to find Big Ivan's nerves and trace them to the roots of his quivering soul. They were certainly doing it. It was inconceivable that a man could suffer so much and yet live. Big Ivan was paying for his low order of nerves. Already he had lasted twice as long as any of the others.

Subienkow felt that he could not stand the Cossack's sufferings much longer. Why didn't Ivan die? He would go mad if that screaming did not cease. But when it did cease, his turn would come. And there was Yakaga awaiting him, too, grinning at him even now in anticipation—Yakaga, whom only last week he had kicked out of the fort, and upon whose face he had laid the lash of his dog whip. Yakaga would attend to him. Doubtlessly Yakaga was saving for him more refined tortures, more exquisite nervewracking. Ah! That must have been a good one, from the way Ivan screamed. The squaws bending over him stepped back with laughter and clapping of hands. Subienkow saw the monstrous thing that that had been perpetrated, and began to laugh hysterically. The

Indians looked at him in wonderment that he should laugh. But
Subienkow could not stop.

This would never do. He controlled himself, the spasmodic
twitchings slowly dying away. He strove to think of other things,
and began reading back in his own life. He remembered his mother
and his father, and the little spotted pony, and the French tutor
who had taught him dancing and sneaked him an old worn copy of
Voltaire. Once more he saw Paris, and dreary London, and gay
Vienna, and Rome. And once more he saw that wild group of
youths who had dreamed, even as he, the dream of an independent
Poland with a king of Poland on the throne at Warsaw. Ah, there
it was that the long trail began. Well, he had lasted longest. One by
one, beginning with the two executed at St. Petersburg, he took up
the count of the passing of those brave spirits. Here one had been
beaten to death by a jailer, and there, on that bloodstained highway
of the exiles, where they had marched for endless months, beaten
and maltreated by their Cossack guards, another had dropped by
the way. Always it had been savagery—brutal, bestial savagery.
They had died—of fever, in the mines, under the knout. The last
two had died after the escape, in the battle with the Cossacks, and
he alone had won to Kamchatka with the stolen papers and the
money of a traveler he had left lying in the snow.

It had been nothing but savagery. All the years, with his heart
in studios and theaters and courts, he had been hemmed in by
savagery. He had purchased his life with blood. Everybody had
killed. He had killed that traveler for his passports. He had proved
that he was a man of parts by dueling with two Russian officers on
a single day. He had had to prove himself in order to win to a place
among the fur thieves. He had had to win to that place. Behind him
lay the thousand-years-long road across all Siberia and Russia.
He could not escape that way. The only way was ahead, across the
dark and icy sea of Bering to Alaska. The way had led from savagery to deeper savagery. On the scurvy-rotten ships of the fur
thieves, out of food and out of water, buffeted by the interminable
storms of that stormy sea, men had become animals. Thrice he had
sailed east from Kamchatka. And thrice, after all manner of hardship and suffering, the survivors had come back to Kamchatka.

There had been no outlet for escape, and he could not go back the way he had come, for the mines and the knout awaited him.

Again, the fourth and last time, he had sailed east. He had been with those who first found the fabled Seal Islands; but he had not returned with them to share the wealth of furs in the mad orgies of Kamchatka. He had sworn never to go back. He knew that to win to those dear capitals of Europe he must go on. So he had changed ships and remained in the dark new land. His comrades were Slavonian hunters and Russian adventurers, Mongols and Tatars and Siberian aborigines; and through the savages of the New World they had cut a path of blood. They had massacred whole villages that refused to furnish the fur tribute; and they in turn had been massacred by ships' companies. He, with one Finn, had been the sole survivors of such a company. They had spent a winter of solitude and starvation on a lonely Aleutian isle, and their rescue in the spring by another fur ship had been one chance in a thousand.

But always the terrible savagery had hemmed him in. Passing from ship to ship, and ever refusing to return, he had come to the ship that explored south. All down the Alaskan coast they had encountered nothing but hosts of savages. Every anchorage among the beetling islands or under the frowning cliffs of the mainland had meant a battle or a storm. Either the gales blew, threatening destruction, or the war canoes came off, manned by howling natives with the war paint on their faces, who came to learn the bloody virtues of the sea rovers' gunpowder. South, south they had coasted, clear to the myth land of California. Here, it was said, were Spanish adventurers who had fought their way up from Mexico. He had had hopes of those Spanish adventurers. Escaping to them, the rest would have been easy—a year or two, what did it matter more or less?—and he would win to Mexico, then a ship, and Europe would be his. But they had met no Spaniards. Only had they encountered the same impregnable wall of savagery. The denizens of the confines of the world, painted for war, had driven them back from the shores. At last, when one boat was cut off and every man killed, the commander had abandoned the quest and sailed back to the North.

The years had passed. He had served under Tebenkoff when Michaelovski Redoubt was built. He had spent two years in the Kuskokwim country. Two summers, in the month of June, he had managed to be at the head of Kotzebue Sound. Here, at this time, the tribes assembled for barter; here were to be found spotted deer-skins from Siberia, ivory from the Diomedes, walrus skins from the shores of the Arctic, strange stone lamps, passing in trade from tribe to tribe, no one knew whence, and, once, a hunting knife of English make; and here, Subienkow knew, was the school in which to learn geography. For he met Eskimos from Norton Sound, from King Island and St. Lawrence Island, from Cape Prince of Wales, and Point Barrow. Such places had other names, and their distances were measured in days.

It was a vast region these trading savages came from, and a vaster region from which, by repeated trade, their stone lamps and that steel knife had come. Subienkow bullied and cajoled and bribed. Every far journeyer or strange tribesman was brought before him. Perils unaccountable and unthinkable were mentioned, as well as wild beasts, hostile tribes, impenetrable forests, and mighty mountain ranges; but always from beyond came the rumor and the tale of white-skinned men, blue of eye and fair of hair, who fought like devils and who sought always for furs. They were to the east—far, far to the east. No one had seen them. It was the word that had been passed along.

It was a hard school. One could not learn geography very well through the medium of strange dialects, from dark minds that mingled fact and fable and that measured distances by "sleeps" that varied according to the difficulty of the going. But at last came the whisper that gave Subienkow courage. In the east lay a great river where were these blue-eyed men. The river was called the Yukon. South of Michaelovski Redoubt emptied another great river which the Russians knew as the Kwikpak. These two rivers were one, ran the whisper.

Subienkow returned to Michaelovski. For a year he urged an expedition up the Kwikpak. Then arose Malakoff, the Russian half-breed, to lead the wildest and most ferocious of the hell's broth of mongrel adventurers who had crossed from Kamchatka. Subienkow was his lieutenant. They threaded the mazes of the great delta of the Kwikpak, picked up the first low hills on the northern bank, and for half a thousand miles, in skin canoes loaded to the gunwales with trade goods and ammunition, fought their way against the five-knot current of a river that ran from two to ten miles wide in a channel many fathoms deep. Malakoff decided to build the fort at Nulato. Subienkow urged to go farther. But he quickly reconciled himself to Nulato. The long winter was coming on. It would be better to wait. Early the following summer, when the ice was gone, he would disappear up the Kwikpak and work his way to the Hudson Bay Company's posts. Malakoff had never heard the whisper that the Kwikpak was the Yukon, and Subienkow did not tell him.

Came the building of the fort. It was enforced labor. The tiered walls of logs arose to the sighs and groans of the Nulato Indians. The lash was laid upon their backs, and it was the iron hand of the freebooters of the sea that laid on the lash. There were Indians that ran away, and when they were caught they were brought back and spread-eagled before the fort, where they and their tribe learned the efficacy of the knout. Two died under it; others were injured for life; and the rest took the lesson to heart and ran away no more. The snow was flying ere the fort was finished, and then it was the time for furs. A heavy tribute was laid upon the tribe. Blows and lashings continued, and that the tribute should be paid, the women and children were held as hostages and treated with the barbarity that only the fur thieves knew.

Well, it had been a sowing of blood, and now was come the harvest. The fort was gone. In the light of its burning, half the fur thieves had been cut down. The other half had passed under the torture. Only Subienkow remained, or Subienkow and Big Ivan, if that whimpering, moaning thing in the snow could be called Big Ivan. Subienkow caught Yakaga grinning at him. There was no gainsaying Yakaga. The mark of the lash was still on his face. After all, Subienkow could not blame him, but he disliked the thought of what Yakaga would do to him. He thought of appealing to Makamuk, the head chief; but his judgment told him that such appeal was useless. Then, too, he thought of bursting his bonds and dying fighting. Such an end would be quick. But he could not break his bonds. Caribou thongs were stronger than he. Still devising, another thought came to him. He signed for Makamuk, and that an interpreter who knew the coast dialect should be brought.

"Oh, Makamuk," he said, "I am not minded to die. I am a great man, and it were foolishness for me to die. In truth, I shall not die. I am not like these other carrion."

He looked at the moaning thing that had once been Big Ivan, and stirred it contemptuously with his toe.

"I am too wise to die. Behold, I have a great medicine. I alone know this medicine. Since I am not going to die, I shall exchange this medicine with you."

"What is this medicine?" Makamuk demanded.

"It is a strange medicine."

Subienkow debated with himself for a moment, as if loath to part with the secret.

"I will tell you. A little bit of this medicine rubbed on the skin makes the skin hard like a rock, hard like iron, so that no cutting weapon can cut it. The strongest blow of a cutting weapon is a vain thing against it. A bone knife becomes like a piece of mud; and it will turn the edge of the iron knives we have brought among you. What will you give me for the secret of the medicine?"

"I will give you your life," Makamuk made answer through the interpreter.

Subienkow laughed scornfully.

"And you shall be a slave in my house until you die."

The Pole laughed more scornfully.

"Untie my hands and feet and let us talk," he said.

The chief made the sign; and when he was loosed Subienkow rolled a cigarette and lighted it.

"This is foolish talk," said Makamuk. "There is no such medicine. It cannot be. A cutting edge is stronger than any medicine."

The chief was incredulous, and yet he wavered. He had seen too many deviltries of fur thieves that worked. He could not wholly doubt.

"I will give you your life; but you shall not be a slave," he announced.

"More than that."

Subienkow played his game as coolly as if he were bartering for a fox skin.

"It is a very great medicine. It has saved my life many times. I want a sled and dogs, and six of your hunters to travel with me down the river and give me safety to one day's sleep from Michaelovski Redoubt."

"You must live here, and teach us all of your deviltries," was the reply.

Subienkow shrugged his shoulders and remained silent. He blew cigarette smoke out on the icy air, and curiously regarded what remained of the big Cossack.

"That scar!" Makamuk said suddenly, pointing to the Pole's neck, where a livid mark advertised the slash of a knife in a Kamchatkan brawl. "The medicine is not good. The cutting edge was stronger than the medicine."

"It was a strong man that drove the stroke." (Subienkow considered.) "Stronger than you, stronger than your strongest hunter, stronger than he."

Again, with the toe of his moccasin, he touched the Cossack— a grisly spectacle, no longer conscious—yet in whose dismembered body the pain-racked life clung and was loath to go.

"Also the medicine was weak. For at that place there were no berries of a certain kind, of which I see you have plenty in this country. The medicine here will be strong."

"I will let you go downriver," said Makamuk; "and the sled and the dogs and the six hunters to give you safety shall be yours."

"You are slow," was the cool rejoinder. "You have committed an offense against my medicine in that you did not at once accept my terms. Behold, I now demand more. I want one hundred beaver skins." (Makamuk sneered.) "I want one hundred pounds of dried fish." (Makamuk nodded, for fish were plentiful and cheap.) "I want two sleds—one for me and one for my furs and fish. And my rifle must be returned to me. If you do not like the price, in a little while the price will grow."

Yakaga whispered to the chief.

"But how can I know your medicine is true medicine?" Maka-muk asked.

"It is very easy. First, I shall go into the woods——"

Again Yakaga whispered to Makamuk, who made a suspicious dissent.

"You can send twenty hunters with me," Subienkow went on. "You see, I must get the berries and the roots with which to make the medicine. Then, when you have brought the two sleds and loaded on them the fish and the beaver skins and the rifle, and when you have told off the six hunters who will go with me—then, when all is ready, I will rub the medicine on my neck, so, and lay my neck there on that log. Then can your strongest hunter take the ax and strike three times on my neck. You yourself can strike the three times."

Makamuk stood with gaping mouth, drinking in this latest and most wonderful magic of the fur thieves.

"But first," the Pole added hastily, "between each blow I must put on fresh medicine. The ax is heavy and sharp, and I want no mistakes."

"All that you have asked shall be yours," Makamuk cried in a rush of acceptance. "Proceed to make your medicine."

Subienkow concealed his elation. He was playing a desperate game, and there must be no slips. He spoke arrogantly.

"You have been slow. My medicine is offended. To make the offense clean you must give me your daughter."

He pointed to the girl, an unwholesome creature, with a cast in one eye and a bristling wolf tooth. Makamuk was angry, but the Pole remained imperturbable, rolling and lighting another cigarette.

"Make haste," he threatened. "If you are not quick, I shall demand yet more."

In the silence that followed, the dreary Northland scene faded from before him, and he saw once more his native land, and France, and once, as he glanced at the wolf-toothed girl, he remembered another girl, a singer and a dancer, whom he had known when first as a youth he came to Paris.

"What do you want with the girl?" Makamuk asked.

"To go down the river with me." Subienkow glanced her over critically. "She will make a good wife, and it is an honor worthy of my medicine to be married to your blood."

Again he remembered the singer and dancer and hummed aloud a song she had taught him. He lived the old life over, but in a detached, impersonal sort of way, looking at the memory pictures of his own life as if they were pictures in a book of anybody's life. The chief's voice, abruptly breaking the silence, startled him.

"It shall be done," said Makamuk. "The girl shall go down the river with you. But be it understood that I myself strike the three blows with the ax on your neck."

"But each time I shall put on the medicine," Subienkow answered, with a show of ill-concealed anxiety.

"You shall put the medicine on between each blow. Here are the hunters who shall see you do not escape. Go into the forest and gather your medicine."

Makamuk had been convinced of the worth of the medicine by the Pole's rapacity. Surely nothing less than the greatest of medicines could enable a man in the shadow of death to stand up and drive an old woman's bargain.

"Besides," whispered Yakaga, when the Pole, with his guard, had disappeared among the spruce trees, "when you have learned the medicine you can easily destroy him."

"But how can I destroy him?" Makamuk argued. "His medicine will not let me destroy him."

"There will be some part where he has not rubbed the medicine," was Yakaga's reply. "We will destroy him through that part. It may be his ears. Very well; we will thrust a spear in one ear and out the other. Or it may be his eyes. Surely the medicine will be much too strong to rub on his eyes."

The chief nodded. "You are wise, Yakaga. If he possesses no other devil things, we will then destroy him."

Subienkow did not waste time in gathering the ingredients for his medicine. He selected whatsoever came to hand such as spruce needles, the inner bark of the willow, a strip of birch bark, and a quantity of mossberries, which he made the hunters dig up for him from beneath the snow. A few dozen roots completed his supply, and he led the way back to camp.

Makamuk and Yakaga crouched beside him, noting the quantities and kinds of the ingredients he dropped into the pot of boiling water.

"You must be careful that the mossberries go in first," he explained.

"And—oh yes, one other thing—the finger of a man. Here, Yakaga, let me cut off your finger."

But Yakaga put his hands behind him and scowled.

"Just a small finger," Subienkow pleaded.

"Yakaga, give him your finger," Makamuk commanded.

"There be plenty of fingers lying around," Yakaga grunted, indicating the human wreckage in the snow of the score of persons who had been tortured to death.

"It must be the finger of a live man," the Pole objected.

"Then shall you have the finger of a live man." Yakaga strode over to the Cossack and sliced off a finger.

"He is not yet dead," he announced, flinging the bloody trophy in the snow at the Pole's feet. "Also, it is a good finger, because it is large."

Subienkow dropped it into the fire under the pot and began to sing. It was a French love song that with great solemnity he sang into the brew.

"Without these words I utter into it the medicine is worthless," he explained. "The words are the chiefest strength of it. Behold, it is ready."

"Name the words slowly, that I may know them," Makamuk commanded.

"Not until after the test. When the ax flies back three times from my neck, then will I give you the secret of the words."

"But if the medicine is not good medicine?" Makamuk queried anxiously.

Subienkow turned upon him wrathfully.

"My medicine is always good. However, if it is not good, then do by me as you have done to the others. Cut me up a bit at a time, even as you have cut him up." He pointed to the Cossack. "The medicine is now cool. Thus I rub it on my neck, saying this further medicine."

With great gravity he slowly intoned a line of the "Marseillaise," at the same time rubbing the villainous brew thoroughly into his neck.

An outcry interrupted his play acting. The giant Cossack, with a last resurgence of his tremendous vitality, had arisen to his knees. Laughter and cries of surprise and applause arose from the Nulatos, as Big Ivan began flinging himself about in the snow with mighty spasms.

Subienkow was made sick by the sight, but he mastered his qualms and made believe to be angry.

"This will not do," he said. "Finish him, and then we will make the test. Here, you, Yakaga, see that his noise ceases."

While this was being done, Subienkow turned to Makamuk.

"And remember, you are to strike hard. This is not baby work. Here, take the ax and strike the log, so that I can see you strike like a man."

Makamuk obeyed, striking twice, precisely and with vigor, cutting out a large chip.

"It is well." Subienkow looked about him at the circle of savage faces that somehow seemed to symbolize the wall of savagery that had hemmed him about ever since the Czar's police had first arrested him in Warsaw. "Take your ax, Makamuk, and stand so. I shall lie down. When I raise my hand, strike, and strike with all your might. And be careful that no one stands behind you. The medicine is good, and the ax may bounce from off my neck and right out of your hands."

He looked at the two sleds, with the dogs in harness, loaded with furs and fish. His rifle lay on top of the beaver skins. The six hunters who were to act as his guard stood by the sleds.

"Where is the girl?" the Pole demanded. "Bring her up to the sleds before the test goes on."

When this had been carried out, Subienkow lay down in the snow, resting his head on the log like a tired child about to sleep. He had lived so many dreary years that he was indeed tired.

"I laugh at you and your strength, O Makamuk," he said. "Strike and strike hard."

He lifted his hand. Makamuk swung the ax, a broad ax for the squaring of logs. The bright steel flashed through the frosty air, poised for a perceptible instant above Makamuk's head, then descended upon Subienkow's bare neck. Clear through flesh and bone it cut its way, biting deeply into the log beneath. The amazed savages saw the head bounce a yard away from the blood-spouting trunk.

There was a great bewilderment and silence, while slowly it began to dawn in their minds that there had been no medicine. The fur thief had outwitted them. Alone, of all their prisoners, he had escaped the torture. That had been the stake for which he played. A great roar of laughter went up. Makamuk bowed his head in shame. The fur thief had fooled him. He had lost face before all his people. Still they continued to roar out their laughter. Makamuk turned, and with bowed head stalked away. He knew that thenceforth he would be no longer known as Makamuk. He would be Lost Face; the record of his shame would be with him until he died; and whenever the tribes gathered in the spring for the salmon, or in the summer for the trading, the story would pass back and forth across the campfires of how the fur thief died peaceably, at a single stroke, by the hand of Lost Face.

"Who was Lost Face?" he could hear, in anticipation, some insolent young buck demand. "Oh, Lost Face," would be the answer, "he who once was Makamuk in the days before he cut off the fur thief's head."

# 4

# THE CESSION OF RUSSIAN AMERICA TO THE UNITED STATES

A<small>FTER</small> several weeks of negotiation between Secretary of State William Henry Seward and Baron Edouard de Stoeckl, Russia's Minister to the United States, the draft of the Treaty of Cession of Russian America to the United States was completed, and on March 30, 1867, was signed at four o'clock in the morning.

The adjournment of Congress had been fixed for noon on that very day. Only eight hours remained in which to obtain the Senate's ratification; but Seward was determined to seek it. Early that forenoon he hastened to the Capitol and was able to persuade the necessary number of senators to agree to an executive session. It was known that at the time there was substantial opposition and that the chances of obtaining the two-thirds vote required for ratification of a treaty were slight. Had a vote been taken at that time, the purchase would doubtless have been defeated.

Senator Charles Sumner, who favored the treaty, in order to gain time, moved that the treaty be referred to the Committee on Foreign Relations, of which he was chairman. In the meanwhile, Sumner studied all the available literature about Russian America and on April 9 delivered a three-hour speech to the Senate. It was a summary of everything that was then known about Russian America. In the course of his speech, dealing with the character of the area and its probable value, he felt "obliged to confess a dearth

of authentic information easily accessible." He added: "Perhaps
no region of equal extent, unless we accept the interior of Africa or
possibly Greenland, is so little known."

Not surprisingly, his address contained a number of mistakes.
He refers to "Mount St. Elias, the highest peak of the continent."
It was not until nearly thirty years later, 1896, that what was truly
the highest peak, Mount McKinley, was identified and its greater
height of over 20,000 feet correctly appraised.

In his concluding summary, Sumner gave the area the name that
has endured. At the conclusion of his speech, the vote was 27 in
favor and 12 opposed, with 6 members absent, a sufficiency, but
only one more than needed. By so narrow a margin was this mo-
mentous decision made. It was then proposed to make the vote
unanimous. This was almost, but not quite, achieved, the final
recorded vote being 37 to 2.

From  •  •  •

## The Works of Charles Sumner, Volume XI

### Summary of Senator Sumner's Speech to the Senate

MR. PRESIDENT,—I now conclude this examination. From a review of the origin of the treaty, and the general considerations with
regard to it, we have passed to an examination of these possessions
under different heads, in order to arrive at a knowledge of their
character and value. And here we have noticed the existing government, which was found to be nothing but a fur company, whose only
object is trade; then the population, where a very few Russians and
Creoles [1] are a scanty fringe to the aboriginal races; then the climate, a ruling influence, with its thermal current [2] of ocean and
its eccentric isothermal line, by which the rigors of the coast are
tempered to a mildness unknown in the same latitude on the Atlantic side; then the vegetable products, so far as observed, chief
among which are forests of pine and fir [3] waiting for the axe; then

[1] Creole, as used in Alaska, is a person of Russian descent born in America,
generally part Aleut, Eskimo, or Indian (E.G.).

[2] Kuroshio, the Japan Current (E.G.).

[3] This was an error. The forests of Alaska are primarily of spruce and hemlock,
not pine and fir (E.G.).

the mineral products, among which are coal and copper, if not iron, silver, lead, and gold, besides the two great products of New England, "granite and ice"; then the furs, including precious skins of the black fox and sea-otter, which originally tempted the settlement, and remain to this day the exclusive object of pursuit; and, lastly, the fisheries, which, in waters superabundant with animal life beyond any of the globe, seem to promise a new commerce. All these I have presented plainly and impartially, exhibiting my authorities as I proceeded. I have done little more than hold the scales. If these incline on either side, it is because reason or testimony on that side is the weightier.

As these extensive possessions, constituting a corner of the continent, pass from the imperial government of Russia, they will naturally receive a new name. They will be no longer Russian America. How shall they be called? Clearly, any name borrowed from classical antiquity or from individual invention will be little better than misnomer or nickname unworthy of the historic occasion. Even if taken from our own annals, it will be of doubtful taste. The name should come from the country itself. It should be indigenous, aboriginal, one of the autochthons of the soil. Happily such a name exists, as proper in sound as in origin. It appears from the report of Cook, the illustrious navigator, to whom I have so often referred, that the euphonious designation now applied to the peninsula which is the continental link of the Aleutian chain was the sole word used originally by the native islanders, "when speaking of the American continent in general, which they knew perfectly well to be a great land." It only remains, that, following these natives, whose places are now ours, we, too, should call this "great land" Alaska.

Another change should be made. As the settlements of this coast came eastward from Russia, bringing with the Russian flag Western time, the day is earlier by twenty-four hours with them than with us, so that their Sunday is our Saturday, and the other days of the week are in corresponding discord. This must be rectified according to the national meridian, so that there shall be the same Sunday for all, and the other days of the week shall be in corresponding harmony. Important changes must follow, of which this is typical. All else must be rectified according to the national meridian, so that within the sphere of our common country there shall be everywhere the same generous rule and one prevailing harmony. Of course, the unreformed Julian calendar, received from Russia, will give place to ours—Old Style yielding to New Style.

An object of immediate practical interest will be the survey of the extended and indented coast by our own officers, bringing it all within the domain of science, and assuring to navigation much-needed assistance, while the Republic is honored by a continuation of national charts, where execution vies with science, and the art of engraving is the beautiful handmaid. Associated with this survey, and scarcely inferior in value, will be the examination of the country by scientific explorers, so that its geological structure may become known, with its various products, vegetable and mineral. But your best work and most important endowment will be the Republican Government, which, looking to a long future, you will organize, with schools free to all, and with equal laws, before which every citizen will stand erect in the consciousness of manhood. Here will be a motive power without which coal itself is insufficient. Here will be a source of wealth more inexhaustible than any fisheries. Bestow such a government, and you will give what is better than all you can receive, whether quintals of fish, sands of gold, choicest fur, or most beautiful ivory.

\* \* \*

Opposition in the United States to the acquisition of Alaska was made clear in the debates in the House of Representatives in 1868 when the appropriation of $7,200,000, the purchase price, was under consideration. Substantial opposition was also expressed in newspaper editorials. "Seward's Folly" was the most widely accepted of several unflattering designations of the transaction.

Little known is that, despite the absolutism of czarist rule, opposition was also manifested in Russia. It was sufficiently voiced so that Baron Edouard de Stoeckl, who had negotiated the Treaty of Cession, felt obliged to justify it. He did so in a letter from Washington, in July, 1867, to the Chancellor, Prince Gorchakov. That the explanation found favor in St. Petersburg is indicated by

Prince Gorchakov's notation that the presentation was "very re-markable" and by Czar Nicholas I's notation of assent, with the suggestion that an extract be made of it and published. The letter was written in French. (At the editor's request, it was translated by Elizabeth Hanunian of the Library of Congress.)

From · · ·

### Russian Opinion on the Cession of Alaska

Letter by Baron de Stoeckl to Prince Gorchakov

Washington, July 12/24, 1867

Very remarkable.[1]

Yes, and one could make an extract and publish it.[2]

MR. CHANCELLOR:

Our colonies in America were little known up to now even in Russia. The only information one had came from documents pub-lished from time to time by the company which had an interest in presenting the state of the country in a satisfactory light. Also the treaty of cession seemed to have given rise to more or less erroneous comments in the Russian newspapers.

I take the liberty, my Prince, of submitting to Your Excellency some details on this matter which my position enabled me to study.

The discovery of America seemed to open up a new era in the world. All of the European Powers, big and small, were rushing to the new continent to exploit the enormous riches which it con-tained. The natives were driven out, or rather, destroyed. Whole empires were founded, but these empires disappeared and left the Powers that founded them without gain.

England was perhaps the only exception. She used her colonies for increasing the sale of her goods and enlarging her navy, the element of her prosperity and power, enormously.

The colonies have always had the tendency to make themselves independent. The thirteen British provinces, which later formed

[1] Notation by Prince Gorchakov.
[2] Notation by the Czar.

the republic of the United States, were the first to shake off the
yoke of the North country. Though England made unheard of efforts to subdue them, she did not succeed. The war of independence
only resulted in increasing the already existing rivalry between
the colonies and the mother country and arousing hostile feeling
between the two nations, which even a century could not erase.

Spain had as its share the finest regions of that continent. The
flag of Castile was waving from Mexico to the Amazon, and over
the entire expanse of the Pacific coasts. What use did Spain make
of all the riches of that vast territory which she owned for almost
three centuries? With the loss of its colonies the Spanish Government is weaker and the nation poorer than the day on which
Christopher Columbus discovered the new world.

France likewise endeavored to found colonies. She was drawn
into long and costly wars. England took Lower Canada away from
her. Later on, she was compelled to sell Louisiana, under permanent threat from the proximity of the United States. It was a great
sacrifice for her; for with Louisiana she lost not only the Mississippi valley, today the most fertile part of the Union, but also the
fifty or sixty thousand French inhabitants of that territory.

Portugal acted more wisely. Seeing that she could not [hope to]
keep Brazil, she parted with it of her own accord, and the two
countries established friendly relations. Brazil achieved her independence without revolution. She preserved the monarchic institutions and thus saved herself from the anarchy which devastated
all of the Latin American republics.

Russia was the last of the European Powers to be attracted by
the new continent. Although the expedition for the exploration of
the Pacific was organized under the reign of Empress Anna, Peter
the Great appears to have been the first to conceive the idea for it.
That Sovereign, whose genius seemed to penetrate into the future,
had foreseen that the shores of Northern Asia were some day to
be a part of His great Empire, and the purpose of the expedition
was obviously the exploration of those shores. Indeed, it was the
direction taken by the Russian ships under Bering's orders. The
discovery of the North American continent did not appear to have
been an accident. One of the ships, under the command of Captain

Tcherikov, which left the expedition, headed eastward and discovered the Aleutian Islands. Later, other Russian ships were traveling along the coasts of America up to the fifty-fourth degree Northern latitude, and that territory became the property of Russia by right of discovery.

Several adventurers visited the Aleutian Islands to trade in furs, but no permanent establishment was set up on the islands or on the continent. In 1799, under the reign of Emperor Paul, the Russian-American Company was organized, which is still in existence.

When it gave that Company extraordinary privileges and entrusted it with the administration of and absolute control over our American possessions, the Government certainly did not intend to turn that territory into the patrimony in perpetuity of a few hundred stockholders. The Imperial Gov[ernmen]t had to expect that the Company, while looking after its interests, would seek to improve the situation of the country so that some day the central government, when taking over its management, would make it into an outlying province useful for the entire nation.

That purpose has never been attained. According to the report of present Councillor of State Kostlivtzov and Captain Golovnin, entrusted in 1861 with a special mission, it was obvious that our colonies were hardly in a satisfactory state. The status of the Indians on the islands under our rule had not been improved either physically or morally, and the tribes on the mainland continued to be as savage and hostile as they were at the time of discovery. The population was composed of barely five hundred Whites, all in the employ or hire of the Company, and about 1,200 Creoles. No effort has been made as yet to explore the interior of the country and to try to benefit by the resources it could offer. On the contrary, the Company had tried to invest its capital in enterprises that had nothing to do with our colonies, such as the tea trade with China, whaling in the Sea of Okhotsk, etc.

I have by no means the intention to attack the Company. I am simply stating facts. But while it is true that with greater ingenuity and energy it could have done more, consideration must be given to the obstacles which it has had to overcome.

Upon expiration of the charter of the Company the question

arose whether our colonies should be administered by the Imperial
Gov[ernmen]t or again be put into the hands of the Company.

In the first case the Imperial Gov[ernmen]t would have to send
a governor and a flock of underlings on the spot and attract emigration [to the colony] to look after the raising of crops and
animals—which is difficult but not impracticable in that country
—establish regular communications, in sum, create [build up]
everything. Needless to say how difficult this undertaking would
have been. In any event, it could have succeeded only in the course
of time and by making incalculable financial sacrifices.

To renew the charter of the Company would have meant to prolong the existing state of affairs, and it was doubtful whether the
Company in [view of] its present situation could have continued
to exist.

In the committee, presided over by the Emperor and in which
it was his Majesty's pleasure to let me participate, the Minister of
Finance furnished detailed information on the present state of the
Company and on the sacrifices to be made by the Government in
order to maintain its credit [uphold its prestige]. Mr. de Reuteren's
clear and precise statement relieves me from the necessity of dwelling on the subject.

Apart from these difficulties, we would have encountered serious
opposition by our neighbors, the Americans.

In my reports I mentioned more than once the position in which
our colonies were placing us with regard to the United States. May
Your Excellency permit me to summarize them here briefly.

Our treaty of April 5/17, 1824, stipulates "that the American
citizens shall not approach, without the permission of the Governor or of the Commandant, any point at which a Russian establishment [settlement] exists, and that, vice versa, the Russian
subjects shall not approach, without permission, any establishment
[settlement] of the United States on the Northwest coast."

In 1824, when the treaty was signed, the United States had no
possessions on the Pacific; later she conquered California and established several ports there. The Americans received our ships in
San Francisco as they did in New York, i.e., without any restrictions, but they requested the same privileges in the ports of our
possessions. After several appeals had been made, the Company

finally opened the port of Sitka to the ships of the United States, but the trade monopoly exercised by the Company rendered this concession illusory, for the Americans could neither bring in and sell their goods, nor buy the products of our colonies.

In step with the growing United States population on the Pacific coasts, these demands were becoming more and more frequent. The Americans said to us: "We do not want to benefit by the restrictions of the treaty; your ships enter our territory without restriction; your Company sends its agents to us, establishes agencies, and trades free from restrictions. All we request is the permission to enjoy the same advantages in your territory."

In line with the instructions given to me on several occasions, I replied to all these demands that, upon expiration of the charter of the Company, the Imperial Government would take measures to settle these matters. I could do no more, for, after all, the fact is that the Americans were only requesting strict reciprocity which is the basic principle of any trade relation between nations.

We had, without a doubt, the right to stand by the terms of the treaty and to maintain the practice of exclusion in our colonies. The Americans never contested it, but they said to us: "The treaty gives us the same right, and we can close our ports and establishments on the Pacific to the Russian subjects and ships," and I should state here that the treaty does not speak of the agents or the vessels of the Company, but of Russian subjects and Russian vessels in general, so that by keeping the stipulations of the convention of 1824 in force, not only the ships of the Company would have suffered, but all vessels under the Russian flag, without distinction. It would have been to sacrifice our national shipping interests to the interests of the Company.

The Government of the United States often supported these complaints, but it did not insist. It never took offense at the refusals which we have been in the position to make more than once, and I am convinced that it would always have shown itself most willing to settle all these matters amicably.

But another danger was hanging over our possessions. I want to speak about the American freebooters who were rapidly multiplying in the Pacific.

However spacious the regions of the United States Federation

may be, they do not seem extensive enough for the feverish activity
and spirit of enterprise of the Americans. They look upon that
continent as their patrimony. Their destiny ("our manifest destiny," as they call it) is forever to expand, and in that expansion,
pursued by that nation with as much perseverance as success, the
adventurers have played the role of prisoners on more than one
occasion. They are the ones who gradually invaded Texas which
later became a State of the Union. New Mexico and some other
parts of the South were acquired in the same manner.

It had been hoped that our colonies' lack of resources would
keep them safe from the greed of the freebooters, but it was not so.
Although the fish, the furs, and some other comparatively insignificant products of our possessions certainly did not measure
up to the rich valleys of the Mississippi and Rio Grande, nor to the
gold-bearing plains of California, they did not escape the covetous-
ness of the Americans.

I shall refrain from listing here the complaints to which their
depredations on our shores gave rise. Their reply to the protests
which we addressed to the Federal Government was always: "We
cannot prevent our citizens from going out of the country; if they
then create disturbances in your territory, it is up to you to defend
it." There was only one way of putting an end to this state of affairs,
and that was by maintaining a large flotilla in that part of the
world.

In spite of the quite formidable resources [naval units] which
Great Britain possesses in the Pacific, her possessions were no
safer than ours from the depredations of the freebooters. Three
years ago,[3] the rumor spread that gold was being found on [along]
the Frazer River in British Columbia. Within a few weeks, four to
five thousand Americans were on the spot, digging [for gold]. The
English Governor, unable to send them back or afraid to do so,
permitted them to remain in the region on condition that they
would comply with the laws of the colony. The Americans refused,
declared that they recognized no other authority than that of the
United States, and formed a provisional government. England did
not interfere with them. Fortunately for her, the gold was not as

[3] In fact in 1848.

abundant as it was thought to be; it was soon exhausted and the Americans drifted off. Otherwise, British Columbia would now be a territory of the United States.

Of all the colonies that once studded the new world, the only ones left, except for the West Indian islands, are the British provinces of Canada and our possessions.

England has only one purpose in mind today, to get rid of Canada, for the maintenance of which she must make enormous sacrifices and expenditures not exactly in proportion with the profits she derives. But what she wants above all is to find herself no longer in contact with [adjacent to] a rival power always ready to defy her.

The British Parliament has just passed a law joining the different provinces of Canada together into a federation governed by a Viceroy. The purpose which England had in mind was to consolidate her colonies in North America and to make them into a State, strong enough and compact enough to become independent. It would be so today if the Canadians wanted it, but they prefer for the time being to be defended and protected by England. However, the separation will take place, one way or another, in the very near future.

We would have been the only one of the European Powers to possess colonies on the continent. But if Spain, France, Portugal and even England have had to lose or cede their colonies without deriving any benefit, could we hope to be luckier? Could we look forward to a better future in that territory which has for almost a century brought Russia only troubles and financial sacrifices? In order to keep those inhospitable shores, was it within our interest to spoil our good relations and even to risk serious complications with a great nation to which England and France—those two great maritime Powers—bow? I leave the answer to these questions to the press which is attacking the treaty of cession.

Far from [instead of] adding to our political weight, the vast territory that was in our possession in those seas made us grow weaker. Our shores began in Japan, ran along Northern Asia to the Bering Strait, and followed from that point the American littoral to the fifty-fourth degree northern longitude, about several thousands of miles long. Was it possible to guard [protect] such extensive coasts, distant as they are, especially, from the center of the Empire?

We must concentrate our resources and energy on the Amur regions, especially on the provinces south of that river. Those lands are fertile and will easily attract emigration. They have magnificent ports, and the proximity of Japan and China guarantees them a profitable trade. That is where our power in the Pacific must be found.

Because of their contiguity to the Empire these provinces are easier to defend. During the Crimean War the Allies did not challenge our Asiatic coasts, and the attack launched by them on Kamtchatka was repelled by Admiral Zavoiko in such a way as to take away their desire to come back; whereas our colonies were at the mercy of the enemy. They were saved only by a fortuitous circumstance. England declared them neutral territory, for fear that we would cede them to the United States.

One of the most important duties of the position which I have the honor to have been holding for such a long time was to look after the interests of our possessions in America, and I devoted all my [energies and] attention to it [that task]. It was impossible for me not to see that the efforts of the Company were unproductive, that the future of that [part of the] country was bare and that, endangered by the proximity of the Americans, our possessions would draw us into serious disputes with the Federal Gov[ernmen]t and would end up with [our] falling prey to the Americans. In reporting to the Imperial Government on the state of our colonies, I have always conscientiously stated the truth, and the whole truth. If by so doing I was a party to the cession of our colonies, I am ready to assume my share of responsibility, entirely confident that I carried out the duties of a [loyal] subject of our August Master [His Majesty] and that I acted within the genuine interest of our country.

I have the honor to be, Mr. Chancellor, with the highest consideration,

Your Excellency's very humble and obedient servant,
STOECKL.

# 5

# THE AMERICANS TAKE OVER

I<small>N</small> 1864 Prince Dimitrii Petrovich Maksutov, formerly assistant governor, was made governor of Russian America. In St. Petersburg he was given every assurance that the colony would remain in Russian hands. Hector Chevigny tells of the events of 1867 and of the military occupation by the United States that led to years of misrule.

From · · ·

*Russian America,* by Hector Chevigny

THE UPROOTING

In May or June of 1867, apparently through San Francisco, Maksutov learned that in April the United States Senate had bought Alaska.

He was coldly, furiously angry. The secrecy told the story. Honor had meant nothing. Much as he probably wished he could express his feelings by resigning, his sense of duty to the colony was too great. His determination was to remain until his usefulness was over. His first task was to inform the colony. He did so when he had the details from Saint Petersburg and Washington.

The word went out to all the stations, carried by the mail boats to the old forts on Cook Inlet and Prince William Sound, to the posts on Bristol Bay, to Saint Michael, Kodiak, and Unalaska.

From those places it was relayed to the many islands, to the crews working afield, to the posts up the inland rivers. At New Archangel the people had the news directly from Maksutov, a thousand of them listening as he spoke to them from the steps of Baranov's Castle.

They had not long to wait, the people learned. The United States planned to take possession in October. It was hoped the San Franciscans interested in the furs would obtain a franchise from their government like that of the Company. That would mean employment for those whose trade was peltry. With the exception of the naval personnel, all who wished to do so could choose to stay in the country. They could choose to stay and become American citizens. The treaty of cession provided that the inhabitants of the ceded territory ". . . with the exception of uncivilized native tribes shall be admitted to the enjoyment of all the rights, privileges and immunities of citizens of the United States and shall be maintained and protected in the free enjoyment of their liberty, property and religion."

A vast sigh of relief surely went up all over the colony at having the greatest of the questions answered in this unequivocal fashion. And not a word about race. The only distinction was between the civilized and the uncivilized. Moreover, there would be opportunity to see what American rule would be like before a decision had to be made whether to stay. Three whole years were provided. Within that time anyone choosing to do so could go to Russia with transportation furnished. Nor was that all to make the news of the sale palatable when the initial shock wore off. Everything possible would be done to enable those wishing to stay to do so. Individuals would be given title to dwellings and lands they occupied. The Company would likewise make over shops, mills, equipment, in short the facilities for carrying on trades and professions. It sounded like heaven. No one could lose by waiting and seeing. Impatience began to mount as October neared.

What was in store for Alaska was a military occupation. Seward, in his haste to take possession of the territory before it was even paid for, secured an executive order placing it under the War

Department. He believed the arrangement would be of short duration, that surely Congress would do the usual in these circumstances, which was to provide the appurtenances of territorial government: a civilian governor, a legislature, courts, and appropriate laws. President Johnson so requested when, in July of 1867, three months before the occupation began, he formally notified the House of the need to pay Russia. But the belief that Alaska was worthless had taken extremely stubborn root in Congress.

Alaska was made a customs district, and that, aside from granting certain corporate privileges, was to be all that Congress was to do about it for seventeen incredible years. No historian was ever to have a good word to say about this "era of no government," during which no one was to be legally entitled to settle, buy or sell, be married or buried, the legislation remaining unprovided. The lawlessness was to be abetted by the military, which was to remain for ten years. That was the shape of the future as Seward prepared to take possession.

There was to be a formal ceremony of transfer at New Archangel, the purchase treaty stipulating the appointment of commissioners to represent Russia and the United States, the one to declare the territory made over, the other to accept. These two commissioners were also to certify to the division of property, agreement having been reached as to what was to pass to private individuals, what the Company could sell, and what was to go to the United States. This last consisted in general of the vacant lands, the town sites, the public buildings. Seward named the commissioner for the United States, and Stoeckl named Russia's, choosing a man from his diplomatic staff. The two appointees took ship for Alaska from New York in late August.

As he planned the ceremony at New Archangel, Seward seems to have envisioned a happy event marked by banquets, toasts, and speeches. He had personally given his commissioner the flag that was to be raised when that of Russia had come down for the last time, the central act of the ceremony. Present would be the troops who would initiate the new occupation. The choice of these troops together with their commander was made by the general commanding the Pacific area, who seems to have been under the impression that Indians were to be fought.

The commander chosen for Alaska had begun his career as a teen-age private fighting Mexicans in the 1840s. He was a tough one even then; the Battle of Buena Vista made him a second lieutenant. His name, not to be confused with that of the Confederacy's great leader, was Jefferson C. Davis. This Jeff Davis fought the Civil War with the Union Army, first as a lieutenant at Fort Sumter during the bombardment. He saw further action at Pea Ridge, Corinth, and Stone River. He was also with Sherman on the march through Georgia. Quick on the trigger, he killed Union General Nelson during a quarrel, but that was somehow forgotten by the end of the war. Brevetted a major-general, he went out West to fight Indians. That was his occupation when, at thirty-nine, he was ordered to Alaska with a force of 250 men. They sailed from San Francisco in mid-September on the transport *John L. Stevens*. On ahead had gone two gunboats with baggage and supplies.

The harbor of New Archangel, a name soon to be dropped in favor of Sitka, was crowded with shipping, most of the Company's fleet having been called in. The two American gunboats had to moor some distance out. So did the *John L. Stevens* when she arrived on October 8. She had had a rough three-week passage but Davis and his boys were not to go ashore just yet, he learned. They had to wait for the arrival of the two commissioners, and when that would be, nobody could say. The Russian governor was being sticky about it. So there was nothing to do but swear at all the rain and speculate about the Russian women in that funny town over there with the onions on the churches.

Sitka was already jammed with people, men, women, and children having come in from all parts of the colony with tons of baggage. They were the officials and their families, who, together with a number in Sitka, were scheduled to leave directly Russian rule was over. The exodus would begin with the departure of the ship being readied for sailing to the Baltic. The town was filled with the sound of hammering and sawing as crates and boxes were made for the shipping of pianos, books, clothing, and other personal belongings. No joy went with the activity. According to an American

witness, the townspeople "... seemed as though they were preparing for the funeral of the Tsar, going about the town in a most
dejected manner."

Maksutov, who would not be leaving until the last day of the
year, was busy with a number of businessmen up from the United
States, most of them representing the California interests hopeful
of persuading Washington to give them a franchise like the Company's. They had come to Sitka to bid on the Company's salable
property: the ships, the machinery, the equipment, the supplies,
ranging from sheepskin coats to sugar in the colony's far-flung
warehouses. Maksutov sold it all cheaply, hoping it would stay in
the country and help the people, hardly foreseeing that to get their
money's worth most of the buyers would have to resell elsewhere.
One ship bought for $4,000 resold for nine times as much.

Although the Company had paid for everything in the colony
short of personal belongings, Maksutov sold nothing that was
necessary for the new administration to use in carrying on. The
donation included the basic furnishings of the governor's residence. The hospitals, the schools, all the public institutions were
left their equipment, the churches their treasures. Church property,
which by the treaty had passed to the ownership of the congregations, was in the custody of Bishop Petr, who with most if not all
his clergy planned to stay, hoping they would be enabled to carry
on their work.

At length, on the morning of October 18, when Davis and his
250 soldiers had waited out in the harbor 10 days, the U.S.S.
*Ossipee* arrived, bringing the commissioners. The one representing
Russia was Captain Aleksei Peshchurov. His American counter-
part was Brigadier-General Lovell Rousseau. Things began happening immediately. Davis, who lost no time seeing Rousseau, no doubt
complained of the length of time his men had been cooped up on
that ship. When he had seen Maksutov, Peshchurov announced that
the transfer ceremony would be held that very afternoon.

The hour was set for three. To the beat of their drums, under
the command of Peshchurov, the 90 sailors and 180 soldiers from
a Siberian regiment who made up the garrison of the town marched
up to the knoll, crossed the parade ground fronting Baranov's

Castle, and were brought to attention before the 90-foot flagstaff flying the imperial emblem. Now more drums were heard. The Americans had come ashore. Presently onto the parade ground came Generals Rousseau and Davis, the commanders of the American warships, and a company of Davis's troops. They too were brought to attention. A nice ceremony had been worked out. As one flag came down and the other went up, the salutes were to be given alternately by the guns of the *Ossipee* and of Sitka. Happily for a day in October, the rain had ceased; the sun shone. There was, nevertheless, a heavy emotional overcast.

Maksutov was there as an onlooker, his face impassive. With him was his wife, her emotions plainly near the breaking point. Few other Russians had brought themselves to attend. The spectators were mostly the San Francisco businessmen. The very first act of the ceremony brought things to a nerve-racking halt. The wind-whipped Russian flag seemed not to want to come down at the will of the man operating the flagstaff ropes. It curled itself around them, the more tightly the harder the ropes were pulled. Finally a bosun's chair had to be rigged in order to get a man up there to cut it loose. It fluttered down on the bayonets of the soldiers below. The overwrought Princess Maksutova crumpled in a faint.

The rest must have seemed anticlimactic. The guns belatedly saluted. The American flag went up without incident. Peshchurov declared the territory made over, Rousseau accepted. "And," wrote a witness, "we stood upon American soil." Out of deference to the feelings of the Russians, Rousseau tried to stop the giving of three cheers, but he could not.

Years numbering 126 had passed since the discovery of the region by Bering, 122 since the arrival of the first Russians in search of furs, 68 since the founding of the Company. The sale was the greatest event of its kind in peacetime history. But no one adverted to these facts. The ceremony was followed by no banquet at which speeches were made and toasts given. What did follow the ceremony, the moment it was over, was an announcement from Davis that he was in command now. The Maksutovs were immediately to make room for him and his wife at the castle. Nor would he wait until the Russian garrison could be shipped home before his troops took over their barracks. By the time October 18, 1867, had passed into history, the new occupation had begun.

The commissioners remained a week, listing the divided properties, making out the deeds to the lands, homes, and shops going to private individuals. Rousseau was impressed by the people of Sitka. He tried to sound a warning when he wrote his report, remarking that the majority would stay "if treated kindly." The pity was that he, a man far above Davis in character and training, had not been put in command of the occupation. That he would be had been Seward's understanding.

The American period seemed at first to promise only prosperity. Would-be settlers began arriving by the boatload soon after the transfer. The papers all over California, Oregon, and Washington had been full of the news. In San Francisco the bookstores displayed Russian dictionaries. Sitka had several hundred new people by mid-November. They were real-estate dealers, cooks, miners, lawyers, homestead seekers, owners of ships and barges, whores, gamblers. They had one thing in common: they knew how to organize a prosperous, self-governing country.

They liked Sitka and its old inhabitants. The idea was that they would all get rich together. They extended the townsite for miles, staking out lots and building shanties, charging newcomers high prices for them. Among the buildings they put up were a restaurant, two saloons, two tenpin alleys. A newspaper was started. A city charter was framed, ordinances drawn up, the plans calling for even a school board. The first mayor was William S. Dodge, who had come to Sitka as Collector of Customs, the only government official aside from Davis. Everybody knew that Alaska did not as yet have the laws that would make these acts valid, but it was inconceivable that Congress would not soon provide proper territorial government. And when that happened the soldiers would go.

Instead, more soldiers arrived, until there were five hundred stationed in various parts of the country, all under Davis, with the largest detachment at Sitka. They caroused, raped and looted. They looted even the cathedral. That exploit was one of the few for which Davis meted out punishment. It was useless to inform Washington. That was discovered by Collector Dodge, who wrote that ". . . many has been the night when soldiers have taken possession of a Russian house and frightened and browbeaten the women into compliance. . . ." Dodge could do nothing, lacking the means of enforcing even customs regulations, but the people could turn to no one else. "Many is the night I have been called upon, by men and women, Russian and Aleutian, in their night-clothes, to protect them. . . . Officers have carried on with the same high hand among the Russian people. . . ."

Among the Tlingits syphilis and drunkenness spread quickly. Contrary to federal law, the military connived at the importation of hundreds of gallons of rotgut and the molasses with which to make it locally. Davis himself got one chief drunk after dressing him up in a cast-off uniform. The chief thought he had been honored until a guard set him straight with a kick. The cost of that incident was four lives. Quiet was not restored until Davis had a Tlingit village shot up.

Even the Americans could not take Davis's rule for long. Sitka's boom began to peter out a year after it started. As for the Russians, they began to leave within months after the transfer. With no amusement could they have recalled that the purchase treaty had assured them the "rights, privileges and immunities" of American citizenship. Some went to British Columbia, some to California, most went to Russia. With the Maksutovs when they departed on December 31, 1867, went 150 men, women, and children. The last ship furnishing free transportation carried 300, twice her supposed capacity. How they fared, the colony-born who had never seen Russia, seems not to be known. In the observation of old Father German, the colony-born tended not to survive in cities for long.

Northern Alaska was spared military rule. That part of the country was given something quite different in 1870, three years after the purchase, something ironic: another monopolistic fur corporation. Washington had recognized that, short of detailing the Navy to patrol the waters against the irresponsible pillagers, there was no other way to protect the fur resources. The Alaska Commercial Company was given a twenty-year franchise over the Pribilof Islands for an annual fee plus a royalty on the products. It was the heir of its Russian predecessor in that, through Maksutov, its organizers had acquired the buildings and other facilities on the islands.

The organization soon extended itself beyond the Pribilofs, building stations all along the Aleutians and trading with the mainland. The Aleuts were saved from want and demoralization. They were paid, housed, schooled, and doctored. The Alaska Commercial Company has been bitterly denounced, but most historians seem to think it ran its house well. It maintained the only mail and passenger service in the territory. Its part of the country was given a prosperity and an order utterly lacking elsewhere. The enterprise, which reaped the harvest of the conservation measures instituted by Wrangell, was enormously profitable, giving the lie to Stoeckl, whose arguments for selling had included the allegation that the fur resources had been hopelessly depleted.

The peace and prosperity in the north emphasized the anarchy elsewhere. Davis made no use of the governmental facilities so carefully bequeathed him by Maksutov. But then Washington had provided him with no ships and no money. The hospitals were staffless. So were the schools. Sanitation had gone unserved. When, in 1877, after ten years, the soldiers were finally pulled out—because of an Indian uprising in Idaho, not because Alaska had as yet been given civilian government—they left the places they had occupied virtually empty of Europeans. Sitka was a ghost town, the old searchlight atop the castle turning crazily with every wind. The families numbered twenty, only five of them Russian. The cost to the United States had been a culture.

The one remnant of the culture is the adherence of many of the natives to Orthodoxy. The Church in Russia sent funds for nearly fifty years through the missionary organization established by Veniaminov after he was made Metropolitan of Moscow the year following the purchase. The fathers in Alaska were enabled to maintain most of their churches, three or four orphanages, and seventeen schools. In 1887, twenty years after the purchase, according to the bitter comment of the territorial governor, the Russian Church was annually spending more on schooling than the $40,000 the United States was spending for the education of both whites and natives in the entire territory.

No more money could be sent from Russia after the revolution of 1917. Still the fathers stayed at their posts, some supporting themselves by laboring with their hands. It was some time before help came from the North American Orthodox Church, which now has jurisdiction. The Liturgy is still celebrated on the Pribilofs, at Unalaska, Kenai, and elsewhere. Sitka still has a bishop. The cathedral retains its old treasures. It is now one of the oldest houses of worship in continuous use on American soil. Three histories meet in this little Byzantine fane. Names such as Benson and Mather are borne by the members of the congregation, who are mostly Tlingits. With characteristic tenacity they have clung to the faith they first adopted. English or Tlingit or both may be heard in the parts of the Slavonic Liturgy given in the vernacular. In that part of the ritual where once the Tsar was prayed for, the petition is now for the President of the United States.

October 18, the anniversary of the transfer, is now called Alaska Day. The ceremony is re-enacted annually at Sitka. Again the old Russian tsarist flag flies from the tall staff that still centers the knoll overlooking the town. Again it is hauled down and replaced by the Stars and Stripes, the thunder of the saluting guns reverberating down the mountains and causing grave consternation among the millions of seabirds. Otherwise the re-enactment bears little resemblance to the original event. The townspeople are all there. No one is sad. The Orthodox bishop gives an invocation. He is followed by notables with speeches. Bands play, the Tlingits sing to the beat of their old drums. It is a holiday throughout the state. Alaskans are like their Russian predecessors in that they have a great passion for the country. It is thanks to that passion, which drove them to work for statehood long, hard, and consistently, that, in 1959, ninety-two years after the purchase, the President proclaimed that Congress had at last agreed to bestow full membership in the Union. For the first time in the two hundred years and more since the coming of the Russians, the land was no longer a colony.

# 6

## CIVIL GOVERNMENT IN THE 1880's

SAMUEL HALL YOUNG (1847–1927), a clergyman, went to
Alaska as a pioneer missionary in 1878, founded Alaska's first
Protestant church in Wrangell, and established Presbyterian missions throughout Alaska. He was chiefly instrumental in converting
the Tlingit Indians to Christianity. His crusading zeal led him to
participate in all the stampedes—the Klondike, Nome, Fairbanks,
and Iditarod-Flat, where he sought to minister to the spiritual needs
of the gold-rushers. Throughout his long service in the Far North
he called attention by writing and lecturing to Alaska's needs and
the Federal government's neglect of them.

In his autobiography, published shortly after his death in 1927,
Young described the misgovernment and consequent frustrations of
the Alaskans.

From · · ·

*Hall Young of Alaska: The Mushing Parson,* by Samuel
Hall Young

The struggle of Alaskans for their rights as American citizens
forms one of the gloomy pages of American history. The beginning of Alaska's early history reminds me of echo's answer in the
old poem to the word "Matrimony"—"matter o' money." After a
struggle between contending companies, the Alaska Commercial

Company got the lease of the fur seal islands. They paid the United States government three hundred thousand dollars annually for the privilege of killing as many fur seals as they wished. While there were government rules and instructions, these did not seriously hamper this company, which made millions of dollars out of its lease and wished, of course, to continue the arrangement indefinitely. United States Senator Miller of San Francisco was the president of the company. Like the old Hudson's Bay Fur Company of England, they did not wish the country to be settled and the way made plain for rival fur companies to come in and compete with theirs. They employed every means to discourage the settlement of Alaska and even the education and enlightenment of the natives. They opposed all attempts in Congress to organize Alaska and grant us protection of life or property, courts and officers. The wilder and more lawless the country, the more furs for them, was the old cry.

It was evident that this company employed several men at good salaries to "write down" the country and decry and belittle its resources. As early as 1868 efforts were made in Congress to provide some sort of rule for Alaska. Propositions were made to annex Alaska to Canada, to annihilate time and space by making it a county of the territory of Washington, to sell it to a private company, and other absurd suggestions.

For twelve years no bill for the government of Alaska was discussed on either the floor of the House or Senate in Washington. The fur company had its way. Among the writers employed by the company, Henry W. Elliott ("Fur Seal" Elliott) was the most notable. About 1874 he submitted a report as special treasury agent, in which the information on fur seals is valuable, but when it touches upon any other interests of the Territory, it shows either dense ignorance or design to fool the American people. Dr. Jeanette Nichols in her history of Alaska gives a number of quotations from his report which would be amusing if they had not been so disastrous in their effect upon the development of Alaska. It was Elliott's judgment that climactic conditions would always "unfit the Territory for the proper support of any considerable population." He says: "There are more acres of better land lying now as wilderness and jungles in sight on the mountain tops from the car windows of the Pennsylvania road than can be found in all Alaska."

In an article in *Harper's* magazine in reply to criticism upon his report, among other mistakes, he says:

> Though we know now that Alaska will never be, in all human probability, the land for us, yet we have one great comfort in its contemplation, for we shall never be obliged to maintain costly mail routes or appoint the ubiquitous postmaster there. We shall never be asked by the people for a territorial form of government with its attendant federal expenses; and, much as the Coast looms upon the map, we shall never have to provide lighthouses for its vacant harbours.

Although these assertions of Elliott's were denied by William G. Morris, special agent of the treasury, and others, yet they shaped public opinion and also blocked our efforts for legislation in the interest of Alaska. The noted Alexander Stephens of Georgia is reported to have bluffed Dr. Sheldon Jackson, who was attempting to secure his interest and aid in providing civil government for Alaska. The little, old statesman, crippled and hobbling upon his cane, paused long enough to cackle a deriding laugh in the face of the little doctor of divinity, who was about of the same height.

"Huh!" sneered the Senator. "That snowbound wilderness—not enough white men there to make a decent country—never will be," and hobbled on into the Senate.

But after our Indian war at Wrangell, the discovery of gold at Juneau brought crowds of eager miners, the establishment of many salmon canneries and other fisheries, and especially of missions and schools. The pressure upon Congress to afford relief to the inhabitants of the Territory compelled action. I have spoken of the First Territorial Convention at Juneau and of my interview with Senator George and Senator Harrison, and the personal efforts on the part of Drs. Lindsley and Jackson and others in this direction. The situation in Alaska was anomalous, the Alaska Commercial Company fighting us at every point. The Government Bill passed in the winter of 1883–84, while very incomplete and faulty, was at least a step towards giving us our rights. An organic act was passed, and a government and laws for Alaska adopted, based on the Oregon Code, but amended and shaped to fit the idea of Congress that Alaska was not and never would be capable of supporting any considerable population or of providing any great means of wealth. The Bill did not call Alaska a territory, but a district. It provided a governor, a judge, a marshal, a district attorney, a clerk and four United States commissioners and deputy marshals. Schools were provided for to a very limited extent, the importation or manufacture of intoxicating liquors was prohibited, mining laws were instituted and, at least, a beginning made of civil government.

Senator Harrison, the chairman of the committee which framed the organic act, excused its inadequacy by pleading that this form of government would bring to the residents of the Territory and their homes "reasonable protection of life, liberty and pursuit of happiness." Therefore, in the summer of 1884, came our newly appointed officers. Dr. Nichols truly says: "In 1884 Alaska became a political preserve for the payment of small debts owed by big politicians to little ones."

The first Governor was J. H. Kinkead, who had been governor of the state of Nevada, but was considered a "worn-out political hack." It was freely said in Washington that his political friends had sent him to Alaska to get him as far out of the way as possible. Governor Kinkead was a very hard drinker, as his bulbous nose indicated. He brought with him an immense supply of cases labeled "Canned Tomatoes." These "tomatoes" were proclaimed as tasting exactly like Scotch whiskey and producing the same effect. His duties as Governor were so limited that beyond a report of eight and one-half pages there is no record of any of his acts.

The judge was Hall McAllister, the nephew of the noted Ward McAllister of the "four hundred" in New York City. This young man, who was a lawyer in San Francisco, and appointed through the influence of the Alaska Commercial Company, was of the newly discovered species, "Dude." He made his Uncle Ward his model, and closely followed that arbiter of fashion in his manner, his dress, his flourishes and all his actions. The whole government and all its acts seemed so farcical that beyond furnishing amusement to both friends and enemies of the Territory, within and without, it did nothing.

The fall of this government, whose officials were appointed by President Arthur, deserves a paragraph: Dr. Sheldon Jackson remained at Sitka the winter of 1884–85. The quarrels between him and the officials became more and more acute. When President Cleveland was inaugurated, these Republican officials still hoped to serve out their term of four years. Dr. Jackson, in an unguarded moment, voiced his provocation by saying that he was going to Washington on the next steamer and was going to have all the officials turned out of office, and new ones appointed. To prevent this they laid a scheme. They connived with Captain Carroll of the monthly steamer. Dr. Jackson had secured his passage and was ready to board the boat, when Marshal Hillier sent a deputy to arrest Dr. Jackson on a charge of misappropriating Russian property. He marched him up to the guardhouse and kept him there until the steamer moved off. One or two of the officials sailed on that steamer, thinking thus to checkmate the little doctor; but it was the mistake of their lives. The doctor was promptly released from jail after the steamer sailed. Rev. Eugene Willard, who was at Sitka, possessed a photographic camera. Dr. Jackson took Mr. Willard to the guardhouse, sat down on the bare floor and posed in dejected attitude with his chin on his hand, while Mr. Willard "took" him.

Dr. Jackson sailed on the next steamer and went to Washington, taking this picture with him. It was published in *Church* and other periodicals with headlines: "Persecuted for Righteousness' Sake." President Cleveland was besieged with demands that the Alaska officials be removed, and they went out awhirling, in spite of the fact that the great Ward McAllister appeared before the mission Board secretaries in New York, dressed immaculately and gently swinging his jeweled cane: "Me nephew Hall is a good boy, don't ye know? He didn't mean any harm to your work. Won't you, now, be good fellows, and let him serve out his term?"

The fates, or bad liquor, pursued President Arthur's appointees even after they left Alaska. The governor broke his arm and had a paralytic stroke, and soon died. The district attorney fell off the train and was killed. The other officers retired to private life, Judge McAllister resuming his practice of law in San Francisco.

In the spring of 1885, President Cleveland replaced these officers with a full set of Democrats. Governor Swineford of Michigan was a much brighter and more active man than Governor Kinkead. He had a mind sufficiently alert to comprehend something of the possibilities of the great Territory. Throughout his term he laboured for more liberal laws and fairer treatment of Alaska. He attacked the persistent and venal misrepresentations of Alaska by the Alaska Commercial Company and the big fishing interests. He was the first governor to advocate a territorial legislature and the freedom of American citizenship for the settlers. He showed that the census taken in 1886 was faulty, underestimating by one-half the civilized citizenship of the Territory. He did justice to the fine character of the miners and other settlers who were moving into the Territory; he advocated better land laws, increased transportation facilities, better rights for the poor fishermen and miners. He was opposed to big monopolies. When his term of office expired he returned to Alaska as editor of a paper in Ketchikan and made the Territory his home until death. He took the part of the schools and missionaries, and was for a number of years an active and progressive friend of Alaska.

The judge appointed by Cleveland was the occasion of the worst scandal in the history of Alaska officials, except that which gathered about Judge Noyes of Nome in 1900–1. The judge (Judge Dawn) was a kind of political and social roustabout. He had been in turn doctor, preacher and lawyer, without taking the trouble of fully educating himself in any of these professions. He was appointed by President Cleveland on the recommendation of Democrats in Salem and Portland, Oregon. After his appointment, one of those who had signed his petition wrote to President Cleveland protesting against the appointment, and claiming that the petition was a sort of joke, signed by him and others to get rid of the applicant, without any thought that it would be successful. This drew from President Cleveland the famous letter in which he scored unmercifully those who knowingly endorsed unworthy applicants for office:

How can you expect the President, 2,500 miles distant, to know more about the qualifications of an applicant for office than you who are on the ground? All the President can do in such cases is to trust to the honesty and good judgment of the endorsers. If the appointee is unworthy, those who recommended him must bear the odium, and not the President.

Judge Dawn came to Sitka on the same boat with Governor Swineford and the other officials. During the interval between the arrival of the boat which brought them to Alaska and the next monthly steamer, Judge Dawn suddenly appeared with two white companions at Wrangell, having come from Sitka by canoe. He was entertained by our mission and made a very pious address to the boys and girls of our training school, exhorting them to be good Christians and to fit themselves to be good American citizens. He instructed a young man who had been appointed deputy marshal to proclaim the court opened every morning and adjourned until he should return. Then he launched his canoe again, steering for Port Simpson in British Columbia. He took with him as a traveling companion an Indian girl, who had been in our school; his two male companions being in like manner provided with young squaws. Thus he disappeared *forever* from the knowledge of the Alaskans. The reason for his sudden departure was revealed when the next steamer arrived, for it brought a United States marshal from Portland with a warrant for the arrest of Judge Dawn on the charge of embezzling fifteen thousand dollars from his father-in-law. Thus we were left without judge and without court.

# 7

## "NORTH OF FIFTY-THREE"

O~N~ two small fog-bound islands in the southern Bering Sea, just north of the fifty-sixth parallel, are the rookeries of the fur seal. Thither every summer the seals migrate from the west coast of the United States. The islands were uninhabited when the Russians came to Alaska and were not discovered till 1786 by one of their number, Gerassim Pribilof, who gave these islands their name. The Russians harvested this valuable peltry and when, in the early days of Russian rule, reckless killing nearly exterminated the herd, imposed conservation measures to restore it. Acquisition of this rich resource was one of the motivations of California interests who supported the purchase of Alaska.

Apart from a law applying the customs and navigation laws to Alaska, the only other legislation relating to Alaska during its first seventeen years under the American flag was one turning over the responsibility for the fur seals to the Secretary of the Treasury, who promptly leased the islands and their product for twenty years to a private company in San Francisco.

In the late 1880's a few vessels found it profitable to take seals at sea. This was a highly destructive procedure since many were lost. Although it was a practice that could be forbidden to our nationals, it could not be enforced on vessels of other countries. Palliative measures proved ineffective, and by 1910 the herd of 3,000,000 seals at the time of the purchase was reduced to 100,000 and faced extinction.

A treaty between the United States, Russia, Japan, and Britain (in behalf of Canada) forbade pelagic sealing, gave the cosigners a share of the pelts, and put the Government of the United States in charge. The herd was then gradually rebuilt.

Politics in its worst aspects and greed characterized the handling of this resource until it was nearly extinct. In addition to pelagic sealing, raiding parties sought to slaughter and steal the skins on the islands. Bloody clashes took place between these raiders and the Pribilof Island authorities. Battles between raiders also took place. One of these forms the theme of Rudyard Kipling's poem, "The Rhyme of the Three Sealers," which owes its fame in part to its famous line, "And there's never a law of God or man runs north of Fifty-three."

## The Rhyme of the Three Sealers, by Rudyard Kipling

*Away by the lands of the Japanee*
  *Where the paper lanterns glow*
*And the crews of all the shipping drink*
  *In the house of Blood Street Joe,*
*At twilight, when the landward breeze*
  *Brings up the harbour noise,*
*And ebb of Yokohama Bay*
  *Swigs chattering through the buoys,*
*In Cisco's Dewdrop Dining Rooms*
  *They tell the tale anew*
*Of a hidden sea and a hidden fight,*
*When the* Baltic *ran from the* Northern Light,
  *And the* Stralsund *fought the two.*

Now this is the Law of the Muscovite, that he proves with shot and steel,
When you come by his isles in the Smoky Sea you must not take the seal,
Where the grey sea goes nakedly between the weed-hung shelves,
And the little blue fox he is bred for his skin and the seal they breed for themselves.

For when the *matkas* [1] seek the shore to drop their pups aland,
The great man-seal haul out of the sea, aroaring, band by band.
And when the first September gales have slaked their rutting-wrath,
The great man-seal haul back to the sea and no man knows their
    path.
Then dark they lie and stark they lie—rookery, dune, and floe,
And the Northern Lights come down o' nights to dance with the
    houseless snow;
And God Who clears the grounding berg and steers the grinding
    floe,
He hears the cry of the little kit-fox and the wind along the snow.
But since our women must walk gay and money buys their gear,
The sealing-boats they filch that way at hazard year by year.
English they be and Japanee that hang on the Brown Bear's flank,
And some be Scot, but the worst of the lot, and the boldest thieves,
    be Yank!
It was the sealer *Northern Light,* to the Smoky Seas she bore,
With a stovepipe stuck from a starboard port and the Russian flag
    at her fore.
(*Baltic, Stralsund,* and *Northern Light*—oh! they were birds of a
    feather—
Slipping away to the Smoky Seas, three seal-thieves together!)
And at last she came to a sandy cove and the *Baltic* lay therein,
But her men were up with the herding seal to drive and club and
    skin.
There were fifteen hundred skins abeach, cool pelt and proper fur,
When the *Northern Light* drove into the bight and the sea-mist
    drove with her.
The *Baltic* called her men and weighed—she could not choose but
    run—
For a stovepipe seen through the closing mist, it shows like a four-
    inch gun
(And loss it is that is sad as death to lose both trip and ship
And lie for a rotting contraband on Vladivostok slip).
She turned and dived in the sea-smother as a rabbit dives in the
    whins,

[1] She-seals.

And the *Northern Light* sent up her boats to steal the stolen skins.
They had not brought a load to side or slid their hatches clear,
When they were aware of a sloop-of-war, ghost-white and very
    near.
Her flag she showed, and her guns she showed—three of them,
    black, abeam,
And a funnel white with the crusted salt, but never a show of
    steam.

There was no time to man the brakes, they knocked the shackle free,
And the *Northern Light* stood out again, goose-winged to open sea.
(For life it is that is worse than death, by force of Russian law,
To work in the mines of mercury that loose the teeth in your jaw.)
They had not run a mile from shore—they heard no shots behind—
When the skipper smote his hand on his thigh and threw her up
    in the wind:
"Bluffed—raised out on a bluff," said he, "for if my name's Tom
    Hall,
"You must set a thief to catch a thief—and a thief has caught us
    all!
"By every butt in Oregon and every spar in Maine,
"The hand that spilled the wind from her sail was the hand of
    Reuben Paine!
"He has rigged and trigged her with paint and spar, and, faith, he
    has faked her well—
"But I'd know the *Stralsund*'s deckhouse yet from here to the
    booms o' Hell.
"Oh, once we ha' met at Baltimore, and twice on Boston pier,
"But the sickest day for you, Reuben Paine, was the day that you
    came here—
"That day that you came here, my lad, to scare us from our seal
"With your funnel made o' your painted cloth, and your guns o'
    rotten deal!
"Ring and blow for the *Baltic* now, and head her back to the bay,
"And we'll come into the game again—with a double deck to
    play!"

They rang and blew the sealers' call—the poaching-cry of the
   sea—
And they raised the *Baltic* out of the mist, and an angry ship was
   she.
And blind they groped through the whirling white and blind to
   the bay again,
Till they heard the creak of the *Stralsund*'s boom and the clank of
   her mooring chain.
They laid them down by bitt and boat, their pistols in their belts,
And: "Will you fight for it, Reuben Paine, or will you share the
   pelts?"

A dog-toothed laugh laughed Reuben Paine, and bared his flench-
   ing-knife.
"Yea, skin for skin, and all that he hath a man will give for his life;
"But I've six thousand skins below, and Yeddo Port to see,
"And there's never a law of God or man runs north of Fifty-three:
"So go in peace to the naked seas with empty holds to fill,
"And I'll be good to your seal this catch, as many as I shall kill!"

Answered the snap of a closing lock—the jar of a gun-butt slid,
But the tender fog shut fold on fold to hide the wrong they did.
The weeping fog rolled fold on fold the wrath of man to cloak,
As the flame-spurts pale ran down the rail and the sealing-rifles
   spoke.
The bullets bit on bend and butt, the splinter slivered free
(Little they trust to sparrow-dust that stop the seal in his sea!),
The thick smoke hung and would not shift, leaden it lay and blue,
But three were down on the *Baltic*'s deck and two of the *Stral-
   sund*'s crew.

An arm's length out and overside the banked fog held them bound,
But, as they heard a groan or word, they fired at the sound.
For one cried out on the Name of God, and one to have him cease,
And the questing volley found them both and bade them hold their
   peace.
And one called out on a heathen joss and one on the Virgin's
   Name,

And the schooling bullet leaped across and led them whence they
    came.
And in the waiting silences the rudder whined beneath,
And each man drew his watchful breath slow-taken 'tween the
    teeth—
Trigger and ear and eye acock, knit brow and hard-drawn lips—
Bracing his feet by chock and cleat for the rolling of the ships.
Till they heard the cough of a wounded man that fought in the fog
    for breath,
Till they heard the torment of Reuben Paine that wailed upon his
    death:

"The tides they'll go through Fundy Race, but I'll go never more
"And see the hogs from ebb-tide mark turn scampering back to
    shore.
"No more I'll see the trawlers drift below the Bass Rock ground,
"Or watch the tall Fall steamer lights tear blazing up the Sound.
"Sorrow is me, in a lonely sea and a sinful fight I fall,
"But if there's law o' God or man you'll swing for it yet, Tom
    Hall!"

Tom Hall stood up by the quarter-rail. "Your words in your
    teeth," said he.
"There's never a law of God or man runs north of Fifty-Three.
"So go in grace with Him to face, and an ill-spent life behind,
"And I'll be good to your widows, Rube, as many as I shall find."
A *Stralsund* man shot blind and large, and a warlock Finn was he,
And he hit Tom Hall with a bursting ball a hand's-breadth over the
    knee.
Tom Hall caught hold by the topping-lift, and sat him down with
    an oath,
"You'll wait a little, Rube," he said, "the Devil has called for both.
"The Devil is driving both this tide, and the killing-grounds are
    close,
"And we'll go up to the Wrath of God as the holluschickie [2] goes.
"O men, put back your guns again and lay your rifles by,

2 The young seal.

"We've fought our fight, and the best are down. Let up and let
    us die!"
"Quit firing, by the bow there—quit! Call off the *Baltic*'s crew!
"You're sure of Hell as me or Rube—but wait till we get through."

There went no word between the ships, but thick and quick and
    loud
The life-blood drummed on the dripping decks, with the fog-dew
    from the shroud.
The sea-pull drew them side by side, gunnel to gunnel laid,
And they felt the sheer-strakes pound and clear, but never a word
    was said.

Then Reuben Paine cried out again before his spirits passed:
"Have I followed the sea for thirty years to die in the dark at last?
"Curse on her work that has nipped me here with a shifty trick
    unkind—
"I have gotten my death where I got my bread, but I dare not face
    it blind.
"Curse on the fog! Is there never a wind of all the winds I knew
"To clear the smother from off my chest, and let me look at the
    blue?"
The good fog heard—like a splitten sail, to left and right she tore,
And they saw the sun-dogs in the haze and the seal upon the shore.
Silver and grey ran spit and bay to meet the steel-backed tide,
And pinched and white in the clearing light the crews stared
    overside.
O rainbow-gay the red pools lay that swilled and spilled and
    spread,
And gold, raw gold, the spent shells rolled between the careless
    dead—
The dead that rocked so drunkenwise to weather and to lee,
And they saw the work their hands had done as God had bade
    them see!

And a little breeze blew over the rail that made the headsails lift,
But no man stood by wheel or sheet, and they let the schooners drift.

And the rattle rose in Reuben's throat and he cast his soul with a
cry,
And "Gone already?" Tom Hall he said. "Then it's time for me
to die."
His eyes were heavy with great sleep and yearning for the land,
And he spoke as a man that talks in dreams, his wound beneath
his hand.

"Oh, there comes no good o' the westering wind that backs against
the sun;
"Wash down the decks—they're all too red—and share the skins
and run.
"*Baltic, Stralsund,* and *Northern Light*—clean share and share for
all,
"You'll find the fleets off Tolstoi Mees, but you will not find Tom
Hall.
"Evil he did in shoal-water and blacker sin on the deep,
"But now he's sick of watch and trick and now he'll turn and sleep.
"He'll have no more of the crawling sea that made him suffer so,
"But he'll lie down on the killing-grounds where the holluschickie
go.
"And west you'll sail and south again, beyond the sea-fog's rim,
"And tell the Yoshiwara girls to burn a stick for him.

"And you'll not weight him by the heels and dump him overside,
"But carry him up to the sand-hollows to die as Bering died,
"And make a place for Reuben Paine that knows the fight was
fair,
"And leave the two that did the wrong to talk it over there!"

*Half-steam ahead by guess and lead, for the sun is mostly veiled—*
*Through fog to fog, by luck and log, sail you as Bering sailed;*
*And if the light shall lift aright to give your landfall plain,*
*North and by west, from Zapne Crest you raise the Crosses twain.*
*Fair marks are they to the inner bay, the reckless poacher knows,*
*What time the scarred see-catchie* [3] *lead their sleek seraglios.*

[3] The male seal.

*Ever they hear the floe-pack clear, and the blast of the old bull-*
*    whale,*
*And the deep seal-roar that beats off-shore above the loudest gale.*
*Ever they wait the winter's hate as the thundering* boorga[4] *calls,*
*Where northward look they to St. George, and westward to St.*
*    Paul's.*
*Ever they greet the hunted fleet—lone keels off headlands drear—*
*When the sealing-schooners flit that way at hazard year by year.*
*Ever in Yokohama port men tell the tale anew*
*    Of a hidden sea and a hidden fight,*
*    When the* Baltic *ran from the* Northern Light,
*And the* Stralsund *fought the two.*

  [4] Hurricane.

# 8

# GOLD RUSH TALES

JACK LONDON (1876–1916), born in San Francisco, grew up
in relative poverty, and his youth was spent in odd jobs and vaga-
bondage. He was unsuccessful as a short-story writer until after
he had joined the Gold Rush to the Klondike in the summer of
1897. Landing at Dyea, he packed over the Chilkoot Pass and
spent a winter on the Yukon. In the following years he wrote three
novels and five collections of short stories which gained him fame
and fortune. *The Call of the Wild,* his most successful novel, had
as its hero a dog called "Buck." After he had endured incredible
hardships on the trail, too exhausted to mush and cruelly beaten,
Buck was saved from further punishment by John Thornton, a
prospector, to whom thereafter he gave unstinted devotion. The
following chapter illustrates this attachment.

From · · ·

*The Call of the Wild,* by Jack London

FOR THE LOVE OF A MAN

When John Thornton froze his feet in the previous December,
his partners had made him comfortable and left him to get well,
going on themselves up the river to get out a raft of saw-logs for
Dawson. He was still limping slightly at the time he rescued Buck,
but with the continued warm weather even the slight limp left him.

And here, lying by the river bank through the long spring days, watching the running water, listening lazily to the songs of birds and the hum of nature, Buck slowly won back his strength.

A rest comes very good after one has travelled three thousand miles, and it must be confessed that Buck waxed lazy as his wounds healed, his muscles swelled out, and the flesh came back to cover his bones. For that matter, they were all loafing—Buck, John Thornton, and Skeet and Nig—waiting for the raft to come that was to carry them down to Dawson. Skeet was a little Irish setter who early made friends with Buck, who, in a dying condition, was unable to resent her first advances. She had the doctor trait which some dogs possess, and as a mother cat washes her kittens, so she washed and cleansed Buck's wounds. Regularly, each morning after he had finished his breakfast, she performed her self-appointed task, till he came to look for her ministrations as much as he did for Thornton's. Nig, equally friendly though less demonstrative, was a huge black dog, half bloodhound and half deerhound, with eyes that laughed and a boundless good nature.

To Buck's surprise these dogs manifested no jealousy toward him. They seemed to share the kindliness and largeness of John Thornton. As Buck grew stronger they enticed him into all sorts of ridiculous games, in which Thornton himself could not forbear to join, and in this fashion Buck romped through his convalescence and into a new existence. Love, genuine passionate love, was his for the first time. This he had never experienced at Judge Miller's down in the sun-kissed Santa Clara Valley. With the Judge's sons, hunting and tramping, it had been a working partnership; with the Judge's grandsons, a sort of pompous guardianship; and with the Judge himself, a stately and dignified friendship. But love that was feverish and burning, that was adoration, that was madness, it had taken John Thornton to arouse.

This man had saved his life, which was something; but, further, he was the ideal master. Other men saw to the welfare of their dogs from a sense of duty and business expediency; he saw to the welfare of his as if they were his own children, because he could not help it. And he saw further. He never forgot a kindly greeting or a cheering word, and to sit down for a long talk with them ("gas" he called it) was as much his delight as theirs. He had a way of taking Buck's head roughly between his hands, and resting his own head upon Buck's, of shaking him back and forth, the while calling him ill names that to Buck were love names. Buck knew no greater joy than that rough embrace and the sound of murmured oaths, and at each jerk back and forth it seemed that his heart would be shaken out of his body so great was its ecstasy. And when, released, he sprang to his feet, his mouth laughing, his eyes eloquent, his throat vibrant with unuttered sound, and in that fashion remained without movement, John Thornton would reverently exclaim, "God! you can all but speak!"

Buck had a trick of love expression that was akin to hurt. He would often seize Thornton's hand in his mouth and close so fiercely that the flesh bore the impress of his teeth for some time afterward. And as Buck understood the oaths to be love words, so the man understood this feigned bite for a caress.

For the most part, however, Buck's love was expressed in adoration. While he went wild with happiness when Thornton touched him or spoke to him, he did not seek these tokens. Unlike Skeet, who was wont to shove her nose under Thornton's hand and nudge and nudge till petted, or Nig, who would stalk up and rest his great head on Thornton's knee, Buck was content to adore at a distance. He would lie by the hour, eager, alert, at Thornton's feet, looking up into his face, dwelling upon it, studying it, following with keenest interest each fleeting expression, every movement or change of feature. Or, as chance might have it, he would lie farther away, to the side or rear, watching the outlines of the man and the occasional movements of his body. And often, such was the communion in which they lived, the strength of Buck's gaze would draw John Thornton's head around, and he would return the gaze, without speech, his heart shining out of his eyes as Buck's heart shone out.

For a long time after his rescue, Buck did not like Thornton to get out of his sight. From the moment he left the tent to when he entered it again, Buck would follow at his heels. His transient masters since he had come into the Northland had bred in him a fear that no master could be permanent. He was afraid that Thornton would pass out of his life as Perrault and François and the Scotch half-breed had passed out. Even in the night, in his dreams, he was haunted by this fear. At such times he would shake off sleep and creep through the chill to the flap of the tent, where he would stand and listen to the sound of his master's breathing.

But in spite of this great love he bore John Thornton, which seemed to bespeak the soft civilizing influence, the strain of the primitive, which the Northland had aroused in him, remained alive and active. Faithfulness and devotion, things born of fire and roof, were his; yet he retained his wildness and wiliness. He was a thing of the wild, come in from the wild to sit by John Thornton's fire, rather than a dog of the soft Southland stamped with the marks of generations of civilization. Because of his very great love, he could not steal from this man, but from any other man, in any other camp, he did not hesitate an instant, while the cunning with which he stole enabled him to escape detection.

His face and body were scored by the teeth of many dogs, and he fought as fiercely as ever and more shrewdly. Skeet and Nig were too good-natured for quarrelling—besides, they belonged to John Thornton; but the strange dog, no matter what the breed or valor, swiftly acknowledged Buck's supremacy or found himself struggling for life with a terrible antagonist. And Buck was merciless. He had learned well the law of club and fang, and he never forewent an advantage or drew back from a foe he had started on the way to Death. He had lessoned from Spitz, and from the chief fighting dogs of the police and mail, and knew there was no middle course. He must master or be mastered; while to show mercy was a weakness. Mercy did not exist in the primordial life. It was misunderstood for fear, and such misunderstandings made for death. Kill or be killed, eat or be eaten, was the law; and this mandate, down out of the depths of Time, he obeyed.

He was older than the days he had seen and the breaths he had drawn. He linked the past with the present, and the eternity behind him throbbed through him in a mighty rhythm to which he swayed as the tides and seasons swayed. He sat by John Thornton's fire, a broad-breasted dog, white-fanged and long-furred; but behind him were the shades of all manner of dogs, half-wolves and wild wolves, urgent and prompting, tasting the savor of the meat he ate, thirsting for the water he drank, scenting the wind with him, listening with him and telling him the sounds made by the wild life in the forest, dictating his moods, directing his actions, lying down to sleep with him when he lay down, and dreaming with him and beyond him and becoming themselves the stuff of his dreams.

So peremptorily did these shades beckon him, that each day mankind and the claims of mankind slipped farther from him. Deep in the forest a call was sounding, and as often as he heard this call, mysteriously thrilling and luring, he felt compelled to turn his back upon the fire and the beaten earth around it, and to plunge into the forest, and on and on, he knew not where or why; nor did he wonder where or why, the call sounding imperiously, deep in the forest. But as often as he gained the soft unbroken earth and the green shade, the love for John Thornton drew him back to the fire again.

Thornton alone held him. The rest of mankind was as nothing. Chance travellers might praise or pet him; but he was cold under it all, and from a too demonstrative man he would get up and walk away. When Thornton's partners, Hans and Pete, arrived on the long-expected raft, Buck refused to notice them till he learned they were close to Thornton; after that he tolerated them in a passive sort of way, accepting favors from them as though he favored them by accepting. They were of the same large type as Thornton, living close to the earth, thinking simply and seeing clearly; and ere they swung the raft into the big eddy by the sawmill at Dawson, they understood Buck and his ways, and did not insist upon an intimacy such as obtained with Skeet and Nig.

For Thornton, however, his love seemed to grow and grow. He alone among men could put a pack upon Buck's back in the summer travelling. Nothing was too great for Buck to do, when Thornton commanded. One day (they had grub-staked themselves from the proceeds of the raft and left Dawson for the head-waters of the Tanana) the men and dogs were sitting on the crest of a cliff which fell away, straight down, to naked bed-rock three hundred feet below. John Thornton was sitting near the edge, Buck at his shoulder. A thoughtless whim seized Thornton, and he drew the atten-

tion of Hans and Pete to the experiment he had in mind. "Jump,
Buck!" he commanded, sweeping his arm out and over the chasm.
The next instant he was grappling with Buck on the extreme edge,
while Hans and Pete were dragging them back into safety.

"It's uncanny," Pete said, after it was over and they had caught
their speech.

Thornton shook his head. "No, it is splendid, and it is terrible,
too. Do you know, it sometimes makes me afraid."

"I'm not hankering to be the man that lays hands on you while
he's around," Pete announced conclusively, nodding his head
toward Buck.

"Py Jingo!" was Hans's contribution. "Not mineself either."

It was at Circle City, ere the year was out, that Pete's appre-
hensions were realized. "Black" Burton, a man evil-tempered and
malicious, had been picking a quarrel with a tenderfoot at the bar,
when Thornton stepped good-naturedly between. Buck, as was his
custom, was lying in a corner, head on paws, watching his master's
every action. Burton struck out, without warning, straight from the
shoulder. Thornton was sent spinning, and saved himself from
falling only by clutching the rail of the bar.

Those who were looking on heard what was neither bark nor
yelp, but a something which is best described as a roar, and they
saw Buck's body rise up in the air as he left the floor for Burton's
throat. The man saved his life by instinctively throwing out his
arm, but was hurled backward to the floor with Buck on top of
him. Buck loosed his teeth from the flesh of the arm and drove in
again for the throat. This time the man succeeded only in partly
blocking, and his throat was torn open. Then the crowd was upon
Buck, and he was driven off; but while a surgeon checked the bleed-
ing, he prowled up and down, growling furiously, attempting to
rush in, and being forced back by an array of hostile clubs. A
"miners' meeting," called on the spot, decided that the dog had
sufficient provocation, and Buck was discharged. But his reputation
was made, and from that day his name spread through every camp
in Alaska.

Later on, in the fall of the year, he saved John Thornton's life in
quite another fashion. The three partners were lining a long and

narrow poling-boat down a bad stretch of rapids on the Forty Mile
Creek. Hans and Pete moved along the bank, snubbing with a thin
manila rope from tree to tree, while Thornton remained in the
boat, helping its descent by means of a pole, and shouting directions to the shore. Buck, on the bank, worried and anxious, kept
abreast of the boat, his eyes never off his master.

At a particularly bad spot, where a ledge of barely submerged
rocks jutted out into the river, Hans cast off the rope, and, while
Thornton poled the boat out into the stream, ran down the bank
with the end in his hand to snub the boat when it had cleared the
ledge. This it did, and was flying down-stream in a current as swift
as a mill-race, when Hans checked it with the rope and checked too
suddenly. The boat flirted over and snubbed in to the bank bottom
up, while Thornton flung sheer out of it, was carried down-stream
toward the worst part of the rapids, a stretch of wild water in
which no swimmer could live.

Buck had sprung in on the instant; and at the end of three hundred yards, amid a mad swirl of water, he overhauled Thornton.
When he felt him grasp his tail, Buck headed for the bank, swimming with all his splendid strength. But the progress shoreward was
slow; the progress down-stream amazingly rapid. From below came
the fatal roaring where the wild current went wilder and was rent
in shreds and spray by the rocks which thrust through like the
teeth of an enormous comb. The suck of the water as it took the
beginning of the last steep pitch was frightful, and Thornton knew
that the shore was impossible. He scraped furiously over a rock,
bruised across a second, and struck a third with crushing force.
He clutched its slippery top with both hands, releasing Buck, and
above the roar of the churning water shouted: "Go, Buck! Go!"

Buck could not hold his own, and swept on down-stream, struggling desperately, but unable to win back. When he heard Thornton's command repeated, he partly reared out of the water,
throwing his head high, as though for a last look, then turned
obediently toward the bank. He swam powerfully and was dragged
ashore by Pete and Hans at the very point where swimming ceased
to be possible and destruction began.

They knew that the time a man could cling to a slippery rock in the face of that driving current was a matter of minutes, and they ran as fast as they could up the bank to a point far above where Thornton was hanging on. They attached the line with which they had been snubbing the boat to Buck's neck and shoulders, being careful that it should neither strangle him nor impede his swimming, and launched him into the stream. He struck out boldly, but not straight enough into the stream. He discovered the mistake too late, when Thornton was abreast of him and a bare half-dozen strokes away while he was being carried helplessly past.

Hans promptly snubbed with the rope, as though Buck were a boat. The rope thus tightening on him in the sweep of the current, he was jerked under the surface, and under the surface he remained till his body struck against the bank and he was hauled out. He was half drowned, and Hans and Pete threw themselves upon him, pounding the breath into him and the water out of him. He staggered to his feet and fell down. The faint sound of Thornton's voice came to them, and though they could not make out the words of it, they knew that he was in his extremity. His master's voice acted on Buck like an electric shock. He sprang to his feet and ran up the bank ahead of the men to the point of his previous departure.

Again the rope was attached and he was launched, and again he struck out, but this time straight into the stream. He had miscalculated once, but he would not be guilty of it a second time. Hans paid out the rope, permitting no slack, while Pete kept it clear of coils. Buck held on till he was on a line straight above Thornton; then he turned, and with the speed of an express train headed down upon him. Thornton saw him coming, and, as Buck struck him like a battering ram, with the whole force of the current behind him, he reached up and closed with both arms around the shaggy neck. Hans snubbed the rope around the tree, and Buck and Thornton were jerked under the water. Strangling, suffocating, sometimes one upper-most and sometimes the other, dragging over the jagged bottom, smashing against rocks and snags, they veered in to the bank.

Thornton came to, belly downward and being violently propelled back and forth across a drift log by Hans and Pete. His first glance was for Buck, over whose limp and apparently lifeless body Nig was setting up a howl, while Skeet was licking the wet face and closed eyes. Thornton was himself bruised and battered, and he went carefully over Buck's body, when he had been brought around, finding three broken ribs.

"That settles it," he announced. "We camp right here." And camp they did, till Buck's ribs knitted and he was able to travel.

That winter, at Dawson, Buck performed another exploit, not so heroic, perhaps, but one that put his name many notches higher on the totem-pole of Alaskan fame. This exploit was particularly gratifying to the three men; for they stood in need of the outfit which it furnished, and were enabled to make a long-desired trip into the virgin East, where miners had not yet appeared. It was brought about by a conversation in the Eldorado Saloon, in which men waxed boastful of their favorite dogs. Buck, because of his record, was the target for these men, and Thornton was driven stoutly to defend him. At the end of half an hour one man stated that his dog could start a sled with five hundred pounds and walk off with it; a second bragged six hundred for his dog; and a third, seven hundred.

"Pooh! Pooh!" said John Thornton, "Buck can start a thousand pounds."

"And break it out? and walk off with it for a hundred yards?" demanded Matthewson, a Bonanza king, he of the seven hundred vaunt.

"And break it out, and walk off with it for a hundred yards," John Thornton said coolly.

"Well," Matthewson said, slowly and deliberately, so that all could hear, "I've got a thousand dollars that says he can't. And there it is." So saying, he slammed a sack of gold dust of the size of a bologna sausage down upon the bar.

Nobody spoke. Thornton's bluff, if bluff it was, had been called. He could feel a flush of warm blood creeping up his face. His tongue had tricked him. He did not know whether Buck could start a thousand pounds. Half a ton! The enormousness of it appalled him. He had great faith in Buck's strength and had often thought him capable of starting such a load; but never, as now, had he faced the possibility of it, the eyes of a dozen men fixed upon him, silent and waiting. Further, he had no thousand dollars; nor had Hans or Pete.

"I've got a sled standing outside now, with twenty fifty-pound sacks of flour on it," Matthewson went on with brutal directness, "so don't let that hinder you."

Thornton did not reply. He did not know what to say. He glanced from face to face in the absent way of a man who has lost the power of thought and is seeking somewhere to find the thing that will start it going again. The face of Jim O'Brien, a Mastodon king and old-time comrade, caught his eyes. It was a cue to him, seeming to rouse him to do what he would never have dreamed of doing.

"Can you lend me a thousand?" he asked, almost in a whisper.

"Sure," answered O'Brien, thumping down a plethoric sack by the side of Matthewson's. "Though it's little faith I'm having, John, that the beast can do the trick."

The Eldorado emptied its occupants into the street to see the test. The tables were deserted, and the dealers and game-keepers came forth to see the outcome of the wager and to lay odds. Several hundred men, furred and mittened, banked around the sled within easy distance. Matthewson's sled, loaded with a thousand pounds of flour, had been standing for a couple of hours, and in the intense cold (it was sixty below zero) the runners had frozen fast to the hard-packed snow. Men offered odds of two to one that Buck could not budge the sled. A quibble arose concerning the phrase "break out." O'Brien contended it was Thornton's privilege to knock the runners loose, leaving Buck to "break it out" from a dead standstill. Matthewson insisted that the phrase included breaking the runners from the frozen grip of the snow. A majority of the men who had witnessed the making of the bet decided in his favor, whereat the odds went up to three to one against Buck. There were no takers. Not a man believed him capable of the feat. Thornton had been hurried into the wager, heavy with doubt; and now that he looked at the sled itself, the concrete fact, with the regular team of ten dogs curled up in the snow before it, the more impossible the task appeared. Matthewson waxed jubilant.

"Three to one!" he proclaimed. "I'll lay you another thousand at that figure, Thornton. What d'ye say?"

Thornton's doubt was strong in his face, but his fighting spirit was aroused—the fighting spirit that soars above odds, fails to recognize the impossible, and is deaf to all save the clamor for battle. He called Hans and Pete to him. Their sacks were slim, and with his own the three partners could rake together only two hundred dollars. In the ebb of their fortunes, this sum was their total capital; yet they laid it unhesitatingly against Matthewson's six hundred.

The team of ten dogs was unhitched, and Buck, with his own harness, was put into the sled. He had caught the contagion of the excitement, and he felt that in some way he must do a great thing for John Thornton. Murmurs of admiration at his splendid appearance went up. He was in perfect condition, without an ounce of superfluous flesh, and the one hundred and fifty pounds that he weighed were so many pounds of grit and virility. His furry coat shone with the sheen of silk. Down the neck and across the shoulders, his mane, in repose as it was, half bristled and seemed to lift with every movement, as though excess of vigor made each particular hair alive and active. The great breast and heavy fore legs were no more than in proportion with the rest of the body where the muscles showed in tight rolls underneath the skin. Men felt these muscles and proclaimed them hard as iron, and the odds went down to two to one.

"Gad, sir! Gad, sir!" stuttered a member of the latest dynasty, a king of the Skookum Benches. "I offer you eight hundred for him, sir, before the test, sir; eight hundred just as he stands."

Thornton shook his head and stepped to Buck's side.

"You must stand off from him," Matthewson protested. "Free play and plenty of room."

The crowd fell silent; only could be heard the voices of the gamblers vainly offering two to one. Everybody acknowledged Buck a magnificent animal, but twenty fifty-pound sacks of flour bulked too large in their eyes for them to loosen their pouch-strings.

Thornton knelt down by Buck's side. He took his head in his two hands and rested cheek on cheek. He did not playfully shake him, as was his wont, or murmur soft love curses; but he whispered in his ear. "As you love me, Buck. As you love me," was what he whispered. Buck whined with suppressed eagerness.

The crowd was watching curiously. The affair was growing

mysterious. It seemed like a conjuration. As Thornton got to his feet, Buck seized his mittened hand between his jaws, pressing in with his teeth and releasing slowly, half-reluctantly. It was the answer, in terms, not of speech, but of love. Thornton stepped well back.

"Now, Buck," he said.

Buck tightened the traces, then slacked them for a matter of several inches. It was the way he had learned.

"Gee!" Thornton's voice rang out, sharp in the tense silence.

Buck swung to the right, ending the movement in a plunge that took up the slack and with a sudden jerk arrested his one hundred and fifty pounds. The load quivered, and from under the runners arose a crisp crackling.

"Haw!" Thornton commanded.

Buck duplicating the manœuvre, this time to the left. The crackling turned into a snapping, the sled pivoting and the runners slipping and grating several inches to the side. The sled was broken out. Men were holding their breaths, intensely unconscious of the fact.

"Now, *mush!*"

Thornton's command cracked out like a pistol-shot. Buck threw himself forward, tightening the traces with a jarring lunge. His whole body was gathered compactly together in the tremendous effort, the muscles writhing and knotting like live things under the silky fur. His great chest was low to the ground, his head forward and down, while his feet were flying like mad, the claws scarring the hard-packed snow in parallel grooves. The sled swayed and trembled, half-started forward. One of his feet slipped, and one man groaned aloud. Then the sled lurched ahead in what appeared a rapid succession of jerks, though it never really came to a dead stop again . . . half an inch . . . an inch . . . two inches. . . . The jerks perceptibly diminished; as the sled gained momentum, he caught them up, till it was moving steadily along.

Men gasped and began to breathe again, unaware that for a moment they had ceased to breathe. Thornton was running behind, encouraging Buck with short, cheery words. The distance had been measured off, and as he neared the pile of firewood which

marked the end of the hundred yards, a cheer began to grow and
grow, which burst into a roar as he passed the firewood and halted
at command. Every man was tearing himself loose, even Matthewson. Hats and mittens were flying in the air. Men were shaking
hands, it did not matter with whom, and bubbling over in a general
incoherent babel.

But Thornton fell on his knees beside Buck. Head was against
head, and he was shaking him back and forth. Those who hurried
up heard him cursing Buck, and he cursed him long and fervently,
and softly and lovingly.

"Gad, sir! Gad, sir!" spluttered the Skookum Bench king. "I'll
give you a thousand for him, sir, a thousand, sir—twelve hundred,
sir."

Thornton rose to his feet. His eyes were wet. The tears were
streaming frankly down his cheeks. "Sir," he said to the Skookum
Bench king, "no, sir. You can go to hell, sir. It's the best I can do
for you, sir."

Buck seized Thornton's hand in his teeth. Thornton shook him
back and forth. As though animated by a common impulse, the
onlookers drew back to a respectful distance, nor were they again
indiscreet enough to interrupt.

\* \* \*

The gold-rushers to the Klondike included vast numbers of
*cheechakos*—the Alaskan equivalent of the tenderfoot of the West
—some of whom paid a heavy price for their lack of experience.

In the following story Jack London tells what happened to one
who ventured on the trail alone at temperatures which a sourdough would have known enough to avoid.

## To Build a Fire, by Jack London

Day had broken cold and gray, exceedingly cold and gray,
when the man turned aside from the main Yukon trail and climbed
the high earth-bank, where a dim and little-travelled trail led eastward through the fat spruce timberland. It was a steep bank, and
he paused for breath at the top, excusing the act to himself by look-

ing at his watch. It was nine o'clock. There was no sun nor hint of
sun, though there was not a cloud in the sky. It was a clear day,
and yet there seemed an intangible pall over the face of things, a
subtle gloom that made the day dark, and that was due to the
absence of sun. This fact did not worry the man. He was used to
the lack of sun. It had been days since he had seen the sun, and
he knew that a few more days must pass before that cheerful orb,
due south, would just peep above the sky line and dip immediately
from view.

The man flung a look back along the way he had come. The
Yukon lay a mile wide and hidden under three feet of ice. On top
of this ice were as many feet of snow. It was all pure white, rolling
in gentle undulations where the ice jams of the freeze-up had
formed. North and south, as far as his eye could see, it was unbroken white, save for a dark hairline that curved and twisted from
around the spruce-covered island to the south, and that curved and
twisted away into the north, where it disappeared behind another
spruce-covered island. This dark hairline was the trail—the main
trail—that led south five hundred miles to the Chilcoot Pass, Dyea,
and salt water; and that led north seventy miles to Dawson, and
still on to the north a thousand miles to Nulato, and finally to St.
Michael, on Bering Sea, a thousand miles and half a thousand
more.

But all this—the mysterious, far-reaching hairline trail, the
absence of sun from the sky, the tremendous cold, and the strange-
ness and weirdness of it all—made no impression on the man. It
was not because he was long used to it. He was a newcomer in the
land, a *chechaquo*, and this was his first winter. The trouble with
him was that he was without imagination. He was quick and alert
in the things of life, but only in the things, and not in the signifi-
cances. Fifty degrees below zero meant eighty-odd degrees of frost.
Such fact impressed him as being cold and uncomfortable, and that
was all. It did not lead him to meditate upon his frailty as a creature of temperature, and upon man's frailty in general, able only
to live within certain narrow limits of heat and cold; and from
there on it did not lead him to the conjectural field of immortality
and man's place in the universe. Fifty degrees below zero stood for

a bite of frost that hurt and that must be guarded against by the use of mittens, ear flaps, warm moccasins, and thick socks. Fifty degrees below zero was to him just precisely fifty degrees below zero. That there should be anything more to it than that was a thought that never entered his head.

As he turned to go on, he spat speculatively. There was a sharp, explosive crackle that startled him. He spat again. And again, in the air, before it could fall to the snow, the spittle crackled. He knew that at fifty below spittle crackled on the snow, but this spittle had crackled in the air. Undoubtedly it was colder than fifty below—how much colder he did not know. But the temperature did not matter. He was bound for the old claim on the left fork of Henderson Creek, where the boys were already. They had come over across the divide from the Indian Creek country, while he had come the roundabout way to take a look at the possibilities of getting out logs in the spring from the islands in the Yukon. He would be in to camp by six o'clock; a bit after dark, it was true, but the boys would be there, a fire would be going, and a hot supper would be ready. As for lunch, he pressed his hand against the protruding bundle under his jacket. It was also under his shirt, wrapped up in a handkerchief and lying against the naked skin. It was the only way to keep the biscuits from freezing. He smiled agreeably to himself as he thought of those biscuits, each cut open and sopped in bacon grease, and each enclosing a generous slice of fried bacon.

He plunged in among the big spruce trees. The trail was faint. A foot of snow had fallen since the last sled had passed over, and he was glad he was without a sled, travelling light. In fact, he carried nothing but the lunch wrapped in the handkerchief. He was surprised, however, at the cold. It certainly was cold, he concluded, as he rubbed his numb nose and cheekbones with his mittened hand. He was a warm-whiskered man, but the hair on his face did not protect the high cheekbones and the eager nose that thrust itself aggressively into the frosty air.

At the man's heels trotted a dog, a big native husky, the proper wolf dog, gray-coated and without any visible or temperamental difference from its brother, the wild wolf. The animal was depressed by the tremendous cold. It knew that it was no time for travelling. Its instinct told it a truer tale than was told to the man by the man's judgment. In reality, it was not merely colder than fifty below zero; it was colder than sixty below, than seventy below. It was seventy-five below zero. Since the freezing point is thirty-two above zero, it meant than one hundred and seven degrees of frost obtained. The dog did not know anything about thermometers. Possibly in its brain there was no sharp consciousness of a condition of very cold such as was in the man's brain. But the brute had its instinct. It experienced a vague but menacing apprehension that subdued it and made it slink along at the man's heels, and that made it question eagerly every unwonted movement of the man as if expecting him to go into camp or to seek shelter somewhere and build a fire. The dog had learned fire, and it wanted fire, or else to burrow under the snow and cuddle its warmth away from the air.

The frozen moisture of its breathing had settled on its fur in a fine powder of frost, and especially were its jowls, muzzle, and eyelashes whitened by its crystalled breath. The man's red beard and mustache were likewise frosted, but more solidly, the deposit taking the form of ice and increasing with every warm, moist breath he exhaled. Also, the man was chewing tobacco, and the muzzle of ice held his lips so rigidly that he was unable to clear his chin when he expelled the juice. The result was that a crystal beard of the color and solidity of amber was increasing its length on his chin. If he fell down it would shatter itself, like glass, into brittle fragments. But he did not mind the appendage. It was the penalty all tobacco chewers paid in that country, and he had been out before in two cold snaps. They had not been so cold as this, he knew, but by the spirit thermometer at Sixty Mile he knew they had been registered at fifty below and at fifty-five.

He held on through the level stretch of woods for several miles, crossed a wide flat of nigger heads, and dropped down a bank to the frozen bed of a small stream. This was Henderson Creek, and he knew he was ten miles from the forks. He looked at his watch. It was ten o'clock. He was making four miles an hour, and he calculated that he would arrive at the forks at half-past twelve. He decided to celebrate that event by eating his lunch there.

The dog dropped in again at his heels, with a tail drooping discouragement, as the man swung along the creek bed. The furrow of the old sled trail was plainly visible, but a dozen inches of snow covered the marks of the last runners. In a month no man had come up or down that silent creek. The man held steadily on. He was not much given to thinking, and just then particularly he had nothing to think about save that he would eat lunch at the forks and that at six o'clock he would be in camp with the boys. There was nobody to talk to; and, had there been, speech would have been impossible because of the ice muzzle on his mouth. So he continued monotonously to chew tobacco and to increase the length of his amber beard.

Once in a while the thought reiterated itself that it was very cold and that he had never experienced such cold. As he walked along he rubbed his cheekbones and nose with the back of his mittened hand. He did this automatically, now and again changing hands. But, rub as he would, the instant he stopped his cheekbones went numb, and the following instant the end of his nose went numb. He was sure to frost his cheeks; he knew that, and experienced a pang of regret that he had not devised a nose strap of the sort Bud wore in cold snaps. Such a strap passed across the cheeks, as well, and saved them. But it didn't matter much, after all. What were frosted cheeks? A bit painful, that was all; they were never serious.

Empty as the man's mind was of thoughts, he was keenly observant, and he noticed the changes in the creek, the curves and bends and timber jams, and always he sharply noted where he placed his feet. Once, coming around a bend, he shied abruptly, like a startled horse, curved away from the place where he had been walking, and retreated several paces back along the trail. The creek he knew was frozen clear to the bottom—no creek could contain water in that arctic winter—but he knew also that there were springs that bubbled out from the hillsides and ran along under the snow and on top the ice of the creek. He knew that the coldest snaps never froze these springs, and he knew likewise their danger. They were traps. They hid pools of water under the snow that might be three inches deep, or three feet. Sometimes a skin of ice half an inch thick covered them, and in turn was covered by the snow. Sometimes there were alternate layers of water and ice skin, so that when one broke through he kept on breaking through for a while, sometimes wetting himself to the waist.

That was why he had shied in such panic. He had felt the give under his feet and heard the crackle of a snow-hidden ice skin. And to get his feet wet in such a temperature meant trouble and danger. At the very least it meant delay, for he would be forced to stop and build a fire, and under its protection to bare his feet while he dried his socks and moccasins. He stood and studied the creek bed and its banks, and decided that the flow of water came from the right. He reflected awhile, rubbing his nose and cheeks, then skirted to the left, stepping gingerly and testing the footing for each step. Once clear of the danger, he took a fresh chew of tobacco and swung along at his four-mile gait.

In the course of the next two hours he came upon several similar traps. Usually the snow above the hidden pools had a sunken, candied appearance that advertised the danger. Once again, however, he had a close call; and once, suspecting danger, he compelled the dog to go on in front. The dog did not want to go. It hung back until the man shoved it forward, and then it went quickly across the white, unbroken surface. Suddenly it broke through, floundered to one side, and got away to firmer footing. It had wet its forefeet and legs, and almost immediately the water that clung to it turned to ice. It made quick efforts to lick the ice off its legs, then dropped down in the snow and began to bite out the ice that had formed between the toes. This was a matter of instinct. To permit the ice to remain would mean sore feet. It did not know this. It merely obeyed the mysterious prompting that arose from the deep crypts of its being. But the man knew, having achieved a judgment on the subject, and he removed the mitten from his right hand and helped tear out the ice particles. He did not expose his fingers more than a minute, and was astonished at the swift numbness that smote them. It certainly was cold. He pulled on the mitten hastily, and beat the hand savagely across his chest.

At twelve o'clock the day was at its brightest. Yet the sun was too far south on its winter journey to clear the horizon. The bulge of the earth intervened between it and Henderson Creek, where the man walked under a clear sky at noon and cast no shadow. At half-past twelve, to the minute, he arrived at the forks of the creek. He was pleased at the speed he had made. If he kept it up, he would certainly be with the boys by six. He unbuttoned his jacket and shirt and drew forth his lunch. The action consumed no more than a quarter of a minute, yet in that brief moment the numbness laid hold of the exposed fingers. He did not put the mitten on, but, instead, struck the fingers a dozen sharp smashes against his leg. Then he sat down on a snow-covered log to eat. The sting that followed upon the striking of his fingers against his leg ceased so quickly that he was startled. He had had no chance to take a bite of biscuit. He struck the fingers repeatedly and returned them to the mitten, baring the other hand for the purpose of eating. He tried to take a mouthful, but the ice muzzle prevented. He had forgotten to build a fire and thaw out. He chuckled at his foolishness, and as he chuckled he noted the numbness creeping into the exposed fingers. Also, he noted that the stinging which had first come to his toes when he sat down was already passing away. He wondered whether the toes were warm or numb. He moved them inside the moccasins and decided that they were numb.

He pulled the mitten on hurriedly and stood up. He was a bit frightened. He stamped up and down until the stinging returned into the feet. It certainly was cold, was his thought. That man from Sulphur Creek had spoken the truth when telling how cold it sometimes got in the country. And he had laughed at him at the time! That showed one must not be too sure of things. There was no mistake about it, it *was* cold. He strode up and down, stamping his feet and threshing his arms, until reassured by the returning warmth. Then he got out matches and proceeded to make a fire. From the undergrowth, where high water of the previous spring had lodged a supply of seasoned twigs, he got his firewood. Working carefully from a small beginning, he soon had a roaring fire, over which he thawed the ice from his face and in the protection of which he ate his biscuits. For the moment the cold of space was outwitted. The dog took satisfaction in the fire, stretching out close enough for warmth and far enough away to escape being singed.

When the man had finished, he filled his pipe and took his comfortable time over a smoke. Then he pulled on his mittens, settled the ear flaps of his cap firmly about his ears, and took the creek trail up the left fork. The dog was disappointed and yearned back toward the fire. This man did not know cold. Possibly all the generations of his ancestry had been ignorant of cold, of real cold, of cold one hundred and seven degrees below freezing point. But the dog knew; all its ancestry knew, and it had inherited the knowledge. And it knew that it was not good to walk abroad in such fearful cold. It was the time to lie snug in a hole in the snow and wait for a curtain of cloud to be drawn across the face of outer space whence this cold came. On the other hand, there was no keen intimacy between the dog and the man. The one was the toil slave of the other, and the only caresses it had ever received were the caresses of the whip lash and of harsh and menacing throat sounds that threatened the whip lash. So the dog made no effort to communicate its apprehension to the man. It was not concerned in the welfare of the man; it was for its own sake that it yearned back toward the fire. But the man whistled, and spoke to it with the sound of whip lashes, and the dog swung in at the man's heels and followed after.

The man took a chew of tobacco and proceeded to start a new amber beard. Also, his moist breath quickly powdered with white his mustache, eyebrows, and lashes. There did not seem to be so many springs on the left fork of the Henderson, and for half an hour the man saw no signs of any. And then it happened. At a place where there were no signs, where the soft, unbroken snow seemed to advertise solidity beneath, the man broke through. It was not deep. He wet himself halfway to the knees before he floundered out to the firm crust.

He was angry, and cursed his luck aloud. He had hoped to get into camp with the boys at six o'clock, and this would delay him an hour, for he would have to build a fire and dry out his footgear. This was imperative at that low temperature—he knew that much; and he turned aside to the bank, which he climbed. On top, tangled in the underbrush about the trunks of several small spruce trees, was a high-water deposit of dry firewood—sticks and twigs, principally, but also larger portions of seasoned branches and fine, dry, last year's grasses. He threw down several large pieces on top of the snow. This served for a foundation and prevented the young flame from drowning itself in the snow it otherwise would melt. The flame he got by touching a match to a small shred of birch bark that he took from his pocket. This burned even more readily than paper. Placing it on the foundation, he fed the young flame with wisps of dry grass and with the tiniest dry twigs.

He worked slowly and carefully, keenly aware of his danger. Gradually, as the flame grew stronger, he increased the size of the twigs with which he fed it. He squatted in the snow, pulling the twigs out from their entanglement in the brush and feeding directly to the flame. He knew there must be no failure. When it is seventy-five below zero, a man must not fail in his first attempt to build a fire—that is, if his feet are wet. If his feet are dry, and he fails, he can run along the trail for half a mile and restore his circulation. But the circulation of wet and freezing feet cannot be restored by running when it is seventy-five below. No matter how fast he runs, the wet feet will freeze harder.

All this the man knew. The old-timer on Sulphur Creek had told him about it the previous fall, and now he was appreciating the advice. Already all sensation had gone out of his feet. To build the fire he had been forced to remove his mittens, and the fingers had quickly gone numb. His pace of four miles an hour had kept his heart pumping blood to the surface of his body and to all the extremities. But the instant he stopped, the action of the pump eased down. The cold of space smote the unprotected tip of the planet, and he, being on that unprotected tip, received the full force of the blow. The blood of his body recoiled before it. The blood was alive, like the dog, and like the dog it wanted to hide away and cover itself up from the fearful cold. So long as he walked four miles an hour, he pumped that blood, willy-nilly, to the surface; but now it ebbed away and sank down into the recesses of his body. The extremities were the first to feel its absence. His wet feet froze the faster, and his exposed fingers numbed the faster, though they had not yet begun to freeze. Nose and cheeks were already freezing, while the skin of all his body chilled as it lost its blood.

But he was safe. Toes and nose and cheeks would be only touched by the frost, for the fire was beginning to burn with strength. He was feeding it with twigs the size of his finger. In another minute he would be able to feed it with branches the size of his wrist, and then he could remove his wet footgear, and, while it dried, he could keep his naked feet warm by the fire, rubbing them at first, of course, with snow. The fire was a success. He was safe. He remembered the advice of the old-timer on Sulphur Creek, and smiled. The old-timer had been very serious in laying down the law that no man must travel alone in the Klondike after fifty below. Well, here he was; he had had the accident; he was alone; and he had saved himself. Those old-timers were rather womanish, some of them, he thought. All a man had to do was to keep his head, and he was all right. Any man who was a man could travel alone. But it was surprising, the rapidity with which his cheeks and nose were freezing. And he had not thought his fingers could go lifeless in so short a time. Lifeless they were, for he could scarcely make them move together to grip a twig, and they seemed remote from his body and from him. When he touched a twig, he had to look and see whether or not he had hold of it. The wires were pretty well down between him and his finger ends.

All of which counted for little. There was the fire, snapping and crackling and promising life with every dancing flame. He started to untie his moccasins. They were coated with ice; the thick German socks were like sheaths of iron halfway to the knees; and the moccasin strings were like rods of steel all twisted and knotted as by some conflagration. For a moment he tugged with his numb fingers, then, realizing the folly of it, he drew his sheath knife.

But before he could cut the strings, it happened. It was his own fault or, rather, his mistake. He should not have built the fire under the spruce tree. He should have built it in the open. But it had been easier to pull the twigs from the brush and drop them directly on the fire. Now the tree under which he had done this carried a weight of snow on its boughs. No wind had blown for weeks, and each bough was fully freighted. Each time he had pulled a twig

he had communicated a slight agitation to the tree—an imper-
ceptible agitation, so far as he was concerned, but an agitation
sufficient to bring about the disaster. High up in the tree one bough
capsized its load of snow. This fell on the bough beneath, cap-
sizing them. This process continued, spreading out and involving
the whole tree. It grew like an avalanche, and it descended without
warning upon the man and the fire, and the fire was blotted out!
Where it had burned was a mantle of fresh and disordered snow.

The man was shocked. It was as though he had just heard his own
sentence of death. For a moment he sat and stared at the spot where
the fire had been. Then he grew very calm. Perhaps the old-timer
on Sulphur Creek was right. If he had only had a trail mate he
would have been in no danger now. The trail mate could have
built the fire. Well, it was up to him to build the fire over again,
and this second time there must be no failure. Even if he succeeded,
he would most likely lose some toes. His feet must be badly frozen
by now, and there would be some time before the second fire was
ready.

Such were his thoughts, but he did not sit and think them. He
was busy all the time they were passing through his mind. He
made a new foundation for a fire, this time in the open, where no
treacherous tree could blot it out. Next he gathered dry grasses
and tiny twigs from the high-water flotsam. He could not bring his
fingers together to pull them out, but he was able to gather them
by the handful. In this way he got many rotten twigs and bits of
green moss that were undesirable, but it was the best he could do.
He worked methodically, even collecting an armful of the larger
branches to be used later when the fire gathered strength. And all
the while the dog sat and watched him, a certain yearning wistful-
ness in its eyes, for it looked upon him as the fire provider, and
the fire was slow in coming.

When all was ready, the man reached in his pocket for a second
piece of birch bark. He knew the bark was there, and, though he
could not feel it with his fingers, he could hear its crisp rustling as
he fumbled for it. Try as he would, he could not clutch hold of it.
And all the time, in his consciousness, was the knowledge that each
instant his feet were freezing. This thought tended to put him in a

panic, but he fought against it and kept calm. He pulled on his mittens with his teeth, and threshed his arms back and forth, beating his hands with all his might against his sides. He did this sitting down, and he stood up to do it; and all the while the dog sat in the snow, its wolf brush of a tail curled around warmly over its forefeet, its sharp wolf ears pricked forward intently as it watched the man. And the man, as he beat and threshed with his arms and hands, felt a great surge of envy as he regarded the creature that was warm and secure in its natural covering.

After a time he was aware of the first faraway signals of sensation in his beaten fingers. The faint tingling grew stronger till it evolved into a stinging ache that was excruciating, but which the man hailed with satisfaction. He stripped the mitten from his right hand and fetched forth the birch bark. The exposed fingers were quickly going numb again. Next he brought out his bunch of sulphur matches. But the tremendous cold had already driven the life out of his fingers. In his effort to separate one match from the others, the whole bunch fell in the snow. He tried to pick it out of the snow, but failed. The dead fingers could neither touch nor clutch. He was very careful. He drove the thought of his freezing feet, and nose, and cheeks, out of his mind, devoting his whole soul to the matches. He watched, using the sense of vision in place of that of touch, and when he saw his fingers on each side the bunch, he closed them—that is, he willed to close them, for the wires were down, and the fingers did not obey. He pulled the mitten on the right hand, and beat it fiercely against his knee. Then, with both mittened hands, he scooped the bunch of matches, along with much snow, into his lap. Yet he was no better off.

After some manipulation he managed to get the bunch between the heels of his mittened hands. In this fashion he carried it to his mouth. The ice crackled and snapped when by a violent effort he opened his mouth. He drew the lower jaw in, curled the upper lip out of the way, and scraped the bunch with his upper teeth in order to separate a match. He succeeded in getting one, which he dropped on his lap. He was no better off. He could not pick it up. Then he devised a way. He picked it up in his teeth and scratched it on his leg. Twenty times he scratched before he succeeded in lighting it.

As it flamed he held it with his teeth to the birch bark. But the burning brimstone went up his nostrils and into his lungs, causing him to cough spasmodically. The match fell into the snow and went out.

The old-timer on Sulphur Creek was right, he thought in the moment of controlled despair that ensued: after fifty below, a man should travel with a partner. He beat his hands, but failed in exciting any sensation. Suddenly he bared both hands, removing the mittens with his teeth. He caught the whole bunch between the heels of his hands. His arm muscles not being frozen enabled him to press the hand heels tightly against the matches. Then he scratched the bunch along his leg. It flared into flame, seventy sulphur matches at once! There was no wind to blow them out. He kept his head to one side to escape the strangling fumes, and held the blazing bunch to the birch bark. As he so held it, he became aware of sensation in his hand. His flesh was burning. He could smell it. Deep down below the surface he could feel it. The sensation developed into pain that grew acute. And still he endured it, holding the flame of the matches clumsily to the bark that would not light readily because his own burning hands were in the way, absorbing most of the flame.

At last, when he could endure no more, he jerked his hands apart. The blazing matches fell sizzling into the snow, but the birch bark was alight. He began laying dry grasses and the tinest twigs on the flame. He could not pick and choose, for he had to lift the fuel between the heels of his hands. Small pieces of rotten wood and green moss clung to the twigs, and he bit them off as well as he could with his teeth. He cherished the flame carefully and awkwardly. It meant life, and it must not perish. The withdrawal of blood from the surface his body now made him begin to shiver, and he grew more awkward. A large piece of green moss fell squarely on the little fire. He tried to poke it out with his fingers, but his shivering frame made him poke too far, and he disrupted the nucleus of the little fire, the burning grasses and tiny twigs separating and scattering. He tried to poke them together again, but in spite of the tenseness of the effort, his shivering got away with him, and the twigs were hopelessly scattered. Each twig gushed a puff of smoke and went out. The fire provider had failed. As he looked apathetically about him, his eyes chanced on the dog, sitting across the ruins of the fire from him, in the snow, making restless, hunching movements, slightly lifting one forefoot and then the other, shifting its weight back and forth on them with wistful eagerness.

The sight of the dog put a wild idea into his head. He remembered the tale of the man, caught in a blizzard, who killed a steer and crawled inside the carcass, and so was saved. He would kill the dog and bury his hands in the warm body until the numbness went out of them. Then he could build another fire. He spoke to the dog, calling it to him; but in his voice was a strange note of fear that frightened the animal, who had never known the man to speak in such way before. Something was the matter, and its suspicious nature sensed danger—it knew not what danger, but somewhere, somehow, in its brain arose an apprehension of the man. It flattened its ears down at the sound of the man's voice, and its restless, hunching movements and the liftings and shiftings of its forefeet became more pronounced; but it would not come to the man. He got on his hands and knees and crawled toward the dog. This unusual posture again excited suspicion, and the animal sidled mincingly away.

The man sat up in the snow for a moment and struggled for calmness. Then he pulled on his mittens, by means of his teeth, and got upon his feet. He glanced down at first in order to assure himself that he was really standing up, for the absence of sensation in his feet left him unrelated to the earth. His erect position in itself started to drive the webs of suspicion from the dog's mind; and when he spoke peremptorily, with the sound of whip lashes in his voice, the dog rendered its customary allegiance and came to him. As it came within reaching distance, the man lost his control. His arms flashed out to the dog, and he experienced genuine surprise when he discovered that his hands could not clutch, that there was neither bend nor feeling in the fingers. He had forgotten for the moment that they were frozen and that they were freezing more and more. All this happened quickly, and before the animal could get away, he encircled its body with his arms. He sat down in the snow, and in this fashion held the dog, while it snarled and whined and struggled.

But it was all he could do, hold its body encircled in his arms and sit there. He realized that he could not kill the dog. There was no way to do it. With his helpless hands he could neither draw nor hold his sheath knife nor throttle the animal. He released it, and it plunged wildly away, with tail between its legs, and still snarling. It halted forty feet away and surveyed him curiously, with ears sharply pricked forward.

The man looked down at his hands in order to locate them, and found them hanging on the ends of his arms. It struck him as curious that one should have to use his eyes in order to find out where his hands were. He began threshing his arms back and forth, beating the mittened hands against his sides. He did this for five minutes, violently, and his heart pumped enough blood up to the surface to put a stop to his shivering. But no sensation was aroused in the hands. He had an impression that they hung like weights on the ends of his arms, but when he tried to run the impression down, he could not find it.

A certain fear of death, dull and oppressive, came to him. This fear quickly became poignant as he realized that it was no longer a mere matter of freezing his fingers and toes, or of losing his hands and feet, but that it was a matter of life and death with the chances against him. This threw him into a panic, and he turned and ran up the creek bed along the old, dim trail. The dog joined in behind and kept up with him. He ran blindly, without intention, in fear such as he had never known in his life. Slowly, as he plowed and floundered through the snow, he began to see things again—the banks of the creek, the old timber jams, the leafless aspens, and the sky. The running made him feel better. He did not shiver. Maybe, if he ran on, his feet would thaw out; and, anyway, if he ran far enough, he would reach camp and the boys. Without doubt he would lose some fingers and toes and some of his face; but the boys would take care of him, and save the rest of him when he got there. And at the same time there was another thought in his mind that said he would never get to the camp and the boys; that it was too many miles away, that the freezing had too great a start on him, and that he would soon be stiff and dead. This thought he kept in the background and refused to consider. Sometimes it pushed itself forward and demanded to be heard, but he thrust it back and strove to think of other things.

It struck him as curious that he could run at all on feet so frozen that he could not feel them when they struck the earth and took the weight of his body. He seemed to himself to skim along above the surface, and to have no connection with the earth. Somewhere he had once seen a winged Mercury, and he wondered if Mercury felt as he felt when skimming over the earth.

His theory of running until he reached camp and the boys had one flaw in it: he lacked the endurance. Several times he stumbled, and finally he tottered, crumpled up, and fell. When he tried to rise, he failed. He must sit and rest, he decided, and next time he would merely walk and keep on going. As he sat and regained his breath, he noted that he was feeling quite warm and comfortable. He was not shivering, and it even seemed that a warm glow had come to his chest and trunk. And yet, when he touched his nose or cheeks, there was no sensation. Running would not thaw them out. Nor would it thaw out his hands and feet. Then the thought came to him that the frozen portions of his body must be extending. He tried to keep this thought down, to forget it, to think of something else; he was aware of the panicky feeling that it caused, and he was afraid of the panic. But the thought asserted itself, and persisted, until it produced a vision of his body totally frozen. This was too much, and he made another wild run along the trail. Once he slowed down to a walk, but the thought of the freezing extending itself made him run again.

And all the time the dog ran with him, at his heels. When he fell down a second time, it curled its tail over its forefeet and sat in front of him, facing him, curiously eager and intent. The warmth and security of the animal angered him, and he cursed it till it flattened down its ears appeasingly. This time the shivering came more quickly upon the man. He was losing in his battle with the frost. It was creeping into his body from all sides. The thought of it drove him on, but he ran no more than a hundred feet, when he staggered and pitched headlong. It was his last panic. When he had recovered his breath and control, he sat up and entertained in his mind the conception of meeting death with dignity. However, the conception did not come to him in such terms. His idea of it was that he had been making a fool of himself, running around like a chicken with its head cut off—such was the simile that occurred to him. Well, he was bound to freeze anyway, and he might as well take it decently. With this new-found peace of mind came the first glimmerings of drowsiness. A good idea, he thought, to sleep off to death. It was like taking an anesthetic. Freezing was not so bad as people thought. There were lots worse ways to die.

He pictured the boys finding his body next day. Suddenly he found himself with them, coming along the trail and looking for himself. And, still with them, he came around a turn in the trail and found himself lying in the snow. He did not belong with himself any more, for even then he was out of himself, standing with the boys and looking at himself in the snow. It certainly was cold, was his thought. When he got back to the States he could tell the folks what real cold was. He drifted on from this to a vision of the old-timer on Sulphur Creek. He could see him quite clearly, warm and comfortable, and smoking a pipe.

"You were right, old hoss; you were right," the man mumbled to the old-timer of Sulphur Creek.

Then the man drowsed off into what seemed to him the most comfortable and satisfying sleep he had ever known. The dog sat facing him and waiting. The brief day drew to a close in a long, slow twilight. There were no signs of a fire to be made, and, besides, never in the dog's experience had it known a man to sit like that in the snow and make no fire. As the twilight drew on, its eager yearning for the fire mastered it, and with a great lifting and shifting of forefeet, it whined softly, then flattened its ears down in anticipation of being chidden by the man. But the man remained silent. Later the dog whined loudly. And still later it crept close to the man and caught the scent of death. This made the animal bristle and back away. A little longer it delayed, howling under the stars that leaped and danced and shone brightly in the cold sky. Then it turned and trotted up the trail in the direction of the camp it knew, where were the other food providers and fire providers.

\* \* \*

Typical of the prospectors of the Gold Rush period is the following story.

### Too Much Gold, by Jack London

This being a story—and a truer one than it may appear—of a mining country, it is quite to be expected that it will be a hard-luck story.

But that depends on the point of view. Hard luck is a mild way of terming it so far as Kink Mitchell and Hootchinoo Bill are concerned; and that they have a decided opinion on the subject is a matter of common knowledge in the Yukon country.

It was in the fall of 1896 that the two partners came down to the east bank of the Yukon, and drew a Peterborough canoe from a moss-covered cache. They were not particularly pleasant-looking objects. A summer's prospecting, filled to repletion with hardship and rather empty of grub, had left their clothes in tatters and themselves worn and cadaverous. A nimbus of mosquitoes buzzed about each man's head. Their faces were coated with blue clay. Each carried a lump of this damp clay, and whenever it dried and fell from their faces more was daubed on its place. There was a querulous plaint in their voices, an irritability of movement and gesture, which told of broken sleep and a losing struggle with the little winged pests.

"Them skeeters'll be the death of me yet," Kink Mitchell whimpered, as the canoe felt the current on her nose and leaped out from the bank.

"Cheer up, cheer up! We're about done," Hootchinoo Bill answered, with an attempted heartiness in his funereal tones that was ghastly. "We'll be in Forty Mile in forty minutes, and then— Cursed little devil!"

One hand had left his paddle and landed on the back of his neck with a sharp slap. He put a fresh daub of clay on the injured part, swearing sulphurously the while. Kink Mitchell was not in the least amused. He merely improved the opportunity by putting a thicker coating of clay on his own neck.

They crossed the Yukon to its west bank, shot downstream with easy stroke, and at the end of forty minutes swung in close to the left around the tail of an island. Forty Mile spread itself suddenly before them. Both men straightened their backs, and gazed at the sight. They gazed long and carefully, drifting with the current, and in their faces slowly gathering an expression of mingled surprise and consternation.

Not a thread of smoke was rising from the hundreds of log cabins. There was no sound of axes biting sharply into wood, of hammering and sawing. Neither dogs nor men loitered before the big store. No steamboats lay at the bank, no canoes, or scows, or poling boats. The river was as bare of craft as the town was of life.

"Kind of looks like Gabriel's tooted his little horn, and you an' me has turned up missing," remarked Hootchinoo Bill.

His remark was casual, as though there were nothing unusual about the occurrence. Kink Mitchell's reply was just as casual, as though he, too, were unaware of any strange perturbation of spirit.

"Looks as they was all Baptists, then, and took the boats to go by water," was his contribution.

"My ol' dad was a Baptist," Hootchinoo Bill supplemented. "An' he always did hold it was forty thousand miles nearer that way."

This was the end of their levity. They ran the canoe in and climbed the high earth bank. A feeling of awe descended upon them as they walked the deserted streets. The sunlight streamed placidly over the town. A gentle wind tapped the halyards against the flagpole before the closed doors of the Caledonia Dance Hall. Mosquitoes buzzed, robins sang, and moose birds tripped hungrily among the cabins; but there was no human life or sign of human life.

"I'm just dyin' for a drink," Hootchinoo Bill said, and unconsciously his voice sank to a hoarse whisper.

His partner nodded his head, loath to hear his own voice break the stillness. They trudged on in uneasy silence till surprised by an open door. Above this door, and stretching the width of the building, a rude sign announced the same as the Monte Carlo. But beside the door, hat over eyes, chair tilted back, a man sat sun-ning himself. He was an old man. Beard and hair were long and white and patriarchal.

"If it ain't ol' Jim Cummings, turned up like us, too late for resurrection," said Kink Mitchell.

"Most like he didn't hear Gabriel tootin'," was Hootchinoo Bill's suggestion.

"Hello, Jim! Wake up!" he shouted.

The old man unlimbered lamely, blinking his eyes and murmuring automatically: "What'll ye have, gents? What'll ye have?"

They followed him inside, and ranged up against the long bar where of yore half a dozen nimble barkeepers found little time to loaf. The great room, ordinarily a-roar with life, was gloomy and quiet as a tomb. There was no rattling of chips, no whirring of ivory balls. Roulette and faro tables were like gravestones under their canvas covers. No women's voices drifted merrily from the dance room behind. Ol' Jim Cummings wiped a glass with palsied hands, and Kink Mitchell scrawled his initials on the dust-covered bar.

"Where's the girls?" Hootchinoo Bill shouted, with affected geniality.

"Gone," was the ancient barkeeper's reply, in a voice thin and aged as himself, and as unsteady as his hand.

"Where's Bidwell and Barlow?"

"Gone."

"And Sweetwater Charley?"

"Gone."

"And his sister?"

"Gone, too."

"Your daughter, Sally, then, and her little kid?"

"Gone, all gone." The old man shook his head sadly, rummaging in an absent way among the dusty bottles.

"Great Sardanapalus! Where?" Kink Mitchell exploded, unable longer to restrain himself. "You don't say you've had the plague?"

"Why, ain't you heard?" The old man chuckled quietly. "They all's gone to Dawson."

"What like is that?" Bill demanded. "A creek? Or a bar? Or a place?"

"Ain't never heerd of Dawson, eh?" The old man chuckled exasperatingly. "Why Dawson's a town, a city; bigger'n Forty Mile! Yes, sir, bigger'n Forty Mile!"

"I've ben in this land seven year," Bill announced, emphatically, "an' I make free to say I never heard tell of the burg before. Hold on! Let's have some more of that whiskey. Your information's flabbergasted me, that it has. Now just whereabouts is this Dawson place you was a-mentionin'?"

"On the big flat jest below the mouth of Klondike," Ol' Jim answered. "But where has you all ben this summer?"

"Never you mind where we all's ben," was Kink Mitchell's testy reply. "We all's ben where the skeeters is that thick you've got to throw a stick into the air so as to see the sun and tell the time of day. Ain't I right, Bill?"

"Right you are," said Bill. "But speakin' of this Dawson place, how like did it happen to be, Jim?"

"Ounce to the pan on a creek called Bonanza, an' they ain't got to bed rock yet."

"Who struck it?"

"Carmack."

At mention of the discoverer's name the partners stared at each other disgustedly. Then they winked with great solemnity.

"Siwash George," sniffed Hootchinoo Bill.

"That squaw man," sneered Kink Mitchell.

"I wouldn't put on my moccasins to stampede after anything he'd ever find," said Bill.

"Same here," announced his partner. "A cuss that's too plumb lazy to fish his own salmon. That's why he took up with the Indians. S'pose that black brother-in-law of his—lemme see, Skookum Jim, eh?—s'pose he's in on it?"

The old barkeeper nodded. "Sure, an' what's more, all Forty Mile exceptin' me an' a few cripples."

"And drunks," added Kink Mitchell.

"No sir-ee!" the old man shouted, emphatically.

"I bet you the drinks Honkins ain't in on it!" Hootchinoo Bill cried, with certitude.

Ol' Jim's face lighted up. "I takes you, Bill, an' you loses."

"However did that ol' soak budge out of Forty Mile?" Mitchell demanded.

"They ties him down, an' throws him in the bottom of a polin' boat," Ol' Jim explained. "Come right in here, they did, an' takes him out of that there chair there in the corner, an' three more drunks they finds under the piany. I tell you alls the whole camp hits up the Yukon for Dawson jes' like Sam Scratch was after them —wimmen, children, babes in arms, the whole shebang. Bidwell comes to me, an' sez, sez he: 'Jim, I wants you to keep tab on the Monte Carlo. I'm goin'.' "

" 'Where's Barlow?' sez I. 'Gone,' sez he, 'an' I'm a-followin' with a load of whiskey.' An' with that, never waitin' for me to decline, he makes a run for his boat, an' way he goes, polin' upriver like mad. So here I be, an' these is the first drinks I've passed out in three days."

The partners looked at each other.

"Gosh darn my buttons!" said Hootchinoo Bill. "Seems like you and me, Kink, is the kind of folks always caught out with forks when it rains soup."

"Wouldn't it take the saleratus out your dough, now?" said Kink Mitchell. "A stampede of tinhorns, drunks an' loafers."

"An' squaw men," added Bill. "Not a genooine miner in the whole caboodle."

"Genooine miners like you an' me, Kink," he went on, academically, "is all out an' sweatin' hard over Birch Creek way. Not a genooine miner in this whole crazy Dawson outfit, and I say right here, not a step do I budge for any Carmack strike. I've got to see the color of the dust first."

"Same here," Mitchell agreed. "Let's have another drink."

Having taken this resolution (and wetted it), they beached the canoe, transferred its contents to their cabin, and cooked dinner. But as the afternoon wore along they grew restive. They were men used to the silence of the great wilderness, but this gravelike silence of a town worried them. They caught themselves listening for familiar sounds—"waitin' for something to make a noise which ain't goin' to make a noise," as Bill put it. They strolled through the deserted streets to the Monte Carlo for more drinks, and wandered along the river bank to the steamer landing, where only water gurgled as the eddy filled and emptied, and an occasional salmon leaped flashing into the sun.

They sat down in the shade in front of the store, and talked with the consumptive storekeeper whose liability to hemorrhage accounted for his presence. Bill and Kink told him how they intended loafing in their cabin, and resting up after the hard summer's work. They told him with a certain insistence, which was half appeal for belief, half challenge for contradiction, how much they were going to enjoy their idleness. But the storekeeper was uninterested. He switched the conversation back to the strike on Klondike, and they could not keep him away from it. He could think of nothing else, talk of nothing else, till Hootchinoo Bill rose up in anger and disgust.

"Gosh darn Dawson, say I!" he cried.

"Same here," said Kink Mitchell, with a brightening face. "One'd think something was doin' up there, 'stead of bein' a mere stampede of greenhorns an' tinhorns."

But a boat came into view from downstream. It was long and slim. It hugged the bank closely, and its three occupants, standing upright, propelled it against the swift current by means of long poles.

"Circle City outfit," said the storekeeper. "I was lookin' for 'em along by afternoon. Forty Mile had the start of them by a hundred and seventy miles. But gee! they ain't losin' any time!"

"We'll just sit here quietlike, and watch 'em string by," Bill said, complacently.

As he spoke, another boat appeared in sight, followed after a brief interval by two others. By this time the first boat was abreast of the men on the bank. Its occupants did not cease poling while greetings were exchanged, and, though its progress was slow, half an hour saw it out of sight upriver.

Still they came from below, boat after boat, in endless procession. The uneasiness of Bill and Kink increased. They stole speculative, tentative glances at each other, and when their eyes met looked away in embarrassment. Finally, however, their eyes met, and neither looked away.

Kink opened his mouth to speak, but words failed him, and his mouth remained open, while he continued to gaze at his partner.

"Just what I was thinkin', Kink," said Bill.

They grinned sheepishly at each other, and by tacit consent started to walk away. Their pace quickened, and by the time they arrived at their cabin they were on the run.

"Can't lose no time with all that multitude a-rushin' by," Kink spluttered, as he jabbed the sour-dough can into the bean pot with one hand and with the other gathered in the frying pan and coffeepot.

"Should say not," gasped Bill, his head and shoulders buried in a clothes sack, wherein were stored winter socks and underwear.

"I say, Kink, don't forget the saleratus on the corner shelf back of the stove."

Half an hour later they were launching the canoe and loading up, while the storekeeper made jocular remarks about poor weak mortals and the contagiousness of "stampedin' fever." But when Bill and Kink thrust their long poles to bottom and started the canoe against the current, he called after them:

"Well, so long, and good luck! And don't forget to blaze a stake or two for me!"

They nodded their heads vigorously, and felt sorry for the poor wretch who remained perforce behind.

Kink and Bill were sweating hard. According to the revised northland scripture, the stampede is to the swift, the blazing of stakes to the strong, and the crown, in royalties, gathers to itself the fullness thereof. Kink and Bill were both swift and strong. They took the soggy trail at a long, swinging gait that broke the hearts of a couple of tenderfeet who tried to keep up with them. Behind, strung out between them and Dawson (where the boats were discarded, and land travel began), was the vanguard of the Circle City outfit. In the race from Forty Mile, the partners had passed every boat, winning from the leading boat by a length in the Dawson eddy, and leaving its occupants sadly behind the moment their feet struck the trail.

"Huh! couldn't see us for smoke," Hootchinoo Bill chuckled,

flinging the stinging sweat from his brow, and glancing swiftly back along the way they had come.

Three men emerged from where the trail broke through the trees. Two followed close at their heels, and then a man and a woman shot into view.

"Come on, you Kink! Hit her up! Hit her up!"

Bill quickened his pace. Mitchell glanced back in more leisurely fashion.

"I declare, if they ain't lopin'!"

"And here's one that's loped himself out," said Bill, pointing to the side of the trail.

A man was lying on his back, panting, in the culminating stages of violent exhaustion. His face was ghastly, his eyes bloodshot and glazed, for all the world like a dying man.

"*Chechaquo!*" Kink Mitchell grunted, and it was the grunt of the old "sourdough" for the greenhorn, for the man who outfitted with "self-risin'" flour and used baking powder in his biscuits.

The partners, true to the old-timer custom, had intended to stake downstream from the strike, but when they saw claim "81 Below" blazed on a tree—which meant fully eight miles below Discovery —they changed their minds. The eight miles were covered in less than two hours. It was a killing pace over such rough trail, and they passed scores of exhausted men who had fallen by the wayside.

At Discovery little was to be learned of the upper creek. Carmack's Indian brother-in-law, Skookum Jim, had a hazy notion that the creek was staked as high as the thirties; but when Kink and Bill looked at the corner stakes of 79 Above, they threw their stampeding packs off their backs, and sat down to smoke. All their efforts had been vain. Bonanza was staked from mouth to source —"Out of sight, and across the next divide," Bill complained that night as they fried their bacon and boiled their coffee over Carmack's fire at Discovery.

"Try that pup," Carmack suggested next morning.

"That pup" was a broad creek which flowed into Bonanza at 7 Above. The partners received his advice with the magnificent contempt of the sourdough for a squaw man, and, instead, spent the day on Adam's Creek, another and more likely looking tributary of Bonanza. But it was the old story over again—staked to the sky line.

For three days Carmack repeated his advice, and for three days they received it contemptuously. But on the fourth day, there being nowhere else to go, they went up "that pup." They knew that it was practically unstaked, but they had no intention of staking. The trip was made more for the purpose of giving vent to their ill humor than for anything else. They had become quite cynical, skeptical. They jeered and scoffed at everything, and insulted every *chechaquo* they met along the way.

At number twenty-three the stakes ceased. The remainder of the creek was open to location.

"Moose pasture," sneered Kink Mitchell.

But Bill gravely paced off five hundred feet up the creek, and blazed the corner stakes. He had picked up the bottom of a candle box, and on the smooth side he wrote the notice for his center stake:

THIS MOOSE PASTURE IS RESERVED
FOR THE
SWEDES AND CHECHAQUOS.
BILL RADER.

Kink read it over with approval, saying:

"As them's my sentiments, I reckon I might as well subscribe."

So the name of Charles Mitchell was added to the notice; and many an old sourdough's face relaxed that day at sight of the handiwork of a kindred spirit.

"How's the pup?" Carmack inquired, when they strolled back into camp.

"To hell with pups!" was Hootchinoo Bill's reply. "Me and Kink's goin' a-lookin' for Too Much Gold when we get rested up."

Too Much Gold was the fabled creek of which all sourdoughs dreamed, whereof it was said the gold was so thick, that, in order to wash it, gravel must first be shoveled into the sluice boxes. But the several days' rest preliminary to the quest for Too Much Gold brought a slight change in their plan, inasmuch as it brought one Ans Handerson, a Swede.

Ans Handerson had been working for wages all summer at Miller Creek, over on the Sixty Mile; and, the summer done, had strayed up Bonanza like many another waif helplessly adrift on the gold tides that swept willy-nilly across the land. He was tall and lanky. His arms were long, like prehistoric man's, and his hands were like soup plates, twisted, and gnarled, and big-knuckled from toil. He was slow of utterance and movement, and his eyes, pale blue as his hair was pale yellow, seemed filled with an immortal dreaming, the stuff of which no man knew, and himself least of all. Perhaps this appearance of immortal dreaming was due to a supreme and vacuous innocence. At any rate, this was the valuation men of ordinary clay put upon him, and there was nothing extraordinary about the composition of Hootchinoo Bill and Kink Mitchell.

The partners had spent a day of visiting and gossip, and in the evening met in the temporary quarters of the Monte Carlo—a large tent where stampeders rested their weary bones, and bad whiskey sold at a dollar a drink. Since the only money in circulation was dust, and since the house took the "downweight" on the scales, a drink cost something more than a dollar. Bill and Kink were not drinking, principally for the reason that their one and common sack was not strong enough to stand many excursions to the scales.

"Say, Bill, I've got a *chechaquo* on the string for a sack of flour," Mitchell announced, jubilantly.

Bill looked interested and pleased. Grub was scarce, and they were not overplentifully supplied for the quest after Too Much Gold.

"Flour's worth a dollar a pound," he answered. "How like do you calculate to get your finger on it?"

"Trade 'em a half interest in that there claim of our'n," Kink answered.

"What claim?" Bill was surprised. Then he remembered the reservation he had staked off for the Swedes, and said, "Oh!"

"I wouldn't be so close about it, though," he added. "Give 'm the whole thing while you're about it, in a right freehanded way."

Bill shook his head. "If I did he'd get clean scairt and prance off. I'm lettin' on as how the ground is believed to be valuable, an'

that we're lettin' go half just because we're monstrous short on
grub. After the dicker we can make him a present of the whole
shebang."

"If somebody ain't disregarded our notice," Bill objected,
though he was plainly pleased at prospect of exchanging the claim
for a sack of flour.

"She ain't jumped," Kirk assured him. "It's number twenty-
four, and it stands. The *chechaquos* took it serious, and they begun
stakin' where you left off. Staked clean over the divide, too. I was
gassin' with one of them which has just got in with cramps in his
legs."

It was then, and for the first time, that they heard the slow and
groping utterance of Ans Handerson.

"Ay like the looks," he was saying to the barkeeper. "Ay tank
ay gat a claim."

The partners winked at each other, and a few minutes later a
surprised and grateful Swede was drinking bad whiskey with two
hardhearted strangers. But he was as hardheaded as they were
hardhearted. The sack made frequent journeys to the scales, followed solicitously each time by Kink Mitchell's eyes, and still Ans
Handerson did not loosen up. In his pale blue eyes, as in summer
seas, immortal dreams swam up and burned, but the swimming and
the burning were due to the tales of gold and propect pans he heard
of, rather than to the whiskey he slid so easily down his throat.

The partners were in despair, though they appeared boisterous
and jovial of speech and action.

"Don't mind me, my friend," Hootchinoo Bill hiccoughed, his
hand upon Ans Handerson's shoulder. "Have another drink. We're
just celebratin' Kink's birthday here. This is my pardner, Kink,
Kink Mitchell. An' what might your name be?"

This learned, his hand descended resoundingly on Kink's back,
and Kink simulated clumsy self-consciousness in that he was for
the time being the center of the rejoicing, while Ans Handerson
looked pleased, and asked them to have a drink with him. It was
the first and last time he treated, until the play changed, and his
canny soul was aroused to unwonted prodigality. But he paid for
the liquor from a fairly healthy looking sack.

"Not less'n eight hundred in it," calculated the lynx-eyed Kink; and on the strength of it he took the first opportunity of a privy conversation with Bidwell, proprietor of the bad whiskey and the tent.

"Here's my sack, Bidwell," Kink said, with the intimacy and surety of one old-timer to another. "Just weigh fifty dollars into it for a day or so, more or less, and we'll be yours truly, Bill an' me."

Thereafter the journeys of the sack to the scales were more frequent, and the celebration of Kink's natal day waxed hilarious. He even essayed to sing the old-timer's classic, "The Juice of the Forbidden Fruit," but broke down, and drowned his embarrassment in another round of drinks. Even Bidwell honored him with a round or two on the house; and he and Bill were decently drunk by the time Ans Handerson's eyelids began to droop and his tongue gave promise of loosening.

Bill grew affectionate, then confidential. He told his troubles and hard luck to the barkeeper and the world in general, and to Ans Handerson in particular. He required no histrionic powers to act the part. The bad whiskey attended to that. He worked himself into a great sorrow for himself and Bill, and his tears were sincere, when he told how he and his partner were thinking of selling a half interest in good ground just because they were short of grub. Even Kink listened and believed.

Ans Handerson's eyes were shining unholily, as he asked: "How much you tank you take?"

Bill and Kink did not hear him, and he was compelled to repeat his query. They appeared reluctant. He grew keener. And he swayed back and forward, holding on to the bar and listening with all his ears while they conferred together to one side, and wrangled as to whether they should or not, and disagreed in stage whispers over the price they should set.

"Two hundred and—hic!—fifty," Bill finally announced, "but we reckon as we won't sell."

"Which same is monstrous wise, if I might chip in my little say," seconded Bidwell.

"Yes, indeedy," added Kink. "We ain't in no charity business a-disgorgin' free an' generous to Swedes an' white men."

"Ay tank we haf another drink," hiccoughed Ans Handerson, craftily changing the subject against a more propitious time.

And thereafter, to bring about that propitious time, his own sack began a seesaw between his hip pocket and the scales. Bill and Kink were coy, but they finally yielded to his blandishments. Whereupon he grew shy, and drew Bidwell to one side. He staggered exceedingly, and held on to Bidwell for support, as he asked:

"They ban all right, them men, you tank so?"

"Sure," Bidwell answered, heartily. "Know 'em for years. Old sourdoughs. When they sell a claim they sell a claim. They ain't no air dealers."

"Ay tank ay buy," Ans Handerson announced, tottering back to the two men.

But by now he was dreaming deeply, and he proclaimed that he would have the whole claim or nothing. This was the cause of great pain to Hootchinoo Bill. He orated grandly against the "hawgishness" of *chechaquos* and Swedes, albeit he dozed between periods, his voice dying away to a gurgle and his head sinking forward on his breast. But whenever aroused by a nudge from Kink or Bidwell he never failed to explode another volley of abuse and insult.

Ans Handerson was calm under it all. Each insult added to the value of the claim. Such unamiable reluctance to sell advertised but one thing to him, and he was aware of a great relief when Hootchinoo Bill sank snoring to the floor, and he was free to turn his attention to his less intractable partner.

Kink Mitchell was persuadable, though a poor mathematician. He wept dolefully, but was willing to sell a half interest for two hundred and fifty dollars, or the whole claim for seven hundred and fifty. Ans Handerson and Bidwell labored to clear away his erroneous ideas concerning fractions, but their labor was vain. He spilled tears and regrets all over the bar and on their shoulders, which tears, however, did not wash away his opinion that if one-half was worth two hundred and fifty, two halves were worth three times as much.

In the end—and even Bidwell retained no more than hazy recollections of how the night terminated—a bill of sale was drawn up, wherein Bill Rader and Charles Mitchell yielded up all right and title to the claim known as 24 Eldorado, the same being the name the creek had received from some optimistic *chechaquo.*

When Kink had signed, it took the united efforts of the three to arouse Bill. Pen in hand, he swayed long over the document; and, each time he rocked back and forth, in Ans Handerson's eyes flashed and faded a wondrous golden vision. When the precious signature was at last appended and the dust paid over, he breathed a great sigh, and sank to sleep under a table, where he dreamed immortally until morning.

But the day was chill and gray. He felt badly. His first act, unconscious and automatic, was to feel for his sack. Its lightness startled him. Then, slowly, memories of the night thronged into his brain. Rough voices disturbed him. He opened his eyes, and peered out from under the table. A couple of early risers, or, rather, men who had been out on trail all night, were vociferating their opinions concerning the utter and loathable worthlessness of Eldorado Creek. He grew frightened, felt in his pocket, and found the deed to 24 Eldorado.

Ten minutes later Hootchinoo Bill and Kink Mitchell were aroused from their blankets by a wild-eyed Swede, who strove to force upon them an ink-scrawled and very blotty piece of paper.

"Ay tank ay take my money back," he gibbered. "Ay tank ay take my money back."

Tears were in his eyes and throat. They ran down his cheeks as he knelt before them, and pleaded and implored. But Bill and Kink did not laugh. They might have been harder hearted.

"First time I ever hear a man squeal over a minin' deal," Bill said. "An' I make free to say 'tis too onusual for me to savve."

"Same here," Kink Mitchell remarked. "Minin' deals is like horse tradin'."

They were honest in their wonderment. They could not conceive of themselves raising a wail over a business transaction, so they could not understand it in another man.

"The poor, ornery *chechaquo,*" murmured Hootchinoo Bill, as they watched the sorrowing Swede disappear up the trail.

"But this ain't Too Much Gold," Kink Mitchell said, cheerfully.

And ere the day was out they purchased flour and bacon at exorbitant prices with Ans Handerson's dust, and crossed over the divide in the direction of the creeks which lie between Klondike and Indian River.

Three months later they came back over the divide in the midst of a snowstorm, and dropped down the trail to 24 Eldorado. It merely chanced that the trail led them that way. They were not looking for the claim. Nor could they see much through the driving white till they set foot upon the claim itself. And then the air lightened, and they beheld a dump, capped by a windlass which a man was turning. They saw him draw a bucket of gravel from the hole, and tilt it on the edge of the dump. Likewise they saw another man, strangely familiar, filling a pan with the fresh gravel. His hands were large; his hair was pale yellow. But before they reached him, he turned with the pan and fled toward a cabin. He wore no hat, and the snow falling down his neck accounted for his haste. Bill and Kink ran after him, and came upon him in the cabin, kneeling by the stove, and washing the pan of gravel in a tub of water.

He was too deeply engaged to notice more than that somebody had entered the cabin. They stood at his shoulder and looked on. He imparted to the pan a deft circular motion, pausing once or twice to rake out the larger particles of gravel with his fingers. The water was muddy, and with the pan buried in it they could see nothing of its contents. Suddenly he lifted the pan clear, and sent the water out of it with a flirt. A mass of yellow, like butter in a churn, showed across the bottom.

Hootchinoo Bill swallowed. Never in his life had he dreamed of so rich a test pan.

"Kind of thick, my friend," he said, huskily. "How much might you reckon that all to be?"

Ans Handerson did not look up, as he replied:

"Ay tank fafty ounces."

"You must be scrumptious rich, then, eh?"

Still Ans Handerson kept his head down, absorbed in putting in the fine touches which wash out the last particles of dross, though he answered:

"Ay tank ay ban worth five hundred t'ousand dollar."

"Gosh!" said Hootchinoo Bill; and he said it reverently.

"Yes, Bill, gosh!" said Kink Mitchell; and they went out softly, and closed the door.

# 9

# *POET OF THE KLONDIKE*

Robert W. Service (1874–1958), was born in England and emigrated to Canada, where he joined the staff of the Canadian Bank of Commerce in Victoria, British Columbia. He was transferred to Whitehorse, Yukon Territory, and then to Dawson. He became a prolific poet and his verses have long been esteemed in the Far North, especially those inspired by the Klondike Gold Rush. Two of these follow.

*Two Poems,* by Robert W. Service

The Law of the Yukon

This is the law of the Yukon, and ever she makes it plain:
"Send not your foolish and feeble; send me your strong and your sane—
Strong for the red rage of battle; sane, for I harry them sore;
Send me men girt for the combat, men who are grit to the core;
Swift as the panther in triumph, fierce as the bear in defeat,
Sired of a bulldog parent, steeled in the furnace heat.
Send me the best of your breeding, lend me your chosen ones;
Them will I take to my bosom, them will I call my sons;
Them will I gild with my treasure, them will I glut with my meat;
But the others—the misfits, the failures—I trample under my feet.
Dissolute, damned and despairful, crippled and palsied and slain,

Ye would send me the spawn of your gutters—Go! take back your
    spawn again.

"Wild and wide are my borders, stern as death is my sway;
From my ruthless throne I have ruled alone for a million years and
    a day;
Hugging my mighty treasure, waiting for man to come,
Till he swept like a turbid torrent, and after him swept—the scum.
The pallid pimp of the dead-line, the enervate of the pen,
One by one I weeded them out, for all that I sought was—Men.
One by one I dismayed them, frighting them sore with my glooms;
One by one I betrayed them unto my manifold dooms.
Drowned them like rats in my rivers, starved them like curs on
    my plains,
Rotted the flesh that was left them, poisoned the blood in their
    veins;
Burst with my winter upon them, searing forever their sight,
Lashed them with fungus-white faces, whimpering wild in the
    night;

"Staggering blind through the storm-whirl, stumbling mad through
    the snow,
Frozen stiff in the ice-pack, brittle and bent like a bow;
Featureless, formless, forsaken, scented by wolves in their flight,
Left for the wind to make music through ribs that are glittering
    white;
Gnawing the black crust of failure, searching the pit of despair,
Crooking the toe in the trigger, trying to patter a prayer;
Going outside with an escort, raving with lips all afoam,
Writing a check for a million, driveling feebly of home;
Lost like a louse in the burning . . . or else in the tented town
Seeking a drunkard's solace, sinking and sinking down;
Steeped in the slime at the bottom, dead to a decent world,
Lost 'mid the human flotsam, far on the frontier hurled;
In the camp at the bend of the river, with its dozen saloons aglare,
Its gambling dens ariot, its gramophones all ablare;
Crimped with the crimes of a city, sin-ridden and bridled with lies,

In the hush of my mountained vastness, in the flush of my midnight
  skies.
Plague-spots, yet tools of my purpose, so natheless I suffer them
  thrive,
Crushing my Weak in their clutches, that only my Strong may
  survive.

"But the others, the men of my mettle, the men who would 'stablish
  my fame
Unto its ultimate issue, winning me honor, not shame;
Searching my uttermost valleys, fighting each step as they go,
Shooting the wrath of my rapids, scaling my ramparts of snow;
Ripping the guts of my mountains, looting the beds of my creeks,
Them will I take to my bosom, and speak as a mother speaks.
I am the land that listens, I am the land that broods;
Steeped in eternal beauty, crystalline waters and woods.
Long have I waited lonely, shunned as a thing accurst,
Monstrous, moody, pathetic, the last of the lands and the first;
Visioning camp-fires at twilight, sad with a longing forlorn,
Feeling my womb o'er-pregnant with the seed of cities unborn.
Wild and wide are my borders, stern as death is my sway,
And I wait for the men who will win me—and I will not be won
  in a day;
And I will not be won by weaklings, subtle, suave and mild,
But by men with the hearts of vikings, and the simple faith of a
  child;
Desperate, strong and resistless, unthrottled by fear or defeat,
Them will I gild with my treasure, them will I glut with my meat.

"Lofty I stand from each sister land, patient and wearily wise,
With the weight of a world of sadness in my quiet, passionless eyes;
Dreaming alone of a people, dreaming alone of a day,
When men shall not rape my riches, and curse me and go away;
Making a bawd of my bounty, fouling the hand that gave—
Till I rise in my wrath and I sweep on their path and I stamp them
  into a grave.
Dreaming of men who will bless me, of women esteeming me good.

Of children born in my borders of radiant motherhood,
Of cities leaping to stature, of fame like a flag unfurled,
As I pour the tide of my riches in the eager lap of the world."

This is the Law of the Yukon, that only the Strong shall thrive;
That surely the Weak shall perish, and only the Fit survive.
Dissolute, damned and despairful, crippled and palsied and slain,
This is the Will of the Yukon,—Lo, how she makes it plain!

### THE TRAIL OF NINETY-EIGHT

I

Gold! We leapt from our benches. Gold! We sprang from our
    stools.
Gold! We wheeled in the furrow, fired with the faith of fools.
Fearless, unfound, unfitted, far from the night and the cold,
Heard we the clarion summons, followed the master-lure—Gold!

Men from the sands of the Sunland; men from the woods of the
    West;
Men from the farms and the cities, into the Northland we pressed.
Graybeards and striplings and women, good men and bad men and
    bold,
Leaving our homes and our loved ones, crying exultantly—
    "Gold!"

Never was seen such an army, pitiful, futile, unfit;
Never was seen such a spirit, manifold courage and grit.
Never has been such a cohort under one banner unrolled
As surged to the ragged-edged Arctic, urged by the archtempter—
    Gold.

"Farewell!" we cried to our dearests; little we cared for their tears.
"Farewell!" we cried to the humdrum and the yoke of the hireling
    years;
Just like a pack of school-boys, and the big crowd cheered us
    good-bye.
Never were hearts so uplifted, never were hopes so high.

The spectral shores flitted past us, and every whirl of the screw
Hurled us nearer to fortune, and ever we planned what we'd do—
Do with the gold when we got it—big, shiny nuggets like plums,
There in the sand of the river, gouging it out with our thumbs.

And one man wanted a castle, another a racing stud;
A third would cruise in a palace yacht like a red-necked prince of
blood.
And so we dreamed and we vaunted, millionaires to a man,
Leaping to wealth in our visions long ere the trail began.

## II

We landed in wind-swept Skagway. We joined the weltering mass,
Clamoring over their outfits, waiting to climb the Pass.
We tightened our girths and our pack-straps; we linked on the
Human Chain,
Struggling up to the summit, where every step was a pain.

Gone was the joy of our faces, grim and haggard and pale;
The heedless mirth of the shipboard was changed to the care of the
trail.
We flung ourselves in the struggle, packing our grub in relays,
Step by step to the summit in the bale of the winter days.

Floundering deep in the sump-holes, stumbling out again;
Crying with cold and weakness, crazy with fear and pain.
Then from the depths of our travail, ere our spirits were broke,
Grim, tenacious and savage, the lust of the trail awoke.

"Klondike or bust!" rang the slogan; every man for his own.
Oh, how we flogged the horses, staggering skin and bone!
Oh, how we cursed their weakness, anguish they could not tell,
Breaking their hearts in our passion, lashing them on till they fell!

For grub meant gold to our thinking, and all that could walk must
pack;

The sheep for the shambles stumbled, each with a load on its back;
And even the swine were burdened, and grunted and squealed
    and rolled,
And men went mad in the moment, huskily clamoring "Gold!"

Oh, we were brutes and devils, goaded by lust and fear!
Our eyes were strained to the summit; the weaklings dropped to
    the rear,
Falling in heaps by the trail-side, heart-broken, limp and wan;
But the gaps closed up in an instant, and heedless the chain went
    on.

Never will I forget it, there on the mountain face,
Antlike, men with their burdens, clinging in icy space;
Dogged, determined and dauntless, cruel and callous and cold,
Cursing, blaspheming, reviling, and ever that battle-cry—"Gold!"

Thus toiled we, the army of fortune, in hunger and hope and
    despair,
Till glacier, mountain and forest vanished, and, radiantly fair,
There at our feet lay Lake Bennett, and down to its welcome we
    ran:
The trail of the land was over, the trail of the water began.

### III

We built our boats and we launched them. Never has been such a
    fleet;
A packing-case for a bottom, a mackinaw for a sheet.
Shapeless, grotesque, lopsided, flimsy, makeshift and crude,
Each man after his fashion builded as best he could.

Each man worked like a demon, as prow to rudder we raced;
The winds of the Wild cried "Hurry!" the voice of the waters,
    "Haste!"
We hated those driving before us; we dreaded those pressing
    behind;

We cursed the slow current that bore us; we prayed to the God
of the wind.

Spring! and the hillsides flourished, vivid in jewelled green;
Spring! and our hearts' blood nourished envy and hatred and
spleen.
Little cared we for the Spring-birth; much cared we to get on—
Stake in the Great White Channel, stake ere the best be gone.

The greed of the gold possessed us; pity and love were forgot;
Covetous visions obsessed us; brother with brother fought.
Partner with partner wrangled, each one claiming his due;
Wrangled and halved their outfits, sawing their boats in two.

Thuswise we voyaged Lake Bennett, Tagish, then Windy Arm,
Sinister, savage and baleful, boding us hate and harm.
Many a scow was shattered there on that iron shore;
Many a heart was broken straining at sweep and oar.

We roused Lake Marsh with a chorus, we drifted many a mile;
There was the canyon before us—cavelike its dark defile;
The shores swept faster and faster; the river narrowed to wrath;
Waters that hissed disaster reared upright in our path.

Beneath us the green tumult churning, above us the cavernous
gloom;
Around us, swift twisting and turning, the black, sullen walls of
a tomb.
We spun like a chip in a mill-race; our hearts hammered under the
test;
Then—oh, the relief on each chill face!—we soared into sunlight
and rest.

Hand sought for hand on the instant. Cried we, "Our troubles are
o'er!"
Then, like a rumble of thunder, heard we a canorous roar.
Leaping and boiling and seething, saw we a cauldron afume;
There was the rage of the rapids, there was the menace of doom.

The river springs like a racer, sweeps through a gash in the rock;
Butts at the boulder-ribbed bottom, staggers and rears at the shock;
Leaps like a terrified monster, writhes in its fury and pain;
Then with the crash of a demon springs to the onset again.

Dared we that ravening terror; heard we its din in our ears;
Called on the Gods of our fathers, juggled forlorn with our fears;
Sank to our waists in its fury, tossed to the sky like a fleece;
Then, when our dread was the greatest, crashed into safety and
    peace.

But what of the others that followed, losing their boats by the score?
Well could we see them and hear them, strung down that desolate
    shore.
What of the poor souls that perished? Little of them shall be
    said—
On to the Golden Valley, pause not to bury the dead.

Then there were days of drifting, breezes soft as a sigh;
Night trailed her robe of jewels over the floor of the sky.
The moonlit stream was a python, silver, sinuous, vast,
That writhed on a shroud of velvet—well, it was done at last.

There were the tents of Dawson, there the scar of the slide;
Swiftly we poled o'er the shallows, swiftly leapt o'er the side.
Fires fringed the mouth of Bonanza; sunset gilded the dome;
The test of the trail was over—thank God, thank God, we were
    Home!

# 10

## *THE RUSH TO NOME*

THE Klondike Gold Rush was followed by others. Rex Beach wrote of the Nome rush in his autobiography, a selection from which follows.

From · · ·

*Personal Exposures,* by Rex Beach

In his newspaper column Westbrook Pegler stated recently that he discounted by some sixty per cent the stories of Alaskan hardships as described by Robert W. Service and me. Inasmuch as Jack London wrote the first and perhaps the most highly colored portrayals of life up there Mr. Pegler must likewise put him down as a willful exaggerator. This brilliant columnist has more readers than Gillette has blades and if that's how he feels some of his followers must feel the same.

I take no offense at being called a fiction writer: I've been called worse things right to my teeth but actually neither London nor any of the rest of us overwrote the hardships of life on the brown bean frontier and I'm sure any sourdough will subscribe to that statement.

Even during the gold-rush days some Alaskans had a fairly pleasant time of it. Some people go through life without a toothache, too, but that is largely a matter of good luck or an ample supply of calcium. The average man who did not den up at the first frost like a ground squirrel and who wrestled with that country, no holds barred, went through a good deal of grief.

Living conditions are pleasanter now, transportation has vastly improved, comforts are obtainable; travelers can tour the country at ease, at least during the summer season, and not only broaden their minds but also their hips. It is the ease of living, not the country itself nor its climate, that has changed for the better. Underneath her modern dress Alaska is the same old evil-tempered squaw we knew.

Before these reminiscences meander aimlessly in another direction altogether it might be worth while to recite a firsthand experience to show how real or how imaginary were some of those rigors and hardships we endured before the coming of roads, radios, airlines, thermos bottles and newspaper columnists.

As an experience it was not uncommon; many a man went through worse. I shall confine myself to the facts and leave the story uncolored by invention. If it doesn't give a pretty good idea of the country, as it was, and spell hardship with a capital H, I'll eat the cloth covers off every Alaskan book that bears my name.

Shortly after navigation closed during the autumn of my last season in Nome, news came of a promising discovery at Candle Creek, on the shores of Kotzebue Sound, and late in November my partner, Jack Leedy, made me a proposal to go up there and investigate it. A party had just come down from the Arctic by dog team and one of them, whom I shall call Captain Pinkus, had propositioned Jack. He claimed to be the owner of several well-located fractional claims on the main creek and these he offered to relinquish for a down payment of a thousand dollars, plus a dog team and sled, the remainder of the purchase price to come out of the pay streak. Jack offered to put up the money against my team and outfit if I would return with the owner, check up on his statements and keep him honest.

I didn't want to part with my team for every dog in it was a pal of mine. Moreover I had taken a winter's lease on some ground that promised a profit and it was close enough to town so that I could run in after supper, dance all night and run out again in time to get breakfast and go to work. In this way, by sleeping on alternate nights, I could catch up on a lot of enjoyment I had missed during the summer. Jack's proposal meant a long, hard trip involving much exposure and extreme discomfort at best, on top of which I had no great enthusiasm for any place farther north than Nome. There was, in fact, every good reason for me to decline his offer, therefore I accepted it.

On Thanksgiving morning he buckled a money belt weighted with fifty twenty-dollar gold pieces around my middle and I set out with Captain Pinkus. Why I chose to leave on that day I can't recall. Possibly it was a wanton exhibition of self-discipline or an attempt to appear businesslike, but more likely it was because nobody had invited me to dinner.

Before Pinkus and I topped the Dexter Creek divide, a few miles back of town, I realized that he was a voluble but not a valuable traveling companion. He was a weazle-faced windjammer, as hollow as a dried gourd; by the time that day was over I could have shot him from ambush and called it good, clean sport.

Nome clings to the south shore of Seward Peninsula, that body of land which thrusts itself out nearly to Siberia and separates Behring Sea from the Arctic Ocean. It is a wilderness of mountain ranges, spurs and valleys. There were no roads but a few places of shelter were scattered along our route and they were connected in winter by trails of a sort—thin pencil tracings which were visible in good weather but which were erased by every snowfall. Roadhouses then did not mean what they do now. They were not dine and dance places. Some of them served meals, at others a traveler was lucky to find a bare bunk for himself and a lean-to for his dogs. Inasmuch as we had to journey some three hundred miles we carried the usual equipment of tent, stove, bedding and provisions, a load so heavy that we could snitch a ride only on bare ice, of which there was little at that time of year. In consequence we had to make the trip on our insteps. Thirty miles a day under such circumstances was good going and we averaged something like that.

Dog teams have become a curiosity in Alaska of late years, for most of the travel, both winter and summer, is by air and where we crept like worms at the cost of infinite exposure and fatigue one can now fly in a dinner jacket and gun-metal dancing pumps. Travel through a timberless region like that along the Behring Sea and Arctic coast was particularly trying and considerably more hazardous than travel along the Yukon where firewood is abundant. Pinkus and I, for instance, had to burrow for our fuel and there was mighty little of it. Much of the country we traversed was entirely bare of vegetation except along the stream banks where in places a narrow fringe of willows and alders managed to subsist. Often this growth was as sparse as a scholarly Chinese beard and not much longer. Certainly it was harder to ignite and that is no exaggeration for once I touched a match to a beard while its owner was asleep and it burned immediately.

Those green willow twigs and sappy stems would not blaze without encouragement, they wouldn't even break out in a gentle perspiration when matches were applied, therefore we carried kerosene rags or pieces of an old rubber boot for kindling. Even then they did little more than sizzle and stew in their own juice and it took nearly as long to prepare a meal over them as to cook it by body heat.

It was necessary to pitch camp while there was light enough to gather a pile of this brush and while one man was so engaged the other unharnessed, unloaded and started to get the tent up. After a fire was finally kindled and the water bucket had begun to thaw Pinkus and I were usually so thirsty that we drained it as fast as the snow melted, which slowed things down. Meanwhile we shook like aspen leaves in our wet clothes until the tent warmed up, after which we steamed in them.

The mere starting of a fire in cold weather is sometimes a problem to trail-weary men, in fact I nearly perished one night on the Yukon before I could do so although the makings were ready. I had pulled a hand sled all day, perspiring freely, and I was pretty tired when I arrived at the empty cabin where I proposed to put up. Firewood was already cut but it was green; by the time I got my stove set up I had begun to shiver violently and my hands were so numb that I couldn't kindle a blaze. My fingers were so stiff and unmanageable that the matches fell out of them and I could not open the blade of my knife to whittle shavings. I tried putting on my mittens but the linings were soaked with sweat and during my fumbling attempts to get a fire started they had frozen stiff.

In the grub box were some candles and one of these I managed to prop upright, then I worked my hands inside my shirt and held them under my armpits while I stamped around the cabin. It took quite a while to bring back into my icy claws enough circulation so that I could strike a sulphur match and hold it to the candle wick. This done I thrust the tips of them into the flame until enough sensation returned so that I could open my knife blade. Next I clamped my fingers around the handle and promptly they set, like cement. That was fine. Soon I had some shavings prepared and managed to stuff them under the green wood without knocking the stove down; with the candle flame I ignited them and my troubles were over. All in all it was a trying ten minutes and it was hours before I got warm inside.

Once Pinkus and I had snugged down for the night and got the wrinkles smoothed out of our stomachs, a two hours' task at the least, it was then necessary to cook supper for the dogs, another interminable task. There being no dried salmon in that part of the country, I carried a huge square dog pan the size of the stove. In this snow was melted and slowly brought to a boil, then corn meal or rolled oats was stirred in and finally an ample ration of salt pork was diced up and added. Since there were ten animals in the team, it took about as long to care for them as for ourselves, and it was late when we got to bed.

November days are short so we rose early and breakfasted by candle light, cursing the man who invented alarm clocks. Actually we worked about sixteen hours and slept eight. Every moment that we were not in bed was devoted to the active, ceaseless effort to keep alive and to keep going.

Always there was the cold to contend with. It was like a constant weight pressing in from all sides and from it there was no escape. There was no exhilaration to it, no deep and grateful inhaling of the breath or pounding of the chest. Nobody ever professed to be glad he was alive on such a glorious morning. In the first place the mornings weren't glorious: if the weather wasn't bad, at the moment, it promised to become so and we talked about little else except that, and our indigestion.

Such remarks as we voiced were unprintable and frequently they were accompanied by violent eructations of gas for we ate heartily of baking-powder bread, undone beans and fat pork. No sooner were these victuals down than they went to war on us: hyperacidity was chronic. The real call of the wild was not the howl of the timber wolf, the maniac laughter of the Arctic loon, nor yet the mating cry of the moose, it was the dyspeptic belch of a miner with sour stomach.

In the mind of a rugged newspaper columnist trifling in conveniences like these above mentioned may not add up to actual hardship but we were weaklings and we complained.

I have met many heels in my meanderings but compared with Captain Pinkus the worst of them was an amateur. He possessed every detestable characteristic and he became a sharp nail in my boot, a sandpaper undershirt, a stone in the kidney. Nevertheless the louse could travel. He was quick and he was tireless. Doubtless it was his ability to start fast and keep going which accounted for his presence: had he not possessed a quick pickup and unusual powers of endurance somebody would surely have run him down and done away with him.

Our fourth day on the trail was a killer, for we followed a senseless, winding river some fifty-five miles to Carpenter's roadhouse. Doubtless the distance was actually much less than that, nevertheless it was plenty for the weather was bitterly cold, the snow was so gritty that the sled runners squealed and the dogs had to pull every foot of the way. There was no wind, nevertheless our noses froze and white spots repeatedly appeared on our cheekbones.

We did not meet a soul on the trail nor pass a human habitation, not a sound except the complaint of our steel-shod sled and our occasional profanities broke the silence. It was long after dark when we arrived at our destination, half dead on our feet, and we would have marched on past it had not the team turned off and scrambled up the bank.

Ahead of us was what looked like a snow-covered Indian mound but in the side of it a door opened revealing a square of lamp light and we drove directly into a warm and roomy barabara.

The floor was of dirt, the sod roof was supported by posts, along one side ran a row of bunks filled with clean wild hay, and at the other end of the place was a cookstove with a fire in it. No migratory birds after a flight from South America were more completely spent than Pinkus and I: had we collapsed upon the stove we would have sat there and dozed. While our wings drooped, Carpenter, the proprietor, unharnessed and fed our team; Billy Vint, his partner, hurriedly set the agate ware.

I liked Carpenter. He was as fine a specimen of manhood as I ever saw. Well over six feet tall he was as lean and restless as a wolf and was reputed to be a prodigious traveler. Later that night he told me that he and his companion were coming to Candle Creek in a week or so to pick up a load of mail and I was pleased when he invited me to join them on the return trip to Nome. They, too, owned a good team and he was confident that we three could set a record between the two places that would take some beating.

Neither of us dreamed that a time would come when the Alaska Derby, perhaps the most grueling and spectacular sporting event ever known, would be run annually from Nome to Candle and return or that special strains of racing dogs would be bred for it and that fortunes would be wagered on its outcome.

I explained the nature of Jack Leedy's and my arrangement with Pinkus and promised to accept Carpenter's invitation if, when the time came to start home, my team had not changed hands.

"He may have some good ground up there," the roadhouse man said doubtfully. "He's the kind who usually gets in on a good thing. But he's a liar and a blowhard. Better keep an eye on him."

I am not certain now whether it was one or two days' march after this warning that Pinkus and I overtook another outfit headed in the direction we were going, but I do distinctly recall our amazement to discover that it consisted of a man and his wife —a young and beautiful woman who looked as utterly out-of-place amid those bleak surroundings as a rose-tinted flamingo.

During the summer the husband had sent a cargo of supplies

and lumber to build a trading post at the mouth of the Imnachuk,
now he was on his way up there to take charge of it. Being uncertain of the route from here on he was glad to see us and asked if
he and his wife could join with us—just in case.

Neither of them seemed capable of coping with any unusual
hardships, so of course we welcomed the proposal. I explained
that the country was as new to me as to them but my companion
had come down from Candle Creek a month before and he was
acting as guide. To this Pinkus added that he knew of a short cut
that would save many miles and would put us on the headwaters
of the Imnachuk by the next night. There were several cabins on
the creek and by following it down we could sleep under a roof.

Having learned to put less than complete trust in any statement
of the Captain's, I queried him in private but he seemed so confident of himself that when we set out in the morning I allowed
him to have his head.

Midafternoon found us on the summit of a hogback high enough
to see Catalina on a clear day, but the day wasn't clear: the sky
was low and snow was falling. We had climbed steadily for hours,
wallowing knee-deep, and we were tired. So were the dogs. From
the flanks of the divide, shallow valleys radiated in all directions,
deepening as they twisted out of sight, nowhere was there any
conspicuous landmark and as far as we could make out the same
confusion of domes and bulging ridges stretched on indefinitely.
The couple behind us were having a hard time—the woman was
pretty well exhausted, nevertheless she smiled bravely and made
no complaint.

Finally when they had dropped back a ways I stopped the team
and walked forward to Pinkus.

"You're lost," I told him.

He denied the accusation until I took off my mittens and reached
for him, then he confessed and I fingered his Adam's apple until
the other sled drew near.

There was nothing to do except trust to instinct, mine not his,
get down off this exposed place as quickly as possible, praying
meanwhile that the valley selected would prove to be the right
one. That we did, and finally about dark discovered an ax blaze

on an alder trunk. By the light of a match we found it to be a
location notice, the pencil writing of which revealed that we were
indeed on a tributary of the Imnachuk and all we had to do to
reach shelter was keep going.

It was late when we came to a cabin and then Pinkus was not
in the least subdued: on the contrary he claimed all credit for our
safe arrival. In fact he boasted of his unerring instinct for direction
which was more trustworthy than a compass. Compasses go wrong
but never Captain Pinkus.

Our traveling companions could not get off their route from
here in so, on the following morning, we said good-by to them,
after complimenting the wife on her courage and her endurance.

Not until we reached the coast and were out on the ice of
Kotzebue Sound did we hit easy going, then our dogs picked up
the scent of a reindeer herd that had preceded us and ran like
whippets. Pinkus and I merely rode the sled, using the ax blade for
a rudder to keep it from slewing. It skidded once and overturned,
throwing us clear. We hit on our respective heads and I nearly
broke my neck, but, alas, he was uninjured.

The town of Candle Creek consisted of a small store, a large
saloon and a few cabins. The storekeeper's wife served meals in
her kitchen, a ladder led up to a loft, or attic, where there was
floor space for a dozen men to sleep. There was no ventilation
but we had enjoyed nothing else since leaving Nome so we did
not complain.

The mining records showed that Pinkus had indeed located
some fractions but from what I learned it was probable that an
accurate survey of the creek would reduce them to microscopic
proportions. That disappointing news was followed by something
else: the recorder asked me if I was acquainted with a local character by the name of Big George Matson, an ex-whaler, and when
I confessed I was not he said, "That's too bad. He licks every
stranger who comes to town."

"Why?"

"I don't know. He just got into the habit, lately. He likes everybody when he's sober and they like him but the minute he starts
drinking, a new face makes him mad. Trouble is he gets drunk

every night. We haven't had many visitors so he's had to work back over the list of early arrivals which is hard on them. They'll certainly be glad to see you."

I assumed this was an attempt to have some fun with me until I discovered that there was indeed a Candle Creek character by the name of Big George and that he was a bully of formidable proportions. From all I could hear he was something of a public embarrassment, a civic liability, and the more I learned about him, the less eager I was to make his acquaintance. However I could think of no way to avoid him.

He showed up in the saloon that night and I looked on him with misgivings. He was not a tall man, nevertheless he was the biggest thing I ever saw on two legs, excepting perhaps a Kodiak bear I once met face to face in a thicket of devil clubs. He was dressed like a native and wore only three articles of clothing, muk-luks, reindeer-hide pants and parka; the last two garments being worn with the hair inside for greater warmth and to absorb perspiration. His face was wide, his shingled head was as round as a grapefruit. Evidently he radiated heat like a base burner for I was told that he never wore a cap and raised his parka hood for protection against the weather only on rare occasions.

He drank for a while, unobtrusively, then I saw him stare in my direction and ask a question of the bartender. I attempted to blend myself into the background like a spotted fawn but evidently my protective coloring was not very good for he continued to eye me. By and by he came toward the rear of the room where I was standing and the floor boards bent under him.

Pinkus spoke to him but he said, "Get away. I don't like you!" Of me he inquired, "What's your name?"

I told him, whereupon he shook his head slowly. "No. That ain't it."

Here it comes, I thought. Several well-intentioned bystanders must have thought the same for they crowded in and attempted to distract the whaler's attention but he swept them aside.

"I know you," he said to me. "We was shipmates." He laid an arm the size of a leg around my shoulder, and to the others he repeated thickly, "I know this boy! We was shipmates!" Evidently there was something deeply sentimental about that relationship and mention of it released some pent-up flow of emotion for his face puckered, he gulped, tears slowly gathered in his eyes and finally overflowed. With his right fore flipper he patted me as a seal would pat its young.

This was the signal for Pinkus to sound his "a." He plucked at George and neighed loudly that I was his partner and had arranged to buy all his claims.

Evidently this struck George as an unholy alliance or an unfair deal. Anyhow it appeared to shock his every sense of decency for, without a word, he reached for the hood of his parka, then with one forward sweep of his arms he stripped it off over his head and sent it flying, leaving himself bare to the waist. Thereupon he gave the gabby Captain precisely what I had lacked the moral force to give; viz., a thorough overhaul. It was not a fight; he merely took the little asafetida pill in hand and rubbed him on the premises as a cook rubs garlic on a salad bowl.

Pinkus yelled but nobody stirred and when the affair was over I shed tears on Big George's shoulder. Shipmates, indeed! I told him we were closer than that, we were Siamese twins and it would kill me to be severed from his side. To this day I don't know for whom he mistook me, what induced him to maul Pinkus, nor why he later went out of his way to be obliging.

For that matter I can't understand why the little Captain walked all the way back to Candle Creek with me just to prove himself a liar. Perhaps it was an overweening desire to strut and pose, even briefly, as a man of means and a favorite of fortune. More likely, of course, he just loved to lie. Once I had him off my back I began to look around for a real opportunity to turn a dollar and here Big George proved his liking for me was sincere. He put me on to several claims which would be open for relocation on New Year's Day and after examining them I decided to wait over and stake them.

When Carpenter and Vint arrived, soon after Christmas, to get their load of mail I advised them that I had some unfinished business on hand and could not take part in the dash to Nome unless they would postpone the start of it for two or three days.

This they decided would be impossible so I wrote Jack Leedy explaining what I was up to and gave the letter to Billy Vint to deliver. It was lucky for me that I didn't go along.

I believe it was early on the morning of the 29th that they left, taking with them as passenger a man who at the last moment decided to return to Nome; on the afternoon of the 31st George and I drove up Candle Creek. Instead of returning that night we camped in order to be on the ground at daylight.

Of all the trail mates I've had he was about the best and it wore me out to keep up my end of the work. He was obliging, tireless and utterly indifferent to discomfort: when he broke a trail it stayed broken for he wallowed it down like a playful walrus. Why it was that he helped me to relocate those properties instead of staking them himself, I still don't know and I doubt if he knew at the time, but it showed that he could go as far to be friendly and helpful as to be quarrelsome and destructive.

It was on our way back to town on the afternoon of New Year's Day that the worst blizzard of the season rushed down upon us. The world became a milky turmoil through which we had to stumble blindly, my dogs refused to face the bitter gale that came roaring out of the north and we had to drag them. I was glad indeed to have the company of a man as mighty as this whaler for without him I might never have found my way into town.

For three endless days battalions of storm demons did their insane dance of death and nobody ventured outdoors except to probe for his dogs, dig them out and feed them. In doing that it was the part of wisdom to stay within groping distance of a building for the world had vanished, it was blotted out under a Niagara of boiling snow particles.

On the morning of the fourth it reappeared: the storm had passed. Two outfits were leaving for Nome and I joined them for all trails had been obliterated and travel was bound to be arduous. It proved to be all of that and more. In crossing the barrens where Pinkus had lost his direction we selected the headwaters of the wrong stream, and followed it for miles before discovering our mistake—an error that cost us a lot of weary steps and an extra night in the open. Just to step up the general enjoyment somebody

had packed the kindling rags in with the food and I found that
even a small amount of kerosene taken in flapjacks will satisfy
the hungriest man. I retched and vomited and in other ways endeavored to rid myself of the taste but decided finally that the only
way to do so was to swallow a wick and light the end.

We were all pretty well spent when we finally got back on our
course and pulled into a tent roadhouse that had just been established. There we got unexpected news of Carpenter and Vint—
news that pretty nearly took out of me what strength I had left.

That New Year's Day storm smote them at the most unfavorable
spot on their entire route, a height of land where there was no
possible escape from its violence. It came with such swiftness and
fury that all they could do was cut their dogs loose to drift ahead
of it, break out their sleeping bags and crawl into them.

Without food, drink or stimulant of any sort those poor fellows
lay on the crest of that divide for two days and nights, then convinced that they were slowly but surely freezing to death they
decided to push on no matter what the risk. They must have realized that their chances of survival were slim but they were not
the sort of men to meet death without a struggle. Accordingly they
crept out of their bedding and stumbled away through the white
smother.

Carpenter, the iron man, was the first to play out, and that is
understandable. As the leader it is presumable that he had taxed
himself far more severely than the others. When he could go no
farther he directed them to cover him with snow and push on for
help.

Hours later Vint fell and lacked the strength to rise.

The third member of the trio, the poorest traveler, the one least
accustomed to exposure, managed to keep going until he finally
arrived at the roadhouse where we received the news. Happily he
had enough strength and sanity left to relate what had happened
and to indicate roughly where his companions could be found. Of
course a relief party set out immediately.

Vint was discovered lying face down as he had fallen. Carpenter was found only when the rescuers beheld a white hand

and arm stiffly upthrust through a mound of snow. The flesh was marble hard.

Both men were still alive, strange to relate, but in such critical condition that they had been rushed to Nome. Their companion, although less seriously injured, needed medical attention badly enough so we selected the freshest animals out of our three teams, shifted loads and sent him on with one of our group.

That catastrophe sobered me for I realized that only chance, in the person of Big George Matson, had spared me a part in it. Had it not been for his alcoholic vagary that night we met, in all likelihood I too would have been on my way to an amputation.

I never saw Carpenter again but on more than one occasion I heard his voice. Both hands and both feet had been removed when I reached Nome, exposure and shock had completely destroyed his mind. He and another unfortunate victim of freezing were housed together and for weeks their hoarse, incessant babblings were dreadful to hear. It was a mercy when death finally stilled their tongues.

Vint fared considerably better: although seriously mutilated and delirious for weeks he finally recovered. The third man, whose name I have vainly tried to remember, suffered only minor injuries.

Long after I left Alaska a party of prospectors somewhere in the wilderness of hills and valleys drained by the upper Kougarok discovered a weather-beaten sled, the lashings of which had rotted away. Its runners were streaks of rust but in the basket was a canvas mail sack, the fabric of which had withstood the attacks of sun, rain and snow. They brought it to Nome, it was opened and its contents were forwarded. In this manner, some six years after it was mailed, Jack Leedy received my letter from Candle Creek and sent it to me in New York, as a souvenir.

I have it among my possessions, a grim reminder of the Alaska I knew before I ever dreamed of writing. It makes interesting reading alongside of Mr. Pegler's commentary on the hardships of that country. He can discount them by sixty per cent and still have something left.

# 11

# THE LOOTING

*The Spoilers*, Rex Beach's most famous novel, tells the story of the claim jumping at Nome in which a Federal judge, Arthur H. Noyes, and his confederates were involved. Not too many are aware that Beach wrote another version of the affair, a factual account that appeared as a series of articles in Appleton's *Booklovers Magazine* in 1906. Beach summarizes the whole affair in the concluding portion of his opening paragraphs.

From • • •

*The Looting of Alaska, or The True Story of a Robbery by Law*, by Rex Beach

The tale is worth the telling if for no other reason than to show what abuses are possible under our much-touted systems where we are supposedly equal in the eye of God and the law. What was done here to Americans close at home can be done more easily to those distant foreigners we are coming to rule, and to whom our doctrines are as darkness.

The outsider who knows Alaska not as a glacier-riven barren but as the greatest mineral possession we have, with centuries of undeveloped resource before it, will be interested in the story of its shame. It is a recital of intrigue and pillage originating in the fertile brains of statesmen beneath the shadow of Washington

Monument, stretching out to the westward and ending among the
gold-bottomed placers of Nome. There is in it the contrast of the
extra old and the ultra new, the foyer and the frontier, the white
vest and the blue shirt. It has a backing of long toms and gold pans,
writs and riots.

In order properly to understand what led to and aroused the
lusts of the titled conspirators, it is necessary to go back through
the early romance of a great gold strike and sketch the history of
its development; to show how, out of a forbidding and unknown
land peopled by Lapp deer-drivers and shanghaied sailors, was
wrought a wonderful country; how these aliens and a wandering
crew of penniless adventurers solved the mystery of a rock-girt
coast and gave to the world such tidings that in a night there sprang
up a city of twenty thousand, with hotels, theaters, brass bands, and
*tables d'hote;* how a sick man dug into the beach sands where he
lay and found such treasure that his fellow-argonauts swarmed
out of the hills, tore down their houses, ripped up their streets,
and burrowed under the city of their making; how, when they had
done this, a crew of political pirates made them walk the plank.

* * *

A group of high-powered, politically influential conspirators
planned and executed a scheme to defraud the gold miners in the
Nome area and by legal strategy to steal their gold. These were no
ordinary conspirators. They were capably led by a powerful
Dakota political boss, Alexander McKenzie, whom Beach characterized as "not the common municipal vote getter, the manipula-
tor of primaries, but the man of riches, respectability and standing,
who plays the game for gold not glory."

McKenzie's scheme was simple, direct and bold. Its success was
to hinge upon his ability either to influence the passage of Congressional legislation or to manipulate a key presidential appointment. To set his scheme in motion, McKenzie formed the Alaska
Gold Mining Company, whose stock was distributed "where it
would do the most good," among his influential friends, several of
them United States senators.

Then McKenzie attempted to carry through Congress on the

shoulders of his senatorial friends legislation enabling his Alaska Company to seize title to all mining claims at any time owned, or owned at the moment, by aliens residing in Alaska, including even claims bought from aliens in good faith by United States citizens.

This legislation was introduced in an amendment to the proposed new code for Alaska by McKenzie's bosom friend, Senator Hansbrough of North Dakota, himself the recipient of stock in the Alaska Company. Since many of the early gold finds in the Nome area were made by foreigners, principally Swedes, the effect of the amendment would have been to enable McKenzie's Alaska Company to seize "legally" most of the gold being panned in the Nome area.

Though the debate was prolonged for a month, the amendment was defeated. Unabashed, McKenzie brazenly and successfully sought to secure control of the newly created Federal Court at Nome.

By exerting extraordinary pressure through his senatorial friends on President McKinley, McKenzie landed the new judgeship for his old friend, a Minneapolis lawyer named Arthur H. Noyes. Noyes, called by Beach "a plastic tool," would hand down the court orders McKenzie wanted, thus securing to the Alaska Company the same advantages which would have accrued to it through the Hansbrough amendment.

The Company would become the receiver of legitimate mining claims, work them feverishly for a quick and huge profit, before the decisions of Judge Noyes could be questioned or reversed by the nearest U.S. Circuit Court at San Francisco, three thousand miles away. Since the placer gold was so easy to mine with simple tools—a shovel and a pan—McKenzie stipulated that he could sell out the Company's stock before the higher court could act, thus, as Beach writes, leaving the victims to bear the fight.

Within a week of Noyes's arrival at Nome in late July, 1900, his court had ground out the orders and injunctions necessary to turn over to the Alaska Company the operation of most of the mines in the Nome area. McKenzie himself was not idle during this week.

Indeed, on the afternoon of his arrival, McKenzie went to

Nome's most important law office and demanded a half interest in all the firm's mining cases, pointing out to startled lawyers that he, McKenzie, controlled the Nome court and that unless they acceded to his demand, he would see to it that their cases never reached a hearing. Threatened with ruin, the lawyers gave in reluctantly, receiving shares in the Alaska Company in return for half of their business.

Thereupon, McKenzie set a corps of stenographers to work, preparing documents appointing him as receiver of the mines to be seized. That evening Judge Noyes dutifully signed the court orders without any notification to the miners whose claims were to be jumped. As Beach writes, the miners "were not only ignorant of any action taken, but were not even cited to appear in their own defense and argue why such orders should not be entered in the court."

Before midnight, McKenzie's posse of hastily organized hirelings had ejected the rightful owners from the first five claims. Two days later, Noyes issued an order empowering McKenzie as receiver to confiscate everything at the mines: "sluice boxes, pumps, excavations, machinery, pipe, plant, boarding houses, tents, buildings, safes, scales and all personal property fixed and movable, gold, gold dust and precious metals, money boxes or coin, and all personal property upon said claims."

McKenzie's Alaska Company was in complete control. The victims of the willful court orders were taken by surprise. On Discovery Claim one miner was ousted from his bed and run out into the night half naked. But as McKenzie's scheme became apparent, the highly independent miners organized themselves and sent representatives to seek redress of their wrongs at the Superior Court in San Francisco.

Two months passed, while McKenzie strengthened his hand, securing the appointment of a corrupt district attorney, suborning a special examiner sent out by the Department of Justice, and working into his plans a U.S. marshal and a corps of Nome attorneys. Finally, the representatives of the wronged miners returned from San Francisco with an order from the Circuit Court directing Noyes to stay all matters in his court and granting the miners the appeal they had requested from Noyes's previous court orders.

Noyes refused to act. Indeed, he went even further, ordering the U.S. Army troops under his authority to defend and protect the seizures by the Alaska Company. The miners' representatives made another long trip to San Francisco. This time they returned with two deputies of the Circuit Court with instructions "to produce the *body*" of McKenzie on a charge of contempt of court.

A year later his coconspirator, Judge Noyes, was charged similarly. Noyes got off with a thousand-dollar fine; McKenzie was sentenced to a year in prison; but President McKinley pardoned McKenzie on grounds of his ill health.

To Alaskans the Beach novel and magazine series symbolized the consequences of Federal mismanagement of Seward's purchase. At the time of which Beach writes Alaska had not yet achieved even territorial status, although owing to the widespread popular interest fostered by the discovery of gold Congress was belatedly considering a set of laws and the granting of territorial status.

The opening statement of the magazine series, quoted below, is a colorful imprecation on corruption and at the same time an invocation of justice, both expressive of the feelings current in Alaskans at that time.

More from · · ·

## The Looting of Alaska

Alaska is the galley slave of the Union. Her chains were forged by some very vile politics. She has been ruined, rifled, and degraded by such practices as have seldom blackened the pages of American corruption.

To accomplish her debauch, our judiciary has been capitalized, and American courts of law exploited as a commercial investment. She writhes today under the same conditions at which our forefathers rebelled in King George's time, being our only possession —State, territorial or foreign—to suffer taxation without representation.

She has been licensed directly from Washington as a mistress for the politically unclean, has presented the unique spectacle of her court officials in jail yet drawing salaries through the bars, of high government servants retained in office long after conviction in their own court of heinous offenses, of others defiled yet protected in their defilement, and she will show for years the print of the boldest political steal ever consummated in this country. Such an unbroken catalogue of disreputable officeholders has been saddled upon her that she now feels, when a man accepts a position in her government, he is, by virtue of his acceptance, a blackleg.

What are we to think of the conspiracy of 1900 wherein a coterie of exalted political pets stole the resources of a realm as large as Great Britain, France, and Germany, set up their marionettes in control, and took the richest gold mines since '49?

We haven't heard about it! Of course not. When the scandal came out, it was smothered and the public kept in ignorance. Criminals were pardoned, records expunged, thieves exalted to new honors. Your Alaskan remembers it, though—remembers when he was bound, gagged, and gone through by the basest officials that ever disgraced an appointment. He remembers how at headquarters the wheels of justice were mysteriously clogged, and how, when judgment of a feeble kind overtook the gang, they squirmed out of punishment. When he sees these men higher in office and more powerful now than then, with Russian fatalism he shrugs his shoulders and says:

"God is far off, and it's a long way to Washington."

# 12

## *ALASKAN JUSTICE*

James Wickersham was appointed a Federal district judge by President Theodore Roosevelt in 1901 to clear up the mess of corruption left by Judge Noyes. Wickersham continued on the bench till 1908, when he was elected as Alaska's Delegate to Congress, and reelected nine times thereafter. He was a man of many facets. In addition to his public service he was an author, a bibliographer, and an explorer.

Before Judge Wickersham's arrival at Eagle on the Yukon there had been in the interior of Alaska only the miners' code, a practical, if extralegal, application of frontier democracy. Each camp had decided matters of common concern by majority vote and meted out justice deemed to fit the crime. Murder was punished by hanging; offenses of the next gravity, such as theft, by whipping or banishment, or both.

Judge Wickersham tells of two such informal cases in the following account.

From • • •

*Old Yukon: Tales—Trails—and Trials,* by James Wickersham

Notwithstanding the want of organized government justice was not unknown, as the following case will show. A young woman

**147**

appealed to the miners at one of the camps to compel a dance hall
fiddler to marry her and to pay hospital and other bills resulting
from her surrender in reliance upon his promise and his subsequent
repudiation of it. A miners' meeting was called at which the miners
from the nearby creeks appeared in numbers and elected a judge
and a sheriff. A warrant was issued and the fiddler was brought
before the assembly. The trial was prompt. The plaintiff told her
story and the defendant was heard in ominous silence. At the close
of all the evidence a miner from the creeks offered the following
verdict which, without debate, was unanimously adopted:

"Resolved, that the defendant pay the plaintiff's hospital bill
$500.00, and pay the plaintiff $500.00, and marry her as he
promised to do, and that he have until 5 o'clock this afternoon to
obey this order; and, Resolved further, that this meeting do now
adjourn till 5 o'clock."

There was no notice of appeal, no bill of exceptions, no stay of
execution. The saloons did a rushing business that afternoon, but
the miners from the creeks were orderly and not unusually intoxicated. The records disclose that when business was resumed by
the court at five o'clock, the Committee, headed by the sheriff,
reported satisfaction of judgment and marriage. Whereupon this
frontier court, led by the judge and the sheriff, escorted by the jury,
adjourned to the bar to congratulate the happy couple. It would
have taken my court two years, with many pleadings, hearings and
arguments, instead of two hours, to give judgment, which in all
probability would have been reversed on some technicality!

Another marital contract performed on the Koyukuk trail some
few years ago may be of interest. In the absence of both Church
and State, recourse was again had to the Common Law of the
Trail, and one French Joe performed the ceremony, wrote the
contract, and made the public record. The ceremony took place at
a night camp of a group of stampeders en route over the mountains to the distant Koyukuk river gold camp. The record is
preserved in the society columns of the *Yukon Press*, March 17,
1899:

"On the evening of November 10, 1898, a romantic union took
place between Frank McGillis and Aggie Dalton, near the mouth of

Dall river. Splicing was done by 'French Joe' (J. Durrant), and the form of the contract was as follows:

> *Ten miles from the Yukon, on the banks of this lake,*
> *For a partner to Koyukuk, McGillis I take;*
> *We have no preacher, and we have no ring,*
> *It makes no difference, it's all the same thing.*
>
> Aggie Dalton.

> *I swear by my gee-pole, under this tree,*
> *A devoted husband to Aggie I always will be;*
> *I'll love and protect her, this maiden so frail,*
> *From those sour-dough bums, on the Koyukuk trail.*
>
> Frank McGillis.

> *For two dollars apiece, in Chechaco money,*
> *I unite this couple in matrimony;*
> *He be a rancher, she be a teacher,*
> *I do the job up, just as well as a preacher.*
>
> French Joe."

History records that the high contracting parties found the pot of gold on the Koyukuk and lived happily together ever afterwards.

* * *

The vigilantism and outlawry of the old West did not occur in Alaska, with two notable exceptions. The principal character of one of these was Jefferson Randolph Smith, known as Soapy Smith, and the scene of his exploits was Skagway and the trails that led over the White and Chilkoot passes to the Klondike. James Wickersham tells us about him also.

## More from · · ·

### Old Yukon

#### VIGILANTE DAYS OF '98 AT DYEA AND SKAGWAY

In midsummer of 1897 two young men, each bearing a heavy pack, waded ashore from a row boat fast on the mud flats at the mouth of the Dyea river and walked briskly towards the Healy & Wilson store on the bank. A slender, bearded, sharp-eyed man of about thirty-six, with a diamond pin in his shirt front, strolled down the trail to meet them. "Hello, fellows," he said, "are you going over the trail to the Klondike?" And by way of encouragement and a closer acquaintance he added: "The last news from there this week is great—gold in every creek by the millions—you are sure to make a stake easily."

The elder of the young men gave the stranger a friendly but silent nod; the younger stared at him for a moment, then smiled and said: "My father lives in Panama; he is very rich and sends me money to give away to lucky men who deserve it." The dark-whiskered man was manifestly startled. Recovering quickly he exclaimed, as he offered his hand, "Well, by God! stranger, I don't know you, but you sure have me located." "The last time I saw you," was the reply, "you were on the street in Denver selling twenty dollar bills, wrapped round cakes of soap, to the suckers for a dollar, and making that come-on speech to them. Do you remember?" "Sure," Soapy Smith added with a laugh, "and I am still giving them away."

When the Klondike gold strike became known in 1897 there were stories about millions in loose gold, stored in tin cans under miners' bunks. Every adventurer, gambler and crook in Canada and the United States determined to head for the Klondike. One of these was, as above indicated, Soapy Smith.

Jefferson Randolph Smith, alias "Soapy," landed at Dyea in 1897 and quickly gathered under his command a band of cappers, crooks, cardsharps, and cut-throats unequalled on the Pacific coast since the Vigilante days at Virginia City. He came of a wealthy and prominent Southern family, was a hail-fellow-well-met sort, and spent his earnings freely. Any criminal, male or female, who was unfortunate enough to be caught in the net of the law was sure of immediate sympathy and assistance from Soapy. His men covered the towns of Dyea and Skagway and both trails to the boundary line on the Chilkoot summits, beyond which they dared not go for fear of Canada's Mounted Police.

In 1898 the mountain trails from Dyea and Skagway were

crowded with men, women, horses, dogs, all going towards the summit without organization or police protection. Packers carried valuable merchandise on their backs, and each of these unprotected travelers necessarily carried a considerable sum of money on his person. This horde, well supplied with money, but with no organized protection, afforded thugs and highwaymen ideal opportunities for fraud, theft, robbery and murder. The whole area between Lynn Canal and the headwaters of the Yukon, including the Dyea and the White Pass trails, had but a single deputy United States marshal for protection, and he quickly became a silent partner of Soapy Smith's. Soapy's boldest highwaymen were stationed in the towns and at advantageous points along the two parallel trails. It is estimated that 20,000 persons passed over the two trails in 1898. Open violent robbery was a daily occurrence. Sure-thing games—the "shell game" being the most prominent—were played at every stream crossing and at every over-night camp. What the crooked gamester missed, the highway robber got.

Lookouts met every steamer at the Skagway dock as regularly as hotel runners and scrutinized new arrivals for profitable victims. Soapy controlled these criminal activities from "Jeff's Place," as his saloon and gambling joint in Skagway was named. Whether he was guilty or not, every crime committed on the trail for which there was not another known agent was imputed to him. Terror reigned in the towns and on the trails. Law-abiding citizens were intimidated, though the bandits were careful to prey upon transients rather than local residents.

The businessmen of Dyea and Skagway were too much engrossed in their own affairs to provide law enforcement. Transients did not stay at any place long enough to organize for their own safety. They were intent upon getting to the gold fields and amassing a fortune as soon as possible. Soapy's gangsters, on the side lines, chose their victims, and boldly robbed them on the unprotected trails. If complaints were made they fell on deaf ears, for the editor of the principal local paper and the deputy U.S. marshal and the justice of the peace, the only law officers in the towns, were notoriously friendly to the criminals and refused to protect travelers or their property.

If a traveler passing through the towns, or along the trails, displayed or appeared to have money, word would be sent ahead to confederates and he was almost certain to lose his money, if not his life, before reaching the safety of the Canadian policemen on the summit. Bandits along the trails were honest-appearing prospectors, with big phoney packs, filled with hay or shavings, to mislead the unwary. Each of these desperadoes carried dangerous weapons and gambling devices, and was always ready to seduce the innocent traveler to join a game with their cappers or confidence men.

A Presbyterian missionary came to Dyea in the fall of '97 en route to Dawson to establish a church there. He was accompanied by a lay brother, who carried the church fund. The latter was both inquisitive and social, and readily talked with strangers about the trails, the scenery, or matters of current interest. One day on the trail he fell behind his shepherd and met a well-dressed and agreeable gentleman who was giving three roughly-garbed men, carrying heavy-looking miners' packs, information about the trail to the summit. Being naturally interested the guardian of the church fund stopped and joined in the conversation. It appeared that the very agreeable gentleman had been eating English walnuts, for some shells were on the ground at his feet. A short piece of board also happened to be nearby. Picking up the board and three half shells, the agreeable gentleman sat down on a boulder and laughingly explained to the simple-minded miners a childhood game called "Where is the pea?" Before the inquisitive lay brother solved that simple problem he had lost the church fund he was carrying to Dawson!

Another story was related to me by a prominent business man of Skagway who assured me of its truth. An evangelist came to town to organize a congregation and build a church. He was told that Colonel Smith was a public-spirited citizen and would be interested in his project. He found the Colonel at Jeff's Place, and stated his business with so much enthusiasm that he received a contribution of $300 and was introduced to some of the Colonel's business associates who also gave him money. Thus encouraged the evangelist collected from others about $3000 more—all of which was stolen from him that night by one of the henchmen of the false Colonel, who was none other than Soapy Smith. In this manner Soapy recovered his donation of $300, plus a huge interest charge, and turned the balance into the thieves' treasury for division according to the rules of the order.

The War with Spain then engaged the attention of the country and the people were filled with patriotism. With that cunning impudence which characterized him, Smith wrote a letter to President McKinley offering to raise a company of Alaska rough riders. Smith received from the President's secretary a courteous letter of acknowledgment that gave no authority to act as an enlisting officer. This letter served Smith's purpose, however, for it was promptly framed and displayed in Jeff's Place, where it was accepted by the ignorant public as proof that Soapy was a patriotic citizen in direct communication with the White House. Quite a crowd of men appeared and offered to enlist. His "lambs," as Soapy called the sneak thieves and highwaymen that composed his town gang, picked clean the pockets of the volunteers when they left their clothing in the disrobing room preparatory to submitting to a pretended medical examination in another apartment.

Soapy also boldly took over the 4th of July celebration. His gangsters controlled in true ward-heeler style the public meeting held to organize the parade, and elected Soapy grand marshal. He led the parade on a spirited gray horse followed by a brass band of dance hall musicians, then by a special body guard of "tigers" and such citizens as marched in loyalty to their country's flag notwithstanding the character of their leader.

It was reported about this time that the Klondike gold miners and the merchants at Dawson were preparing to send their gold dust out of, and bring their freight into, that camp over the Yukon river steamboat lines, running between Dawson and St. Michael, on account of the control of the Dyea and the Skagway trails by Soapy's highwaymen. When Skagway businessmen and the White Pass railroad officials realized that the existence of their trade route was threatened they developed a patriotic appreciation of law and order that had remained dormant when only the lives and property of transients were involved. It makes a difference, it seems, whose ox is gored. They now determined to curb Soapy's violence by greater violence.

Shortly before the 4th of July there was posted a notice, signed "Committee of 101," stating that a meeting would be held at a specified time and place to organize the citizens of Skagway in favor of law and order and the suppression of crime. Soapy met this threat frankly with a counter-notice purporting to be issued by a "Law and Order Committee of 303" which, for a time, compelled the timid Vigilantes to refrain from public action. However, three days after the Fourth of July parade, in which Soapy had ridden at its head as the representative citizen of Skagway, a match quite unexpectedly set off an explosion that killed the leader and scattered his forces to the four winds.

A simple-minded Klondike miner named Stewart brought in over the trail a small poke of gold dust worth about $2700. Having safely walked through the danger zone from the summit to Skagway, he deposited his little fortune in a merchant's safe. Upon hearing the news two of Soapy's lambs formed an acquaintance with Stewart and persuaded him to take his poke to Jeff's Place for examination. There a quarrel was started by cappers, the poke was seized, and Stewart was thrown into the street. Stewart at once complained to his merchant friend who ran to the secret committee of the Vigilantes with the facts. A small group of businessmen sent for Soapy and begged him to return the poke and gold dust to the owner. He refused to do so, stating that Stewart had lost his gold in a square game. Thereupon the Vigilantes declared war.

Frank H. Reid, a prominent citizen, civil engineer, and official town surveyor, was one of the most courageous and active members of the Vigilantes. Soapy feared him and looked upon him as the leader of the law and order forces. An incident related to me by a young man employed by one of the newspapers at that time shows Reid's quality and Smith's appreciation of it. In the forenoon of the eighth of July, the day after the robbery of Stewart, as Reid was passing by a crowd of which Soapy and his men formed the larger part, Soapy berated Reid so bitterly that every one expected Reid to strike him. Reid, however, after a moment's pause continued on his way. An hour later he explained to my informant that the incident had been planned to provoke an assault upon Soapy so that Reid might be shot by Soapy's henchmen. Reid said that he was unarmed at the time, but that having armed himself he was going to Jeff's Place to kill Soapy. At Jeff's Place, Reid asked Clancy, the barkeeper, for Soapy. Clancy replied that Soapy was in the back-room with friends and at Reid's request went to inform Soapy that Reid wished to speak to him. Reid waited and waited but Soapy stayed in the back-room.

The robbery of Stewart, following upon so many similar crimes by the bandits, stirred the Vigilantes to action. The members were notified that there would be a meeting that night at nine o'clock, at the Sylvester dock warehouse, to consider active measures for the suppression of the criminals. When they met, four of the members were stationed at the town approach to the dock with instructions not to allow any one except members of the Committee to enter the warehouse. One of these outer guards was Reid.

Soapy learned from a spy that the meeting was to be held and boldly announced that he would attend it. He determined to break it up with a display of force and arms, aided by his body guard of "tigers." He left Jeff's Place, followed by fourteen ruffians in military order. Two big revolvers hung from his belt, and a double-barrelled repeating Winchester rifle lay in the crook of his arm. He insolently shouted to the people standing on the sidewalks to "chase yourselves home to bed"; passed on and stepped upon the end of the dock facing the Vigilante guards. None of these guards were armed except Reid, who still carried the revolvers with which he had armed himself to kill Soapy.

Soapy walked rapidly past the two outer guards, for he saw Reid twenty feet further on. As he approached Reid the latter said to him, "You can't go down there, Smith." The outlaw replied, "Damn you, Reid, you have been at the bottom of this," and struck at him with his rifle barrel. The Vigilante chief caught the descending weapon with one hand, quickly thrust his other hand into his coat pocket and attempted to discharge his revolver from that position. Smith jerked his rifle back from its position near Reid's head, who held on as it was lowered. When the rifle was forced down to the middle of Reid's body, Smith pulled the trigger and at the same time Reid fired. Each fired four shots in as many seconds and both fell together on the wharf—Smith dead, Reid mortally wounded.

While Reid was holding to the rifle barrel with one hand and attempting to draw his revolver with the other, Soapy cried out "Don't shoot!" but continued his efforts to get the rifle in position for a fatal shot.

When Soapy fell his henchmen drew their revolvers and rushed forward to avenge his death. Reid's companion guard, a brave little Irishman named Murphy, seized Soapy's Winchester and faced the advancing gang. Just then the Vigilantes came running from their meeting, calling as they came, "Get your guns, men, and kill them." The gang broke and ran, without discharging a gun. Before morning the jail was filled with highwaymen and their abettors, including the editor of the local newspaper, the deputy U.S. marshal and all known accomplices and criminals. When Soapy's clothing was searched at the morgue a note was found in his pockets from the spy who had kept him posted and sent him to his death. It read: "The crowd is angry, if you want to do anything do it quick." It was signed by a letter "S," and was in the handwriting of one "Billie" Saportas, a reporter for a New York paper. He was arrested, jailed and deported with others of Soapy's gang on the first boat going to Seattle. The most prominent of Soapy's bandits were taken to the Juneau jail for trial. Stewart's poke of gold dust was found by the Vigilantes in Soapy's trunk at Jeff's Place, and returned to its owner, the deficit in its quantity being supplied from dust taken from Soapy's till. Turner Jackson, the leader of Soapy's body guard, who thrust his revolver against Si. Tanner, the first Vigilante guard on the dock, with a threat to kill, was convicted and sentenced to ten years in the penitentiary (102 Fed. 473); George Wilder was sentenced to seven years in the penitentiary, and several others accused of misdemeanors were sentenced to from one to three years in the Territorial penitentiary at Sitka. Some thirty-five more were deported on the first boat leaving Skagway for Seattle—where the police arrested all of them, and upon inspection of their records found some escaped convicts among them and men accused of murder and other felonies in different states, where they were sent for trial.

The shot that killed the bandit leader cleared the trails to the Dyea and the White Pass summits of organized highwaymen. The Skagway Vigilantes erected over the body of Frank H. Reid a monument that bears the inscription: *"He gave his life for the honor of Skagway."*

\* \* \*

One of Judge Wickersham's opinions, *McGinley v. Cleary*, has become justly celebrated as a classic example of a judicial verdict spiced with humor.

*The Case of . . .*

## McGINLEY v. CLEARY.

Third Division.　Fairbanks.　August 8, 1904.

### No. 125.

1. CANCELLATION OF INSTRUMENTS—FRAUD—GAMING CONSIDERATION—INTOXICATION.

Equity will grant relief where the transfer of a valuable property has been fraudulently extorted, for a grossly inadequate consideration, from a person in such a state of intoxication as not to be in his right mind or capable of transacting any business or entering into any contract.

2. GAMING—EQUITY—FRAUD.

Plaintiff was the proprietor of a saloon. He gambled with defendant therein with dice, and lost $1,800. To pay his loss he conveyed the premises in dispute. Upon a suit in equity to recover, *held*, that equity will not assist a gambler to recover losses at his own game.

On the 29th of last November the plaintiff was, and for some time previous thereto had been, one of the proprietors of that certain two-story log cabin described in the pleadings as the "Fairbanks Hotel," situate upon lot 1, Front street, in the town of Fairbanks, Alaska. The opening scene discovers him drunk, but engaged on his regular night shift as barkeeper in dispensing whisky by leave of this court on a territorial license to those of his customers who had not been able, through undesire or the benumbing influence of the liquor, to retire to their cabins. The defendant was his present customer. After a social evening session, the evidence is that at about 3 o'clock in the morning of the 30th they were mutually enjoying the hardships of Alaska by pouring into their respective interiors unnumbered four-bit drinks, recklessly expending undug pokes, and blowing in the next spring cleanup. While thus employed, between sticking tabs on the nail and catching their breath for the next glass, they began to tempt the fickle goddess of fortune by shaking plaintiff's dicebox. The defendant testifies that he had a $5 bill, that he laid it on the bar, and that it constituted the visible means of support to the game and transfer of property which followed. That defendant had a $5 bill so late in the evening may excite remark among his acquaintances.

Whether plaintiff and defendant then formed a mental design to gamble around the storm center of this bill is one of the matters in dispute in this case about which they do not agree. The proprietor is plaintively positive on his part that at that moment his brains were so benumbed by the fumes or the force of his own whisky that he was actually non compos mentis; that his mental faculties were so far paralyzed thereby that they utterly failed to register or record impressions. His customer, on the other hand, stoutly swears that the vigor and strength of his constitution enabled him to retain his memory, and he informed the court from the witness stand that while both were gazing at the bill, the proprietor produced his nearby dicebox, and they began to shake for its temporary ownership. Neither the memory which failed nor that which labored in spite of its load enabled either the proprietor or the customer to recall that any other money or its equivalent came upon the board. The usual custom of $500 millionaires grown from wild cat bonanzas was followed, and as aces and sixes alternated or blurringly trooped athwart their vision, the silent upthrust of the index finger served to mark the balance of trade.

They were not alone. Tupper Thompson slept bibulously behind the oil tank stove. Whether his mental receiver was likewise so hardened by inebriation as to be incapable of catching impressions

will never be certainly known to the court. He testified to a lingering remembrance of drinks which he enjoyed at this time upon
the invitation of some one, and is authority for the statement that
when he came to, the proprietor was so drunk that he hung limply
and vine-like to the bar, though he played dice with the defendant,
and later signed a bill of sale of the premises in dispute, which
Tupper witnessed. Tupper also testified that the defendant was
drunk, but according to his standard of intoxication he was not
so entirely paralyzed as the proprietor, since he could stand without holding to the bar. Not to be outdone either in memory or
expert testimony, the defendant admitted that Tupper was present,
that his resting place was behind the oil tank stove, where, defendant testifies, he remained on the puncheon floor in slumberous
repose during the gaming festivities with the dicebox, and until
called to drink and sign a bill of sale, both of which he did according to his own testimony. One O'Neil also saw the parties plaintiff
and defendant about this hour in the saloon, with defendant's arm
around plaintiff's neck in maudlin embrace.

After the dice-shaking had ceased, and the finger-tip bookkeep-
ing had been reduced to round numbers, the defendant testifies
that the plaintiff was found to be indebted to him in the sum of
$1,800. Whether these dice, which belonged to the bar and seem
to have been in frequent use by the proprietor, were in the habit
of playing such pranks on the house may well be doubted; nor is
it shown that they, too, were loaded. It is just possible that mistakes
may have occurred pending lapses of memory by which, in the
absence of a lookout, the usual numbers thrown for the house were
counted for the defendant, and this without any fault of the dice.
However this may be, the defendant swears that he won the score,
and passed up the tabs for payment.

According to the defendant's testimony, the proprietor was also
playing a confidence game, whereupon, in the absence of money,
the defendant suggested that he make him a bill of sale of the
premises. Two were written out by defendant. The second was
signed by plaintiff and witnessed by Tupper, and for a short time
the defendant became a tenant in common with an unnamed person and an equitable owner of an interest in the saloon. The plain-

tiff testifies that during all this time, and until the final act of
signing the deed in controversy, he was drunk, and suffering from
a total loss of memory and intelligence. The evidence in support
of intelligence is vague and unsatisfactory, and the court is unable
to base any satisfactory conclusion upon it.

Above the mists of inebriety which befogged the mental landscape of the principals in this case at that time rise a few jagged
peaks of fact which must guide the court notwithstanding their
temporary intellectual eclipse. After the dice-throwing had ceased,
the score calculated, and the bills of sale written, and the last one
conveying a half interest in the premises signed by the plaintiff, he
accompanied the defendant to the cabin of Commissioner Cowles,
about a block away, on the banks of the frozen Chena, and requested that official to affix his official acknowledgment to the document. Owing to their hilarious condition and the early hour at which
they so rudely broke into the judicial slumbers, the commissioner
refused to do business with them, and thrust them from his chamber. He does not testify as to the status of their respective memories
at that time, but he does say that their bodies were excessively
drunk; that of the defendant being, according to the judicial eye,
the most wobbly. He testifies that the plaintiff was able to and did
assist the defendant away from his office without any official acknowledgment being made to the bill of sale. The evidence then
discloses that, in the light of the early morning, both principals
retired to their bunks to rest; witness Sullivan going so far as to
swear that the plaintiff's boots were removed before he got in bed.

The question of consideration is deemed to be an important one
in this case. Defendant asserts that it consisted of the $1,800 won at
the proprietor's own game of dice, but Tupper Thompson relapses
into sobriety long enough to declare that the real consideration
promised on the part of the defendant was to give a half interest
in his Cleary creek placer mines for the half interest in the saloon;
that defendant said the plaintiff could go out and run the mines
while he remained in the saloon and sold hootch to the sourdoughs,
or words to that effect. Tupper's evidence lacks some of the ear-
marks; it is quite evident that he had a rock in his sluice box. The
plaintiff, on the other hand, would not deny the gambling con-

sideration; he forgot; it is much safer to forget, and it stands a better cross-examination.

The evidence discloses that about 3 or 4 o'clock P.M. on the evening of the 30th the defendant went to the apartment of the proprietor, and renewed his demand for payment or a transfer of the property in consideration of the gambling debt. After a meal and a shave they again appeared, about 5 o'clock, before the commissioner; this time at his public office in the justice's court. Here there was much halting and whispering. The bill of sale written by Cleary was presented to the proprietor, who refused to acknowledge it before the commissioner. The commissioner was then requested by Cleary to draw another document to carry out the purpose of their visit there. The reason given for refusing to acknowledge the document then before the commissioner was that it conveyed a half interest, whereas the plaintiff refused then to convey more than a quarter interest. The commissioner wrote the document now contained in the record, the plaintiff signed it; it was witnessed, acknowledged, filed for record, and recorded in the book of deeds, according to law.

The deed signed by McGinley purports to convey "an undivided one-fourth ($\frac{1}{4}$) interest in the Fairbanks Hotel, situate on lot No. one (1) Front street, in the town of Fairbanks." The consideration mentioned is one dollar, but, in accordance with the finger-tip custom, it was not paid; the real consideration was the $1,800 so miraculously won by the defendant the previous night by shaking the box. Plaintiff soon after brought this suit to set aside the conveyance upon the ground of fraud (1) because he was so drunk at the time he signed the deed as to be unable to comprehend the nature of the contract, and (2) for want of consideration.

It is currently believed that the Lord cares for and protects idiots and drunken men. A court of equity is supposed to have equal and concurrent jurisdiction, and this case seems to be brought under both branches. Before touching upon the law of the case, however, it is proper to decide the questions of fact upon which these principles must rest, and they will be considered in the order in which counsel for plaintiff has presented them.

Was McGinley so drunk when he signed the deed in controversy that he was not in his right mind, or capable of transacting any business, or entering into any contract? He was engaged, under the ægis of the law and the seal of this court, in selling whiskey to the miners of the Tanana for four bits a drink, and more regularly in taking his own medicine and playing dice with customers for a consideration. Who shall guide the court in determining how drunk he was at 3 o'clock in the morning, when the transaction opened? Tupper or the defendant? How much credence must the court give to the testimony of one drunken man who testifies that another was also drunk? Is the court bound by the admission of the plaintiff that he was so paralyzed by his own whiskey that he cannot remember the events of nearly 24 hours in which he seems to have generally followed his usual calling? Upon what fact in this evidence can the court plant the scales of justice that they may not stagger?

Probably the most satisfactory determination of the matter may be made by coming at once to that point of time where the deed in question was prepared, signed, and acknowledged. Did the plaintiff exhibit intelligence at that time? He refused to acknowledge a deed which conveyed a half interest, and caused his creditor to procure one to be made by the officer which conveyed only a quarter interest; he protected his property to that extent. Upon a presentation of the deed prepared by the officer, he refused to sign it until the words "and other valuable consideration" were stricken out; thus leaving the deed to rest on a stated consideration of "one dollar." Upon procuring the paper to read as he desired, he signed it in a public office, before several persons, and acknowledged it to be his act and deed.

Defendant says that the deed was given to pay a gambling debt lost by the plaintiff at his own game, and his counsel argues that for this reason equity will not examine into the consideration and grant relief, but will leave both parties to the rules of their game, and not intermingle these with the rules of law. He argues that they stand *in pari delicto*, and that, being engaged in a violation of the law, equity ought not to assist the proprietor of the game to recover his bank roll. It may be incidently mentioned here, as it has been suggested to the court, that the phrase *pari delicto* does not mean a "delectable pair," and its use is not intended to reflect upon or characterize plaintiff and defendant.

BION A. DODGE, for plaintiff.
CLAYPOOL & COWLES, for defendant.

WICKERSHAM, District Judge. The plaintiff prays judgment that the transfer made to the defendant, Cleary, be vacated as fraudulent and void (1) because he was intoxicated at the time it was made, signed, and delivered, and (2) because no consideration was paid therefor. Equity will grant relief where the transfer of a valuable property has been fraudulently extorted, for a grossly inadequate consideration, from a person in such a state of intoxication as not to be in his right mind, or capable of transacting any business or entering into any contract. Thackrah v. Haas, 119 U.S. 499, 7 Sup. Ct. 311, 30 L. Ed. 486.

The evidence in this case raises the single question, will a court of equity set aside a deed made by the keeper of a saloon in payment of a gambling debt contracted by him to one of his customers when no other fraud is shown? By the common law no right of action exists to recover back money which has been paid upon a gambling debt. 8 Am. & Eng. Ency. of Law (1st Ed.) 1021. In Brown v. Thompson, 14 Bush (Ky.) 538, 29 Am. Rep. 416, the court held that the keeper of a faro bank, who sued to recover losses against one who had won by betting against the bank, was not within the spirit of the Kentucky statute, although his claim was within the letter, and accordingly refused to maintain his action. The general policy of the courts in suits to recover gambling losses is clearly stated by Judge Ross in Gridley v. Dorn, 57 Cal. 78, 40 Am. Rep. 110, where he says:

> The impropriety of the court's entertaining such actions as this is well illustrated by the circumstances of the present case, for it appears from the record to have been conceded in the court below that the right of the plaintiff to recover depended upon the question whether the wager made was a "by bet" or a "time bet." To determine this question several witnesses were introduced, who gave their opinion in the matter, and we have been cited by counsel to the "Spirit of the Times" and the "Rules of the Na-

tional Trotting Association" as authorities upon the proposition. These are, we believe, standard authorities in turf matters, but cases which depend upon them have no place in the courts. If, notwithstanding the evil tendency of betting on races, parties will engage in it, they must rely upon the honor and good faith of their adversaries, and not look to the courts for relief in the event of its breach.

There are cases where courts will assist in the recovery of money or property lost at gambling, but this is not one of them. The plaintiff was the proprietor of the saloon and the operator of the dice game in which he lost his property. He now asks a court of equity to assist him in recovering it, and this raises the question, may a gambler who runs a game and loses the bank roll come into a court of equity and recover it? He conducted the game in violation of law, conveyed his premises to pay the winner's score, and now demands that the court assist him to regain it. Equity will not become a gambler's insurance company, to stand by while the gamester secures the winnings of the drunken, unsuspecting, or weak-minded in violation of the law, ready to stretch forth its arm to recapture his losses when another as unscrupulous or more lucky than he wins his money or property. Nor will the court in this case aid the defendant.

The case will be dismissed; each party to pay the costs incurred by him, and judgment accordingly.

# 13

# ON THE TRAIL OF THE GOLDSEEKERS

Hamlin Garland (1860–1940), author and poet, joined the Gold Rush in 1898 and recorded his four months on the trail in prose and in verse in a little volume entitled *The Trail of the Goldseekers*.

Already an author of note, he went not to join those who, returning, "carried great bags of nuggets and bottles of shining dust which they had burned, at the risk of their lives, out of perpetually frozen ground, so far to the north that the winter had no sun and the summer midnight has no dusk"—he went for other and rarer reasons. He left his home in Wisconsin because he said,

> I believed that I was about to see and take part in a most picturesque and impressive movement across the wilderness. I believed it to be the last great march of the kind which could ever come in America, so rapidly were the wild places being settled up. I wished, therefore, to take part in the tramp of the goldseekers, to be one of them, to record their deeds. I wished, therefore, to return to the wilderness also, to forget books and theories of arts and social problems, and come again face to face with the great free spaces of woods and skies and streams. I was not a goldseeker, but a nature hunter, and I was eager to enter this, the wildest region yet remaining in Northern America. I willingly and with joy took the long way round, the hard way through.

Unlike Jack London and Rex Beach, Garland did not find in these experiences the literary treasure that would bring him fame. But some of his verses were born of his northern experiences.

### Two Poems, by Hamlin Garland

#### The Goldseekers

I saw these dreamers of dreams go by,
I trod in their footsteps a space;
Each marked with his eyes on the sky,
Each passed with a light on his face.

They came from the hopeless and sad,
They faced the future and gold;
Some the tooth of want's wolf had made mad,
And some at the forge had grown old.

Behind them these serfs of the tool
The rags of their service had flung;
No longer of fortune the fool,
This word from each bearded lip rung:

"Once more I'm a man, I am free!
No man is my master, I say;
To-morrow I fail, it may be—
No matter, I'm freeman to-day."

They go to a toil that is sure,
To despair and hunger and cold;
Their sickness no warning can cure,
They are mad with a longing for gold.

The light will fade from each eye,
The smile from each face;
They will curse the impassible sky,
And the earth when the snow torrents race.

Some will sink by the way and be laid
In the frost of the desolate earth;
And some will return to a maid,
Empty of hand as at birth.

*But this out of all will remain,*
*They have lived and have tossed;*
*So much in the game will be gain,*
*Though the gold of the dice has been lost.*

## Do You Fear the Wind?

Do you fear the force of the wind,
The slash of the rain?
Go face them and fight them,
Be savage again.
Go hungry and cold like the wolf,
Go wade like the crane:
The palms of your hands will thicken,
The skin of your cheek will tan,
You'll grow ragged and weary and swarthy
But you'll walk like a man.

# 14

## *LAYING THE LINE*

I<small>N</small> the summer of 1901 a promising young first lieutenant, William Mitchell, was sent to investigate delays in the laying of the Alaska line, an attempt to build an overland telegraph across wild and largely unexplored territory.

Mitchell reported that the work on the line was proceeding slowly because it was carried on only during the summer months and "the thing to do is to work through the winter getting the material out: the wire insulators, poles, food supplies, and forage; then to actually construct the lines in the summer, when we could dig holes in the ground and set telegraph poles."

This recommendation pleased Mitchell's superiors, especially Brigadier General A. W. Greely, a famous Arctic explorer who was head of the Signal Corps. Mitchell returned again to Alaska, journeying to Fort Egbert, near the town of Eagle City on the Canadian border, which was to be his lonely outpost for the next two years.

More than anyone else, it was Mitchell who first called attention to the strategic importance of Alaska, which continued to be overlooked and ignored by the military strategists in Washington until almost the very eve of Pearl Harbor, December 7, 1941. Yet as far back as February 13, 1935, in what was virtually his last public appearance, Billy Mitchell testified before the Military Affairs Committee of the House of Representatives and vigorously called attention to the strategic importance of Alaska in the com-

ing era of air power, whose prophet he had been: "Japan is our
dangerous enemy in the Pacific," Mitchell declared, with uncanny foresight. "They won't attack Panama. They will come right
here to Alaska. Alaska is the most central place in the world for
aircraft, and that is true either of Europe, Asia, or North America.
I believe in the future he who holds Alaska will hold the world,
and I think it is the most important strategic place in the world."

The following selection from Billy Mitchell's memoirs of his
Alaskan experience appeared in *American Heritage* in 1961.

## From · · ·
### Billy Mitchell in Alaska

I found the garrison at Fort Egbert in rather a poor state of
discipline. There were a great many recruits and a few older non-
commissioned officers. On account of the cold, drills were held ir-
regularly, and little target practice was carried on. The men did
not like to work on the telegraph line, or anywhere in the cold,
for that matter. It is difficult to handle a group of men without
giving them plenty of work, and in the North it is hard to find
enough work for them to do while in garrison.

No trails existed over the mountains where the telegraph lines
were to go, nor was their course definitely located, so the first thing
we had to do was to survey their route. The first line would be
between Eagle City and Valdez, where the submarine cable from
the United States ended, a distance of almost four hundred miles
through a trackless wilderness, with no means of subsistence for
men or animals except game, which could only be found at certain
seasons of the year.

My orders specified that all transportation in the post should be
turned over for my use, and I made preparations to get my outfits
out on the trail as soon as possible. I began to buy dogs to use for
light sledding and reconnaissance work, selecting each one myself.
The first dog I obtained was a MacKenzie husky leader called
"Pointer," owned by a squaw man named Jack Lawrence, a mail
carrier. My attention had first been drawn to Jack when he neg-

lected his squaw for a week or so, to remain in Eagle City celebrating. She came up with a long knife, found where he was, grabbed him by the nape of the neck, and marched him home.

Pointer was the greatest dog I have ever seen. He weighed about 120 pounds and was perfectly sure on the trail. He could feel through the snow with his feet for an old trail and unerringly find it. We could depend on him to protect the sled and the team under all conditions. He was so fierce that we had to cut his fangs off to keep him from chewing up the other dogs. He became tremendously attached to me, and from that time on during every trip, Pointer was my constant companion and friend.

Gradually we got together wonderful teams. I selected the best ones, mated in size, gaits, and weight, and organized them into two teams. Taking a man named Emmet with me, I made a reconnaissance to see for myself where the lines should go and how we could stand the weather. When doing this advance reconnoitering, we always traveled light, often not carrying a tent but digging a hole out with a snowshoe and banking up a fire of logs opposite it, sleeping in the reflected heat of the embers. Sometimes we slept in a hole in the snow with the dogs lying on top of us.

It was necessary to push through to the south and find where the men working under Captain Burnell were located. He was supposed to work north from Valdez over Thompson's Pass in the Alaska Range of mountains, and meet me somewhere on the Tanana River, more than 150 miles from each of us.

Emmet and I sought and found the Mentasta Pass, south of the Tanana River. Just south of the pass lies Mentasta Lake, the headwaters of a small river called the Tokio, which is fed by warm springs.

We traversed the lake without much trouble, but once down the precipitous sides of the Tokio River, on whose treacherous icy surface we had to travel, we began to break through. The temperature was around 60 degrees below. There was layer upon layer of ice, with about three feet of water between them. When our moccasins and trousers were wet, they would freeze instantly and become hard as boards the minute we got out of the water. In one place I broke through with my sled, clear to my shoulders, and if my leader Pointer had not gotten a foothold on the ice beyond and pulled out Hunter, the second dog, and the rest of the team, I would probably have been there yet. Emmet avoided that hole, but broke through in another up to his waist. We were both thoroughly wet and the dogs were encased in ice, biting at their feet to get it off. If we did not act quickly, we would be frozen to death in a few minutes.

Fortunately for us, I spied a dry tree leaning over the river, as if it had been put there by Providence. Shouting to Emmet to start chopping the tree, as he was the least wet, I drove the team ahead, breaking through the ice as I went, and began turning the dogs loose from their harness, jumping in the water meanwhile to keep from freezing stiff. I got two candles from the sled and lighted them with matches we carried in a shotgun cartridge case to keep them dry.

Emmet grabbed a double-bitted axe and went for the tree, but on raising it for the first stroke, the axe handle broke in two from brittleness caused by the intense cold. Emmet was now beginning to freeze. I told him to jump in the water while I tackled the tree. After having chopped it about half way through, my axe handle broke. Things looked bad. I had a little tin of kerosene, but that had frozen. We had placed the lighted candles in a sheltered place and warmed our hands over them, because if our hands became stiff we would be unable to light the matches. I jumped back in the water, as Emmet came up with his second axe, with which he got the tree down, stripping off the branches in a second, and setting them ablaze.

In the meantime, three of his dogs had chewed through the traces and gotten loose before I had been able to let them out. But in a moment we had a roaring fire, and everything was changed. Before long, I had a fine meal ready.

Within a few hours we had dried everything, repaired the harnesses where the dogs had chewed through, and prepared the dogfood of equal parts of bacon, rice, and king salmon. I always carried the best food obtainable for the dogs and fed them in individual dishes so as not to lose any of the substance in the snow and ice. Each dog was trained to come to his own dish, while I stood over them with a twenty-foot whip, ready to pounce on any animal that tried to steal his neighbor's food or make trouble.

We whittled out a couple of new axe handles from spruce wood, and started out again next morning. There was a mail station somewhere in the vicinity, and we expected to meet the mail carrier coming north from Valdez at any time. We should have met him the day before, but I figured he had been delayed. Soon I could see by the action of my lead dog that he smelled a habitation. It is remarkable how these animals show by their actions what lies ahead of them. We were running along at the base of a steep bank when I noticed ahead of us a place where a sled had evidently broken into the ice.

Peering over the bank, I could see the top of a tent. It was about lunchtime. Yelling "gee" to the leader, I jumped up the bank with the team. There in front of the tent was a sled on which a man was sitting, with his head leaning over on his hands. Sitting in front of him, immovable, was a large, black dog. I called to the man but received no response, and going closer found that he was frozen to death. The mail was in the sled under him. Between his teeth was a match, and between his knees was a box on which he had tried to scratch the match when his hands had frozen.

Pieces of harness showed where four of his dogs had bitten out and left; his only remaining companion was this half-bred dog with all four feet frozen. We put the body of the mail carrier in his tent, which we laced up, and shot his dog. Then we proceeded on down the river.

In a couple of days we arrived at Copper Center, where there was a settlement of Indians. I noticed one especially handsome large Indian with reddish hair and blue eyes. I asked him his name, and he answered, "Me named Cross River Joe."

"Who your papa?" I asked.

"Long time ago big soldier chief, he come here. He my papa," Joe replied. "Now me chief of tribe."

"Where your mama?" I went on, inspired by some curiosity.

"She live in cabin up river," he answered. I told him I would like to see his mama tomorrow, so the following day she appeared, decked out in very handsome beaded caribou-skin clothes, with a large aneroid barometer hanging around her neck, like a jewel. It was of brass, polished till it shone. The barometer had been given her as a magic talisman by the "soldier chief" who was Joe's father.

Copper Center was just north of the Coast Range, and here I encountered a sergeant from Valdez who had some telegraph supplies in his charge. Proceeding south from there, I came to the Thompson Pass in the Coast Range, where I met Captain Burnell.

I had now traversed the whole route over which the telegraph line was to run from Eagle City to the coast. We made all arrangements possible between ourselves for its completion. I returned over the trail we had broken and fortunately got by the Tokio River without breaking through again.

On this trip I fell in with the Middlefork Indians on the Forty Mile Creek, whose chief, Joseph, became one of my great friends and companions later on. He had thirteen families under him. Their country began about one hundred miles south of the Yukon and extended over to the Tanana divide. They were great hunters, trappers, and fishermen.

Every Indian tribe had its own clearly defined hunting grounds and boundaries, and each hated every other tribe. The only time they got together was in their general hate for the white man. All of them, however, respected the soldiers, especially the "soldier chiefs." I was the first officer to come into Chief Joseph's camp. As he heard my men calling me lieutenant, he always afterward addressed me as "Chief Klutina," that being his rendition of the word "lieutenant." I was later known by that name to all the Indians in that part of the country.

.    .    .    .    .    .    .    .    .    .    .    .

Gradually the streams showed signs of breaking, and we came back from the trail to Fort Egbert, putting our dogs in the corral for the summer. The snow melted from the hills and ran down, forming pools of water. From the south, ducks began to arrive, first by tens, then by hundreds and thousands. In May, the Yukon River was still frozen.

One night we heard a tremendous cracking like cannon shots. It was the ice in the river. People began yelling and discharging firearms. Next morning when I looked out, I saw that it had broken, and the river had begun moving. This is the great annual event in the North. All winter long, private bets had been laid, specifying the day, hour, and minute when the breakup would come and the ice begin moving at a certain point. A stake was erected on one bank and a tree or rock selected on the opposite side, from which a sight could be taken by two or three people, to decide when the river actually moved. Each settlement had a pool made up as to when the river would break up.

Everyone who is able to gives a party, and they visit between cabins at all hours of the day and night, drinking each other's health for the coming season.

The grandeur of the breakup at Eagle City is impossible to convey by words. A great bend in the river here has as its background an enormous mass of rock called Eagle Cliff, against which the ice piles up for more than one hundred feet. Great cakes from five to ten feet thick grind and crash together with a noise like an artillery preparation for attack, for two or three days. Every day the river moved more and more and finally was clear.

One day while shooting ptarmigan on a hill near Eagle City, I suddenly came upon the body of an Indian with the whole side of his head torn off. He had a bow in one hand and a quiver of arrows on his back. Near him was a hole between some rocks on a hillside, and the snow all around was covered with blood and bear tracks. Putting buckshot into both barrels of my shotgun, I followed the bear's trail into a little open stretch of spruce timber. Within a hundred yards I came upon him, stone dead, with an arrow piercing his heart.

This is probably what had happened: the Indian saw the breath of the bear rising from his den as he prepared to come out from his winter hibernation. Going to the mouth of the cave, the Indian shot him through the heart as he emerged, then ran. But the bear, enraged at the pain, saw him, and being more active than the Indian had calculated, jumped out and happened to catch him right on the head with the first blow.

It was now the latter part of May, and instead of darkness, the days were all light. Before the snow had half gone, the mosquitoes made their appearance. Wild flowers began to cover every inch of ground.

Soon we were able to get out on the trail with saddle horses and pack mules, and get the men started digging post holes. The earth was still frozen, and we tried many methods for getting the holes down. Blasting did no good; the ground was so springy that it just bounced away and closed up again. Using steam points from a boiler was too cumbersome, because it took too much equipment to carry a boiler along and too much work to get fuel. So we used very sharp digging tools, which were sharpened and tempered every few days by blacksmiths who went from place to place with their pack mules.

Our next project was a trip from Eagle, on the Yukon, to the Tanana River, then down the Tanana to locate the mouths of the north and south tributaries of the river and determine the best place for crossing it with the telegraph lines. We were to travel by pack mule 150 miles to the Tanana, where we would build a whip-sawed boat to take us down the river to Fort Gibbon. None of my acquaintances in Alaska had gone down the Tanana; it was just as mysterious a country to us then as the center of Greenland or the Antarctic continent is today.

While making my arrangements, I received a telegram from the commander of the Canadian Mounted Police across the border in Dawson that Major F., my superior officer, who was on the way up from the Yukon from Skagway to inspect the lines, was acting strangely, and that two plain-clothes Mounted Police had been detailed to accompany him. This seemed very odd to me, and I could not imagine what was the matter.

I went down to the wharf to meet Major F. as he came off the steamer. He greeted me with his usual cordiality. I noticed, however, that he was very nervous and kept looking all around suspiciously. Going out to my cabin at the military post, he was immediately called upon by the commander and other officers. As soon as they left, I spoke to him of the trip I was about to make, of the arrangements I had made for it, and suggested that it would be a good thing for him to accompany me, as he would get an excellent idea of the country.

Major F. said he would like to go to my office and look over all phases of our work. As soon as we were alone, he said, "I want to tell you what has happened to me recently, and then I want your candid opinion about it.

"About a month ago, I was in my room in the hotel at Juneau, when I heard two men talking in the next room. I could hear one of them saying, over and over: 'Now we have him. We will kill him tonight.' After a while, I heard my own name mentioned. I listened further and when I was sure that they were after me, I took my pistol, broke the door, and jumped into the room, intending to arrest the men and take them to the town marshal. There was nobody in the room whatever. I went out and walked around the streets. Everybody stared at me. As I passed different groups of men, they eyed me peculiarly and absolutely stopped talking.

"I went back to my room and thought it over. I thought I had better consult a doctor. I went to one, and he gave me some medicine to take, but it made my brain so inactive that I stopped it." Here the Major paused a moment, and I asked him how he knew it made his brain inactive.

"Because I took a simple problem in integral calculus, and it was perfectly impossible for me to work it out. I was sure then that the stuff was affecting my brain. Again I heard the men talking in the next room during the night. The door of the room was open, and I rushed in, but again they avoided me. There was no one there. So I determined to come up here to you. I kept my departure a secret. Just before the steamer was to leave Juneau for Skagway, I ran down and jumped on board. As the steamer pulled out, I could see people running down to the wharf with the evident intention of getting me.

"When I arrived at Skagway, I went to the cable office and looked over the messages received that day, to see if anyone had wired ahead that I was coming and to look out for me. I found only one suspicious message which was in code. It was addressed to the Canadian Bank of Commerce. I went to the bank and asked them to let me see their cipher, so I could decode the message, which they did. It said that a shipment was being made to the bank and to look out for it. It did not say what the shipment was or anything else about it, and I drew from that, that it might mean me. I seemed to be followed everywhere, through the streets, mostly by the rougher element, who always kept their eyes on me.

"I went to White Horse on the White Pass Railway, and at that place I asked the Canadian Mounted Police authorities for an escort. Two men were detailed to accompany me, in plain-clothes, and they took the river steamer with me. A few cows were being shipped down the river, and as I looked in at them through a window, I heard the two men who were taking care of them say, 'We'll get him before long; he is going down the river now.'

"When I arrived at Dawson, the commander of the Mounted Police met me at the wharf, and as there was another boat ready to leave, I did not go into the town but came to you right away. I saw how everybody looked at me when I got off the boat. I am sure that I am being watched and followed, and that the first opportunity will be taken to make away with me."

He stopped speaking, and I could see that my old friend was in a terribly excited state of mind. He had always been one of the bravest of men, and to see him in abject fear was a strange thing to me.

Unquestionably Major F. had lost his mind. If we confined him or restrained him physically, he would certainly go all to pieces. But if I got him out in the wilderness where he would get plenty of fresh air and exercise, I thought I might cure him. So I suggested that we start on the trip for the Tanana River the next morning.

He wanted to know if there were many Indians and if I thought they knew about the plot. I replied that there were a few, but I knew them all. They were my friends and would do more for me than for any other white man. He then asked what kind of an outfit I was going to take, and I told him one packer, four pack mules, and our saddle horses. He asked to see the packer, and I had the man, Hall by name, come in. He was a great big fellow, about six feet three in height, with blue eyes and a blond beard, as fine and straightforward in appearance as any man I have ever seen. Major F. was satisfied with him.

Next morning we got away. Major F. would look behind every tree, thinking he might find an Indian waiting to shoot him. At our first camp that night, the mosquitoes were terrible. I built smudges, around which the horses and mules stood, and put up our silk tent, which had a floor to it and a hole with a puckering string to close it up. In the middle of the night a bear or wolf came near the camp, and the horses made a lot of noise. Major F. thought the camp was attacked and made a bolt for the hole in the tent, knocking the whole thing down on top of us. Once disentangled, Major F. took a pistol in each hand and began running all around. I thought he would certainly shoot Hall and myself before I could persuade him there was nothing to be feared.

The next day we ran into a small herd of caribou. We made a careful roundabout stalk and I brought Major F. within range of a nice bull, which he killed. This pleased him greatly, not only because he was glad to make the kill, but also because he was satisfied he could hit whatever he aimed at.

For several days we journeyed on and saw nobody, but one afternoon, just as we were making camp, an Indian from the Middlefork Tribe came up. Indianlike, he approached me, gave me one grunt and then sat down on his haunches to watch what was going on. After having made our camp and started the fire, I gave him a little tobacco and papers for cigarettes, and poured him a cup of tea with some sugar.

"Long time me no see you, Klutina," he said. "What for you bring stranger here?"

"He is very big soldier chief," I replied, "much bigger than me. He is chief of all the soldier chiefs in the North. All the Indians who see him must remember he is a very big soldier chief and do everything for him they can, as he likes all Indians."

Major F. had heard him say, "What for you bring stranger here?" and immediately he was off again, thinking the Indians were in league against him. For several days after this we saw nobody, and again he was becoming quiet, although he would frequently get up at night with his weapons and look around.

Arriving at our little station on the Tanana River, I ordered the two men there to whipsaw some lumber and make a boat for us to descend the Tanana River. We then proceeded south through Mentasta Pass to meet Captain Burnell's party.

A few days later we met a large and well-appointed pack train with the supplies from Valdez. Captain Burnell had accompanied them, and we conferred again about our plans for joint action. After their hard journey, the men were certainly a tough-looking lot in their buckskin clothes, leather chaps, and long beards, their faces covered with running sores caused by mosquito bites. The mules and horses looked more like skeletons than the sleek animals one sees in the United States. I could see that Major F. was becoming nervous again. He took me aside and said he thought we had better get away from that rough crowd, as he feared he might be grabbed up by them at any moment. Here in the wilderness nobody would ever know what had happened!

We returned to the Tanana River station, where we found our boat completed, so we started down the river. For twelve days we traveled on, catching fish, both salmon and trout, and seeing many animals on the banks: bears, wolves, beaver, caribou, otter, and moose. I purposely avoided Indians on this trip, because at the mouth of the Tanana we would run into another military garrison, and I thought it best to keep the Major from seeing anyone as long as possible. He had said not a word about his hallucinations during this stage of the trip, and I thought he might be over them.

When we finally arrived at Fort Gibbon, we looked pretty tough. Our clothes were in rags. I had lost my hat in the river, and my head was shaggy. Our bearded faces were full of sores from mosquito bites, but we were in fine physical condition. The exercise and fresh air had done Major F. a great deal of good.

Upon our arrival, one of the officers began to jolly us about our appearance, and immediately Major F. was off again. He took this as an indication that the officer was linked up with the gang who were after him. His fears redoubled, and they had to send him out of Alaska under guard. Fortunately, with a year of quiet and good care, he recovered his health, and was sent back to full duty with his organization. In due course he retired from the Army, and afterward became a professor in a large university.

.    .    .    .    .    .    .    .    .    .    .    .    .

No white man had ever been down the Goodpaster River, and few Indians in our vicinity knew anything about it, because the

Middlefork Indians' domain stopped at the divide at the head of the river, and the Goodpaster Indians, who live on the Tanana, did not come over on the north side of the divide. I had consulted several times with Chief Joseph of the Middlefork tribe about the trip I proposed to make down this river. I wanted him to accompany Dutch and myself, to help break the trail down there. He always said it was a terrible trip, and it was a tradition among his people that anybody who went down it in wintertime never came back.

These Indians were very bad, he explained. If they looked at you intently, they made you sick, and they stole from graves. I assured him that I could protect him against these things, that he need not worry because I had fine dogs, good toboggans that we would use on the snowshoe trails, good rifles and snowshoes, and the best of food in the North. We had become great friends, having hunted and fished a great deal together, and for that reason he agreed to go with me.

Just before Christmas I made a trip with Dutch to my various stations to see how things were going, and to make sure the men were well taken care of and would have whatever we could give them for Christmas. We had a wonderful horse trail made across the country, and with our sleds light, we went along at a great rate, often at a dead gallop. I was crossing the Forty Mile Creek on the way back, when I looked down the trail and saw a lone figure running toward me with a springy step and waving his hand. I brought the dogs to a halt, and he handed me a letter from the commander of the Mounted Police in Dawson, asking me to come there and spend Christmas with them.

We had to travel hard to get to Dawson in two days. Turning my teams in the trail, I made for the metropolis of the North. The dogs seemed to know that they were on the way to holiday and a rest. We jingled down the Forty Mile with our bells echoing from the hills on either side. That night we reached the little town of Forty Mile on the Yukon and stayed at the roadhouse, setting off early next morning.

The Yukon River trail was rough in spots, but we made good time. The winter trail along a large river follows the smooth ice as far as possible. On each side, broken fragments and high ridges of ice were heaped up where the water had pressed them aside before they froze solid. Behind them, the high and precipitous river banks thrust upward, heightening the boldness and grandeur of the scene. In some places the ice had no snow on it, and the wind whistled over the frozen surface with biting fierceness.

About three o'clock in the afternoon, the dogs showed that they smelled the town lying around the bend of the river ahead of us. We went straight down the main street at a gallop, our bells jingling merrily.

The Christmases at Dawson were renowned all over the Northland. I put up with Captain Cosby of the Mounted Police, one of the finest fellows I ever knew, while Dutch went with the non-commissioned officers, and our teams were carefully housed in a section of the Mounted Police dog corral where they could not fight the other dogs. Our teams were the envy of all the dog mushers in Dawson who gathered to inspect them.

The parties given by the various prosperous citizens were endless and all very well done. The ladies had as fine Paris gowns as could be found anywhere and wore wonderful jewels. At one dinner, we ate raw oysters on the half shell that cost one dollar apiece. I learned afterward that the shells had been brought in separately, and the oysters put on them, but they were very good indeed.

Most of the music consisted of fiddles, played by musicians who knew all the old-time dances. There were some accordions, guitars, and mandolins, and a few upright pianos.

On Christmas Eve, the Mounted Police gave a great ball. All turned out in their full-dress uniforms. As I had none with me, I wore one of Cosby's, red coat and everything else, and had just as much fun as if it had been my own.

We stayed seven [sic] days, which was plenty long enough. Had we remained longer and accepted the lavish hospitality extended to us, both the dogs and ourselves would have lost our "trail condition."

The temperature had been falling constantly, and when we left Dawson on January 2, the thermometer registered 62 degrees below zero. In weather as cold as that, when one exhales the breath, the moisture congeals instantly, and a distinct pop can be heard. It is practically impossible for wind to blow at this temperature. If it did, it would freeze you just the way a hot iron burns.

Having a long nose that protruded whenever it had a chance and was constantly being frozen on the end, I hit upon the scheme of putting a little piece of snowshoe rabbit fur on it, the hairs of which stick out about an inch and a half. The moisture from my face held it there.

Ice formed all over our parka hoods from the moisture of our breath and had to be knocked off every little while. Long beards and mustaches become instantly caked with ice, and are not only an inconvenience but a menace, as they might freeze one's face. That is why men in the North shave clean in winter, after having let their beards grow long in the summer to keep the mosquitoes off.

One often hears inexperienced men say that after it gets below 40 degrees, a further drop does not make much difference. This is not so. Forty degrees below is not particularly cold, or even 45, but for every degree below 50, the intensity of the cold seems to double.

In spite of the intense cold, we made excellent time, going by way of Forty Mile, and in three days I reached the head of the Middlefork River and scaled the high divide where I had ordered a cache of supplies to be made. Here I was met by Chief Joseph. He had brought an excellent outfit with him, good snowshoes, caribou-skin clothing, and a 30/30 carbine. He seemed quite melancholy, however, and told me that he might never see his own people again as he was going with me into the country of the bad Indians. Although I did not expect to encounter any very unusual conditions, I knew that a long snowshoe trip with the temperature below 60 degrees was a serious thing, particularly if we ran into any warm springs and broke through the ice. The temperature had been falling steadily. It was now under 70 degrees below zero.

We found the Goodpaster to be a beautiful stream, gradually broadening out between washed-down hills, with excellent timber. We threaded our way through groves of spruce trees, birches, and alders, and as we descended the river course, we began to get more and more into the bed of the stream.

The terrible cold continued, constantly around 70 below. The wise huskies would stop every little while and bite the snow out of their feet to keep them from freezing. A snowshoe trail in cold weather is extremely hard on dogs, because even after it has been broken, the dogs go in almost up to their bellies. As their feet go down through the snow, their toes spread out, with the web and hairs projecting so as to offer the greatest surface possible. The snow sticks to the hair between the toes, and in a little while it is a good deal the same as marbles between them.

We made about fifteen miles a day, which we considered good, as the snow was quite deep compared to the Yukon. On our fifth day out we ran across a trail which Joe at once pronounced to be made by an Indian, one of his tribe, he thought, who had left his own country and gone into the forbidden territory because it was so rich in furs. The trail went ahead of us down the river. Soon we saw the smoke of a fire rising through the spruce trees, and getting closer, saw an Indian wickiup, a lodge built something in the form of a beehive, covered with bark and spruce boughs.

"Him David house. I guess he die," said Joe, meaning that the lodge belonged to a man of his tribe named David, who was probably starving to death.

Leaving Dutch with the dogs, Joe and I went to the wickiup and looked in. There sat David with his head in his hands, emaciated and pale. Three children, practically unable to move, were on the other side of him, while his squaw was just able to put wood on the fire. Three dogs were in the lodge, two of them hardly able to move, but one came toward the door to try to attack us. He was so weak he fell into the fire on the way and had to be pulled out.

Joe talked to David and elicited the information that David had come across with his family at the first snow. It had grown cold so quickly that he had been unable to get sufficient caribou meat to last him through the winter. The snow was so light that the game ran right through it, but it offered the maximum impediment to snowshoes. He had only killed a couple of caribou since the middle of November, and for over a month they had subsisted on moosehide from their moccasins and the sinews out of their snowshoes, had eaten one dog, and were about to kill the others. All these Indians seemed perfectly numb, mentally and physically, so exhausted were they. A white man under the same conditions would have frozen and died long before.

We had been hitting a terrific gait along the trail. Dutch was getting tired, but Indian Joe was becoming much more so, although neither of them said anything about it. I therefore decided to give them a day's rest and at the same time try to save this Indian family. If I split my own meager store of provisions with them at that time, they would eat everything up in a few days; so I gave them only meals that we cooked ourselves during the day we were there, and left them just enough food to last for ten days, by which time I expected to return.

Naturally this was cutting down our own supply pretty low, but I knew I could get to the mouth of the Goodpaster in four or five days, and I expected the Indians there to have some dried salmon left and possibly some game. We chopped an additional store of wood for David's family and fixed up his lodge. The effect of a little food on the dogs was even more marked than the effect on the Indians.

The day's rest had stiffened up both Joe and Dutch, who showed increasing signs of fatigue. Dutch kept lagging behind, so I sent him forward where I could watch him. When cold begins to seize people, they become very pleasant, and everything seems rosy to them. They want to lie down and take it easy, and when they do, they freeze to death in a couple of minutes.

The second day out from the camp of the starving Indians, Dutch began to lag behind worse than ever. As we rounded a turn in the river, I looked back and did not see him. I could tell by the action of the Indian that he was worried. A little way down the stream we saw a dry spruce tree, sticking over the bank above the ice. I told Joe to go down there and make a fire instantly while I ran back on my snowshoes to look for Dutch. I found him about 150 yards back, lying in the snow. I spoke to him, asking him why he had not kept up. Dutch answered that he was so tired he had to lie down and take a rest, and he didn't believe it was possible for him to move, that he was perfectly comfortable there in the snow.

It was a typical example of the stage where circulation begins to slow up, preparatory to freezing. I jumped squarely on his face with both my snowshoes and wiggled them around, then jumped on his chest and kicked him in the stomach, all the time abusing him verbally, trying to make him get up and fight me. At last I got him on his feet and slapped him in the face as hard as I could with my open hands, to make him so mad that he would exert himself. Dutch was a good man physically, and ordinarily would take no foolishness from anybody, but I had a terrible time trying to rouse his ire and get him started down the trail. At last I succeeded and walked along with him, hitting him every few moments and dragging him along. As he rounded the turn, I saw that Joe had gotten the fire started in a jiffy. Flame and smoke were rising from the dried spruce boughs.

The sight seemed to work a transformation in Dutch. His eyes stuck out, and he made straight for the fire. When he got there, he jumped squarely into it. We had to drag him out to keep him from burning himself. As it was, he burned a part of one snowshoe and one moccasin, and it took us an hour to repair them. He now began to tingle all over and appreciate how cold he was.

I had two bottles of Perry Davis Pain Killer in each sled. This is the greatest medicine ever invented for use in the North. I do not know the ingredients, other than alcohol and some laudanum, but I would hazard a guess at red pepper, turpentine, and tabasco juice. You can take it internally or rub it on as a liniment. For man or dog, it is one of the best remedies I know for frost bite.

I gave Dutch a good swig of it and rubbed some on his neck and chest. In a little while he was well heated up. We ate a good hearty lunch, and I filled him full of hot tea. Then I put him ahead of the sleds and kept him there for the rest of the trip.

Five days out from David's house, or ten days away from the head of the Goodpaster River, we reached its mouth, a distance of 170 miles. Rounding a point, we came all at once on the Indian village, which consisted of ten or twelve log cabins, with caches outside of them. Birchbark canoes were piled up for the winter outside the houses, and sleds and dogs were in front of the doors.

As the dogs heard our bells, they put up a great hue and cry. An Alaskan dog cannot bark, it can only howl. If one does hear a bark in the North, it is an unmistakable sign that the dog is of an outside breed.

As we came up the bank to the village, these Indian dogs ran up to my leader, Pointer, apparently with the idea of biting him. Pointer grabbed one of them by the throat and threw him five or six feet, never looking at him at all, but keeping right on the trail. The dog beat a hasty retreat, and none of the others came near us again.

The Indians seemed tremendously astonished to see us, and eyed my Indian, Joe, curiously. He spoke an entirely different language from their own, but he made himself understood by signs and a few words common to all Indians. Several of the Goodpaster Indians spoke quite a few words of English, having been down to the mouth of the Tanana River to trade their furs.

I explained to them that I was a soldier chief, engaged in putting up a "talk string"—as they called the telegraph wire—which I said would be a great assistance to them when installed. One asked me if it would bring more white men into the country, and I told him it probably would not, because the "talk string" would do the work of many mail carriers who otherwise would have to go through that country. One Indian said he had heard that game would not cross the "talk string," and that therefore the migration of the caribou would be changed, much to their disadvantage.

This was really so. The caribou at first were very much afraid of the right of way that we chopped through the country and of the wire that was laid on the ground, because when they came into contact with it, it cut their legs. We found that caribou had become entangled in our wire in several places and pushed it a hundred feet away from its original location, but afterward let it severely alone. Gradually they became used to it and after a while crossed the right of way without hesitation. I explained this to the Indians and told them it would make no difference with the caribou migration. In addition, the telegraph line went straight from point to point and would always afford them a fine winter trail.

They asked me why I had brought an Indian of another tribe

with me, because he might find out things there which they did not wish him to know. I replied that I was a soldier chief, and he was an Indian chief, that we were great friends and companions, hunted and fished together, and I had made him come with me against his will, to assist me on this trip.

The Indians seemed satisfied with these explanations and told me they were glad to see me, that I was the first white man who had ever come down the river, and they were greatly surprised that I came through in this terribly cold weather. They themselves had even stopped trapping, they told me.

After having provided for our dogs and eaten a good meal ourselves, we settled down to smoke, and I gleaned from the Indians all the information I could about the country. I asked when they thought the breakup would come in the spring, and where they thought was a good place for us to build boats. The conversation shifted to when the salmon would come, whether there were many of them, how much game there was in the country, and where it was located. The Goodpaster, they told me, was the best place for marten, or Alaska sable, but the Delta River, the mouth of which was about ten miles below, was the best place for foxes, particularly black and silver tips, several of which they had obtained during the last month.

Finally, an Indian who was telling me about the Delta River, said, "Me come back yesterday from line of traps, Delta River, me catchum two white men. They heap sick, too much eat."

This was astonishing information, two white men in the country at that time of the year, and sick from eating too much! I could get no more out of him except that he had left two Indians with them, that he had given them frozen salmon to eat, and that they had been on the trail a long time, coming from the Copper River. Joe elicited the information that these men were nearly frozen to death and in a very bad condition.

I determined to push down there at once and see what the trouble was. Telling one of the Goodpaster Indians to start down ahead of me, I borrowed a sled from them to use instead of my toboggan, hitched my team to it, took a little rice and bacon with me, and left Dutch to look after things at the Goodpaster village.

In a couple of hours I reached the Indian camp, a little above the mouth of the Delta. Sure enough, I found two white men, one an Irishman and the other a Swede. The Indians had built a nice wickiup for them, with a comfortable fire which made it quite warm. The Irishman's face and hands were entirely black from freezing, and his ears were all shriveled up and sloughing off. The front teeth of both men were broken off from having tried to bite into the frozen fresh salmon which the Indians had given them, and both were very sick at their stomachs from having eaten so much of it. The Swede was in much better condition than the Irishman. His toes and fingers were a little frozen, but his face, except for the nose and ears, was pretty clear of frost, as were his legs, arms, and back.

I looked over the Irishman. The Indians had taken off his trousers and were rubbing him with snow to try and save him, but I saw at once that his legs were gone and probably his arms. He had worn suspenders to hold up his trousers, and these had frozen from the moisture. There was a black streak on each side of his chest and down his back where they had extended. I did not see how the man could have lived.

I gave him a little Perry Davis Pain Killer, and cooked some rice, bacon, and salmon for them. It would have been impossible to get these men back to my working parties or to Eagle City, but there was a trading station at a little place called Chena, about a hundred miles below, where a gold strike had just been made. I therefore told the Indians that they must mush these men on down there, and they would be paid liberally for their efforts by the government or by private individuals. Both the frozen men said they had plenty of money and produced an order from the Northern Commercial Company to give them practically anything they wanted.

In the meantime, the Swede, whose vitality seemed enormous, began telling me what had happened to them. To begin with, he and his partner had determined to go into the upper Tanana River country, as they thought it offered the best chance for making a strike. During the summer they hired some packers to take them up the Chestachina River, and carried a good outfit across the divide, which is without timber for about thirty miles. They made a good strong cache for it, which would resist wolverines or any other animals, then crossed the divide and waited for the freeze in a cabin on the Chestachina about fifty miles from their cache.

When the freeze came, they crossed the divide under great difficulty, then found that their cache had been robbed by the Delta Indians of everything except a little corn meal. They debated whether they should go back or go ahead, and decided that the trip back was almost as bad as the trip ahead. As they were both good shots, they thought they could kill game sufficient for their subsistence, but little did they know about hunting at that time of the year in northern Alaska. They saw sheep several times but could get nowhere near them, and in a week's hunting only killed two rabbits.

Still they decided to push ahead. Soon their scanty supply of corn meal was exhausted. They went several days without eating, and their dogs became so exhausted that they could go no further. A dog can work from four to seven days without anything to eat. After that he dies if he is not fed. So they killed one dog, ate some of it, and fed the rest to the other dogs. This carried them on a little further. Two dogs ran away, which left them only two others. These they also killed. Pulling their own sled, they still made from six to eight miles a day.

Eventually, the terribly cold weather overwhelmed them. Their clothing and outfit were not sufficient to stand it. The Irishman began to freeze more and more every day and could not thaw out properly. When all their dog meat was gone, they chewed the dog hides, then ate all the webbing out of their snowshoes. They ate their moccasins and attempted to make sandals for their feet out of birchbark. Finally they ate their moosehide mittens, leaving only the woolen linings to wear, which of course soon became wet and froze their hands. By that time they were nearing exhaustion and really had expected to die in the camp where the Indians found them.

I urged the Indians to make all haste to take them down the

river. They did it and did it well, sending two sleds with two
Indians each. I afterward found that they got the men to Chena
in about four days, in as good condition as could be expected.
The Swede lost only two or three fingers and the ends of a few
toes. The Irishman lost both legs and both arms. I saw him several
months afterward, and he remarked in a jocular way that he did
not know whether it was better to be dead or alive in that condition.
His face was a mass of scars and his ears practically eaten away.

I went back to Central, to find the boats practically finished.
There were five quite large ones, about eighteen feet long, which
would hold one ton of cargo, four rowers, and a steersman; and
for my own use, a double-ender, twelve feet long. Despite their
crude tools and equipment, the men had built excellent boats.

I organized the crews and practiced them in rowing and steering.
I put our best men with the two boats containing our reserve food
supplies, so as to insure their getting through in good shape. They
were to stop at the mouth of the Goodpaster, opposite the Indian
village, and organize a camp from which supplies could be distributed up and down the river.

I started the pack trains through the water while the ice was
still floating on it. They carried the working parties along the line
where they were to erect the poles, put on the insulators, and tie the
telegraph wire on. Our wire had now been laid all along the right
of way from the head of the Goodpaster to the Tanana, and it remained for me to determine the course of the line from that point
on down to where we met the other party.

We had practically continuous light at this time. I started out in
the lead with my boat, ordering the others to come at two-hour
intervals so that if anything happened to us in front, we would have
sufficient time to run upstream and signal to them what to do.

Old Dutch was at the oars in my boat, and he proved to be a
pretty fair oarsman. I manned the two steering sweeps in the
stern, which I used to avoid drifts, rapids, or "sweepers," that is,
trees which had fallen into the water but whose roots had not been
detached from the earth. They would be carried downstream by

the current, then would spring back and repeat the operation. It was a very dangerous thing to get caught under one of them.

I sat in the stern, with Dutch in front of me at the rowing bench. The Goodpaster was beautiful; the trees were beginning to take on their summer aspect, and the bushes were completely clothed with bright green leaves. Wild flowers covered the ground. We were so confident now that we would finish the telegraph line that summer that we had ceased to talk about it.

That night we made camp at the mouth of the Goodpaster. I decided to wait there until the other boats arrived and reorganize the expedition. Mosquitoes were beginning to get bad. It is impossible to convey to one who has not been in the North how terrible these insects really are. At night we built long smudges, or slow-burning fires, around which the mules and horses stood to escape the mosquitoes. After a while the animals got so they would not even leave the smudge to feed or graze, so great was the pain inflicted by the bites. Two of my mules were literally killed by mosquitoes on this expedition. They were bitten so severely that they would not leave the smudges to feed and grew constantly weaker. Later, trying to avoid the mosquitoes, they got into the swift water of the Tanana and were swept away and drowned.

Dutch and I worked down the river ahead of the working parties. When I found a suitable place to land, I would get out on the bank, strike the line where the telegraph should go, then with my prismatic compass lay a straight line from one point to another, and blaze the trail through myself, alone. I laid out from five to ten miles a day in this way. It was difficult working through the underbrush, bogs, and wet moss, with the mosquitoes and insects to contend with, but much easier and quicker than carrying a big outfit and several men along with me.

Rounding the promontory which is at the mouth of the Delta River, we entered Bates' Rapids of the Tanana. The water here was much swifter than I had supposed. The river was wide, with an interminable number of sloughs. The current ran at a prodigious rate, carrying with it whatever trees or other floating material got into it. These things lodged on the bends, bars, or on projections along the banks and made a great heap like a log jam under which the current raced and roared. If a boat got under them, it would be all off with it.

We had only about one hundred miles more to go to finish the line, so I determined to take one of the large grub boats and handle it myself, to be sure that nothing happened to it on the way down. I had one of my other men take my own boat while I took Dutch and three others, all of them at the oars, two on each side. One was an ex-constable of the Canadian Mounted Police, a very good man on the water. I stood up in the stern and had a twenty-foot sweep with which to steer the boat. The channels were crooked and in many places "sweepers" fifty feet long hung over them, going down with the water, then rising with a swish and falling again.

We made very good time, and I was able to avoid both "sweepers" and the great piles of drift on the bars. I had never before seen such swift water, nor have I since. Suddenly the channel narrowed, and the speed of the current increased. I could see there was a sharp turn ahead, on the other side of which there would be an eddy, due to the water hitting the point and then swirling on the other side. Directly opposite this point was a long "sweeper," a green spruce tree. Green trees are much more limber than dead ones, and whip in and out of the water with an incredible swing. If this "sweeper" hit us, we would certainly be swamped and lose our grub, and thus be delayed another year on the work. It was the supreme moment of test, on which hung the success of our expedition.

Shouting to the men to put on all the speed they could so as to get steerage, away we shot for the point. I planned to swing the boat as we got there, aiming it to the right and trusting it would hit the eddy on the other side and carry us to safety. As we neared the point, I thought I would make it. Standing in the stern, I pulled my steering sweep with all my might, but just as I did so, the spruce caught me squarely across the waist and lifted me from the boat.

Below us was a great pile of driftwood on a projection of the bank under which the water swirled. I knew if I let go of the tree, I would be carried under the driftwood and never be heard from again. The tree carried me under the icy water, then flopped up about fifteen feet in the air, then fell again and went under the current. I could hear Dutch telling me to hold on, and the other men shouting as they pulled for the shore. A quarter of a mile below me the boat landed. By that time I had wrapped both my arms and legs around the trunk and found that I could hold my breath while the "sweeper" went under the water. I thought I could hang on for fifteen or twenty minutes at least, but if I were swept off at the end of that time, I would have so little strength left I could not avoid going under the drift pile.

I saw three men leave the boat the instant it touched the shore, while a fourth made it fast to the trunk of a tree. One of them had a big coil of rope, another an axe. Never have I seen men work faster or to better effect. Going to the bend about thirty feet upstream from me, they tied the rope around Dutch, over his right shoulder and under his left arm, then took a turn around his body. They snubbed the rope around a tree, and Dutch jumped into the raging current, being let down gradually by the other three until he got to the point where the "sweeper" carried me upstream and down into the water. As I came up, he grabbed me around both shoulders, and I grabbed him. Holding on to each other like vises, we were pulled in by the other three men.

As we landed, Dutch said to me, "I don't know if we are even, but you saved me from freezing last winter, and I have pulled you out of a bad place in this river." If it had not been for men like these, I doubt if I would have been rescued.

We completed the trip twenty miles down the river that day without further mishap. Here we stayed several days, while I ran the course of the line up and down. Then Dutch and I took our small boat and dropped down to the mouth of the Salcha River, a few miles below. Again I ran the course of the line, meeting my men about twenty miles up the river as they worked chopping out the right of way. Never have I seen greater physical strength or endurance displayed by a group of men. There were twenty in each working party, great bearded fellows in blue denim clothing, high horsehide boots and slouch hats, with remnants of mosquito netting around the edges. Their faces were running sores from the terrible assaults of the mosquitoes and black flies. As they attacked the spruce trees, the forest seemed to fall in front of them. Without such men, the lines in the North could never have been completed.

For a couple of weeks we worked with great speed. Already our parties had gotten in touch with those of Lieutenant Gibbs working up the river. July was approaching, and now I had no doubts that we would finish the telegraph system that summer. At last my wire crossed the Salcha River. Because of lack of transportation, Gibbs had fallen a little behind in his work, and I had to extend on beyond, but at length we reached the end of his wire. I made the last connection of the Alaska system myself.

Then from St. Michael and Nome on the Bering Sea, clear through to New York and Washington, the electric current transmitted our messages with the speed of light. Alaska was at last open to civilization. No longer was it the land of the unknown, sealed tight by the God of Everlasting Snow and Frost. We had forced open the portal with which he shut out the white man from the North.

# 15

## THE ERUPTION OF KATMAI

On June 6, 1912, Alaska was rocked by one of the most tremendous volcanic explosions in recorded history. Dr. Robert F. Griggs, leader of a series of expeditions organized by the National Geographic Society, reported that if such an eruption had occurred at New York City it could have been heard as far as Chicago, and that, if the winds were right, sulfuric acid in the fumes could have ruined clothes hanging on the line in Denver. As a result of Dr. Griggs's expeditions, reported in successive numbers of the *National Geographic*, President Woodrow Wilson set aside Katmai National Monument in 1918.

Containing some 4,215 square miles, Katmai is the largest of all U.S. national parks and monuments. For thirty years nothing was done to make this monument to one of nature's most violent rampages available to the public. In the early 1950's Northern Consolidated Airlines began developing fishing camps on some of the beautiful and abundant lakes within the area. In 1963 the National Park Service made its first contribution to making Katmai's natural phenomena accessible by constructing a twenty-one-mile jeep trail from Brooks Lake Camp into the famed Valley of Ten Thousand Smokes, from which hikers can now visit the craters of Mount Katmai and Mount Novarupta and other vestiges of the great upheaval.

While much has been written about the eruption of Katmai in both popular and scientific publications, perhaps the most vivid account was by Rex Beach in Chapter VII of his autobiography.

More from ⋅ ⋅ ⋅

### *Personal Exposures,* by Rex Beach

On June 6, 1912, the little steamer *Dora,* teammate of the *Newport* which had taken Roy Norton and me to Katmai, Alaska, was passing through Shelikof Straits between Kodiak Island and the mainland when it sighted a heavy cloud of smoke arising from the neighborhood of Mount Katmai. This smoke spread rapidly until it covered the sky and obscured the sun; then came a rain of ashes so thick and so continuous that daylight disappeared completely and that part of the world for hundreds of miles in many directions was blanketed in a darkness deeper and more terrible than the blackness of the darkest night. That inky gloom of mysterious origin lasted for days, lightnings flashed pallidly, thunders roared, reverberations and explosions occurred so tremendous that they were audible for nearly a thousand miles. To the people who cowered beneath this terrifying pall it seemed that the world had come to an end.

Plainly one of the greatest eruptions of all time was occurring but for a long while its precise location was not known. Happily it took place in a region only sparsely settled, otherwise the loss of life would have been tremendous. The size of that cataclysm may be gauged by comparison. Based on data assembled later by actual exploration, Dr. Robert F. Griggs of the National Geographic Society makes some calculations that are significant. In his book, *The Valley of Ten Thousand Smokes,* he states that if that eruption had occurred on Manhattan Island, the column of smoke and steam would have been visible in Albany and the sound of it would have been heard in Chicago. Evil-smelling fumes would have swept west to the Rocky Mountains and as far away as Toronto an acid rain would have scalded human flesh. In Philadelphia, the streets would have been covered a foot deep with ashes and for nearly three days and nights Philadelphians would have groped through darkness so impenetrable that an electric globe would have been invisible at arm's length. An area larger than New York City would have opened in yawning chasms, each vomiting a fiery fountain of steam and gas and quantities of molten lava sufficient to overflow all but the tops of skyscrapers like the Empire State and Radio City. For months thereafter no one could have approached closer than Paterson.

This is language the ordinary man can understand and it affords a faint conception of the violence and the scope of the catastrophe.

In 1815 there was a similar eruption in the East Indies during which more than fifty thousand people lost their lives. In this Alaskan upheaval not a single human being was killed.

The people nearest to the scene were my Indian acquaintances in Katmai Village and in Savonoski, over on the north side of the barrier range. All but six of the former, fortunately for them, were some miles away fishing and those who had remained behind were frightened away by the early portents of impending disaster.

Across the range on the Behring Sea side, American Pete, the Chief of Savonoski, was perhaps the closest observer if not the only eyewitness of the start of the cataclysm. When the first eruption occurred he happened to be in the upper part of that peaceful valley into which the storm drove Roy Norton and me and according to him:

"Katmai blow up with plenty fire and fire come down from mountain with big smoke. We go fast Savonoski. Everybody get in skin boat quick and paddle hard. Dark. No can see. Hot ashes fall. Too bad. Never can go back. Everything burn up."

That's a pretty flat and disappointing firsthand description of such a spectacular phenomenon, but it's all there is.

On the Pacific side of the peninsula where the Katmai residents were fishing was a Russian who wrote a letter as follows:

My dear wife Tania:

We are awaiting death at any moment. A mountain has burst near here so that we are covered with ashes in some places ten feet deep. We can't see daylight and we have no water. All the rivers are covered with ashes. Ashes mixed with water. Here are darkness and hell, thunder and noise. I do not know whether it is day or night. Perhaps we shall see each other again. God is merciful. Pray for me.

Your husband,
Ivan.

Bits of fragmentary description like these came from other near-by sources and they piece together a darkly blurred but frightful picture. On Kodiak Island, a hundred miles away, there were cannery towns and settlements and from them comes a more detailed story. Soon after the eruption started, Kodiak Village was cut off from communication with the outside world by electrical disturbances which put all wireless apparatus out of business. The sky rained ashes, a pitch darkness enveloped the island, streams and wells became choked until there was no water to drink. Nobody had the faintest idea what had happened. Day and night were alike. The air was heavy with sulphurous fumes and ashes fell in such quantities that they accumulated on the neighboring hills and slid off in avalanches, filling the air with suffocating dust. They descended from the sky in torrents, crushing roofs beneath their weight; the air grew hot, sultry and stuffy, dust filled the nostrils, eyes burned with acid.

The darkness was more awful than words can describe: people with lanterns in hand felt their way about and bumped into each other. Despairing birds fluttered blindly through space and fell screaming to earth. Hidden lightnings glared and there was a constant boom of thunder. In Dante's description of the Inferno there is nothing to compare with this.

When, after two days and three nights of unbroken darkness, the murk lifted a little and the pallid light shone through, the inhabitants of Kodiak beheld a new and terrible world, a world of gray, dead ash in which the very shape and contour of things had been hideously altered. Nowhere was there a sign of the lush, green life for which the island was famous.

Mountains and valleys had become deserts, villages were half buried: every spruce tree was a tent, its branches bent to the ground with a burden of ash. Streams were choked, bays were clogged with masses of floating pumice thick enough to support a man: gasses blown high from the bowels of the earth combined with the moisture of the clouds to produce sulphuric rains which burned human flesh, killed vegetation and ate the metal work of buildings.

Ash to the depth of twelve inches fell over an area of three thousand square miles and it has been estimated that when dignified old Mount Katmai went on its drunken rampage it pulverized and blew into the sky over six cubic miles of molten rock.

Figures like these cannot be grasped by the human mind.

Naturally every form of animal, bird, fish and insect life in the neighborhood of the disaster was destroyed. Every growing thing was killed to the ground and what had been a pleasant world teeming with life became a no man's land where only the sound of wind and water broke the deathlike silence.

The Katmai region remained unexplored for a long while. The natives, believing it accursed, refused to return: it was remote from the world of the white man and the waters of the North Pacific thereabouts, as I have explained earlier, are among the most treacherous known. Of course there was considerable curiosity as to what had actually happened under that pall of blackness and the first attempt to solve the mystery was made by two venturesome sourdoughs from Anchorage, Messrs. Horner and Hesse. They were not equipped for extensive exploring hence they did not get far or see a great deal but they did bring back photographic evidence of colossal destruction. It was not until three years after the eruption that an expedition from the National Geographic Socity made a thorough reconnaissance of the devastated area.

Dr. Griggs and his venturesome associates were the first to report in detail upon the effects of the volcanic upheaval. It is from their account that the facts, figures and most of the descriptive matter herein set down has been culled. Aside from them and Father Hubbard, previously mentioned, few, if any, qualified observers have ever laid eyes on this phenomenal valley and none, so far as I know, have written about it.

My own experiences, coupled with the fact that certain scenes and incidents in *The Silver Horde* were laid in the Katmai region caused me to read with avid interest every word I was able to find.

The first expedition landed about where Norton and I had gone ashore. They found that the sea, after three years, was still full of floating pumice and the mouth of the river was clogged. The valley itself was deep in ashes over which lay an ankle-deep covering of soft, sticky mud. The origin of this mud was mysterious.

The hardships of those explorers were intense for the desolation around them beggared description. They had to carry their supplies on their backs through mud fields and ghost forests utterly bare of leaf—forests stricken by gasses and acid rain. They wallowed through quicksand waist- and armpit-deep, they crossed bottomless, shifting streams which ran icy water and liquid ashes. They fought terrific windstorms which filled the air with blinding particles sharper than pulverized glass.

Many surprises greeted them as they struggled deeper into this uncanny land of death. They found new volcanoes where none should be, one of which belched a column of steam a thousand feet in diameter, more than a mile high; they encountered great ash slides, made up of particles so sharp that they ground away their finger tips; out of the overloaded brooks they strained their drinking water but they couldn't wash their faces in the water they drank for it was too dirty. Neither could they wash in the streams themselves, for the water carried such a burden of volcanic material that it cut and scratched their flesh.

Mile after mile they traveled in an absolute silence unbroken by any sound; where Norton and I had traversed a timbered country full of game there was no vestige even of insect life.

Such desolation was awesome and each day brought new marvels to wonder at. They discovered where an enormous landslide had jammed the mile-deep Katmai Canyon until the upper river became a lake which finally burst through and rushed down the lower valley in a tidal wave six miles wide and ten feet deep. It had uprooted the skeleton forests or sheared off the dead trunks; it had carried a burden of boulders with it, one of which they estimated to weigh more than a hundred tons. It was a topsy-turvy place indeed, for these boulders lay on top of the ash and the snow drifts, not under them. They beheld evidence that this flood, at its height, had exceeded the volume of Niagara and that it had been thirty-five times greater than the Johnstown flood which cost some fifteen thousand [sic] lives. Truly they had entered a freakish world where titanic forces had been at play.

They had come to see Mount Katmai but the dismal fogs and

low hurrying clouds obscured it. Those clouds parted finally, however, and revealed a sight which stunned them. Where once had stood a majestic, three-peaked mountain was now only a low, broken stub. Its upper half had been completely blown away.

They were unable to scale the mountain that year but returned the following summer and climbed its mud-plastered slopes to look down into an abyss of such immensity that they could not guess its size. In the bottom, nearly four thousand feet below, lay a wonderful lake of weird, vitriolic blue—a lake which gave off wisps of steam. It was rimmed by towering precipitous cliffs of rock, their ragged summits capped in places with sheer walls of glacial ice. The tremendous dimensions of that crater, more than eight miles around, its incredible depth, make it one of the world's curiosities. Mind you, this enormous cavity was created when infernal fires and superheated gasses surged up from the depths of the volcano, melting the rock and tossing it out in a series of thunderous reverberations.

How majestic, how terrible must have been that scene.

The earthquake shocks which accompanied it actually split mountains apart and shattered them. These scientists found towering peaks which, three years after the upheaval, were still crumbling and sending down battalions of galloping boulders. They found where great shoulders of rock and earth, thousands of feet high, had broken away and rushed down the valleys like streams of water. I am not writing fiction; these words are theirs.

Imagine, if you can, dry rivers of granite boulders plowing down toward the sea like so much liquid! And yet that is precisely what had occurred. One of those land and rock slides had run for a distance of five miles—an irresistible, thundering torrent of solid matter sufficient in weight and velocity to wipe out a city: a hundred million cubic yards of broken granite rushing at railroad speed until its force was spent! Another spectacle too stupendous to visualize.

Astounding and awesome as were these evidences of volcanic fury, the most spectacular discovery was reserved for the second year and even then only a glimpse of it was had.

Shortly before the expedition was ready to return home, three of its members decided to cross Katmai Pass and discover, if possible, the source of some peculiar clouds that had aroused their suspicions. I judge they must have been camped near where Norton and I had rested while we waited to make our twenty-five-mile midwinter dash from timberline to timberline.

Having ascended the pass to its summit where I played out, they were about to turn back when Dr. Griggs, the leader, caught sight of a tiny puff of vapor emerging from the earth. He rubbed his eyes and looked again at this miniature volcano for to a scientist that little steam jet issuing out of the floor of the pass was as significant as some of the major phenomena he and his fellows had discovered.

Proceeding onward they found the earth broken into fissures from which poured other jets of steam. In places the vapor came with the roar of an escape valve and it was hot. Gratefully they warmed their hands over it. That steam was evil-smelling stuff, as if the chef of the infernal regions was cooking rotten eggs for lunch. Further down the slope and over the crest of an obstructing hill they saw more steam rising so they hurried on.

Remember, not since American Pete fled from this valley had any human being set foot therein. When Dr. Griggs and his companions climbed that hillock and looked down they beheld one of the most amazing visions ever seen by mortal eye. The whole valley, as far as they could see, was filled with hundreds, thousands, tens of thousands of smokes, some large, some small. Some were mere tiny jets, others sent up columns of superheated steam and gasses which rose five hundred feet in height. For a dozen miles, to a point where the lonesome valley turned behind a mountain near the old village of Savonoski, the place boiled and eddied with clouds of vapor as if all the steam engines in the world had popped their safety valves at once.

It was a breath-taking sight and quite unlike anything on the face of this globe. A burnt and scalded mountain valley, pockmarked with pitholes which spouted steam and smoke; a lonesome, snow-encircled place that boiled and simmered amid Arctic desolation.

Later exploration revealed the true sublimity of this spectacle. That valley was a beautiful but also a dreadful place, for visitors stood with their feet on the very lid of hell. They walked on ground that rang hollow and beneath them were gas-filled chasms of unknown depth hot enough to melt metal. When they broke through the mud crust around those vents, live steam burst forth. There were bubbling pools of scalding mud like pots of porridge; they froze their food in snow drifts and cooked it over steaming fumaroles near by. Bacon could be fried over many of the vents—provided one held his frying pan so securely that it couldn't fly aloft; camps were pitched on sand so warm that a thermometer thrust six inches into it rose to the boiling point and one had to sleep on top of his bedding to keep cool.

A nightmare place, truly. A place of contradictions. One of the first explorers says, "It is uncannily unreal. Hot streams issue from beneath banks of snow, glaciers hobnob with steaming fumaroles; icebergs and hot water are found in the same lake. Enormous mud flows appear to have run uphill. A stick chars when thrust into a jet of steam. The valley is a huge chemical manufacturing plant roofed over by a permanent cloud of vapors."

Extraordinary as all this sounds, the most peculiar thing about this valley is the fact that preceding the Katmai eruption it opened up and belched forth a river of white-hot sand which flowed like a stream of viscous fluid, destroying everything in its path and leaving on its margins forests of charcoal.

Too bad the world can never visualize what that spectacle looked like, but those scientists have reconstructed it from a study of its effects. Here is the way Dr. Griggs imagines American Pete might have seen it had he remained longer and had he been equipped with a gas mask and asbestos underclothes.

First came a series of earthquakes increasing in volume and in frequency until, near the head of the valley of the Ukak, the face of Falling Mountain let go with a thunderous roar, pouring millions of tons of rock into the low land as a farmer spills loose wheat out of a bag. That rushing river of rock forced ahead of it a hurricane of wind which bent and whipped the forest. A great dust cloud arose lending a gloomy and portentous aspect to the scene.

Soon, during a more violent quake, the valley floor broke open and through the cracks came seething, white-hot magma—molten

rock—struggling for release from its prison; another convulsion
and new fires gushed forth, the valley opened up for its full length,
spouting out the melted viscera of the earth in fiery cascades.

No man can imagine what it looked like while those fountains
were at play but presumably the sky was filled with a pyrotech-
nical display such as no human eye has ever seen and the hills
shook with the sound. Huge blocks of red-hot lava were hurled
high into the air, enormous glowing bombs of superheated rock
soared above the surrounding mountains. There was a rain of
incandescent pumice; horrible, burning, billowing clouds arose
above the jets of frothing lava.

Snows and the lower parts of the glaciers round about were
melted and turned to steam with an almost explosive suddenness,
then the bushes began to crackle, the forest ignited and roaring
fires swept up the mountains; gales of hurricane force rushed into
the valley. In the space of a few minutes moose, caribou, bears,
birds, fish and every form of living thing were cremated in that
holocaust.

Meanwhile the floor of the valley was rising as this white-hot
sand gushed out of the earth. Expanding gases tossed it into a
terrible turmoil and it began to flow—a river of incandescent
grains hundreds of feet deep which ran with a mighty roaring.
This tumbling torrent rolled down the valley, consuming everything in its path. A dozen miles below it encountered a belt of
hills which dammed it up temporarily but like water it found its
way through the lowest notch and continued for another three
miles before it came to rest.

Nothing ever seen could possibly compare with such a sight as
this. And yet it was no more than the gentle overture to that unbelievable, indescribable catastrophe which followed, when Mount
Katmai itself began to boil and finally erupted. Then indeed the
earth rocked, cliffs fell down and hills were tossed about.

The dramatic stories of those scientists, beautifully illustrated
in the *National Geographic Magazine*, created a great stir and the
entire area around the Valley of Ten Thousand Smokes was set
aside by the government as a National Monument, or Park, and
tentative plans were made to open it up for tourists. Those plans
were never carried out, however, for the smokes gradually lessened

and later explorers forecast an ultimate disappearance of the phenomena.

The man who first predicted the gradual cooling of this steaming cauldron was Father Bernard R. Hubbard, the famous "Glacier Priest" of Santa Clara University, who has devoted years to the study of the entire eighteen-hundred-mile Alaskan volcanic rift. Himself a geologist, he has led several foot parties of his students into the valley, enduring the same incredible hardships as the earlier visitors. As a matter of fact they overcame greater hazards and discomforts by reason of the fact that they made their studies both in winter and in summer and were at all times poorly equipped.

The exploits of this smiling, bareheaded Jesuit priest and his hand-picked group of student explorers read like fiction of the wildest sort and one hesitates to credit them until he actually meets the Father and his gang. They are the huskiest and most self-reliant outfit I ever encountered; each one is an athlete, they have developed an Alpine technique of their own and when the country won't support them they appear able and willing to live off their own fat for an indefinite time. Father Hubbard and any three of his young behemoths would probably constitute a winning Rose Bowl football team.

He and one of his lads climbed Mount Katmai late one fall, just to keep an eye on it, and here is how he describes the sight:

> Finally we made it—the top of Katmai! Below and around us was the world's most colorful and impressive crater. . . . As we crawled exhausted, inching our way on torn knees and bleeding hands towards the crater's edge projecting three thousand feet above the crater bottom, clouds were beginning to form in earnest and a cold wind was starting up.
>
> Everything was pouring into Katmai when we got there. Clouds were pouring in, waterfalls were pouring in, rocks were pouring in. Even Ed Levin almost poured in when he crawled near the icy edge and peered down to the water of the lake below; so I spiked his belt with the end of my ice-pick and held him until he had seen enough. . . .
>
> Scores of waterfalls—the lowest of them higher than proud Yosemite—sent their slender threads of water thousands of feet

down the precipitous walls of Katmai, blending their individual
sounds into a collected roar that came, now soft, now loud, to our
ears as some wind current allowed. . . . Rocks, loosened from the
mighty cliffs that held in their titanic eight-mile embrace this
nightmare of unleashed chaos, crashed down the walls hurling
landslides into the watery depths. . . . The glaciers that we had
noticed four years earlier forming on the inner side of this great
hole were larger and more active, cascading in beautiful ice falls
down to the edge of the lake.

On one of his backbreaking, starvation-haunted trips into this
region Father Hubbard and a companion descended to the blue
vitriol lake at the bottom of this amazing pit. To me this account
sounded like a hare-brained undertaking and when I asked him
how they managed to negotiate those treacherous hanging ice
fields he shrugged and grinned.

"It was easy! The principal hazards going down were the crevasses, but the ice slopes steeply so we laid on our backs and slid.
In that way we shot over the cracks that were too wide to jump!"

Having had some experience with Alaskan glaciers my hair
flew up like a fright wig but this amazing man appears to be
immune to perils and gaily indifferent to hardship or fatigue. On
one occasion, at the close of a sixteen-hundred-mile dog-team trip,
he raced the spring thaws for days while delirious and in a high
fever from an attack of the flu, picked up on an errand of mercy.
In an open walrus-skin boat he cruised from Behring Straits to the
Mackenzie delta. He has explored Alaska's glaciers and from
Cook's Inlet to Bogoslof (that steaming island which overnight
rose out of the sea and sinks, rises or changes its position), he has
followed her festoon of volcanic fires. He has studied volcanoes,
climbed them, flown into them and lived inside their erupting
craters.

He was the first to explore mighty Aniakchak, largest active
crater in the world, and gave warning to the country that it was
about due to let go as Katmai had done. Sure enough it promptly
blew a three-mile hole out of its floor, sending its infernal fires
seven thousand feet aloft. While it was still vomiting gas and
smoke he arranged with a daredevil pilot to fly him into its maw

so that he could observe the changes that had occurred. A down-draft sucked them into the very hell pit out of which noxious vapors roared, and only by good luck did they escape.

On a later trip he flew in with another pilot and landed on a lake which must have been boiling not long before. Groping through steam he finished his explorations only to learn that the plane's fuel tanks held barely enough gasoline for twenty minutes' flying, whereas it would require a half hour to spiral up out of the crater and reach the coast.

Alaskan fliers are resourceful. Necessity has taught them to use their wits. This one, after due study, took off and flew directly at the volcanic vent and so maneuvered his ship that the super-heated air and gases belching from it tossed the airplane high enough to clear the crater's cliffs.

For years Father Hubbard has been doing things like this but it is not only the thirst for knowledge and the urge for adventure that drives him; he has a very definite purpose in mind. Upon his support largely depends the education and welfare of hundreds of Alaskan Mission Indians. They are his children and to them he dedicates the earnings from his lectures, his motion pictures and his writings about our Arctic wonderland. Equipped with a soup stick, a camera and his breviary he is ever ready to tackle any hazard, any test of endurance the North affords, and his motive is as fine as that of those other Jesuit Fathers, who, cross in hand braved the dark wilderness of the New World to found an empire "with no arms save those of virtue."

Of all the picturesque Alaskans I have met, not excluding those legendary fellows of the glamorous gold-rush days, none was as arresting, as vital and as colorful as this modern Marquette.

"It's a pity that the Valley of Ten Thousand Smokes has quit smoking," he says regretfully, "for while it lasted there was no sight like it in the world. Now plant and animal life is returning and soon it will resemble the country you passed through. But that great volcanic rift is still active. One of these days some other mountain will blow up. Perhaps I'll have the luck to be there when it happens."

# 16

# *THE LINDBERGHS VISIT NOME*

In 1931 the Lindberghs, Charles Augustus and his wife, Anne Spencer Morrow Lindbergh, took off on an exploratory flight from New York to Tokyo. Charles Lindbergh, who had amazed and thrilled the world with his solo flight from New York to Paris in 1927, was pioneering the Great Circle route. A consultant to Pan American Airways, he had been assigned this mission by them. His wife, Anne, acted as his radio operator. They flew across Canada, spent a night at Barrow, the northernmost point in their flight, were down the next night in a lagoon off the northern coast of Seward Peninsula, and in Nome the next day and night. There they witnessed an Eskimo kyak race and a dance by the visiting King Islanders. The story of their flight was written four years later by Anne Lindbergh and published under the title: "North to the Orient."

From · · ·

*North to the Orient,* by Anne Morrow Lindbergh

The King Islanders

*The Nugget,* Nome's daily telegraph bulletin, lay on the table, its front page announcing the day's entertainment. We had arrived in this old Alaskan mining town after a short flight from Shishmaref Inlet. The night mists had melted when we woke the morning

---

ESKIMO SPORTS

Tomorrow Afternoon at 4 P.M.

At Barracks Sq. and Water Front

ESKIMO "WOLF DANCE" IN COSTUME

At Arctic Brotherhood Hall 8 P.M.

Public Invited

LINDBERGHS BE GUESTS OF HONOR

---

after our adventure with the duck hunters. In front of us glistened a promised land. This was the Alaska we had read of. Snow-capped mountains climbed ahead of us instead of flat wastes. Green valleys cut the morning light. And the sea, the Bering Sea, rising in the gap between two hills as we approached, burned brilliant blue. We followed the beach, a gleaming white line, toward Safety Harbor. A second white line ran parallel to the shore, like foam or scattered flowers. As we came nearer I saw it to be a tangled trail of drift-wood, polished white by the surf after its long journey down the Yukon River, out into Norton Sound, and up the coast to Nome. Pounding, dancing, tossing, all the way they had come, these white arms, these branches from an alien forest, to flower on a bare coast that had never known a tree. They were as startling to see here as the waxen stems of Indian pipe in the heart of green woods, ghostly visitors from another world.

No trees yet. We had come far south from Barrow, but there were still no trees on these green hills falling to the water's edge. A broad trail cut its way over the slope, rippling up and down, like a whip cracking in the air. An Eskimo trail, I supposed, until I saw a black beetle crawl around the corner. A car! A road! We had not seen a road for so long that I hardly recognized one.

A little later we were bumping along the same road on our way into town. It had been a trail in the Gold Rush days. Old road-houses were stationed along the side, a day's dog-team journey apart over winter snow; we had already passed the second one

in forty minutes. Dilapidated shingled buildings they were, fast
becoming useless; for the airplane on skis is replacing the dog
team. It is cheaper per pound to fly.

Nome has changed since the Gold Rush days when in the 1890's
the precious metal was discovered in creeks and on the coast, and
the great trail of prospectors swarmed over the mountains to that
far cape of Alaska; when all the beach for miles—that white line
we had seen from the air—was black with men sifting gold from the
sand; when banks, hotels, theaters, and shops sprang up overnight
and busy crowds thronged up and down the plank streets. Twenty
thousand people once filled the town; now there are hardly more
than a thousand.

But there were still signs of the old life. We passed a deserted
mining shack by a stream. Fireweed, yarrow, and monkshood
sprawled over the rusted machinery. On the beach two men were
shoveling sand down long wooden sluice boxes, "washing" gold.

"Just about manage a day's wage that way," explained our host
as we passed. Ahead was a gold dredge in action; the water pipes
or "points" plunged deep into the ground to thaw it out before
dredging.

The banks, the hotels, the shops, were still there as we rattled
over the plank streets of Nome. Empty shells of buildings, many
of them, gray, weather-beaten, sagging like an old stage set, tattered
banners of a better day. But Nome was still busy. Besides a number
of stores selling drugs and provisions, there were little shops
showing moccasins and ivory work. One large window was a mass
of climbing nasturtiums grown from a window box. There were
boats coming in, trade and tourists. There was the loading and unloading of lighters in the harbor. That was what brought the King
Islanders.

This Eskimo tribe from King Island in the north came to Nome
in the summer to get what work they could as longshoremen and,
perhaps, selling trinkets to tourists. They paddled eighty miles
down the coast in huge "umiaks," walrus-skin boats holding twenty-
five or thirty people. When they put to shore they tipped their
boats upside down and made tents of them. Here under a curved
roof they sat—those of the tribe who were not working in the

harbor—and filed away at walrus-tusk ivory, making bracelets and cigarette holders.

Not today though. Today they were all down at the wharf, as we were, to see their Chief win the kyak race. For, of course, he would win. That was why he was Chief. He was taller and stronger and stood better and danced better and hunted better than anyone else in the tribe. When he ceased to excel, he would cease to be Chief. I wondered, looking at him, if he had to be browner than the rest of them, too. He stood quite near us on the dock, shaking his head and sturdy shoulders into a kind of raincoat, a hooded parka made of the gut of seals. His head emerging from the opening showed a streak of white across the dark crop of hair, and, looking at his face, one was shocked to see the same splash of white on the side of brow and cheek, as though the usual Eskimo brown were rubbing off. It was not a birthmark, they told me, but some strange disease which was slowly changing the color of his skin. Would it detract from his superiority or increase it? He seemed quite invincible as he stood there, his broad shoulders thrown back, his head well set. Even his features were stronger than those of his men; firmer mouth, more pronounced cheekbones, unusually deep-set eyes. He belonged to those born rulers of the earth.

The three men who were to race squeezed into their kyaks (a native boat entirely sealskin-covered except for a hole where the man sits). Each one then tied the skirt of his parka around the wooden rim of the opening so that no water could enter. Man and boat were one, like Greek centaurs. Then they were launched. A cold rain was driving in our faces and the bay was choppy, but the three kyaks, far more delicately balanced than canoes, rode through the waves like porpoises. It was difficult to follow the race. Sometimes the waves hid a boat from view, or breaking over one, covered it with spray. But the Chief won, of course. The crowd on the beach shouted. He did not come in; merely shook the water from his face and started to turn his kyak over in a side somersault. A little flip with the paddle and he was upside down. "That's how easily they turn over," I thought. For one horrible second the boat bobbed there in the surf, bottom up, like one of those annoying come-back toys with the weight stuck in the wrong end. A

gasp from the crowd. Then, "A-a-ah!" everyone sighed with relief.
He flipped right side up, smiled, shook the water off his face. What
was he thinking as he shoved in to shore after that triumph? He
had won. He had turned a complete somersault in rough water.
No one else could do it as well. He was Chief of the King Islanders.

We saw him again at night. The bare raftered hall was jammed
with the Eskimo and white inhabitants of Nome. Around the walls,
as in an old-fashioned dancing school, sat a row of Eskimo mothers.
Leaning over their calico skirts they peered at the audience and
at the same time kept watch of their black-eyed children who
sprawled in and out among the slat chairs. There was much giggling
and rustling of paper programs. As the curtain rose one noticed
first the back wall hung with furs, one huge white bearskin in the
center. The stage itself was empty except for a long box, like a
large birdhouse, in which were five portholes. On top of the box
over each hole squatted an Eskimo in everyday dress: skin trousers,
boots, and parka. Out of the holes suddenly popped five wolves'
heads. Ears erect, fangs bared, yellow eyes gleaming, the heads
nodded at us. Nodded, nodded, nodded, insanely like a dream, this
way and that, to the rhythmic beat of a drum. For now in the background of the stage sat some Eskimo women and a few old men
chanting and pounding out the rhythm of those heads. Every little
while when a head became awry, the Eskimo on top leaned over and
jerked it straight by pulling at an ear. The snarling heads began to
look childish. Weren't those squatting figures just like the nurses in
Central Park? "Tony! Anne! Christopher! come here—what have
you done to your coat? Look where your hat is! There now—go
along." They apparently had no part in the drama, these nurses.
Like the black-hooded figures who run in and out on the Japanese
stage, they were, I assumed, supposed to be invisible, and only
there for convenience.

Pound, pound, pound—out of the holes leaped the wolves (who
were dressed in long white woolen underwear below their fierce
heads). On all fours they stared at us. Pound, pound, pound—
they nodded this way, that way, this way, that way, unceasingly,
like a child who is entranced with a new trick and cannot shake
himself free of it, but repeats it again and again, a refrain to his life.

Pound, pound, pound—they were on their feet and shaking their bangled gauntlets this way and that. The wolf in the center tossed his head and glared at us—the Chief of the King Islanders. Pound, pound, pound, the nodding went on and on. Pound, pound, pound, their movements were sudden and elastic, like animals. There was more repose in their movement than in their stillness, which was that of a crouching panther, or of a taut bow. One waited, tense, for the inevitable spring. Action was relief. Pound, pound, pound —legs in the air and a backward leap. They had all popped into the holes, dissappeared completely. The cross-legged nurses merely nodded approval. And the curtain fell.

The Chief of the King Islanders came out from a door to the left of the stage. The wolf's head lay limp in his hand. Sweat ran down his face. He stood a head above the rest of the group and had that air of being looked at which is quite free from any self-consciousness, as though stares could reflect themselves on the face of the person beheld even when he is unconscious of them. The Chief did not notice the eyes turned toward him, for he was watching the sports now beginning in the hall.

Chairs pushed back, the Eskimo boys were kicking, with both feet together, at a large ball suspended from the rafters. Their toes often higher than their heads, they doubled up in a marvelously precise fashion like a jackknife. Now the girls' competition. The ball was lowered from the ceiling to meet their height. A thin strip of a girl was running down the aisle, her black braids tossing arrogantly. Stop, leap, and kick—the ball shot into the air and spun dizzily. That was an easy one. "The Chief's daughter," someone whispered to me. The ball was raised; the contestants fell out; one fat girl tried and sat down on the floor; everyone laughed.

There were only two left now. A run, a jump, and a leap—the ball floated serenely out of reach. Three times and out. Only the Chief's daughter left. A run, a jump, and a leap—the ball gleamed untouched. She missed it. She ran back shaking her braids. The ball was still. Several people coughed, rustled their programs. I saw her sullen little face as she turned. A run, a jump, and a leap. We could not see her touch it but the ball quivered slightly and began to spin. She had grazed it. "Hi! Hi!" shouted the Eskimos, and the crowd clapped. Her expression did not change as she wriggled back into her seat. But the Chief of the King Islanders was smiling, an easy, arrogant smile.

The next morning we walked down the plank streets of Nome to the King Islanders' camp. The town was quiet after the excitement of the night before. Life in camp was going on as usual. In the shade of their long curved "umiaks" sat whole families, mothers nursing their babies, old men filing at ivory tusks, while near by were young men curing fish, hanging long lines of them up to dry in the sun. We stopped and talked to one of the ivory filers. He had a half-finished match box in his hand. A pile of white dust lay at his feet. He was, we were to discover, the Chief's brother.

"That was a wonderful dance of yours last night." A broad smile accentuated his high cheekbones. Then gravely he looked up at us.

"My," he said simply.

" 'My,' " we echoed. "What do you mean?"

"*My*," he repeated with emphasis, putting down his file, "*my* brother, *my* son, *my* nephews—" He took a long breath. "*My.*"

That was it, I thought, as we walked back. That was what the Chief of the King Islanders felt, shaking the water from his face after his somersault. That was what he thought tossing his wolf's head. That was what he meant by that smile when his daughter made the ball quiver—simply, "*My.*"

# 17

# THE BATTLE OF THE
# KOMANDORSKI ISLANDS[1]

THE Aleutians theater in the Pacific war might well be called
the Theater of Military Frustration. No flag or general officer on
either side, with the exception of Rear Admiral McMorris, won
fame or fortune there."

Thus wrote Rear Admiral Samuel Eliot Morison, for forty years
professor of history at Harvard University, and official historian
of naval operations in World War II, in his monumental *History
of U.S. Naval Operations in World War II*. His account of the
only major naval engagement incidental to Alaskan operations
follows.

[1] Action Reports of CTG 16.6 (Rear Adm. McMorris) and of individual ships;
Admiral William S. Pye's Report on the battle, as a result of putting it on the game
board at the Naval War College; Cominch Secret Information Bulletin No. 7 "Battle
Experience Solomon Islands and Alaskan Areas March 1943"; Buships War Damage
Report on *Salt Lake City*; conversations with Rear Adm. McMorris, Cdr. W. S. Bitler
and other officers of *Salt Lake*, 7 Nov. 1943. On the Japanese side, a detailed account
by Cdr. M. Okumiya in *Inter. Jap. Off*. 399-402, with chart contributed by C.O. of
*Tama*; personal narratives by Cdr. K. Miura and Cdr. S. Hashimoto of Admiral Hosogaya's staff on pp. 98-100, 111-15, and by Cdr. T. Kuwahara on pp. 207-08 of same,
and the U.S. Army Hist. Div. translations listed in chap. i footnote 1, above; Salomon
does. obtained through SCAP in Tokyo, 1946.

From · · ·

*History of U.S. Naval Operations in World War II*, by
Samuel Eliot Morison

26 March 1943 [2]

Off the Komandorski Islands between lats. 53° and 53° 30′ N
there took place on 26 March 1943 a naval battle that has no
parallel in the Pacific war. A small task group under Rear Admiral Charles H. McMorris fought a retiring action against a Japanese force, under Admiral Hosogaya, of twice its size and fire
power; the battle lasted without a break for three and a half hours
of daylight; the contestants slugged it out with gunfire at ranges
of eight to over twelve miles, without the intrusion of air power or
submarines. It was a miniature fleet action of the sort that the
Navy, after World War I, had expected to fight in "the next war,"
with one important difference, that neither side did the other any
great hurt.

Admiral McMorris's task group had been cruising on a north-
south line west of Attu for several days in order to intercept Japanese reinforcements. He flew his flag in 22-year-old light cruiser
*Richmond,* Captain Theodore M. Waldschmidt. Destroyer Squad-
ron 14, Captain Ralph S. Riggs, comprising *Bailey, Coghlan,
Dale* and *Monaghan,*[3] acted as screen. A recent and fortunate
accession to the group was *Salt Lake City,* Captain Bertram J.
Rodgers; "Swayback Maru," as the crew called this thirteen-year-
old heavy cruiser because of her pronounced sheer. She had spent
six months being repaired after the Battle of Cape Esperance, and
with a new crew, almost half of them fresh from boot camp, had just
relieved *Indianapolis.* On 11 March, when assigned to the North
Pacific Force, she had had but a week of intensive firing practice.

[2] The action took place west of the international date line; but as the North Pacific
Force operated on Z plus two time, with date as if in long. W, I have followed their
practice. Subtract 3 hours to get approximate sun time for the position of this fight.
The Japanese used Tokyo time (Z minus 9) and date 27 March.

[3] Commanded respectively by Lt. Cdr. John C. Atkeson, Cdr. Ben. F. Tompkins,
Cdr. Anthony L. Rorschach, Lt. Cdr. Peter H. Horn.

Eleven days later she joined McMorris, who had commanded *San Francisco* in the Battle of Cape Esperance and knew what to expect of *Salt Lake*. Although she had never worked with these ships before, she was destined to become their sword, their shield and their buckler in time of trouble.

Ot 0730 March 26, an hour before sunrise, this task group lay 180 miles due west of Attu and 100 miles south of the nearest Komandorski Island. The ships were strung out in scouting line six miles long, steering N by E. Destroyer *Coghlan* was in the van, flagship *Richmond* next, followed by *Bailey* flying Captain Riggs's pennant, then *Dale*. *Salt Lake City* steamed next to last in the column, *Monaghan* in the rear. They were making 15 knots and zigzagging. Temperature was just above freezing point. The Arctic day was breaking, light SE airs barely ruffled the surface of a gently heaving sea, and visibility was so good under a 2500-foot overcast that lookouts reported fish broaching many miles away. As one stood on the bridge or forecastle, there was nothing but the swish of a bow wave to break the sweet silence of the sea, so seldom experienced in high-speed naval operations.

The crews had just finished breakfast and were going to dawn general quarters when the van destroyer and the flagship, almost at the same moment, made radar contact on five vessels between 7½ and 12 miles due north. Admiral McMorris promptly ordered his ships to concentrate on *Richmond*. In the dim morning twilight lookouts aloft and radar men at their scopes below vied with each other to make out what manner of ships these were. They appeared to be transports or cargo carriers screened by destroyers and perhaps one light cruiser. As light increased with the coming day, more and more ships were sighted; but, as McMorris later confessed, he still anticipated a "Roman holiday." Gunners saw that ready boxes were filled and gave their pieces a final polish. Prisoners were released from the brig, messmen sliced bread for sandwiches, cooks put coffee on to boil, and all preparations were made for a morning's battle.

A few minutes after 0800 the prospect changed radically and most unpleasantly. First one heavy cruiser and then another was made out, rapidly approaching gunfire range on McMorris's star-

board bow; the auxiliaries were now on his port bow. And soon a
couple of light cruisers hove into sight.

McMorris had run into Admiral Hosogaya's entire fleet. He was
running reinforcements into Attu under escort of every combatant
ship at his disposal. Heavy cruiser *Nachi* led a column composed
of heavy cruiser *Maya*, light cruiser *Tama*, destroyers *Wakaba* and
*Hatsushimo*, light cruiser *Abukuma*,[4] destroyer *Ikazuchi*, two fast
and heavily armed 7000-ton converted merchant cruisers, *Asaka
Maru* and *Sakito Maru*, which were doubling as transports; destroyer *Inazuma* in the rear. They were on a northerly course
approaching a rendezvous with slow freighter *Sanko Maru* which
had been sent ahead with one destroyer as escort.

About the same time that the Americans made their first radar
contact, the navigating officer of *Asaka Maru* sighted the masts of
a ship against the southern horizon $13\frac{1}{2}$ miles distant. Presently
more masts appeared. Hosogaya then ordered his force to turn
southeastward and engage, while the two *Marus* continued on their
course out of the way. The turn had already begun when the
Americans identified them.

They outnumbered the American force more than two to one.
*Maya* was longer, heavier and three years newer than *Salt Lake
City;* both she and *Nachi* were rated at $35\frac{1}{2}$ knots' speed as against
*Salt Lake's* $32\frac{3}{4}$. And at 0810 *Salt Lake* was still more than three
miles behind *Richmond*, endeavoring to catch up. Should McMorris
accept battle against these odds? And if he did, how would he
fight? Or if he retired, in what direction? He decided on the bold
course of trying to catch and sink the transports while his own force
was under long-range gunfire, and then to retire at high speed. It
was rather a thin hope that Admiral Hosogaya would let him close
the transports near enough to damage them; but the Japanese might
make a mistake, and even if they did not, the United States bomber
patrol flying from Amchitka and Adak, who were promptly notified, might catch the transports.

These were some of the thoughts that passed through the Admiral's mind, and some of the elements in his decision; but the

[4] Flagship of Desron I, with Rear Adm. Tomokazu Mori in command. These cruisers,
completed 1920-21, were slightly smaller than *Richmond*, and carried seven 5.5-inch
guns in their main batteries as compared with her ten 6-inch.

main factor was probably that McMorris wanted a fight badly, and knew that his men felt the same way. Not for nought did his parents name him Horatio! And wisely, as Nelson would have done, he informed Captain Rodgers of *Salt Lake City* that flagship *Richmond* would conform to the movements of the more powerful heavy cruiser.

No spotting planes were launched by the Americans, as McMorris decided to conserve the flagship's against possibly greater need at a later hour, and *Salt Lake's* one available plane had been degassed. *Nachi* launched a spotting plane, possibly two; but owing to poor communications and brisk anti-aircraft fire from the American ships it did the Japanese little good.

At 0840, before the American ships had had time to close into battle order, the enemy opened fire on *Richmond* at 20,000 yards, made a close straddle on the second salvo, and then shifted to *Salt Lake City*. Throughout the action "Swayback Maru" received most of the enemy's attention; he would not waste ammunition on ships whose main batteries could not reach him at extreme ranges. *Salt Lake* commenced return fire with her forward turrets at 0842 and at a range of over 20,000 yards made hits on *Nachi* with her third and fourth salvos, starting a fire that looked serious but was quickly brought under control.

Nevertheless, Hosogaya by changing course and closing range had frustrated the American attempt to get at the transports. McMorris regretfully decided to turn away and forget the auxiliaries for the time being; his chance might come later. So at 0845 he ordered 25 knots' speed and a 40-degree turn to port in order to confuse enemy gunfire. Within three minutes the Japanese had so closed the range that he had to bend on 3 more knots and continue turning until he was retiring in a southwesterly direction with the enemy in hot pursuit on his port quarter.

*Nachi* now ceased firing because her engineers' carelessness had caused a failure of electric power when the guns were at maximum elevation,[5] but *Maya* was firing steadily with her main battery. A

[5] According to Cdr. Miura, one of her staff officers (*Inter. Jap. Off.* p. 99), generator steam supply was shifted too early to a boiler that was just getting up steam, and half an hour passed before things were straightened out. The flagship should of course have had all boilers on the line at that time of day in those waters.

salvo of eight torpedoes, launched by *Nachi* at 0846, failed to score because of the extreme range. Four minutes later she received two 8-inch shell hits.[6] One severed communications on the mainmast and the other exploded on the starboard side of the bridge, killing several men and wounding a score. Two minutes later a third shell exploded in her torpedo tube compartment, creating more casualties. Near-misses drenched the bridge; *Salt Lake* was doing some fancy shooting at a range of almost nine miles.

Flagship *Richmond*, seldom firing at this range, led her by 2000 to 3000 yards. Both ships zigzagged, but *Salt Lake* was making the most abrupt zigs and zags as Captain Rodgers "chased the salvos." [7] He chased them to very good purpose, too; as his "exec," Commander Worthington S. Bitler, described it:

> The skipper would ask, "Well, Worthy, which way shall we turn next?" I'd answer, "Your guesses have been perfect so far, Captain. Guess again!" He'd swing right or left, and the spot we would have been in had we gone the other way would be plowed up with ten or fifteen 8-inch shells. The skipper would then look at me with a grin just like a schoolboy that's got away with something in school. "Fooled 'em again, Worthy!" He did so, too; it was uncanny.[8]

*Salt Lake* now concentrated on *Maya*, which got the range as *Nachi* maneuvered to avoid masking her gunfire. Those who witnessed the action compared these two big cruisers to a pair of graceful fencers, thrusting and parrying for three and a half hours over an ocean dueling ground. Captain Rodgers, as calm as if he were directing peacetime maneuvers, inspired complete confidence; even when his ship went dead in the water, the men on the bridge had no doubt of eventual victory.

The American destroyers did not waste ammunition in long-range firing, and the enemy destroyers, which (with light cruiser

[6] Cdr. K. Miura insisted these were 6-inch shells, but he must have been wrong, as *Richmond* was not firing at that time.

[7] This means that when the enemy makes a near-miss one alters course and steers the ship right into the splashes, so that when the enemy corrects his range, on the assumption of his target continuing same speed and course, his corrected salvo will miss.

[8] John Bishop in *Saturday Evening Post*, 5 Feb. 1944 p. 10.

*Abukuma*) were ordered to make a torpedo attack, played a cautious game. At about 0902 light cruiser *Tama* was observed to have peeled off from the main formation. She hung on McMorris's starboard quarter, apparently to stay between him and the auxiliaries, and then retired out of sight. *Nachi* and *Maya* with four destroyers now made a wide sweep southward in order to get between McMorris and his Aleutian bases. *Maya,* after launching eight torpedoes which failed to score, at 0910 made her first hit, on *Salt Lake's* starboard plane amidships. Lieutenant Commander Winsor C. Gale and Fireman James F. David were killed; flames burst out but were soon brought under control and the plane was jettisoned.[9] Ten minutes later *Salt Lake* and *Nachi* hit each other at a range of about 24,500 yards; the Japanese cruiser slowed down and was seen to be smoking heavily.[10] Apparently the shell that stopped her was a destroyer's 5-inch which passed through a gun port of No. 1 turret, exploded inside and killed the entire gun crew; other 5-inch shells burst above the main deck and killed men topside.

All enemy ships now checked fire. McMorris, hoping that he had knocked out the smoking cruiser, and bent on getting a crack at the transports, made a wide right turn, bringing his column around to due north, between 0926 and 0953. At 0930, when *Nachi's* main battery resumed working, she, *Maya* and the four destroyers straightened out in pursuit, crossing the American wakes at 0952 about five miles to the rear. All this time both sides were slugging their best. Although *Maya* and *Nachi* were faster than *Richmond* and *Salt Lake,* they took it out in zigzagging; for a pursuing ship in a stern chase can come bows-on only at the expense of masking her stern guns, and must reckon with running into torpedo water if she closes. Hosogaya's tactics were to concentrate on *Salt Lake* with a minimum of risk to his ships.

Captain Rodgers, observing that light cruiser *Tama* had worked

[9] Capt. Rodgers's Report states that the 0910 hit was below waterline and flushed shaft alleys No. 3 and 4; but officers on board *Salt Lake* told the writer that that was a different hit.

[10] About this time the float plane from *Nachi* was spotted and fired on by both cruisers and destroyers; it disappeared into a cloud, smoking, at 0831 and did not again tangle with them; but Cdr. Hashimoto says that it spotted for the Japanese forces throughout the action.

up to about 18,000 yards on his starboard quarter, an excellent position to spot for *Nachi* and *Maya*, obtained permission from the Admiral to sheer out and take her under fire at 0945. *Salt Lake* fired 8 salvos at the light cruiser and forced her to make a 360-degree turn to evade. *Richmond's* officers on the bridge had time for a good laugh over a dispatch from Admiral Kinkaid at Adak, sent to McMorris half an hour earlier, "suggesting that a retiring action be considered." He added cheerfully that Army bombers would be due to arrive in about five hours' time!

*Salt Lake's* steering gear, which had given trouble before, came near letting her down badly at 1002, just as *Maya* and *Nachi* began to straddle her. The hydraulic unit on the steering engine was carried away by the shock of her own gunfire. This limited rudder changes to 10 degrees for the rest of the action; even that was possible only by use of a diesel boat engine that the ship's crew had rigged in preparation for just such an accident. Her movements became erratic but she kept up a high rate of fire from her after turrets. *Maya* and *Nachi*, both apparently in the best of health, closed range under 20,000 yards, steering so as to throw full salvos. The enemy cruiser which fired blue-dyed projectiles was particularly obnoxious; some 200 of her shells fell within 50 yards of *Salt Lake City*, which again and again was concealed from view of her consorts by the splashes; many times they thought she was lost, but she emerged intact from this shower of 8-inch armor-piercing projectiles, except for one high-trajectory hit at 1010 which penetrated her main deck and passed out through her hull just below the waterline.

The last hope of working around the enemy's van toward his transports had now vanished; McMorris's one object was to save his ships. Captain Rodgers, now that *Salt Lake* was taking water and steering with difficulty, expected the enemy to close and requested a smoke screen, which the Admiral promptly ordered. Conditions were ideal for laying smoke: a retiring action on a windless day, with high humidity and the temperature just above freezing. *Bailey, Coghlan* and *Salt Lake* used both chemical and funnel smoke very effectively from 1018 until the end of the fight. At 1028 the Admiral changed course to 240° in order to take advantage of this cover. The enemy fired whenever he caught sight of his quarry through holes in the smoke, or on information relayed by his light forces, which now and again closed range although promptly slapped down by *Richmond* and Riggs's destroyers whenever they did. *Maya* fired four torpedoes at so great a range that no American ship even sighted their wakes.

As eleven o'clock approached, McMorris was pushing westward at 30 knots in the direction of Kamchatka. *Richmond* was in the van with *Salt Lake* 3000 yards astern; and the four destroyers on *Salt Lake's* port beam and quarter were diligently making smoke. They had now arrived at a point about 550 miles from Adak but only 420 miles from the Japanese base at Paramushiro. The Army bombers were not due for another four hours; Mitsubishis from the Kuriles might well get there much earlier. The enemy was making about two knots' more speed than the Americans. "The chance of breaking away to the south with a view to later turning east seemed fair," observed Admiral McMorris. "Determined to act accordingly," at 1100 he ordered a turn southward inside of the Japanese track, to course 210°. *Maya* and *Nachi*, presumably baffled by the smoke screen, continued for several minutes westward before turning south, and when they did so the flagship fired eight torpedoes; the light cruisers cut the corner, taking the inside track, and at 1115 *Abukuma* fired four torpedoes. None of these caught up with the Americans.

*Salt Lake* received her fourth and last hit at 1103,[11] as a result of which the after gyro room and engine room flooded, the latter to a depth of four feet.[12] Valiant work was done by damage control, men calking leaks in the outer skin with their own shirts while standing chest-deep in oil sludge and icy water. The flooding was serious enough to give her a five-degree list to port, yet she never ceased firing, and was still able to keep up full speed. But when the after fireroom went out of commission at 1125, as a result of

[11] Capt. Rodgers's Action Report states that she was hit also at 1059 on the starboard plane, which was jettisoned; but the "exec.," navigator and gunnery officers with whom the writer conversed on 6 Nov. 1943 were positive that the plane was hit and jettisoned at 0910 and that there was no hit at 1059.

[12] To control this flooding, the main circulator pump of No. 3 main engine was periodically used to take suction on the after engine room bilge. When the main circulator was so used, the engine was stopped.

damage to the after oil manifold, speed fell to 20 knots. McMorris ordered a torpedo attack by three destroyers, then canceled the order at 1138 because *Salt Lake's* speed had picked up as the fuel oil system was unsplit and suction was taken on the forward fuel line. The enemy managed to close only about 3000 yards during this slowdown, as he did a "ships right" to avoid the torpedo attack that he expected from the destroyers' movements, but which was never launched.

At 1150, *Salt Lake's* situation became very unhappy. Arctic sea water in the fuel oil snuffed out all the burners,[13] steam pressure stopped, power was lost, main engines stopped and she drifted to a halt. At 1155, the signal "Speed Zero" was hoisted, and also went out over voice radio after an 8-inch projectile passed through the "Zero" flag. The ship was then 105 miles south of the Komandorski Islands and 190 miles west of Attu. Few impartial observers would have bet five dollars on her chance of survival. *Maya* and *Nachi* were at 19,000 yards' range on her port quarter, firing steadily and closing rapidly, The light cruisers were at about the same range on her starboard quarter. Japanese destroyers would soon be at effective torpedo range; *Hatsushimo* in fact sent a spread of six torpedoes her way at 1154, but they failed to score. "Swayback Maru" was still firing with her after turrets, but her ammunition was 85 per cent expended, and as a "sitting duck" she had little chance against two healthy hunters of her own class.

Yet within five minutes the picture completely changed.

At 1154, when his ship went dead in the water, Captain Rodgers asked the Admiral to order a torpedo attack and McMorris promptly complied. He also closed the stricken cruiser in *Richmond* with the object of taking off her crew, and Captain Riggs sent *Dale* on the same rescue mission. *Salt Lake* still lay behind the destroyers' smoke screen, her plight concealed from the enemy, when at a minute or two before noon [14] *Bailey, Coghlan* and *Monaghan* reversed course to deliver a torpedo attack on *Maya*

---

[13] This happened because the engineers, attempting to correct the list by pumping salt water ballast from port tanks, inadvertently connected the ballast-transfer line to the one fuel line in use.

[14] The time given by Capt. Riggs is 1154, but his clock must have been a bit slow or else *Salt Lake's* were fast. Admiral Pye thought the time was 1159.

and *Nachi,* distant 17,000 yards. It was a "magnificent and in-
spiring spectacle." The destroyers had some distance to go under
fire before releasing torpedoes, but before they had been gone five
minutes there occurred what seemed almost a miracle: the enemy
column turned from a southerly to a westerly course.[15] Could
Hosogaya be breaking off the action? That is exactly what he was
doing.

There were several reasons for this decision by the Japanese
commander. His fuel supply was low and he wished to be certain
of enough to get home. His ammunition was "below the minimum
prescribed by doctrine." [16] He was disgusted with the performance
of his destroyers. Nobody told him that *Salt Lake* lay dead in the
water because the only Japanese who could see her through the
smoke was the pilot of *Nachi's* spotter plane, who either could
not get through to the Admiral with this vital piece of news, or did
not try. Hosogaya figured that American bomber-plane support, already overdue, might arrive at any moment. Indeed, he thought
it was already there. *Salt Lake,* which had been firing blue-dyed
armor-piercing shells, ran out of them at this point, and the white
plumes raised by near-misses of her undyed HC shells looked to
Captain Rodgers like splashes from aerial bombs dropped from
above the overcast. Obviously the Japanese thought so too, as they
were observed to be firing their anti-aircraft guns at high elevation.
Finally (in the words of a participant),[17] "Our flagship, the *Nachi,*
was hit by effective shots from an outstandingly valiant United
States destroyer, which appeared on the scene toward the end of
the engagement."

*Bailey,* the "outstandingly valiant destroyer," with *Coghlan* and
*Monaghan,* tried her best to overtake *Nachi* and *Maya.* The Japanese returned the destroyers' gunfire briskly, apparently smother-
ing them with splashes; it seemed impossible that they could survive, but still they bore in. Lieutenant Commander Atkeson,
*Bailey's* skipper, chased the salvos expertly. Presently an 8-inch

---

[15] The time, as far as we can make out, was 1203.

[16] Cdr. Hashimoto in *Inter. Jap. Off.* p. 112. If figures in "Northern Area Operations"
p. 32 are correct, *Nachi* had expended only 59 per cent and *Maya* 75 per cent of her
8-inch ammunition, but *Salt Lake* had expended 85 per cent of hers.

[17] Name unknown; the account is the one Mr. Salomon obtained through SCAP.

shell exploded at the galley door on *Bailey's* starboard side.[18] Captain Riggs decided to launch torpedoes immediately at a range of 10,000 yards, rather than risk destruction of the ship before he could get them away. At 1203, just as her five torpedoes hit the water, *Bailey* received a second hit which cut all electric power; she turned away and her sister destroyers followed, without launching. Captain Riggs wished to send them back in, but Mc-Morris, knowing how difficult it is to score with torpedoes in a stern chase, ordered them to retire with him.

*Salt Lake City* remained dead in the water only four minutes. In complete darkness and during the heat of battle, damage control purged the salted fuel lines, cut in other oil tanks and relighted fires in the forward fireroom. At 1158 the forward engines began to show life. When eight bells struck, she was making 15 knots, which gradually built up to 23 as power was restored to the after engines. Captain Rodgers resumed gunfire with his after turrets at 1202, but the enemy was now opening range so rapidly that he ceased firing at 1204; *Richmond* and some of the destroyers continued until 1212, when the action broke off.

By 1215 the Japanese ships were hull-down. *Salt Lake,* with five feet of water in the after engine room bilges, was capable of making 30 knots and fighting until her ammunition was exhausted —as it almost was. Admiral McMorris gave his group the course for Dutch Harbor.

Thus *Salt Lake* was extricated from her predicament, and with her sister ships lived to fight another day. They had conducted a brilliant retiring action against heavy odds, and were able to get home under their own power. Their casualties were incredibly low, 7 killed (2 in *Salt Lake,* 5 in *Bailey*); 7 hospital cases and 13 minor injuries.[19] All sailors topside were soaked through their winter "zoot suits" by the shell splashes, and thoroughly chilled,

[18] The torpedo attack developed so quickly that only a part of *Bailey's* crew were warned, and when this shell exploded the damage control party was in the galley gangway getting lunch to serve to the gun crews. The key damage control men were killed or wounded.

[19] Japanese casualties were 14 killed, 26 or 27 wounded, all but one in *Nachi* (WDC No. 160623 NA No. 11,784 "Tabular Records of Japanese Heavy Cruisers"). Cdr. Miura in *Inter. Jap. Off.* p. 99 says 40 men were killed topside; he must have meant total casualties.

for the water temperature was 28° and that of the air 30° to 40°. All hands in *Salt Lake* were served a shot of "medicinal alcohol" and worked cheerfully at damage control for hours before securing; but there was none of that for the destroyer sailors. *Bailey's* men, with a demolished galley, had cold comfort from a diet of ham, crackers and apple juice until they reached port. She and *Salt Lake* went on to Mare Island for repairs; and when *Bailey* was dry-docked a good third of her underwater plates were found to be wrinkled and dented from near-misses.

Air participation in this action was limited to one or two float planes from *Nachi*. Why no Japanese bombers came out from Paramushiro has never been explained, but there were plenty of "alibis" for the American air forces. Two PBYs on routine patrol were ordered by Admiral Kinkaid at 0844 to make and keep contact with *Asaka Maru* and *Sakito Maru*, but did not find these ships until 1410; they carried no bombs and their contact reports were poor and belated. A minor strike of B-25s from Amchitka, the new emergency airstrip 450 miles from the scene of the action, was delayed owing to the necessity of installing auxiliary gas tanks. Three B-25s and eight P-38s took off at 1330 and received a report from Admiral McMorris telling where to find the two *Marus*, but turned back for lack of fuel; a second strike also failed. The Adak-based bombers 150 miles farther eastward, were even more tardy. McMorris's first contact report found them armed with general-purpose bombs, readied for a strike on Kiska. An attack on ships required the substitution of armor-piercing bombs. These had to be gathered from various storage places where they were frozen in, and auxiliary tanks had to be installed in the B-25s. Four hours were spent in making the change, and then a snowstorm socked Adak in for two hours. The bombers finally took off in time to view McMorris's force on its homeward passage, when they had insufficient fuel to pursue the enemy.[20] But the two Japanese transports and the freighter returned to Paramushiro without touching Attu; their mission was thwarted. So, by any standards, Admiral McMorris had won.

[20] Cominch "Battle Experience Solomons and Alaska" pp. 43-2 [sic]; Craven and Cate *Army Air Forces in World War II*, IV 377.

Radio Tokyo claimed the usual annihilating victory, and took great umbrage at the American radio release claiming that the Japanese had fled,[21] but Admiral Hosogaya's conduct was not pleasing to his superior officers. They saw no reason why he should not have disposed of *Salt Lake City*, relieved him within a month, and sent him into the reserve. Flagship *Nachi* retired to Sasebo for repairs.

Although retiring actions never seem as glorious as advancing ones, the odds against which McMorris fought, his bold handling of the task force, and the magnificent manner in which all ships responded to his leadership should make Komandorski a proud name in American naval history. That moment in the gray sub-arctic noon just as the enemy turned away, when *Salt Lake City* lay dead on a glassy sea but still firing, with *Richmond* firing as she closed, and three destroyers going in for a torpedo attack, deserves to be depicted by a great marine painter.

As one bluejacket remarked, "The way Captain Rodgers handled the ship had a good deal to do with it, but there was more to it than that." Ensign F. R. Lloyd, USNR of *Salt Lake* thus concluded her log for 26 March: "This day the hand of Divine Providence lay over the ship. Never before in her colorful history has death been so close for so long a time. The entire crew offered its thanks to Almighty God for His mercy and protection."

21 "We had purpose in that our fleet went in westerly direction in order to pursue American fleet. There is only shock at such base means of propaganda taken by America." (Tokyo broadcast 30 March 1943.)

# 18

## BUSH PILOTS

ALASKANS are the "flyingest" of all Americans, measured
by the number of flights and miles flown per capita. A larger percentage of Alaskans have pilots' licenses and fly their own planes
than do their fellow citizens in any other state. Necessity, the lack
of highways (one of the discriminations suffered by Alaska as a
territory was exclusion until 1956 from the Federal aid highway
legislation adopted by Congress in 1916), and likewise the Alaskans' pioneering spirit, caused them to take to the air.

The "bush pilot" is distinctively and uniquely an Alaskan character and his service is a peculiarly Alaskan institution. Every
intra-Alaskan airline and two of the four lines connecting Alaska
with "the lower 48" were initiated and developed by early bush
pilots. But while these modern airlines now connect Alaska with
the outside and serve effectively within Alaska, the bush pilot is
still indispensable.

Richard L. Neuberger, who served in the United States Army in
Alaska during World War II, wrote this vivid tribute to the in-
trepidity, ingenuity, and valor of the bush pilots in 1948. Its va-
lidity is little changed, although their planes are now better and
their flying safer, partly due to subsequent airstrip construction—
much of it through the efforts of Tony Schwamm, a bush pilot and
World War II aviator who headed the Territory's Department of
Aviation from 1949 to 1954.

Dick Neuberger, elected to the United States Senate in 1954, was a dedicated supporter of the cause of Alaskan statehood and was presiding over the Senate when the statehood bill passed on June 30, 1958. He died of cancer in 1960, on the eve of his campaign for reelection. A 7,500-foot peak in Alaska was named for him by vote of the Alaska legislature.


From · · ·

### Beating the Alaskan Bush, by Richard L. Neuberger

... The bush pilot is the taxicab man of the North Country. From Cape Prince of Wales along the Bering Sea, on across Alaska and the Canadian Arctic for 3,000 miles to Hudson Bay, he provides standard transportation. You either travel with him or you crawl along laboriously by snowshoe, dog sled and canoe. River packets, cutting wood for fuel as they churn along, operate on the Yukon and Mackenzie, but only during the few months of open water from May until the last of September.

No metropolitan fleet of taxis has a greater variety of customers than does the average Alaskan bush pilot. In the morning he may fly a hopeful prospector to diggings so promising that the pilot must swear on a dog-eared Old Testament never to reveal where he has been. That afternoon the bush pilot may rush the pregnant wife of a trapper over in the next valley to a Fairbanks hospital just in time. The following day he may rescue half a dozen beleaguered U.S. Army fliers, as did William Munz and Frank Whaley a few months ago on the bleak tundra north of Nome.

Nothing feezes a bush pilot—not even the urgent message that came to Fairbanks calling for a plane to hurry to a lonely settlement in the Tanana region, to take away a shapely female of dubious morals before she disrupted the community for keeps.

Alaska is as dependent on its bush pilots as Venice is on gondoliers. The Territory has 2,827 miles of "usable roads," according to the House Committee on Public Lands, and 528 miles of railways. These cover Alaska about as thoroughly as a diaper would cover an elephant. Sweden, less than one third of Alaska's size, has more than 50,000 miles of roads and 10,000 miles of railway. In many Alaskan communities men pay $3,000 for automobiles, shipped north at the world's highest ocean freight rates, which they can drive only four or five miles out of town before the road trickles off into muskeg or jack pine.

In Alaska, you fly or you stay put. Such giants of the airways as Pan American and Northwest link Alaska with continental United States. But when you fly within Alaska itself, the chances are your life will be in the hands of one of the nonchalant men known as "bush pilots." The wilderness in the North is not the wilderness. It is "the bush," a term first applied by a band of Australians who struggled across Chilkoot Pass in the great gold rush of 1898. Dozens of Alaskans soar out over these solitudes in tiny planes, bringing mail and medicines and fresh food to backwoods outposts, and so they are "bush pilots."

Not to fly in Alaska is the equivalent of not riding a horse in Wyoming. It carries with it a social stigma. Unkind words are passed behind one's back. . . . Indeed, more than one robust Alaskan looks back on a nativity in the cramped cabin of a bush plane. Jim Dodson flew his Stinson through a snow flurry with one hand, and with the other helped a homesteader's wife give birth to a six-pound girl. The pilot became the baby's godfather. The famous bush pilot Joe Crosson, who thrilled the world when he rushed 280,000 units of diphtheria serum to stricken Barrow, landed a woman in labor at Fairbanks less than five minutes before her child was born.

"You should have circled, Joe," a mechanic told him. "You could have collected two fares instead of one."

A young American newspaperwoman from New England, Jean Potter, created a phrase in which Alaska takes pride. "Alaskans are the flyingest people," said she. Statistics prove her point. The boom town of Anchorage, with more than 12,000 inhabitants, is now Alaska's largest city, having overtaken the capital of Juneau since the 1940 census. In one month in 1945, Merrill Field, just outside Anchorage, had 10,000 airplane landings and take-offs. This exceeded the number of civilian operations at La Guardia Field, New York City (pop. 7,000,000).

A preponderance of the flights at Merrill Field were by bush pilots. Appropriately enough, this most intensively used of all airports under the American flag was named in memory of a bush pilot, Russell Merrill. He disappeared over Cook Inlet flying a compressor unit to a Kenai Peninsula gold mine.

The airplane in Alaska nearly occupies the place of the automobile in "the States," and the bush pilot is the man at the stick. In fact, Alaska has 116 times as many planes per capita as the nation proper. George Sundborg, manager of the Alaska Development Board, supplements this with further statistics: "Airplanes in Alaska fly 70 times as many miles as those in the United States for each person, they carry 23 times as many passengers, they fly 18 times as many passenger miles, they carry 1,034 times as much freight and express and 48 times as much first-class mail."

The air over Alaska is full of planes: Fokkers, Bellancas, Norsemen, Lockheeds, Ford Tri-motors, Piper Cubs, Vegas—anything that will hold together in the sky. These seem frail against the cosmic distances they seek to conquer, yet conquer they have. Fred Milligan remembers when he ran the mail from Nenana down the Kuskokwim behind a team of 14 Huskies. It took him three weeks. Then Fred saw an old Fairchild fly the route in four hours. "I decided then and there," he said, "that Alaska was no country for dogs."

Pioneer miners decided Fairbanks was the "golden heart" of Alaska. Bush pilots call it "the hub." From Fairbanks they fly in every direction of the compass. They take prospectors to the creeks and trappers to the mountain valleys where marten, fox, lynx and ermine are found. The pilot invariably makes an appointment to pick up the trapper on a certain day the following spring. God willing, the pilot will be there. It might mean death for the trapper if the date were broken because the winter's grub supply is sure to be almost gone.

With his last choking breath, a bush pilot dying of pneumonia told a nurse about the half-breed trapper up the Koyukuk expecting him within the week. The dead pilot's pal kept the appointment. Oscar Winchell was 10 days late picking up a trapper and his wife at Post Lake "when the ceiling dropped down lower than the doorstep of a one-story cabin." Oscar, formerly an Arizona cowpuncher, felt so remorseful that he dipped into his own funds to bring his anxious customers a planeful of fresh oranges and the best steaks available in Fairbanks.

Nothing surprises a bush pilot. He may be asked to fly a cow to a Matanuska dairy herd, or he may be paid $500 to return a mail-order bride to the steamer dock at Seward because she doesn't turn out to be the winsome bathing beauty whose picture was sent to a lonely trader. He may be commissioned to overtake the Alaska Railroad's pretentious new streamliner AuRoRa on its way to McKinley Park, and he may wing a fabulously valuable cargo of furs off a ship wedged in the ice pack for the next six months.

People crack mentally in the winter darkness of the bush, and bush pilots fly them out. No assignment makes the fliers of the North more nervous, but as Joe Crosson once said, "What about the marshals and Canadian Mounties who used to be six and eight weeks along the trail with those poor people on dog sleds?"

Bush flying has been a marginal business. Two hundred miners in the remote and inaccessible Iditarod region, busting their britches to get to town, may represent fares of $75,000 to divide among a few pilots. But gross income and net income in bush flying are far apart.

Until the Japanese army crouched in the outer Aleutians, and the United States government spent billions to dot Alaska with airfields, the average Alaskan plane suffered two or three crack-ups annually. These were not necessarily the terrifying impacts which leave no survivors, but merely broken landing gear, splintered propellers, a strut or nose smashed by a 20-pound Canadian goose. On two or three occasions Les Cook rigged a makeshift propeller out of sledge boards and moose glue, and it took him home.

Yet such misfortunes idle a plane, and while it is laid up for repairs the exchequer of the pilot increases not.

"When I went into this," said a bush flier in southeastern Alaska, "I figured I'd be a rich man if I could keep the plane in the air half the days of the year. Well, I'm not a rich man. Too many logs in the water to prick pontoons, and too many nicked fenders, I guess."

Alaskans go in and out of the flying business, as businessmen in the United States will take a fling at farming and then perhaps give it up as too fettering a pastime. Jimmy Rodebaugh, freight conductor on the Alaska Railroad, was one of the pioneers of Alaskan aviation. Many ex-fliers are now prosperous mine owners and trading post proprietors. Nick Bez, the burly Yugoslav immigrant who is Alaska's dominant salmon packer and a bosom pal of President Truman, was operating planes over the timbered Inside Passage before he acquired his first cannery.

Today, Alaska has 18 certificated air carriers which fly under authorization of the Civil Aeronautics Board. The scores of bush pilots have no such official sanction. Last year the C.A.B. grounded some of them. The resulting uproar was as loud as a thousand hungry Kadiak bears in mass chorus. Alaskans insisted the bush pilot was absolutely essential. "TERRITORY CANNOT SURVIVE WITHOUT BUSH AIR OPERATIONS," warned a wire from one chamber of commerce.

"To ground the bush pilot in Alaska," said Delegate E. L. (Bob) Bartlett on the floor of Congress, "would be to leave lonely settlements at the mercy of epidemics, to leave the expectant frontier mother to undergo her ordeal alone, to isolate trappers and prospectors in fastnesses they might never quit alive." And C.A.B. Examiner Raymond W. Stough wrote an amen to Bartlett's words by recommending that the bush pilots be exempted from the workings of the certification law because of the unique nature of their operations.

The bush pilots frequently serve as feeders for the authorized air lines, but between the two factions there is considerable jealousy. William Munz, one of the Nome pilots who rescued the six survivors of the crumpled B-29 Clobbered Turkey, runs a comparatively small air undertaking which has a C.A.B. certificate. As a member of the Territorial Senate, Munz sponsored a bill last year setting up an Alaskan Aviation Board on which only "officers of certificated air carriers" would have been eligible to serve. The rank-and-file bush pilots banded together in a powerful opposition lobby and the bill died.

The bush pilot has a real status in Alaska. Parents are proud to make him godfather of their offspring, and girls consider him a prize catch. This is a real tribute, for Alaskan girls, outnumbered more than 2 to 1 by the male population, can pick and choose as they please. The bush pilot is a glamor boy in any Northern town. In fact, more than one attractive mail-order bride has ended up in the arms of a bush pilot instead of in the possession of the lonely trader or miner who paid her passage north.

Some measure of the standing of bush pilots may be gained from the fact that both the men who rescued the stranded Army fliers above Nome are influential in Alaskan politics. Munz was elected to the Territorial Senate in 1946 when Alaska went Republican for the first time in more than 15 years. Frank Whaley, one of the most spectacular pilots along the Bering Sea Coast, served in the Territorial House and Senate as a Democrat, but the G.O.P. slogan "Had Enough?" caught up with him at the last election. In the legislative halls at Juneau the two men looked at bills from an aerial perspective.

While opposing a Soil Conservation Service enabling act, Senator Munz told his colleagues, "I've flown over a whole lot of Alaska and I've seen the country, and if there is any one thing we in Alaska have got plenty of and don't need to conserve, it's soil."

Alaska is close to its flying past. Only 25 years have gone by since Carl Ben Eielson, the first great bush pilot of the North, arrived in Fairbanks from North Dakota to teach school. Men still are flying in Alaska and the Canadian Arctic who gave Eskimo tribes their original look at a flying machine. C. H. (Punch) Dickins set a Fokker cabin monoplane down on the Mackenzie delta in 1929. "I don't believe it—wings no flap," said an old Eskimo crone. And Dickins swears he was told by a leader of the tribe: "It is big bird all right, but no meat on it."

Alaska now has 91,000 people. This seems a skimpy population, indeed in a land more than twice the size of Texas. Yet it represents a 48 per cent increase in the number of whites since 1940. Governor Gruening maintains that "without aviation, and particularly the individual bush aviator who will fly anywhere, at any time, there would be no real prospect of settling Alaska within our lifetime." Gruening is the only governer ever to visit every settlement, Indian and white, in the Territory, a feat he attributes to "the resourcefulness and skill of bush pilots." The governor's own son, Hunt, is a senior pilot for Alaska Coastal Air Lines.

Bush flying in the North got its real impetus from World War I. Men who had learned aviation in the American and Canadian armies bought flimsy crates stuck together with glue and baling wire, and flew them in the world's worst flying weather. The bush pilots pioneered routes which were to become major air operations of Pan American and Canadian Pacific. They demonstrated that the month's journey from Fairbanks to Nome by dog team could be reduced to seven hours, and that expensive though bush fares might be, they still were less than the cost of the food alone for 14 ravenous Malemutes.

Of course, the bush fliers took chances. They navigated, as one of them from Texas explained, "by guess and by gosh." They had no reliable maps, so they followed rivers and the tenuous thread of the Alaska Railroad. Noel Wien flew along the Yukon because a prospector said he could land on the wide sand bars. But the sand bars were 10 feet under water at flood stage. Wien came down on a tiny baseball diamond at Ruby. The landing shattered his propeller. The shaken passengers transferred to a stern-wheeled river boat. Wien gloried in the fact that he repaired the Fokker and arrived in Nome ahead of them. The next time they were not so timid.

On another occasion, with smoke from a forest fire billowing across the land, Wien clung to the railroad right of way as a guide. He was afraid to fly high for fear he would lose the track, and this vast realm of mountains and spruce solitudes was strange to him.

Once he nearly rammed a freight train, leaving the engine crew thinking it had seen an apparition.

In Fairbanks, Wien was asked what he did when he came to the 60-foot overhead bridge which crossed the railroad at Dead Man's Slough. He turned white. "Bridge?" he gasped. "Was there a bridge? I guess I must have flown under it. I know I never saw it!"

World War II has brought about the greatest advance in Alaskan bush flying. The Army is surrounding Fairbanks with "atomic airfields" which have 15,000-foot runways. In Anchorage alone 900 people work for the C.A.B. Man-and-wife weather stations stud the Territory and give some warning of the storms which drop the thermometer to 65° below in the Tanana Valley and drench the "panhandle" with 155 inches of rain a year.

The bush pilots are ubiquitous. They will hedgehop a homesteader across a narrow river full of slush ice, or they will fly a miner 700 miles to catch a boat ready to lift anchor for Seattle. If a trading post needs a generator or an Indian school must have smallpox vaccine, the bush pilot is on his way. In a prodigious domain with only a few roads and but one twisting railway, the flier represents comfort, food, health and even life itself.

No week passes in Alaska without a bush pilot completing some errand of mercy. It may be a radio from the Noatak Valley that gangrene is killing a trader caught on the trail at 50° below. The flier may see a homesteader frantically waving a blanket, and come down to find a woman in need of surgery. More than once the word *help*, formed of trimmed spruce saplings lying in the snow, has brought succor from the skies.

Bush pilots charge stiff fees for their services. With Alaska in the midst of a great defense boom, the second in less than a decade, many of them report incomes above $10,000. Numerous Alaskans have paid $150 to fly the 500 miles from Fairbanks to Point Barrow, northernmost settlement under the Stars and Stripes. But these tolls the general run of Alaskans do not resent. In the first place, everything is high in Alaska. Even before the war eggs were $1.25 a dozen, milk 28 cents a quart, haircuts at Fairbanks $1.50.

More fundamental than this, however, the people of Alaska realize the bush pilot has no sinecure. Risks are standard to his trade. Sometimes the risks are too great. Ben Eielson crashed in Siberia taking furs off the icebound American motor ship *Nanuk*. Earl Borland died with him. Les Cook came down in flames in the Yukon Territory. Merrill disappeared over the sea. Most bush pilots are fatalists. Few of them wear parachutes. They do not brood over comrades who will fly no more. But they are conscious of the hazards they run, and fees are assessed accordingly. On his fatal venture, the rangy Eielson was to have received $50,000 to get the *Nanuk*'s furs and passengers to the Alaskan mainland.

A prospector, grizzled and cantankerous, protested to a bush pilot over his $350 ferrying charge. The pilot was indignant, for the journey had been 230 miles through a pelting snowstorm. Now he had to fly another 230 miles back to base.

"Brother," said he, "you walk out of here and then decide what I'm worth."

Four months later, the miner, gaunt, emaciated, but cantankerous no longer, staggered into a trading post on the Yukon. Gunny sacks wrapped his frostbitten feet. He lost four toes in the mission hospital, then said he had decided what the bush pilot was worth.

"He's worth my whole dang' claim," the prospector continued. "He got me there in three hours. It took me six weeks of unmitigated frozen hell to walk out."

Bush pilots often compete for passengers as vociferously as Times Square bootblacks try to drum up a shine. When the miners come in off the boats at Nome or clamber down from the coaches of the streamlined AuRoRa at Fairbanks, bush pilots frequently hawk their wares. Some promise fast service, others more roomy planes, a few even offer cut rates. Occasionally a pilot will grubstake a prospector and get a share of his strike.

Fliers vie to serve a full-blooded Indian trapper known through the bush as "McTavish," who always runs a lush trap line. McTavish invariably fills a plane with a heavy pay load of pelts. He knows no English, and sometimes the pilot must bargain for him with the fur buyers. Many bush pilots understand the Indian lingo and the singsong jargon of the Eskimo tribes.

Fliers at Ladd Field, on the thinly timbered fringes of Fairbanks, noticed that one particular bush pilot was dominating the flights north of town. It took a long time to get onto the secret of his success. At a camp on the shores of a small lake, two girls were dedicating the late summer to sun-bathing. DDT evidently had taken care of the mosquitoes. The men being away all day at the diggings, the bathers resolved not to have the sun tan stripped by the marks of swimming suits. The girls paid no attention to the little red monoplane high in the sky, for they did not know of the powerful binoculars the pilot was passing around among his satisfied passengers.

Some Air Corps officers have been known to be offended by the nonchalance and the indifference to protocol of the average Alaskan bush pilot. The *"Mukluk* telegraph," which is Alaskan for redhot gossip, has it that Munz and Whaley, the bush pilot heroes of the Nome rescue, were permitted by the Army to take off only after many precious days had been lost. Residents of Nome claim all the marooned fliers could have been saved had the bush pilots been allowed to go into action immediately. And C. Dewey Anderson, a Nome member of the Territorial legislature, contends Munz actually was reprimanded by the Army for landing without field clearance when he returned with four survivors!

Munz wanted Sam Mogg, an Eskimo dog musher, to handle rescue work on the ground. Anderson charges that the Army sent its own dog teams, but forgot to take along food for the Huskies!

Charges of this sort are as thick around Nome as gulls and terns on the Bogoslof Islands. Yet between the average bush pilot and the rank-and-file Army aviator there is a genuine highball-drinking, address-swapping friendship. The feudin' and the fightin' begin only when the bush pilot confronts the top-level Air Corps brass.

If Alaska ever is crisscrossed with roads, the reign of the bush pilot may ebb. Today he is monarch of the North, and with only 2,827 miles of road in a land 586,400 square miles in area, many decades must pass—even if the most feverish highway construction program is begun—before bus and truck can reduce the plane in Alaska to an auxiliary role. The ratio of 116 times the number of planes per capita in Alaska as compared with the United States probably will continue. Perhaps the proportion may increase as Alaska's population expands and the far-flung reaches of the hinterland are settled.

On skis in winter, pontoons in summer and wheels in between, the bush pilot is to be Alaska's taxicab driver for at least a generation to come—and he knows it. Should the U.S. and the U.S.S.R. ever come to blows at the narrow gap of Bering Strait, the bush pilot will be more important than ever, for the North is his realm. Absorbed into the American Army Air Forces, he will be the kind of sky scout that Kit Carson and Jim Bridger were on land with the old blue-coated cavalry a century ago.

Bush pilots are fully aware of their talents and usefulness. One from the lower Yukon made an emergency landing deep in the bush. When he got ready to take off, the sticky slush of late spring would not allow the plane to rise. He tried for three days to fly without success. He ate the last of his sandwiches, finished the final package of cigarettes. Then he tied a rope to the switch, and got behind the plane and pushed.

The plane moved, but twice it nearly went aloft without the pilot. He desperately pulled the switch just in time. The third time the plane started he managed to scramble through the door on his belly before it took to the air.

"It sure gave me a funny feeling to see that ship start to leave the ground without me," he told his cronies when he eventually got back to his home hangar near Bristol Bay. "All of a sudden I realized what it must be like to be in the bush without an airplane. How'd they ever get along in Alaska before we went into business?"

# 19

# *A GERMAN JOURNALIST'S VIEW*

A FOREIGNER'S view of contemporary Alaska is presented by the German Hans Otto Meissner, journalist and big-game hunter, in his book, *Bezaubernde Wildnis* ("Enchanted Wilderness"). A more understanding appraisal of Alaska and its people has seldom been written. (The translation is by George Starosolsky.)

From · · ·

*Bezaubernde Wildnis* ("Enchanted Wilderness"), by Hans Otto Meissner

May I introduce Alaska, the forty-ninth state of the United States of America. It is seven times larger than the Federal Republic, but has only 250,000 inhabitants, of which more than one half live within the two biggest towns.

The rest of the huge country is nearly uninhabited.

In this enormous country I roamed, wandered, stalked, hunted, and won wonderful trophies. I made friends with white Americans, Aleuts, Eskimos, and Indians, and had unforgettable adventures. Finally, when I had to leave, I left my trunk in Alaska.

· · · · · · · · · · · · ·

The name *"Alaska"* itself sounds somehow cold and white and makes one think of a land of ice and snow. Also, we often hear that

Eskimos live there and that everybody who does not go around in
thick fur coats must freeze to death. In reality, it is only half that
bad; Alaska has approximately the same climate as East Prussia
or Scandinavia, has a really warm summer, and, afterward, four
to five months of a hard, honest winter. True, the temperature goes
down to 30 and 40 degrees below zero. Yet in July and August, the
temperature on the Yukon may rise to 40 degrees centigrade above
zero and this is a nearly equatorial temperature.

In addition, we must consider the diversity of this big country,
which reaches from the year-round ice-free southeast shores with its
relatively warm Japan current, to far beyond the Arctic Circle.
Accordingly, the climate in the various parts is different and so
is the vegetation. From densely moss-grown rain-conditioned forests
to treeless tundra, every variation is there. The highest mountain
peaks of America are there, the most beautiful prairies, the steep-
est coastlines. There are volcanoes, glaciers, mighty rivers, uncounted lakes; one can enjoy lovely countryside and be frightened
by terrible precipices. Hot springs invite bathing, landslides come
down with crashing noise, blooming water lilies glitter on thousands of dark ponds with no human eye ever looking at them.

There is a tremendous number of wild animals in Alaska that
do not have equals as to power and size in all the world. No grizzly
is more fierce than the Alaskan grizzly; none more powerful than
the Kodiak bear; nowhere does a moose carry stronger antlers.
White wild mountain sheep and silk-furred mountain goats enliven
the mountains, uncounted herds of caribou roam the tundra, lynx
and wolves live in the woods. Bisons pasture in the prairies, musk
oxen stand in the Arctic islands and polar bears inhabit the cold
shores. Sea otter and walrus splash in the bays, whales plow
through the seawaters, and two million fur seals live on the Pribilof Islands. And all these wild animals thrive and multiply. . . .
You can hardly imagine a country more beautiful, healthier, more
refreshing than Alaska. It has not yet been discovered by travel
agencies, hardly touched by human exploit, still is 99 percent as
it was created by God. And yet this enchanted wilderness is only
ten flying hours away from us. . . . However, less than one half
of the present-day residents were born in Alaska and only one

fourth can boast that their father or mother were. Since nearly everybody is a foreigner in one way or another, a dislike of foreigners is unknown. Most of the Alaskans have come here as foreigners and every foreigner can become an Alaskan very fast. This openheartedness manifests itself also in respect to people who do not intend to remain here. Every visitor is received with open arms not just because he brings in money but simply because he is here. After a few weeks, you belong here and have a great circle of friends. Only those who move on the next day, who stay in a hotel and have no time to talk to the Alaskans, are regarded as regular tourists. Since I stayed for four months and returned after every trip back to Anchorage where I had a room with friends, I was accepted into the community without any effort on my part. I took part in social events and nearly every evening I was the guest of a nice family. I was asked to lecture and was a member of several clubs. I was even offered jobs. If it were my wish and will, I would have been well off there. The press greeted me as a colleague, and even now I contribute to the *Anchorage Times* from Munich. Unfortunately, however, I cannot write to most of my friends in Alaska because I know only their first names or nicknames. This is the custom in Alaska; at introductions, the last name, position, or title are either not mentioned at all or are immediately forgotten. All call each other by their first names. If there were a difference in the English usage, as there is in the German, between "you" and "thou," they would address you by "thou."

Alaska has accomplished in the practical life a classless society, whose theoretical accomplishment is being aspired to by so many people. This was brought about first of all by the general wealth in which everyone participates directly or indirectly. There are in fact very few very rich people, and nobody who is really poor. The needy receive such substantial support that by our standards they are not needy any more. Skilled workers earn quite a lot, often more than the managing employees and high officials. On the other hand, the top earnings are greatly reduced by taxes. Under such circumstances, the striking financial differences between people are considerably eliminated, at least as far as the

outer appearance of their way of life is concerned. There is no
"society," no exclusive circles, and nobody who would want to be
distinguished.

All people wear good but practical clothing, nearly all families
live in their own houses, and no one is without a car. There are
no extra-luxurious establishments, everybody can afford to visit
any place and have a drink. In a country which is composed almost entirely of wilderness and where people are constantly on
the move, the outer appearance does not matter at all. Social forms
are limited to a minimum and are replaced by cordiality. The
servants make conversation with their employers and the employers with the servants. Because most of the women, unless they
have too many children, take a job, it is possible that the waitress
may be the wife of the district attorney or the bus driver the husband of a woman doctor and it is probable that the driver and the
waitress earn more money than their academically educated
spouses. Nobody has so far come to the crazy notion that certain
occupations are "finer" than the others.

For example, while I had dinner with the manager of the largest
bank, his oil-heating system was being repaired. The mechanic
and his helper simply stayed for dinner. This appeared quite
natural to our host, since they happened to there at that time. And
everybody was called by his first name.

Contrary to the rest of the United States, wealth is not being
shown off. It would be in bad taste to indulge in luxury; the notion of a "playboy" is quite unknown. Therefore there is no social
envy, since every provocation to it is absent.

Naturally, a country with so few inhabitants and such small
towns does not know mass congestion. Here everybody is treated
as a personality and enjoys the human warmth of those surrounding
him without his neighbor's curiosity bothering him too much. Since
nobody can disappear in the anonymity of the mass, everybody
must watch his "standing," it means that he must bear in mind
his reputation and good name. Lack of reliability or dubious behavior in business matters will be talked about and make the doer
unacceptable. Therefore everywhere in Alaska people act honestly
and correctly. Burglary, theft, and cheating are very rare crimes.

You don't see any policemen on the street and you do not lock your car.

... In no other country did I find dealing with government authorities so pleasant; the officials show a simply astonishing helpfulness. Nor are they overworked, because personal conversation is a part of every office visit. For the most part, official contact with an official leads to personal acquaintance. Since due to my hunting trips I had much to do with the game warden's office, I soon became friends with most of his employees. We ate together and visited each other.

"Cold" Alaska radiated human warmth and cordiality such as I never experienced in any other country. Whoever has lived there even for a short time will feel attracted to Alaska for the rest of his life.

I, too, fell in love with this country and can hardly wait to be there again.

# 20

# *EDNA FERBER HELPS*
# *THE CAUSE OF STATEHOOD*

In the early 1950's Edna Ferber became interested in the cause of Alaskan statehood. She visited Alaska several times, and her novel, *Ice Palace*, appeared in the early spring of 1958. The title refers to a large apartment house in an Alaskan city. The book had a markedly beneficial impact on the cause of Alaskan statehood. People who had not read serious prostatehood arguments did read this novel and were impressed through it by the justice of Alaska's quest for the full equality which admission to the Union would bring. Not a few wrote their senators and congressmen urging them to support the pending statehood legislation. Their pleas had a distinct effect on the votes in both House and Senate, which took place in the late spring and early summer of that year. Indeed, *Ice Palace* was referred to by one of the newspaper reviewers as the *Uncle Tom's Cabin* of the statehood struggle.

Edna Ferber laid the scene in a mythical city which she called Baranof, which, while it includes aspects of various Alaskan towns, has more of the characteristics of Fairbanks than of any other community. Her impressions of Alaskans and their way of life found sprightly expression in the opening paragraphs of the first chapter.

From · · ·

*Ice Palace,* by Edna Ferber

Every third woman you passed on Gold Street in Baranof was young, pretty, and pregnant. The men, too, were young, virile, and pregnant with purpose. Each, making his or her way along the bustling business street, seemed actually to bounce with youth and vitality. Only an occasional old sourdough, relic dating back to the gold-rush days of fifty years ago, wattled and wary as a turkey cock, weaving his precarious pedestrian way in and out of the frisky motor traffic, gave the humming town a piquant touch of anachronism.

An exhilarating street, Gold, though the stores and office buildings that lined it—one- or two-story cement or wooden structures—were commonplace and even shabby. The enlivening quality was inexplicable, but ardent Alaskans sometimes attributed it to the piercing quality of the Arctic light and the dryness of the atmosphere. Middle-aged tourists, weary after thousands of miles of travel over this seemingly boundless territory—whether by plane or by a combination of plane, train, ship and automobile—were puzzled and plaintive as they viewed the haphazard town of Baranof for the first time.

"Everybody walks as if they had springs in their shoes. Or maybe it's because you're all so young."

If the visitor's guide happened to be Ott Decker, Secretary of the Baranof Chamber of Commerce, he would reject this with the mysterious lightheartedness that seemed to suffuse most near-Arctic citizens.

"Young's got nothing to do with it. Around here you can live to be a hundred, easy, unless you're shot, or your plane cracks up on you, or a bear sees you first."

"Well, it's something. A kind of a crazy something. No offense. I just mean, what makes them bounce?"

"My opinion, it's the violet rays or the magnetic pole—we're not so far from the North Pole, you know, when it comes right down to geography—or it's the radiant northern, uh, isotopes or something."

"Now wait a minute. Just a minute. Radiant. I always understood you had winter about eight months in the year, and no sun to speak of."

"That's right. But you feel great. And summers! Say—summers! Like today. Daylight round the clock twenty-four hours. And you know what? You don't need sleep. You feel hopped up all the time. Take the Eskimos up there in Kotzebue and Oogruk and Barrow and around where it's really tough going. Always laughing their heads off. For what! They got nothing to laugh at. They just feel good. Everybody feels good. I don't know. It's a kind of a balloon feeling."

It was true that everything in Baranof seemed exaggerated. Edges sharper. Skies bluer. Mountains higher, snow deeper, temperature lower, daylight longer, sunlight briefer, depending on the season. The very air sometimes seemed more utterly still than anywhere else in the world, yet it pulsed almost palpably with life. When the wind blew it blew harder. Down in southeast Alaska—the region facetiously called the Banana Belt—the Taku screeched and whistled about your ears in season. In the remote north villages on the Bering Sea or the Arctic Ocean the polar blasts in February could strangle the breath in your throat and force it back into the reluctant lungs. Deceived by the dry air you could freeze your face and walk about, unknowing. Baranof wore parkas, fur-hooded, through the winter. This gave pedestrians the anonymity of dominoes at a masquerade. There was a favorite joke, often quoted. "Winters in Baranof, speak to anything that moves. If it's standing still, call the ambulance."

Off to school on the bitter black winter mornings the children were round bundles of wool and fur, their eyes peering out like those of small woodland creatures in a nest. Mothers, standing briefly in the doorway, would call, "Now remember, don't run! Even if you're late—don't run." They knew the danger of the quick intake of breath like icy knives into the warm scarlet lung tissue.

Across the winter sky swept the northern lights, eerie dazzling curtains of swaying green and blue and orange. Then, miraculously, June came, it was summer, it was daylight round the clock. The thermometer that had registered sixty below zero in January now might show ninety above. Yet there was Baranof and much more of Alaska besides, dry and cool, energetic and somewhat crazily high-keyed in an agreeable way under the constant compulsion of the weird Arctic sun. Up, up far north in Barrow on the shore of the frozen Arctic Ocean the United States flag whipped aloft in the wind for eighty days and eighty nights, for there was during that period no sunset hour in which to lower it. If you happened to be soaring in a comfortably cosy plane above Bering's ice-locked coast, nibbling a ham sandwich and sipping hot strong coffee, you could see just over there, beyond the two island dots that were the Big Diomede and the Little Diomede, the black strangely menacing line that was the coast of Siberia.

But here in mid-Alaska a kind of carefree mood took hold. Baranof stayed out of doors every possible minute. You played baseball at midnight. Your wife tended her garden at eleven P.M. Your children frisked like leprechauns far into the night. Perhaps you slept from midnight through the hour or two of rosy twilight until, like a blindingly dazzling scimitar thrust through a scarlet velvet curtain, the sun rose again at one or two o'clock in the morning. This brief interlude of repose seemed, magically, to suffice, both for the sun and you.

If you were young and in love you might stroll hand in hand down to the water's edge to delight romantically in the glorious color above and the pastel reflection below. Mount McKinley, king of all the peaks on the North American continent, white-crowned in the summer, white-robed in the winter, looked in this midsummer midnight light like the gods' Valhalla—or a gigantic scoop of raspberry and orange sherbet. Baranof citizens adjusted to this summer-winter variant of one hundred and fifty degrees as nonchalantly as they digested the local moose steaks in January or the monster home-grown strawberries in August.

# 21

## ALASKA'S ESKIMO PEOPLE

THE theme of hospitality is at the heart of many writings
about Alaska's Eskimos. Vilhjalmur Stefansson, one of the world's
foremost authorities on the peoples of the Arctic, when testifying
before a Senate committee on February 24, 1948, delivered a
memorable encomium on the Eskimo:

> I have heard of the merits of the Golden Rule from my Sunday-
> school days up, but I have never seen it practiced as consistently
> as it is by the uncivilized Eskimos.

Stefansson's remarks were reiterated by another traveler, First
Lt. David H. Jarvis, who commanded a relief expedition to Alaska.

> The hospitality of these people I have never seen equaled
> elsewhere. It is never grudging; it is thrust upon you. The best
> they have and the best place in the house are at your disposal.
> It is so universal that it comes as a matter of course, and as a
> result does not seem to be properly recognized or appreciated.
> Often it is embarrassing, for the natives are so insistent and
> generous that it is hard to refuse to accept their offers and go
> about your business in your own way. Never in all our journey
> did we pass a house where the people did not extend a cordial
> welcome and urge us to go in; and hardly a hut that we did go
> into, but the place was cleared out for us and our belongings.
> What this means to a tired, cold, and hungry traveler cannot be
> fully appreciated save by those who have experienced it, and
> my former good impressions of the Alaskan Eskimo were but

intensified by this winter's journey. All that we ever gave in return for such hospitality, and all that was expected, was a cup of tea and a cracker to the inmates of the house after we had finished our meal.

In recent times the Eskimos have found a spokeswoman in Sally Carrighar, who once said of them: "They're so balanced. They've never allowed themselves to be corrupted. Many of our wrongs would be righted if we lived more intuitively, as they do."

Miss Carrighar spent three years in Alaska (1948–1951), writing most of her book, *Icebound Summer*, in the back room of a trader's warehouse at Unalakleet. The selection which follows is a chapter from her second book, *Moonlight at Midday*.

# From · · ·
## *Moonlight at Midday,* by Sally Carrighar

### THE PROUD ESKIMO IGLOO-WIFE

The familiar cartoons in which Stone-Age men drag their women around by the hair might be revised if the artists would visit Alaska. Except for a few routine customs the Eskimo women are truly emancipated. In proportion to numbers more of them vote than white women do; they have clubs; they hold auctions to buy new clocks for their churches, to get funds to help elderly people in need, and such purposes. They think for themselves, and all these abilities are not new. Eskimos are well out of the Stone Age by now, but not long out. They were still in it when "Sinuk Mary, the Reindeer Queen," was born. She died at Unalakleet in 1949, while I was there.

Sixty years earlier, about 1890, the Eskimos of Alaska were facing starvation. The hunger was largely due to the fact that the whaling ships, which came into the Northern waters each summer, had depleted the whales. In Siberia, less than a hundred miles away, reindeer had been domesticated and were being herded successfully, almost like cattle, by Eskimos. In Alaska the climate and forage were practically the same, and therefore the officers of our revenue cutter, the *Corwin*, suggested that we should import some of those deer and teach our Eskimos how to herd them. Urged by a missionary, Dr. Sheldon Jackson, our federal Bureau of Education set up the project.

In order to buy the reindeer it was necessary to have an interpreter. At Sinuk, a village just north of the present city of Nome, was a young Eskimo woman, Mary Ana-chah-look, who knew the Siberian dialect. Perhaps her family had come from Siberia. She boarded the cutter and went to Siberia with the officers, and the deal was arranged. When the ship returned to Alaska she was asked whether she would rather be paid in money or with a few deer. She chose the deer.

Her ability with the animals was uncanny; none of the other herders was so successful. Increasing numbers of deer were brought in, some from Europe too, and Siberian and Lapp herders were employed to teach the Alaskan Eskimos. The Siberians went back home before long, and the Laplanders did only middling well in this alien land; many reindeer ran off and joined the wild caribou herds, and wolves brought down others. Commercial interests took over the deer, with the intention of selling reindeer meat in the States. But that had not been the purpose of bringing the deer to Alaska: they were to furnish the Eskimos with a stable food supply, and the government therefore took back the herds. Some of the deer still remain and still are a disappointment and subject of controversy.

Meanwhile, as the other herds waxed and waned, Mary's prospered. I have seen a picture of Mary; she had the straightforward glance of a clear thinker and doer. She set about breeding and herding her reindeer, and they multiplied until at one time, according to estimate, she had 85,000 of these Northern cattle. She could not manage so many personally and she was not able to find assistants who had her ability. Dividing her animals, sending small herds farther away to avoid exhausting the forage, she lost many. Her wealth declined. At the time she died she had less than 1,000 deer.

Meanwhile she led a respected and useful life. She and her husband, Charlie Ana-chah-look, were childless, but they adopted twenty-two children. One of them, Eunice, was the daughter of a girl that Mary had adopted a generation earlier. Eunice is now married to Frank Ryan, the postmaster at Unalakleet. When I came, Sinuk Mary, helpless in her last illness, lived with the Ryans. In what seemed a typical selfless gesture of an Eskimo woman, Frank's mother persuaded the family to move Sinuk Mary into her cabin. "You are young," she said, "but I am old, and so it is proper that I have the burden."

Sinuk Mary died and was buried during a blizzard. The grave was hewed out with picks in the solidly frozen ground, and the coffin was made by the Dorcas Society, a volunteer group of men who take responsibility for the funerals. In the blowing snow Mary's coffin was pushed on a sled to the cemetery a mile away, with the Eskimos following in their parkis and bright parki covers. Due to three weeks of bad weather we were cut off from the rest of the world at that time. When communications again were restored, most newspapers in the States carried the story that Sinuk Mary, the Reindeer Queen, had died.

There have been other famous Eskimo women. Some have been shamans, or witch doctors, able to foretell the future, so it was believed, and work magic and cure sick people. It is said of a "medicine woman" still living in the mountains east of Kotzebue that in her younger days she performed operations on eyes and restored sight to more than a few blind persons. She is supposed to have used a jade knife.

If the Eskimos had a matriarchal society, this high status accorded their women would not seem unusual. But they don't have; the husband is the accepted head of the family. He is not the head in any overpowering degree, however. In most ways the marriages seem like partnerships, and that state of affairs may be due to the attitude that the Eskimo women have in regard to work.

I first noticed it in Matilda, the eleven-year-old daughter of Charlie Traeger and Eula. Matilda loved to work. Every day she would press her own clothes and even the slacks of her small brother, Clairon. She could cook, and she helped her mother in many other ways. Yet she never seemed like a little busybody —it was just that the work was enjoyable. She reminded me of what Margaret Mozee, the wife of the U.S. marshal, had told me in Nome. An Eskimo girl was scrubbing her stairs one day, and she looked down with a flashing smile and said, "Isn't this *fun*, Mrs. Mozee!"

Matilda's father, born in Ohio, had had a good education before he came to Alaska during the gold rush. Her mother had more pride, of race and station, than any other Eskimo woman that I have met. In Matilda the best of both strains were combined. She was a sensitive little aristocrat. In school, when marching lines passed, some of the smaller girls would reach out and touch Matilda's coat. In the second grade, when the teacher asked the pupils how many knew their birthdays, few could tell their own but they all knew Matilda's—March 11.

She often came in to see me late in the afternoon, and it was our custom that one day she would tell me a story and the next day I would tell one. Hers included many incongruous details from the two cultures she had in her life, and from things she had read. Her father had sent away, for example, for books of fairy tales.

One story, especially, showed the ideal that she had absorbed from her mother and the Eskimo women who were their neighbors. As Matilda told it, a prince came riding into the village on his horse. Two girls competed for his love, and most of the story concerned the girl he chose and their life after he took her away to his kingdom. He spent every day out of doors, riding around with other princes, and while he was gone his bride "stayed in the palace and made him the most beautiful parkis and *mukluks*." But on some days "she went out on the tundra and hunted for wild celery and *masu* roots, and she picked barrels and barrels of blueberries for the prince, and she cut up and dried his fish and his seal and whale meat just right." Even though he was gone from home almost all the time, "she did not mind—because she was doing her work."

As I was hearing this little tale I was thinking that if it were told by a child in the States, the princess probably would have been sitting all day on a velvet cushion, or playing a harp, or embroidering on silk with gold thread and pearls. At least, that would have been my imagining when I was small. But Matilda's princess not only was doing productive labor; there was something in the child's telling that made the work sound like a privilege. It was evident that the princess was proud to be picking those berries and drying those fish. "She was doing her work." As Matilda said it, "work" sounded as if it were an honor and a fulfillment.

Soon after Matilda had told her story, I was in one of the Eskimo cabins one afternoon and I picked up, to examine with admiration, a girl's parki made of ground-squirrel skins. How many skins were there in it, I asked the girl's mother, who of course made the parki. Eighty, she said. The skins were sewn together with the most minute, even stitches, sinew being the thread. I knew by then that preparing the sinew was in itself a task. By sinew the Eskimos mean the shredded muscle fibres from along the spine or legs of a reindeer or caribou, or along the spine of a seal. After the muscles are pulled from the carcass, they are hung up to dry, and in this process they become tangled and bunched. The women patiently separate them into fine, silklike strands, and they make their sewing thread by winding together two of these with a skillful rolling motion, one palm down across the other.

The squirrels had had to be caught, in the first place—in the spring, out in the "squirrel camps" to which all the families go with the most contagious joy as soon as the snow melts from the hillsides and the squirrels wake up from their hibernation. The squirrels are taken with snares at the holes of their dens, and even small children help. But the animals have to be skinned and the hides prepared, and those are a woman's tasks. The parki I held was trimmed around hood, wrists, and hem with wolverine fur, and therefore the mother had skinned out a wolverine too and had tanned the pelt. Every member in that large family had one of these parkis, and I said of the one in my hands, "A lot of effort went into this."

"Not too much," said the Eskimo housewife. "Anyway, that's my work."

My work: her tone was the same as Matilda's, the same that a serious painter would use when he spoke of his pictures, or a composer his music. Work: there is no way to convey in print the self-respect, the head-high pride.

I thought at the start that the Eskimo women led easy lives—

they could relax so completely and quickly. Whenever they came
to see me, they dropped immediately into a mood of contented
leisure. So comfortably they would sit in my room, their hands
never restless, capable hands but quiet in the wide laps, hardly a
muscle in all their bodies that was not taking a chance to rest.
Though their faces were animated, their bright talk and merry
eyes seemed the flowering of a sense of peace.

As the winter wore on and I spent more and more time in their
cabins, they continued to work when I was there, as they did
with their other neighbors, and I was impressed with the sheer
volume of their accomplishments.

An Eskimo woman makes all of her family's outside clothing
and footwear. Since the parkis are worn hair side in, with cloth
covers, the covers must also be made. The housewife does not
have a pattern. Either she measures her subject with her eye or
she measures, the length of an arm perhaps, with the repeated
span of her hand. Then she lays out her cloth and, working very
fast, cuts it by guess, we would say, including the elaborately
fitted hood. The garment is not simple. It has a ruffle around the
bottom, a double pocket across the front, the hood, which can
turn with the head, and intricate bands of trimming. The man's
cover is made of drill; the women's and girls' are usually of
percale or Indianhead, though the trader's wife, who was conscious of her prestige, had a wine-colored velveteen parki cover
embroidered with sequins. Most people have several. I know one
man who has five. And the *igloo*-wife makes them all, besides the
fur parkis beneath.

Boots are a famous product of Eskimo women's skill, and some
women make them to sell. Tourists buy them readily. White people, and Eskimos when they talk to us, call them *mukluks*. That
is a Russian word, introduced at the time the Russians had trading
posts in Alaska. The Eskimo word for boot, differing somewhat
according to tribe, is pronounced something like *kommick*. The
plural is *kommahk*.

In one version, Lapp boots, the soles as well as the legs are of
fur. I tried a pair but gave up; they slip so much on the snow
that half the time I was coasting—and not on my feet. The soles

of the typical Eskimo boots are of sealskin, the hair having been removed. The uppers are fur of seals, reindeer fawn, or caribou legs. Removing the hair from sealskin for the soles is done by rotting it off with warm oil. If the skin is to be bleached, it is soaked for three days in fresh snow water, frequently being wrung out. "If our men will help with the wringing, we appreciate that," said one Eskimo housewife. Then the skin is stretched on a rack and hung out of doors to freeze and thaw, after which it is scraped, and finally it is put back on the rack to bleach in the winter weather. In Alaska extreme cold is considered a good bleaching agent for anything, sealskin to sheets. Preparing the sealskin is thus a laborious process, but the skin at the end is almost as fine as white parchment.

The soles of the boots are cut large enough so the edges can bend up around the foot, and the edges are finely crimped where they will be sewed to the uppers. The crimping was formerly always done with the teeth, wherefore many old women have worn their teeth to the gums. Most of the younger women are using pliers. In making the boots, the small measurements are computed by the joints of a woman's thumb, and the fur for the uppers is cut, as the women do with all fur, by laying it hair-side down and slicing just through the skin with an *ulu*. Most *mukluks* are about eight inches high, topped with trimming composed of fine mosaics of different-colored fur, or bands of the skin of wolf fish, or beading on felt, beads having come in with the Russians and felt with the Laplanders. The Siberian Eskimos do embroidery, but this art has never caught on with Alaskan Eskimos. As a finish the *mukluks* may have draw-strings of wool ending in bright yarn tassels. The fanciest *mukluks* often are seen on young men, made by devoted brides or fond mothers.

During the summer a woman will gather quantities of fine grass and dry it for pads in the *mukluks*. These pads are not only warm; they absorb the perspiration from a man's feet when he is hunting out on the sea ice. Moist feet freeze most quickly, and frosted feet probably are the North's greatest hazard. Only last winter a trapper was found dead on his trail, where he had lain down and crossed his hands on his chest, probably because frozen feet would not carry him the two last miles to his cabin. Sometimes when an Eskimo hunter knows that he will be out on the ice for many hours, he takes extra pads of grass to replace those in his boots.

In addition to parkis, parki covers, and boots, most *igloo*-wives knit the mittens and gloves and sometimes the sweaters their families wear. They also knit these to sell, and their skill baffled me. One could say to them, "I'd like a sweater with a dog team" —or man in his kayak, or a bear, seal, beaver, anything that they know—"in a different color across the front and back," and the woman picks up her needles and starts to knit with no design, nothing to follow. When she has finished the sweater, the picture in wool will be the right size, perfectly centered, and often with some attractive extra detail, like a bear's tracks behind him.

Tradition rigidly regulates the separate duties of men and women. In the government boarding school to which native high-school children are sometimes sent, it was thought logically that tanning would be a good trade to teach Eskimo boys. They were not willing to learn because, they said, "tanning is women's work."

In the securing of food, however, the work of the men and women is complementary. A woman will gather the berries and herbs; she *may* hunt with her husband, though rarely if ever out on the sea ice; she *may* have a trapline, though she seldom does; she probably does do a share of the fishing; and assuredly she will butcher the meat that her husband kills, short of walrus and whales. In even the case of those monstrously large animals, occasionally she will help. If the seal killed on the ice is one of the bearded species, up to ten feet long, a man usually finds it necessary to cut it up partly, in order to get it home. In any event, he has probably walked several miles over hummocky ice, at perhaps 30° below zero or colder; he has dragged home possibly three hundred pounds of meat, and he arrives much too tired to carve up and hang the seal. Therefore the wife takes over.

Sometimes the women will work at this job in pairs—a mother and daughter, or sisters, or friends. The one helping will be rewarded with part of the meat.

First they sharpen their *ulus*.

If the skin will be wanted all in one piece, for a poke to hold oil or a float to be used in whale-hunting, the skin is deftly slipped off the animal over its head. Otherwise the seal is laid on its back and a median slit is made from its chin to tail. The blubber adheres to the skin, and this layer is spread out in a sheet at the sides of the animal. The viscera are removed and, while the rest of the carving goes on, some elderly woman (the older ones frequently offer to do tasks like this) cleans the intestines. She does this by pouring water into the upper end and working it down, again and again repeating the process until the casing is sanitary, as it would be for our sausage.

The intestines of seals formerly had picturesque use. Before canned milk was brought to the North, it was a crucial time when a child was being weaned and could hardly digest the heavy meat diet of older Eskimos. Sometimes a mother would chew the meat for her child, her saliva thereby starting the digestive process, as some birds and perhaps wolves do for their young. She also would make a broth of fish or meat, fill a short length of cleaned intestine with it, and hang it around her neck to keep it warm for the child's next feeding: the Eskimos' baby bottle.

The rest of the seal's carcass is cut up in pieces, much as a butcher would do with our meat. At the end there is a very dexterous separating of blubber from skin with the *ulu*.

On one of my earliest days at Unalakleet I watched an elderly woman, Mrs. Shafter, flensing the excess fat from a white-whale stomach. The stomach, bright red, was perhaps five feet long. It was hung from an overhead pole, and Mrs. Shafter had put a stovepipe into the upper opening to hold it in shape. With her *ulu* she was flecking off any tissues that stuck to the membrane, and her skill was so interesting to watch that I wished I could try what she was doing. I asked what the stomach was used for, and she said that when it was dry, slabs of the white-whale skin would be stored in it. The skin, like all whale skin, is called *muktuk*. It is eaten, and many civilized people like it.

When we think of carving a seal, whale, or caribou, our minds don't go far beyond the picture of slicing meat. But this is the way one of the older generation of Eskimos uses a caribou: meat for food; hide for parki, trousers, or mattress; leg skins for *muk-luks;* head for soup and butter; sinew for thread; leg bones and meat for stew; bone marrow for butter; hoofs and bones boiled to eat as soup, or with lye for soap, or glue, or as a source of grease; eyes for pudding; fat from viscera for food; stomach eaten, including contents; intestines washed and dried for storage of food, or split and sewn into raincoats and windows; heart, liver, lungs, and kidneys eaten on the spot.

Up on the farthest-north coast, where the really enormous whales are secured, and also walrus, each of which may provide more than a ton of meat, the problem of keeping these vast supplies would be complicated if it were not for the fact that in many locations along the shore there are ice caves. The meat stored in those caves quickly freezes and keeps for a year or more. Thus, after a season when several whales are caught, a village looks forward to many months of security.

As a special treat when the whale meat is fresh, some is covered with blubber and allowed to sour behind the stove for a week or so. The resulting strong flavor is much enjoyed.

Incidentally, the Eskimos are very sensitive about the fact that most of their white neighbors do not like native foods. I think that the Eskimos could have taken this difference in taste philosophically, as they have taken the difference in dress, if so many white people had not expressed frankly their feelings of queasiness: "How can you eat that *revolting* blubber?" The Eskimos in Alaska are quite well informed about the way the Russians treat their kinsmen on the other side of the Bering Sea, and they dislike many things that the communists do; but our Eskimos say rather wistfully, "The Russians do eat our kind of food."

One time Colonel M. R. Marston, who formerly commanded the Eskimo Scout Battalion of the Alaska National Guard, asked if I'd like to meet with some of these men who are guarding our most remote shores. For this gathering, which would include the wives, Colonel Marston had provided a large slab of raw *muktuk,* the black skin of one of the giant whales, and he said to me, "If you go, you must promise to eat the *muktuk* and promise to keep it down. If you refused their delicacy, my Eskimo friends would be hurt."

By then I had tried beaver, seal, arctic hare, reindeer, owl, ptarmigan, and the skin of the white beluga whale, and the only three that I liked, the only three that my not very robust stomach could even hold on to, were the hare, reindeer, and ptarmigan. It was therefore a precarious promise I made, but Colonel Marston accepted it, and we set out for the Eskimo home where the meeting was held.

The Eskimos feel at ease with the Colonel, and since I was sponsored by him, they accepted me, even though I was strange to that particular group. I was a little tense, thinking about the *muktuk* to come, but I enjoyed the evening.

When the talking was over, several plates were brought in with neatly cut one-inch squares of black rubbery-looking meat with about an equal amount of what appeared to be suet adhering. I took one of the squares, chewed it, swallowed it—and quickly reached for another. And then another, and another. When all the Eskimos were through, I was still eating *muktuk*. They were much pleased, of course. I actually had enjoyed the meat, which tasted rather like fine-grained beef. The blubber in that case was more like gristle than grease, and it did take some chewing. The *muktuk* probably came from one of the baleen whales, which nourish their mammoth bodies on plankton, the most minute plants and animals of the sea. The whales that eat fish, I found later, have skin and flesh that taste fishy, and I cannot eat them.

Among Eskimos, cooking is almost never a very elaborate process. Some of the women at Unalakleet baked bread (delicious), and they made pies and cakes too, but not often. To prepare a meal usually meant little more than putting some meat on the stove to boil—perhaps not even that. The meat, boiled or raw, may be placed on a single dish and the family gather around and dip into it. The smoked salmon strips never are cooked. Many a white Alaskan carries a strip in his parki pocket, from which he takes a bite or two any time he feels hungry, and Eskimo children always do. Salmon strips are known as Eskimo candy.

Cooking and dish-washing are therefore no burden for most

Eskimo housewives. But one dish does take time: their famous "ice cream." The recipe can be found in a little cook book prepared by the schoolchildren of Shishmaref, who allow it to be sold for the benefit of the Alaska Crippled Children's Association. Along with some rather startling recipes, such as that for boiled bears' feet, is this for the "ice cream":

> *Grate reindeer tallow into small pieces. Add seal oil slowly while beating with hand. After some seal oil has been used, then add a little water while whipping. Continue adding seal oil and water until white and fluffy. Any berries can be added to it.*

Due to the heat of the beating hand, the tallow does become white and fluffy, and when a quantity of wild berries are added, the "ice cream" at least looks like ours. Sometimes in winter it is put outside to freeze, but in summer is eaten warm. Any white newcomer is a *cheechako* (tenderfoot) until he has tried it.

Many Eskimos keep their homes simple—by preference, it seems. When they don't, they feel smothered. The white husband of one native woman I know allowed her to send to the mail-order companies for an overstuffed living-room set, tables, lamps, extra chairs: what would be the complete furnishings of a civilized house. When they came and had been installed, she pushed everything back against the walls "so there would be some space." The family of an Eskimo CAA operator, who were given furnished government housing, put most of the furniture in their storage locker. They did not want the clutter.

The average Eskimo woman therefore seldom has knickknacks to dust or carpets to sweep, few lamps, draperies, coffee or end tables, pictures, books, fine cooking utensils that add up to housekeeping as most Stateside women know it. Considering also that her meals are no burden, she largely escapes a routine, and that is the way she wants it. The production of something new is the kind of work that lifts the morale of an Eskimo *igloo*-wife. She would rather be making clothes than mending them, rather pick berries than cook them, rather bleach sealskins for *mukluks* than scrub a floor. When these women are doing a washing, they don't speak of "my work" with the same bright voices as when they are helping to fill the caches with winter food.

It seems to me they have hold here of something basic to human happiness: the need not to be bored. There are signs that life for the civilized woman, too, tends in the same direction. Modern interiors are less crowded, family meals are becoming more simple. We still make a fetish of cleanliness, beyond what is needed aesthetically or for health, but if we can cultivate a little indifference, all our household machinery will free women from grinding monotony.

In deciding what we shall do with that leisure, again there are hints from the Eskimo *igloo*-wife. For she uses her mind, as well as her hands, creatively.

An eight-year-old boy told me: "Last year we find a dead crane in the marsh. When my mamma cut open its stomach, she see many seeds, not the kind here. She plant them, because she want us to know what kind of weeds grow in the white-man's country."

"Did they grow?"

"Yes, but we did not know the names of the weeds."

I asked him to describe them, and one sounded like clover, a different kind from the arctic plant.

"Not clover, my mamma said, because no bees come to it." He added hopefully, "Maybe next year we find another crane and you will tell us the names."

"If I know them."

He looked at me with surprise.

"You will know them. Because they are white-man's weeds."

But would I? I was only a naturalist, not an Eskimo mother.

Even the five-year-olds had an amazing knowledge of nature. A group of small children were with me one day on the bank of the slough behind town, watching a flock of terns diving into the water. I asked, "What are they diving for?"

"Needlefish," said one of the little girls. "Have points sticking out of their backs. The papa fish make the nest in a ditch, away from the sea. The mamma come there and all she do, she lay eggs. Then she go away. The papa bring food to his baby fish, he take them out for a swim, he teach them everything." Sticklebacks, of course, whose habits are exactly as the child had described them. How did she have all that information, which I had acquired in biological laboratories?

"I see them. My mamma show them to me."

In other ways too the women's minds strike new paths—in courtesy, for example. A public-health nurse arrived, one who would be staying at Unalakleet. On her first Sunday afternoon some of the Eskimos came to call. Mrs. Oliver Anawrok greeted her:

"We would not want to have to ask your help before we had welcomed you to our village."

The women, as well as the men, were trying to think out the problems that arise in adjusting their culture to ours. Mrs. Miles Gounangn, daughter of Nashoalook, the last head man of the village, said this:

"Eskimos always used to be generous, always giving, always helping. When a man catch a seal, his wife cook a big meal, and they send the children to every family, say, 'Kah-kheim! Come! Come and eat!' Now—no! We do not share very much now. That is because of money. We always owe to the store. We know debts are not right, and if we give our seals to our neighbors, we have to buy food and our debts will get bigger. When we cook a meal now, we call our children inside and we eat alone."

But it still is true that all who need it are given help.

I had heard before I went to Alaska that there have been few societies in which a woman has had as much independence as among Eskimos. And from the beginning I enjoyed seeing these husbands and wives together, talking and seeming so unrestrainedly to be sharing anything that was in their minds. Few women had even a trace of coyness. They often were shy with outsiders; some who were far from young appeared shy in the trading post. But with their own men their manner could be summed up by saying that they were just natural—feminine, always concerned to look pretty at every age, up to the oldest, and yet with a dignity that was akin to the men's.

All that is true, although from our standpoint the traditional life of an Eskimo woman has been a strange mixture of freedom and subservience. Not too long ago a husband might offer his wife to a visiting stranger—merely a gesture of hospitality, and in some cases a wife could refuse. And in the old culture a wife did not eat until after her husband was served; a very old woman in Nome always walked a few steps behind her husband when they came downtown together; and I have heard that some women on St. Lawrence Island do not wear gloves—they pull their hands up into their parki sleeves to keep them warm, because "gloves are a luxury reserved for men."

Formerly—less today—Eskimo women assumed an inferior position in these outward ways. And yet one could become a Reindeer Queen, not because she had blond hair but because she had built up a herd of eighty-five thousand deer. These women do not, as Francis Fergusson phrases it, "define their actions and their beings only with reference to their men."

The Eskimo men don't admire incompetence in a woman. They assume that their wives and daughters will want to do most of the things that men do, such as to shoot well. Many Eskimo women have their own rifles. They drive dog teams. I have seen little girls of ten and twelve driving in sled-dog races, although Northern dogs, most of which have some wolf blood, often are dangerous. When outboard motors came into the country, women as well as men learned to repair them. A woman can set a net and bring in a boatload of fish, and now when the summer freighters arrive, the Eskimo wives sometimes do more of the longshoring than husbands do, and no one thinks they have sacrificed their femininity because they have strong arms and backs. The lovely Matilda, who has recently finished high school, said a few months ago, "Sometimes I think the greatest happiness is the knowledge that one has done something well."

We hear often of vicious circles. There are benign circles too. Because an Eskimo wife has so many valuable skills, her husband treats her in most ways as an intelligent human being. Thus encouraged, she has self-respect and the wish to develop more skills. Wherefore her husband treats her as an intelligent human being. . . .

When the weather is too bad for hunting, the men spend most

of their days together, usually in the trading post. In the post at Unalakleet a stairway rose from the store to the living quarters above. Although I could not see the men, I could hear them. They often were silent, but occasionally they would laugh. Eskimos' laughter grows out of small, immediate happenings—they see the humor in a situation and chuckle. I did hear that, but not once in a year the particular laughing tone which, in many men elsewhere, means that the subject is women.

# 22

## *ALASKAN SCENERY*

CONCLUDING his article on "General Geography" in Volume II of the report of the Harriman Alaska Expedition of 1899, Henry Gannett, chief geographer of the United States Geological Survey, wrote:

There is one other asset of the Territory not yet enumerated—imponderable and difficult to appraise, yet one of the chief assets of Alaska, if not the greatest. This is the scenery. There are glaciers, mountains, and fiords elsewhere, but nowhere else on earth is there such abundance and magnificence of mountain, fiord, and glacier scenery. For thousands of miles the coast is a continuous panorama. For the one Yosemite of California Alaska has hundreds. The mountains and glaciers of the Cascade Range are duplicated and a thousand-fold exceeded in Alaska. The Alaska coast is to become the show-place of the earth, and pilgrims, not only from the United States, but from far beyond the seas, will throng in endless procession to see it. Its grandeur is more valuable than the gold or the fish or the timber, for it will never be exhausted. This value, measured by direct returns in money received from tourists, will be enormous; measured by health and pleasure, it will be incalculable.

There is one word of advice and caution to be given those intending to visit Alaska for pleasure, for sightseeing. If you are old, go by all means; but if you are young, stay away until you grow older. The scenery of Alaska is so much grander than anything else of the kind in the world that, once beheld, all other scenery becomes flat and insipid. It is not well to dull one's capacity for such enjoyment by seeing the finest first.

Henry Villard, president of the Northern Pacific Railroad, wrote in *A Journey to Alaska,* published in 1899:

> It may be said without exaggeration that no other part of the earth known to man surpasses Alaska in imposing and beautiful scenery. The most traveled of those who behold the extent and variety of its scenic magnificence and whose souls are open to such appeals of nature will readily admit that they have never seen the like of it and that nothing they ever saw impressed them so deeply.

John Muir (1838–1914), the naturalist and explorer, made the first of several journeys to Alaska in 1879. He was enchanted with the region, as can be seen in the following description of the Alexander Archipelago.

From · · ·

*Travels in Alaska,* by John Muir

ALEXANDER ARCHIPELAGO

To the lover of pure wildness Alaska is one of the most wonderful countries in the world. No excursion that I know of may be made into any other American wilderness where so marvelous an abundance of noble, newborn scenery is so charmingly brought to view as on the trip through the Alexander Archipelago to Fort Wrangell and Sitka. Gazing from the deck of the steamer, one is borne smoothly over calm blue waters, through the midst of countless forest-clad islands. The ordinary discomforts of a sea voyage are not felt, for nearly all the whole long way is on inland waters that are about as waveless as rivers and lakes. So numerous are the islands that they seem to have been sown broadcast; long tapering vistas between the largest of them open in every direction.

Day after day in the fine weather we enjoyed, we seemed to float in true fairyland, each succeeding view seeming more and

more beautiful, the one we chanced to have before us the most
surprisingly beautiful of all. Never before this had I been em-
bosomed in scenery so hopelessly beyond description. To sketch
picturesque bits, definitely bounded, is comparatively easy—a
lake in the woods, a glacier meadow, or a cascade in its dell; or
even a grand master view of mountains beheld from some commanding outlook after climbing from height to height above the
forests. These may be attempted, and more or less telling pictures
made of them; but in these coast landscapes there is such indefinite,
on-leading expansiveness, such a multitude of features without
apparent redundance, their lines graduating delicately into one
another in endless succession, while the whole is so fine, so tender,
so ethereal, that all pen-work seems hopelessly unavailing. Tracing
shining ways through fiord and sound, past forests and water-
falls, islands and mountains and far azure headlands, it seems as
if surely we must at length reach the very paradise of the poets,
the abode of the blessed.

Some idea of the wealth of this scenery may be gained from the
fact that the coast-line of Alaska is about twenty-six thousand miles
long, more than twice as long as all the rest of the United States.
The islands of the Alexander Archipelago, with the straits, channels, canals, sounds, passages, and fiords, form an intricate web
of land and water embroidery sixty or seventy miles wide, fringing
the lofty icy chain of coast mountains from Puget Sound to Cook
Inlet; and, with infinite variety, the general pattern is harmonious
throughout its whole extent of nearly a thousand miles. Here you
glide into a narrow channel hemmed in by mountain walls, forested
down to the water's edge, where there is no distant view, and your
attention is concentrated on the objects close about you—the
crowded spires of the spruces and hemlocks rising higher and
higher on the steep green slopes; stripes of paler green where
winter avalanches have cleared away the trees, allowing grasses
and willows to spring up; zigzags of cascades appearing and disap-
pearing among the bushes and trees; short, steep glens with brawl-
ing streams hidden beneath alder and dogwood, seen only where
they emerge on the brown algæ of the shore; and retreating hollows,
with lingering snow-banks marking the fountains of ancient gla-

ciers. The steamer is often so near the shore that you may distinctly
see the cones clustered on the tops of the trees, and the ferns and
bushes at their feet.

But new scenes are brought to view with magical rapidity.
Rounding some bossy cape, the eye is called away into far-reaching
vistas, bounded on either hand by headlands in charming array,
one dipping gracefully beyond another and growing fainter and
more ethereal in the distance. The tranquil channel stretching
river-like between, may be stirred here and there by the silvery
plashing of upspringing salmon, or by flocks of white gulls floating
like water-lilies among the sun spangles; while mellow, tempered
sunshine is streaming over all, blending sky, land, and water in
pale, misty blue. Then, while you are dreamily gazing into the
depths of this leafy ocean lane, the little steamer, seeming hardly
larger than a duck, turning into some passage not visible until
the moment of entering it, glides into a wide expanse—a sound
filled with islands, sprinkled and clustered in forms and composi-
tions such as nature alone can invent; some of them so small the
trees growing on them seem like single handfuls culled from the
neighboring woods and set in the water to keep them fresh, while
here and there at wide intervals you may notice bare rocks just
above the water, mere dots punctuating grand, outswelling sen-
tences of islands.

The variety we find, both as to the contours and the collocation
of the islands, is due chiefly to differences in the structure and
composition of their rocks, and the unequal glacial denudation
different portions of the coast were subjected to. This influence
must have been especially heavy toward the end of the glacial
period, when the main ice-sheet began to break up into separate
glaciers. Moreover, the mountains of the larger islands nourished
local glaciers, some of them of considerable size, which sculptured
their summits and sides, forming in some cases wide cirques with
cañons or valleys leading down from them into the channels and
sounds. These causes have produced much of the bewildering
variety of which nature is so fond, but none the less will the
studious observer see the underlying harmony—the general trend
of the islands in the direction of the flow of the main ice-mantle

from the mountains of the Coast Range, more or less varied by
subordinate foothill ridges and mountains. Furthermore, all the
islands, great and small, as well as the headlands and promontories
of the mainland, are seen to have a rounded, over-rubbed appearance produced by the over-sweeping ice-flood during the
period of greatest glacial abundance.

The canals, channels, straits, passages, sounds, etc., are subordinate to the same glacial conditions in their forms, trends, and
extent as those which determined the forms, trends, and distribution of the land-masses, their basins being the parts of the pre-
glacial margin of the continent, eroded to varying depths below
sea-level, and into which, of course, the ocean waters flowed as
the ice was melted out of them. Had the general glacial denudation
been much less, these ocean ways over which we are sailing would
have been valleys and cañons and lakes; and the islands rounded
hills and ridges, landscapes with undulating features like those
found above sea-level wherever the rocks and glacial conditions are
similar. In general, the island-bound channels are like rivers, not
only in separate reaches as seen from the deck of a vessel, but
continuously so for hundreds of miles in the case of the longest
of them. The tide-currents, the fresh driftwood, the inflowing
streams, and the luxuriant foliage of the out-leaning trees on the
shores make this resemblance all the more complete. The largest
islands look like part of the mainland in any view to be had of
them from the ship, but far the greater number are small, and
appreciable as islands, scores of them being less than a mile long.
These the eye easily takes in and revels in their beauty with ever
fresh delight. In their relations to each other the individual members of a group have evidently been derived from the same general
rock-mass, yet they never seem broken or abridged in any way as
to their contour lines, however abruptly they may dip their sides.
Viewed one by one, they seem detached beauties, like extracts
from a poem, while, from the completeness of their lines and the
way that their trees are arranged, each seems a finished stanza in
itself. Contemplating the arrangement of the trees on these small
islands, a distinct impression is produced of their having been
sorted and harmonized as to size like a well-balanced bouquet. On

some of the smaller tufted islets a group of tapering spruces is planted in the middle, and two smaller groups that evidently correspond with each other are planted on the ends at about equal distances from the central group; or the whole appears as one group with marked fringing trees that match each other spreading around the sides, like flowers leaning outward against the rim of a vase. These harmonious tree relations are so constant that they evidently are the result of design, as much so as the arrangement of the feathers of birds or the scales of fishes.

Thus perfectly beautiful are these blessed evergreen islands, and their beauty is the beauty of youth, for though the freshness of their verdure must be ascribed to the bland moisture with which they are bathed from warm ocean-currents, the very existence of the islands, their features, finish, and peculiar distribution, are all immediately referable to ice-action during the great glacial winter just now drawing to a close. . . . Never before in all my travels, north or south, had I found so lavish an abundance of berries as here. The woods and meadows are full of them, both on the lowlands and mountains—huckleberries of many species, salmon-berries, blackberries, raspberries, with service-berries on dry open places, and cranberries in the bogs, sufficient for every bird, beast, and human being in the territory and thousands of tons to spare. The huckleberries are especially abundant. A species that grows well up on the mountains is the best and largest, a half-inch and more in diameter and delicious in flavor. These grow on bushes three or four inches to a foot high. The berries of the commonest species are smaller and grow almost everywhere on the low grounds on bushes from three to six or seven feet high.

\* \* \*

John Burroughs (1837–1921), one of the scientists invited to join the Harriman Alaska Expedition in 1899, describes an entirely different type of scenery in westward Alaska.

From · · ·

## *Far and Near,* by John Burroughs

### IN GREEN ALASKA

We entered [Cook Inlet] under bright skies, and dropped anchor behind a low sandspit in Kachemac Bay, on the end of which is a group of four or five buildings making up the hamlet of Homer. There was nothing Homeric in the look of the place, but grandeur looked down upon it from the mountains around, especially from the great volcanic peaks, Iliamna and Redoubt, sixty miles across the inlet to the west. The former rises over twelve thousand feet from the sea and, bathed in sunshine, was an impressive spectacle. It was wrapped in a mantle of snow, but it evidently was warm at heart, for we could see steam issuing from two points near its summit.

Our stay in Cook Inlet was brief. Our hunters had hoped to kill some big game here, but after interviewing an experienced hunter who had a camp on shore, they concluded that on our return in July the prospects would be better. On the afternoon of June 30, therefore, we left the inlet and were off for the island of Kadiak, a hundred miles to the southwest.

We were now about to turn over a new leaf, or indeed to open a new book, and to enter upon an entirely different type of scenery —the treeless type. Up to this point, or for nearly two thousand miles, we had seen the mountains and valleys covered with unbroken spruce forests. Now we were to have two thousand miles without a tree, the valleys and mountains green as a lawn, and to the eye as smooth—all of volcanic origin; many of the cones ideally perfect; the valleys deepened and carved by the old glaciers, and heights and lowlands alike covered with a carpet of grass, ferns, and flowers.

The forests begin to fail at the mouth of Cook Inlet. As we came out, my eye was drawn to rolling heights, where were groups and lines of trees amid broad, green expanses. The suggestion of hill farms at home with orchards and groves, and trees along the fences, was very strong, but one looked in vain for the houses and barns of the farmers. We were going into a milder climate, too.

But balmier skies awaited us; the warmer currents of the Pacific flowing up from Japan and the southern seas were soon to breathe upon us; that pastoral paradise, Kadiak, was soon to greet us.

All the afternoon we steamed along the coast in smooth seas, in full view of lofty, snow-covered mountains with huge glaciers issuing from out their loins. Late at night, off against Kukak Bay, we put off a party of five or six men who wished to spend a week collecting and botanizing on the mainland. It looked like a perilous piece of business, the debarkation of these men in the darkness, in an open boat on an unknown coast many miles from shore. Might they not miss the bay? Might they not find the surf running too high to land, or might not some other mishap befall them? But after a hard pull of several hours, they made the shore at a suitable landing-place, and their days spent there were in every way satisfactory.

On the morning of July 1, we woke up in Uyak Bay on the north side of the Island of Kadiak. The sky was clear and the prospect most inviting. Smooth, treeless, green hills and mountains surrounded us, pleasing to the eye and alluring to the feet. Two large salmon canneries were visible on shore, and presently a boat came off to us with fresh salmon. Here we left a naphtha launch with a party of six men, heavily armed, bent on finding and killing the great Kadiak bear, the largest species of bear in the world, as big as an ox. They had been making up their mouths for this monster bear all the way, and now they were at last close to his haunts. In two or three days we were to return and pick them up and hoist their game aboard with the great derrick. In the delicious sunshine we steamed out of Uyak, bound for Kadiak village on the east end of the island, one hundred miles away. Kadiak Island lies nearly south from Cook Inlet, about fifty miles from the mainland. It is one hundred and fifty miles long and one third as broad. It would just about fill up Cook Inlet, out of which it may have slipped some time for aught I know. It is treeless except upon the east end, which faces toward the great Alaskan forests, from which the tree infection may have come.

How beautiful and interesting the shores we passed that day! Smooth, rounded hills, as green and tender to the eye as well-kept lawns, recalling the hills we saw in May upon Snake River; natural sheep ranges, such as one sees in the north of England, but not a sign of life upon them.

I warn my reader here, that henceforth I shall babble continually of green fields. There was no end to them. We had come from an arboreal wilderness to a grassy wilderness, from a world of spruce forests to a world of emerald heights and verdant slopes. Look at the map of Alaska, and think of all the peninsulas from Cook Inlet and all the adjacent islands, and the long chain of the Aleutians sweeping nearly across to Asia, as being covered with an unbroken carpet of verdure—it must needs be the main feature in my descriptions. Never had I seen such beauty of greenness, because never before had I seen it from such a vantage-ground of blue sea.

We had not been many hours out of Uyak that afternoon when we began to see a few scattered spruce-trees, then patches of forest in the valley bottoms. At one point we passed near a large natural park. It looked as if a landscape gardener might have been employed to grade and shape the ground, and plant it with grass and trees in just the right proportion. Here were cattle, too, and how good they looked, grazing or reposing on those long, smooth vistas between the trees! To eyes sated with the wild, austere grandeur of Prince William Sound the change was most delightful. Our course lay through narrow channels and over open bays sprinkled with green islands, past bold cliffs and headlands, till at three o'clock we entered the narrow strait, no more than twice the ship's length in width, upon which is situated the village of Kadiak, called by the Russians St. Paul. We could see the wild flowers upon the shore as we passed along, barn swallows twittered by, a magpie crossed the strait from one green bank to the other, and as we touched the wharf a song sparrow was singing from the weather-vane of a large warehouse—a song sparrow in voice, manners, and color, but in form twice as large as our home bird. The type of song sparrow changes all the way from Yakutat Bay to the Aleutian Islands, till at the latter place it is nearly as large as the catbird; but the song and general habits of the bird change but very little. How welcome the warmth, too! We had stepped from April into June, with the mercury near the seventies, and our spirits rose accordingly. How we swarmed out of the ship, like boys out of school, longing for a taste of grass and of the rural seclusion and sweetness! That great green orb or half orb of a mountain that shone down upon us from just back of the town, the highest point in its rim at an altitude of twenty-three hundred feet—how our legs tingled to climb it!—and the green vale below, where the birds were singing and many rare wild flowers blooming; and the broad, gentle height to the north; threaded by a grassy lane, where groves of low, fragrant spruces promised a taste of the blended sylvan and pastoral; or the smooth, rounded island opposite, over which the sea threw blue glances; or the curving line of water sweeping away to the south toward a rugged mountain-wall, streaked with snow; or the peaceful, quaint old village itself, strung upon paths and grassy lanes, with its chickens and geese and children, and two or three cows cropping the grass or ruminating by the wayside—surely, here was a tempting field to ship-bound voyagers from the chilly and savage north. The town itself had a population of seven or eight hundred people, Indians, half-breeds, and Russians, with a sprinkling of Americans, living in comfortable frame cottages, generally with a bit of garden attached. The people fish, hunt the sea-otter, and work for the Alaska Commercial Company. We met here an old Vermonter, a refined, scholarly looking man, with a patriarchal beard, who had married a native woman and had a family of young children growing up around him. He liked the climate better than that of New England. The winters were not very cold, never below zero, and the summers were not hot, rarely up to 80° Fahrenheit. There were no horses or wheeled vehicles in town, and the streets were grassy lanes. Such a rural, Arcadian air I had never before seen pervading a town upon American soil. There is a Greek church near the wharf, and its chime of bells was in our ears for hours at a time. The only incongruous thing I saw was a building with a big sign on its ridge-board: CHICAGO STORE. I went in and asked for some fresh eggs; they had none, but directed me to a cottage near the beach.

I found here a large Russian woman who had the eggs, for which, after consulting with a younger woman, she wanted "four bits." The potatoes in her garden had tops a foot high, but her currant bushes were just in bloom. Our stay of five days in this charming place was a dream of rural beauty and repose: warm summer skies above us, green, flower-strewn hills and slopes around us—our paths were indeed in green pastures and beside still waters. One enticing trail left the old Russian road half a mile north of the village, and led off northwest across little mossy and flowery glens, through spruce groves, over little runs, up a shoulder of the mountain, and then down a few miles into a broad, green, silent valley that held a fine trout brook. The path was probably made by the village anglers. In looking into such a peaceful, verdant sweep of country, one almost instinctively looked for farmhouses, or for flocks and herds and other signs of human occupancy; but they were not there. One high mountain that cut into the valley at right angles had a long, easy ridge, apparently as sharp as the ridge-board of a building. I marked it for my own and thought to set my feet upon it, but the way was too beguiling, and I did not get there. The mountain looked as though it had just had a priming coat of delicate green paint.

But the mighty emerald billow that rose from the rear of the village—we all climbed that, some of us repeatedly. From the ship it looked as smooth as a meadow, but the climber soon found himself knee-deep in ferns, grasses, and a score of flowering plants, and now and then was forced to push through a patch of alders as high as his head. He could not go far before his hands would be full of flowers, blue predominating. The wild geranium here is light blue, and tinges the slopes as daisies and buttercups do at home. Near the summit were patches of a most exquisite forget-me-not of a pure, delicate blue with yellow centre. It grew to the height of a foot and a handful of it looked like something just caught out of the sky above. Here, too, was a small, delicate lady's-slipper, pale yellow striped with maroon; also a dwarf rhododendron, its large purple flowers sitting upon the moss and lichen.

The climber also waded through patches of lupine, and put his feet upon bluebells, Jacob's ladder, iris, saxifrage, cassiope, and many others. The song-birds that attracted our notice were the golden-crowned sparrow and the little hermit thrush. The golden-crown has a strangely piercing, plaintive song, very simple, but very appealing. It consists of only three notes, but they come from out the depths of the bird's soul. In them is all the burden of the mystery and the pathos of life.

In the spruce groves to the north opened up by the old grassy road, besides the birds named, one heard the pine grosbeak, the gray-cheeked thrush, and the weird strain of the Oregon robin. This last bird was very shy and hard to get a view of. I reclined for two hours one day upon the deep dry moss under the spruces waiting for the singer to reveal himself. When seen he looks like our robin in a holiday suit. His song is a long, tapering note or whistle, at times with a peculiar tolling effect. . . .

While here Mr. Harriman had the luck to kill the long-expected Kadiak bear; he shot a mother and cub. He and his guide, an old Russian named Stepan Kondakoff, found her grazing near the snow-line on the mountain-side about ten miles to the south. She was eating grass like a cow, Mr. Harriman said. She was a large animal, but below the size of the traditional Kadiak bear. Her color was a faded brown. A much larger one was seen far across a difficult valley.

On July 3, which was bright and warm, a number of us visited Wood Island, a few miles to the east, where the North American Commercial Company has its headquarters, and where are large old spruce woods and lakes of fresh water. Charles Keeler and I heard, or fancied we heard, voices calling us from out of the depths of the woods; so we left the party and took ourselves thither, and lounged for hours in the mossy, fragrant solitudes, eating our lunch by a little rill of cold water, listening to the song-birds and ravens, and noting the wood flowers and moss-draped trees. Here we heard the winter wren at our leisure, a bubbling, trilling, prolonged strain like that of our eastern bird, but falling far short of it in melody and in wild lyrical penetration. In other words, it was the same song sung by a far inferior voice. The elusive note of the Oregon robin, as though the dark, motionless spruces had found a voice, was also heard here and there. These woods were not merely carpeted with moss, they were upholstered; the ground was padded ankle-deep, and under every tree was a couch of the most luxurious kind.

The 4th of July found us, as it usually finds Americans, wherever they are, overflowing with patriotism, bunting, and gunpowder hilarity. Our huge Graphophone played very well the part of a brass band; Professor Brewer, upon the hurricane deck, discharged admirably the duties of the orator of the day; he was followed by Mr. Keeler, who shaded the picture the speaker had drawn by a stirring poem, touching upon some of the nation's shortcomings; songs and music, followed by a boat race and general merriment, finished the programme.

Kadiak, I think, won a place in the hearts of all of us. Our spirits probably touched the highest point here. If we had other days that were epic, these days were lyric. To me they were certainly more exquisite and thrilling than any before or after. I feel as if I wanted to go back to Kadiak, almost as if I could return there to live—so secluded, so remote, so peaceful; such a mingling of the domestic, the pastoral, the sylvan, with the wild and the rugged; such emerald heights; such flowery vales, such blue arms and recesses of the sea, and such a vast green solitude stretching away to the west and to the north and to the south. Bewitching Kadiak! the spell of thy summer freshness and placidity is still upon me.

\* \* \*

Hudson Stuck (1863–1920) was an English Episcopal clergyman who came to this country in 1885 and in 1904 was appointed Archdeacon of the Yukon. He was one of a party of four men who made the first successful ascent of Mount McKinley, which he described in *Ascent of Mount Denali* (its Indian name); other books included *Voyages on the Yukon and Tributaries* and *A Winter Circuit of Our Arctic Coast*. The following extract presents his observations on still another part of Alaska—the Far North.

From · · ·

## *Ten Thousand Miles with a Dog Sled,* by Hudson Stuck

### "Sunrise and Sunset"

The days were nearing the shortest of the year, when, in
these latitudes, the sun does but show himself and withdraw again.
But, especially in very cold weather, which is nearly always very
clear weather, that brief appearance is preceded by a feast of rich,
delicate colour. First a greenish glow on the southern horizon,
brightening into lemon and then into clear primrose, invades the
deep purple of the starry heavens. Then a beautiful circle of blush
pink above a circle of pure amethyst gradually stretches all around
the edge of the sky, slowly brightening while the stars fade out
and the heavens change to blue. The dead white mirror of the
snow takes every tint that the skies display with a faint but
exquisite radiance. Then the sun's disk appears with a flood of
yellow light but with no appreciable warmth, and for a little space
his level rays shoot out and gild the tree tops and the distant hills.
The snow springs to life. Dead white no longer, its dry, crystalline
particles glitter in myriads of diamond facets with every colour
of the prism. Then the sun is gone, and the lovely circle of rose
pink over amethyst again stretches round the horizon, slowly
fading until once more the pale primrose glows in the south against
the purple sky with its silver stars. *Thus sunrise and sunset form
a continuous spectacle, with a purity of delicate yet splendid
colour that only perfectly dry atmosphere permits.* The primrose
glow, the heralding circle, the ball of orange light, the valedictory
circle, the primrose glow again, and a day has come and gone.
Air can hold no moisture at all at these low temperatures, and
the skies are cloudless.

# 23

# THE CHALLENGE
# OF THE MOUNTAINS

No area of the United States and few areas elsewhere on
earth offer so many varied and challenging opportunities to the
mountaineer as does Alaska. This is due not only to the galaxy
of unclimbed high peaks, but because Alaska is a relatively newly
discovered land where mountain climbing as a sport developed
only in this century.

The earliest of the known great Alaskan ascents came in 1899,
when Luigi Amedeo, Prince of Savoy and Duke of the Abruzzi,
with a well-organized expedition, surmounted the 18,008-foot
giant Mount St. Elias and named a number of adjacent peaks,
including a 16,421-footer after his yacht, *Bona,* and a 17,147-
footer after the Cunard liner on which he had crossed the Atlantic,
*Lucania.*

When, following the Gold Rush at the turn of the century, the
Federal government began sending its geologists to Alaska, they
were, in the pursuit of their calling, among the early mountaineers,
and some of Alaska's noblest peaks appropriately bear their names.
But mountaineering in Alaska is still in its adolescence, as the
following article appearing in the *Alaska Review* indicates. Its
author, William E. Davis, an assistant professor of psychology at
Alaska Methodist University in Anchorage, has to his credit eight
first ascents in the St. Elias Range and has done considerable other
climbing in Alaska.

From · · ·

*The Unclimbed Mountains of Alaska,* by William E. Davis

In Alaska there are more than sixty-five mountain peaks with an altitude over 10,000 feet. The number in this altitude range which are unnamed is not known. The highest and best known peaks have been climbed, although some of them only by one party. The rest remain mostly unknown and certainly unclimbed.

Some expeditions came in the early days of mountaineering to assault the highest peaks. The Duke of Abruzzi came with an extensive retinue in the latter part of the nineteenth century and was successful in the first ascent of Mt. St. Elias, the third highest peak on the North American continent. Mt. Blackburn, the highest summit in the Wrangell range, was climbed in 1912 by an expedition led by a woman. The stories of these early assaults are some of the most thrilling in mountaineering history.

Other expeditions have visited only recently. Mt. Huntington, located in the McKinley massif, was described by the *American Alpine Club News* as "one of the greatest prizes in the Alaska range." It was climbed for the first time in the summer of 1964 by a team led by the famous French guide, Lionel Terray.

Climbing these great giants requires organization of a mountaineering expedition. As James Ramsey Ullman notes, "The Alaskan mountains are in every sense arctic mountains. . . . Mountaineering here is far more than a matter of mere climbing. It is pioneering and exploration as well." Even to approach the peaks, supplies must be carried over great distances or ferried in by aircraft at great expense. Yet once these difficulties are overcome, the actual climb need not be overwhelming.

Herein is one of the ironies of Alaskan mountaineering. The technical climbing problems on the highest peaks are few. The battle is in getting to them and then having the time to wait for good weather. To climb Mt. McKinley by the West Buttress route requires good equipment, adequate food, plenty of time, acclimatization, and perseverance. A knowledge of snow and ice climbing techniques is required but extensive technical difficulties simply do not exist on this route.

But just the opposite holds for peaks in the 10,000 to 14,000 feet altitude range. Many of these are reasonably accessible (by Alaskan standards). They can be approached after a modest backpack often from a road or from a point easily reached by airplane. The costs are modest, too, when compared to mounting an expedition for a massive assault on the high peaks. Yet these summits pose some of the most formidable technical challenges in current mountaineering.

Most of the high peaks are massive mounds of snow and ice. Once a feasible route is located, they are climbed by a long and arduous walk. Not so the smaller mountains. They present sheer precipices on every side capped with thin, serrated ridges. Snow and ice routes are interspersed with rock outcroppings. On some, even locating a potential route may involve extensive reconnaissance.

The composition of the mountains adds to the difficulty. Most of the rock in Alaska is noted for its unstable and treacherous nature. The hard, smooth, firm granite of the Colorado Front Range or Yosemite National Park is nowhere to be found. Instead loose, ragged, shifty scree and talus are everywhere. Every peak worthy of the title has at least one chute down which the rocks pour at a persistent rate.

The snow and ice sometimes is not much better. On the really narrow ridges it is always corniced and often rotten. I can recall one that was completely made of rime ice. It looked as if someone had bunched up about a million lace tablecloths and scattered them along the ridge, and it felt about as stable as a filigree.

The technical climbing problems associated with these conditions are obvious. Prudent climbers enjoy protection on exposed ridges, especially if the drop-off is in the neighborhood of 2,000 or 3,000 vertical feet. The rock, however, does not lend itself to the placement of pitons. Instead of searching for a crack that will accept a safety point, one becomes content with finding a foothold that is stable enough to stand on for longer than a minute. Handholds that are not readily detached from the mountainside also are welcomed.

Similarly with the snow and ice, it often is hard to find an area that is stable enough to accept a piton or ice screw. With perseverance, one can stomp down a foothold that will stay in place and shave off enough filigree to chop a handhold but comfortable belay positions often are few and far between.

The great overburden of snow and ice on the higher mountains covers these technical difficulties. Of course it is possible to go out of your way to find these problems on the giant peaks. The north face of Logan, the Wickersham Wall on McKinley, and Mt. St. Elias from Columbus Glacier all pose severe technical challenges. But these are not the easiest routes, and my point is that even the easiest routes on the lesser peaks involve difficult technical problems.

It depends, I will admit, on the type of problem one wants to tackle. The highest peaks demand organizational skill, months of planning, and physical stamina. The smaller peaks require less expeditionary involvement but demand greater abilities with rope and hardware, in leadership, and technical skill. If you want to combine all of these problems in a single packet, then you choose one of the technical routes on the giants.

Where can these lesser-known peaks be found? In all of the significant mountain ranges in Alaska. Within a 150 mile radius of Anchorage, two perfect examples exist. To the west, across Cook Inlet, the northern end of the Chigmit Mountains has proven a mecca for local mountaineers. Mt. Gerdine (10,756') was considered the highest summit for a number of years. The first attempt to climb the mountain was made in 1961, the second and third in 1963. The third attempt was finally successful. The value of the prize was somewhat lessened when a new map of the area was published which lopped 2,000 feet off the previously given altitude. This change elevated one of Mt. Gerdine's neighbors, Mt. Torbert, from 10,600' to 11,413' and made it the highest peak in the range. Needless to say, Mt. Torbert was climbed shortly after the new map's publication.

To the east of Anchorage lie the Chugach Mountains. Accessibility by automobile road is one of their advantages. At the east end of Eklutna Lake is a series of peaks that has attracted local climbers for the past decade. Those who pioneered these summits have the pleasure of knowing that their names for the peaks should persevere. The U.S. Board of Geographic Names accepted the names submitted by the Mountaineering Club of Alaska including such descriptive ones as Bold Peak, Bashful Peak, Baleful Peak, Bellicose Peak, Peril Peak, and White Lice Mountain.

Everyone who drives the Richardson Highway from Glennallen to Valdez is impressed by the peaks of the Chugach Range visible from the road. My mountaineering friends from the South 48 who come to Alaska as tourists keep asking me why I don't have a drive-in outing in the area. I can't give them a satisfactory answer. All of the advantages of the lesser peaks exist in this area.

Fairbanks enjoys a similar proximity to the mountains if you measure the distance in air miles. Unfortunately, the driving distance is longer. The peaks of the Alaska Range east of the McKinley massif are the most readily accessible. Mt. Hayes (13,740') and Mt. Deborah (12,540') are the highest summits and have been climbed. But both east and west of the Richardson Highway are plenty of other tempting summits, and the Denali Highway opens up the approaches from the south to the Cathedral Peaks.

South and west of the Haines Cutoff are the northern peaks of the Fairweather Range. This is an area that has seen activity lately by interested mountaineers. Like some of the other places where the lesser-known peaks can be found, this location requires an assist from a bush pilot. A lot of slogging through bush and muskeg carrying an impossible load of supplies can be avoided by the airlift and airdrop.

Mt. McKinley National Park has a special place on my list. The peaks east of The Great One can be reached by a day's backpack from the park road. Rotten rock, corniced ridges, and jumbled icefalls can be found on nearly every one. An added bonus greets the climber on most summits (providing, of course, that the weather is cooperative) since McKinley itself is visible from this direction.

I suspect that not too many of these mountains remain unclimbed. McKinley Park rangers have a notable penchant for climbing everything in sight. The attractive peaks of the Alaska Range within the Park are often in plain sight from the rangers' front yard. This area thus may not provide the attraction of a technically difficult climb plus a first ascent. For my money, a view of McKinley is worth the loss of a first ascent.

If you are not concerned about an approach from an automobile highway, the possibilities multiply manyfold. The area west of Anchorage and across Cook Inlet has already been mentioned. Further south in the Aleutian Range volcanoes are most prominent. Volcanoes are less apt to be surrounded by the rugged lesser peaks but even so there are some rugged-looking summits visible across from the Kenai Peninsula.

For that matter, the Kenai Peninsula itself is not without some attractions. I have never seen the southern part of the Harding Ice Field but I have cast some longing glances at the northern part.

And of course the St. Elias Range holds untold numbers of lesser peaks. You can approach from the west by flying out of Cordova; you can approach from the north by jumping off from Chitina, Nabesna, or Chisana; or you can go from the south by flying out of Yakutat. There are so many unclimbed peaks in the 10,000 to 14,000 ft. range in this area that they defy description. A few that I have seen looked to me unclimbable. However, I am not fool enough to suggest that there is any mountain in Alaska that cannot be climbed. In the St. Elias Mountains, there are some that will provide exciting and technically magnificent ascents for someone; ascents that will push one to the limits of his skill.

The mountains of the Alaskan panhandle can be included in our catalogue. Again access is available only by air although the development of logging roads may open new areas as it has in British Columbia. The border between the United States and Canada follows generally the crest of the coastal range. The Coast Mountains have not gotten a great deal of attention from mountain climbers so that the extent of the lesser peaks is not known. The ones I have seen from the air compare in every favorable respect with the qualities I have attributed to these mountains.

So the unclimbed mountains of Alaska can be found anywhere you look. Some mountaineer colleagues have tried to argue with me that there isn't anything left in Alaska worth the time and trouble involved in making the climb. Their contention is that since the mightiest have all been climbed, there is little left to tempt one to spend a lot of money just for an exciting climb.

True, the possibility of a first ascent over 18,000 feet seems nil. But just consider the possibilities of first ascents without the altitude limitation. And then add the challenge of technical difficulty. This is the heart of my argument. To be sure, the chance of becoming famous on the mountains of Alaska may not be too great. But the chance to have a thrilling climb is immense. The technical problems are there and they involve snow, ice, and rock. They can be complicated if you want to make an expedition out of it. The potential of these Alaskan mountains has barely been touched.

\*    \*    \*

Mount McKinley, often referred to as "the monarch of the continent," is the loftiest peak in North America. The lateness of its discovery, identification, and measurement suggests the recency of much else in the way of discovery about central Alaska. Considerable literature on Mount McKinley exists, although a definitive history of these experiences remains to be written by some competent alpinist who has climbed Mount McKinley and has also devoted much time and thought to its exploration, geography, and geology, such as Henry Bradford Washburn, Jr., who is probably the foremost authority on the subject.

In selecting "The Great One" by James Ramsey Ullman, the editor has found what he considers the best account of the earlier pioneering ascents.

From · · ·

*High Conquest,* by James Ramsey Ullman

"THE GREAT ONE": THE STORY OF MOUNT MCKINLEY

In the faraway, frozen heart of Alaska stands the highest mountain in North America. We know it as Mount McKinley.

Men of other races, however, have had other, and better, names for it. To many of the aboriginal Indian tribes of the region it was known as Denali—"The Home of the Sun." Others knew it as Tralaika, still others as Doleyka, and the Russians, when they came, called it Bulshaia Gora. Significantly these three names, in three different tongues, meant the same thing—"The Great One."

For this remote snowpeak in our own northwest is not merely the culminating point of the North American continent; it is also one of the greatest single mountains on earth. The giants of the Himalayas and Andes are higher—22,000 to 29,000 feet, as against McKinley's 20,300—but these figures indicate total heights above sea level, and the mountains usually rise from lofty plateaus that are themselves 10,000 to 15,000 feet high. McKinley, however, has no such headstart. The valley of the Yukon River, from which its northern slopes spring, is a scant 1500 feet above the sea, and the wilderness of forests and glaciers to the south is only slightly more elevated. The mountain soars up in one gigantic, unbroken sweep of rock and ice to its full height—almost four miles straight up from base to peak.

But the greatness of McKinley is more than a matter of arithmetic. Every traveler who has laid eyes on it, from near or far, has declared it to be one of the most impressive sights in the world. From Cook Inlet on the Pacific, two hundred miles to the south, its snowy crest dominates the northern horizon; from Fairbanks, a hundred and fifty miles north, it appears like a great white giant crouched against the sky. Except for its immediate neighbor, 17,000-foot Mount Foraker, it has not a single rival. Its cloud-hung battlements tower, lone and immense, over 300,000 square miles of central Alaska.

This colossus among mountains has been conquered twice. The records of these two ascents, together with those of the several unsuccessful efforts, make a story that, for achievement and disappointment, tragedy and comedy, heroism and even villainy, are unsurpassed in the annals of mountaineering.

So far as we know, the first white man to look upon McKinley was the English navigator, George Vancouver. While exploring the southern coast of Alaska in 1794 he saw "distant, stupendous snow mountains" to the north. He did not, however, approach any nearer, nor did any other white men, so far as we know, for almost a hundred years. The Russians, who owned and occupied the territory for the first two-thirds of the last century, obviously knew of the peak, since they gave it a name, but there is no record of any exploration in its vicinity. In 1867 the United States purchased Alaska for what then seemed the enormous sum of $7,200,000—the famous "Seward's Folly." During the next twenty years traders and prospectors trickled in, and towns and trading posts were established. But they hugged the coasts. It was not until the 1890's that the interior wilderness began to be opened up, and Americans discovered that they had acquired not only a vast arctic storehouse of gold, fish and fur, but the highest mountain on the continent as well.

Most of the pioneers of central Alaska were men in search of gold. One of these, Frank Densmore, penetrated the McKinley region in 1889 and returned with such glowing descriptions of the mountain that it was known for years among the Yukon prospectors as "Densmore's Peak." Another, W. A. Dickey, followed in 1896, reaching the outer edge of the mountain's great skirt of glaciers. Presumably Dickey was ignorant of the already existing names for the peak—or perhaps he was merely a good Republican. In either case, he named it in honor of William McKinley, who was then candidate for President of the United States. And the name stuck.

In the next ten years several individuals and expeditions approached the mountain, among them George Eldridge and Robert Muldrow, of the U.S. Geological Survey, who measured the mountain by triangulation and fixed its height at 20,300 feet. The first actual attempt at ascent took place in 1903. Under the leadership of Judge Wickersham, one of the foremost citizens of the new boom town of Fairbanks, a party of four men packed in to the base of the mountain and began to climb it. They were unfortunate in their choice of route, however, for they were halted almost immediately by unscalable walls of ice, and soon turned back. Thereafter Judge Wickersham was often heard to declare that the summit would never be reached except by an airplane or a balloon. Thereafter, that is, until it was climbed.

The next man to enter the expanding saga of McKinley was one of the strangest figures in the history of exploration and mountaineering. This was Dr. Frederick Cook, who was later to win worldwide notoriety as the bogus "Discoverer of the North Pole." At this time, however, Dr. Cook was concentrating on becoming the equally bogus "Conqueror of Mount McKinley." His first expedition to the mountain was in the same year as Judge Wickersham's, but it was little more than a reconnaissance of the surrounding passes and glaciers. In 1906, however, he returned, and this time plunged energetically into the business of making his own particular brand of history.

Ironically, Cook's companions at the outset of this second venture were two men of complete honor and integrity. They were Herschel Parker and Belmore Browne, whose later battles with McKinley—as we shall see—form one of the brightest, most heroic chapters of mountain history. On this occasion, however, they and Cook bogged down in the great wilderness south of the peak and were forced to withdraw without finding even a way of approach to the heights.

Then began Cook's audacious hoax. With only one companion, a packer named Edwin Barill, he returned to the base of the mountain, was unheard from for a few weeks, and then reappeared with the claim that he had reached the summit. Neither Parker, Browne nor anyone else who knew McKinley well believed him. He had not, for one thing, had enough time for the ascent, and, furthermore, his description of his experiences did not tally with their own observations. But Cook was a fraud who knew his business. Undeterred by suspicions and accusations, he returned to civilization and began systematically to reap the rewards of his "feat." He wrote a book called *To the Top of the Continent*, in which he described his struggles on the ascent and the magnificence of the view from the top. He showed photographs which he said he had taken on the summit. He lectured before great public gatherings and learned societies. As far as the world was concerned, he was what he claimed to be—the conqueror of McKinley.

Seven years passed before the fraud was finally exposed. Parker and Browne could not conclusively prove their suspicions, and it remained for Hudson Stuck and his companions, who in 1913 made the true first ascent, to settle the matter once and for all. Stuck was Archdeacon of the Yukon, a man above suspicion in every way, and his description of McKinley refuted Cook's in countless details. Cook had spoken of "the heaven-scraped granite and frosted rocks" of the summit. Stuck reported that there was no rock of any kind on the peak above 19,000 feet, but only a permanent sheath of snow and ice. Cook devoted pages of his book to vivid descriptions of the view from the top and referred to McKinley as standing utterly alone. Stuck declared that the dominant feature of the view, "bursting on the eye and filling all the middle distance," was the great mass of Mount Foraker. And so on, throughout the account of his ascent.

From this point on the evidence piled up rapidly. Barrill, Cook's packer, after years of silence, signed a sworn statement that his employer's claims were untrue. An insignificant foothill peak was found, which coincided so completely with Cook's supposed photographs of McKinley's summit that it became obvious they had been made there. Within a short time the "conqueror's" claims were thoroughly discredited. Then, a few years later, came the still more sensational exposure of his faked discovery of the North Pole, and Cook's fantastic career reached its end. He dropped into obscurity—a dishonored, broken man.

Meanwhile the fight against "The Great One" went on. The bogus conquest had, if nothing else, aroused widespread interest in the greatest American mountain, and the attack was on in full force.

First in the field was a group of men who put even the incredible Dr. Cook to shame. They are known in climbing history as "the sourdough expedition," and no stranger or more haphazard exploit than theirs has ever occurred on any major mountain in the world. By every accepted standard they should not only have made a ridiculous failure of their attempt, but all should have been killed five times over. Instead, they missed immortality by a hairbreadth—or, to be accurate, 300 feet—and, in addition, per-formed what is undoubtedly one of the greatest exploits in the annals of mountaineering.

The sourdoughs of McKinley were a half dozen prospectors and miners of the vicinity of Fairbanks. None of them had ever been on a mountain in his life, but they were typical Alaskan frontiers-men, with frontiersmen's strength and pride, and when they heard of Cook's claims they snorted in disbelief and decided it was high time they took a hand in the affair themselves. "If McKinley is going to be climbed," they decided in effect, "we're the boys who are going to do it."

And in the spring of 1910, off they went.

The whole venture was organized in a way that would make a good Alpine Club member's hair stand on end. Or, rather, it wasn't organized at all. The $500 which was the bulk of their capital was put up by one Billy McPhee, a public-spirited saloon-keeper of Fairbanks. There was no leader, no prearranged plan of attack, and by the time they reached the base of the mountain half the party had come to blows with the other half and left for home. There was no scientific knowledge among them, no proper clothing or equipment, in fact nothing whatever of the things which a mountaineer is supposed to possess—save two. They had pluck and they had luck.

Their first great good fortune was in selecting the Muldrow Glacier as their way of approach. This vast tongue of ice extends from the northern foothills up into the very heart of the McKin-ley range, and to this day it is the only practicable route that has been found giving access to the upper reaches of the mountain. The sourdoughs obviously did not know this, but their instinct was right. Day after day, week after week, they toiled up the gigantic ice-slope of the Muldrow, hacking steps, bridging cre-vasses, moving slowly on and up into a silent, frozen world where no living thing had ever moved before.

At last they reached the glacier's head. They were now 11,000 feet above the sea, but barely at the base of the mountain proper, and above them the great white ridges and precipices of McKin-ley towered almost another two miles into the sky. By this time only three members of the expedition were left—Pete Anderson, Billy Taylor and Charley McGonogol—but these three, as they were soon to prove, were men of herculean strength and determination. For several days they camped at the head of the glacier, studying the vertical wilderness above them and awaiting favorable weather. Then, at two in the morning of April tenth, they started up.

A word is necessary here about the usual methods of scaling great peaks. Climbing itself is only one of the problems involved; more than half the battle is the establishment of high camps and the bringing up of reserve supplies, so that the climbers will not starve or freeze to death in the event of a mishap or a storm. On the great Himalayan peaks, as we shall see, the insurmountable difficulty has always been that of porterage. On McKinley, every regular expedition has spent weeks preparing the way for the final assault. Such finicky, tenderfoot precautions, however, were not in the line of the Messrs. Anderson, Taylor and McGonogol. With the food and equipment that an average person might take along for a picnic lunch, they climbed from their glacier camp to within 300 feet of the highest point of North America and back— *all in one day*.[1]

The sourdoughs, unlike most mountaineers, have left no written record of their venture, and the details of their astonishing ascent are very vague. It is known, however, that their route was roughly that followed in all subsequent expeditions: from the head of the Muldrow, up the great ice-spine that was later to be called Karstens Ridge, and into the upper ice-basin near the mountain's summit. It was when they reached this basin—now known as Harper Glacier—that they made a choice that was to cheat them of worldwide fame. McKinley is a mountain of two peaks—the south, or true summit, 20,300 feet high, and the north, a scant 300 feet lower. Standing between them on that day, already at 17,000 feet and with victory in their grasp, the sourdoughs chose the wrong one!

---

[1] In the Arctic, in spring and summer, the climbing day is limited only by the endurance of the climbers. Instead of darkness, nighttime brings merely a gray twilight, and it is possible to climb safely at any hour.

What prompted their choice has never been satisfactorily explained. It may have been that they thought the North Peak was the higher. It may have been the knowledge that half the population of central Alaska was watching through telescopes in Fairbanks, from which the North Peak alone is visible. At all events, the North Peak it was. McGonogol, near collapse, had to turn back within 500 feet of the goal, but Anderson and Taylor struggled on up the fearful ice-slope, in sub-zero cold, until they reached the top. There they unfurled the Stars and Stripes on a fourteen-foot flagstaff they had miraculously carried with them and planted it firmly on the topmost pinnacle. This done, they started down, picked up the exhausted McGonogol, and descended the 9000 feet to the Muldrow Glacier without a single stop. And in another week or so they were safe and sound in Billy McPhee's Fairbanks saloon, telling all about it to anyone who would buy them a drink.

Confronted with a performance like this, the usual rules and standards of mountaineering collapse into the wastebasket. Indeed, the whole story of their ascent seemed so fantastic that for several years it was generally disbelieved—those same years, ironically, during which Dr. Cook was still a national hero. It remained again for Archdeacon Stuck to clear things up. In his ascent of the true summit in 1913 he had ample opportunity to view the top of the North Peak, and what he saw completely vindicated the claims of the sourdoughs. The American flag was gone, to be sure, long since torn to shreds in the wild arctic winds; but the flagstaff was still there—"plain, prominent and unmistakable."

The sourdoughs never went back to McKinley. They were prospectors, not mountaineers, and one fling at "The Great One" was enough for them. That they could have reached the true summit had they tried no one who has known them or the mountain has ever doubted. But the fact remains that they didn't. The highest point in the continent still stood, lofty and untrodden, awaiting its next attackers.

They were not long in coming.

Indeed, in the same year as "the sourdough climb" Herschel Parker and Belmore Browne were again in the vicinity of the mountain. As in 1906, they approached it from Cook's Inlet, on the south—this time at the head of a party from the Explorers' Club of New York—and again they found that their route lay through almost impassable country. For weeks on end they struggled up icy, raging rivers, through tangled forests and wild boulder-choked gorges until at last they came out on a wide snow-plain at the very foot of the mountain. Through all their long ordeal, however, they had gained only 5000 feet in altitude, and here at their seventeenth camp, when they were already near exhaustion, McKinley's summit was still 15,000 feet above them.

Worse yet, it was immediately apparent that the southern side of the mountain was unclimbable. Its face rose in a series of ice-hung precipices to which a fly could not have clung—much less a man—and even the two ridges which they discovered ended hopelessly under huge outcropping cliffs and hanging glaciers. As if this were not enough, the whole expanse above them was scoured by avalanches. The south face of McKinley, unlike the north, is exposed to the moist winds from the Pacific, with the result that the snow upon it seldom freezes. There was no surface into which an ax or crampon-spike could bite, but only three vertical miles of roaring, crumbling destruction. Convinced that "The Great One" could never be climbed from that side, the expedition turned away and began the long struggle back to the coast.

But Parker and Browne were not through yet. McKinley had cast its spell upon them, and in 1912, six years after their first attempt, they were back again for their third and last. This, as it was to turn out, was one of the most magnificent, and at the same time, heartbreaking, assaults ever made on a great mountain.

This time, profiting from experience, they approached McKinley from the north, by the same general route that the sourdoughs had used. But there any resemblance between their expedition and that of the doughty pioneers ended. Both of them were thoughtful, highly educated men—Parker a physicist and university professor and Browne a distinguished painter—and their attack was as reasoned and carefully planned as the sourdoughs' had been haphazard. For months in advance they pored over maps, planned their marches and camps, assembled their supplies and equipment.

Then, with Merle La Voy and Arthur Aten, two sturdy Alaskans who had been with them in 1910, they set out for their goal.

From late February until late May they mushed in by dog-sled from Seward, on the coast, to the inner fastnesses of the mountain. After much reconnoitering they found a pass through the northern ridge, came out on the Muldrow Glacier and began its steep, laborious ascent. The Muldrow was long and broad, but it could never be mistaken for a paved avenue. It lunged down from the heights like a colosal ski-jump, and its surface was an ice-choked wilderness of humps and hollows. In some places huge seracs, a thousand feet high, had to be surmounted; in others were yawning, seemingly bottomless crevasses that they circumvented. Often the sled-dogs would tumble headlong into them and hang howling by their harnesses until they were pulled out.

Back and forth, back and forth, endlessly, went the men and dogs and sleds, establishing camps and bringing up supplies. But slowly they advanced, and at last, in the first week of June, they reached the head of the glacier. Here, at 11,000 feet, the great northeast ridge of McKinley began its skyward climb. Leaving the dogs behind, with Aten to take care of them, Parker, Browne and La Voy set foot at last upon the mountain proper.

Almost immediately they encountered the frightful weather that was to plague them during their whole ordeal on the peak. A blizzard howled down violently, the ice cliffs cracked and groaned, and avalanches roared about them like artillery. For four days the men huddled in their tent, rubbing one another's bodies to keep from freezing to death, clinging to the guy ropes so that they would not be blown into eternity. When the storm had passed they resumed the ascent, undaunted, and for a week crept upward. Uncounted thousands of steps had to be hacked in the glazed snow of the ridge. Backbreaking loads had to be carried in relays to higher camps. At one point their food supply ran so low that they had to descend all the way to the glacer to replenish it. But they pushed on doggedly and at last gained the upper basin, at a height of about 16,000 feet.

Here another savage storm imprisoned them for days, but they bided their time hopefully, for they were confident that the worst of McKinley was beneath them. And, indeed, when the weather finally cleared, the last 4000 feet of the South Peak appeared as merely a gentle slope into the sky, easy of access and presenting no major difficulties. At six in the morning of June 29 they began the summit dash with high hearts.

Dash, to be sure, is scarcely the word. It was still necessary for them to hack out footholds in the glaring cone of ice and to halt every few steps, gasping, in the thin, freezing air. But they made steady progress and within four hours had gained half the distance. The summit point of North America stood out near and clear above them. "It rose," Browne declared later, "as innocently as a tilted snow-covered tennis court, and as we looked at it we grinned with relief—we *knew* the peak was ours."

Then the last blow fell. With paralysing suddenness the wind sprang up into a howling gale, the sky darkened and the blizzard resumed. By the time they had struggled up another thousand feet they could no longer see one another at five yards through the blinding snow, and the sixty-mile wind threatened to hurl them at any moment from the mountainside. Bent double, frost-crippled, scarcely able to breathe, they still crept on until they reached the limit of human endurance. To have gone another step upward would have been suicide. At a height of 20,000 feet—a mere 300 from their goal—they turned back.

Somehow they succeeded in descending to their highest camp, and two days later they made a second attempt. But again the elements defeated them. A thick, freezing fog closed in about them, in which they could neither see nor breathe, and they were stopped at 19,300 feet. The next day, both their supplies and strength exhausted, they began the descent of the mountain. "I remember," said Browne, "only a feeling of dull despair."

Thus ended one of the most gallant unsuccessful ventures in the history of mountaineering. That it did not end in final and complete tragedy was merely a stroke of the greatest luck. For in that summer of 1912 the volcano Katmai, 400 miles away, was in eruption, and the shock of its explosions was felt throughout the plains and ranges of central Alaska. Only a few days after they had descended to the lowlands, the weary, discouraged men were startled by a vast thunder of sound, so great that it seemed the earth itself were splitting open. And, indeed, it was. Behind them, as they watched, the whole north face and ridges of McKinley, on which they had so recently stood, gave a monstrous shudder, detached themselves from the main mass of the mountain and plunged wildly into the valleys below.

That was their last view of McKinley—roaring defiance at its challengers.

Mountains are not greatly concerned with human concepts of justice. Parker and Browne devoted years of their lives to the exploring and ascent of McKinley, only to meet ultimate defeat. Its next assailants spent a total of two months on its forbidding terrain —and conquered it.

Not that there was anything undeserved in the triumph of Archdeacon Hudson Stuck. He and his companions were mountaineers of the first order; he had made many ascents in the American and Canadian Rockies, and for years past, during his farflung journeys among the Indians of Alaska, he had seen McKinley from afar and yearned to climb it. When at last he did, he brought to it the same resolution and courage, the same simplicity and integrity of spirit that consistently marked him in his life's work.

In the spring of 1913 Stuck received leave of absence from his churchly duties and set out from the tiny mission station of Nenana to achieve his great ambition. His companions were Harry Karstens, a sturdy sourdough who had come to Alaska in the Klondike gold rush and was later to become superintendent of McKinley National Park; Robert Tatum, a 21-year-old missionary from Tennessee; Walter Harper, a strong, cheerful, young halfbreed, who had been Stuck's dog-driver and interpreter for several years; and two Indian youngsters from the Nenana mission school named Johnny and Esaias.

With dogs and sleds they mushed across the vast white plains of central Alaska, crossed the outer spurs and ridges that guard McKinley and came out at last on the Muldrow Glacier, as the other expeditions had done before them. Here Esaias, having done his bit, was sent back to Nenana, Johnny remaining to take care of the dogs. Slowly and carefully the little party threaded its way up the steep maze of the glacier, probing and zigzagging endlessly to avoid the great crevasses, suffering greatly from cold and snow-storms and the fierce wind that swooped down on them from the frozen heights.

Ironically, though, neither mountain nor elements was responsible for their only serious mishap. Returning one day from a scouting expedition they saw with horror that their camp was afire, and before they could extinguish it a large part of their food and equipment had been burned. The worst loss of all was that of their entire supply of sugar. There is no food more essential than sugar to men struggling in the cold and often close to exhaustion, and in the days to come they were to have ample occasion to bemoan their bad luck.

At last, however, they reached the head of the glacier and, like Parker and Browne and the sourdoughs in earlier years, stood staring upward at the huge white wilderness of the upper mountain. But, as they stared, they realized something was wrong. The great ridge which was to be their route was not at all as the previous expeditions had described it—a thin, clean knife-edge cutting into the sky. What they saw instead was an indescribable chaos of pinnacles and chasms and great tumbled ice-masses piled crazily upon each other as far as the eye could see. And presently they realized what had happened. The great earth tremors of the previous year, from which Parker and Browne had barely escaped with their lives, had indeed blown to bits what had formerly been the northeast ramparts of the mountain. The ridge that the other parties had ascended had completely ceased to be. Instead of fol-lowing a route which others had pioneered before them, they were faced with the necessity of becoming pioneers themselves.

What Stuck and his companions did then was quite simply this: they cut a three-mile staircase in the ice. With magnificent patience and endurance they hacked and chopped and clawed their way from the 11,000-foot altitude of the Muldrow's head to the 16,000-foot heights of the upper basin. They surmounted ice-blocks as large as three-story houses, they edged around cornices that hung in space a mile above the glaciers; they struggled up with their supplies on their backs, descended again, struggled up with more. None of them ventured to count the thousands or tens of thousands of steps they cut, but Stuck later estimated that each member of the party, in going back and forth, had climbed at least 60,000 feet—or three times the total height of McKinley.

After days of unrelieved toil the savage earthquake-shattered ridge was at last behind them. On June third they camped at 16,500 feet in the middle of the upper basin, between the twin peaks of the mountain, and three days later at 18,000 feet on the slopes just beneath the summit. And now the blessing that had been so cruelly withheld from Parker and Browne was granted to them: the day of the final assault was clear and fine.

They started at three in the morning and for hour after hour toiled upward through the frozen gray silence of the arctic heights. Sometimes it was still necessary to hack steps with their axes; at other times their crampons sufficed, biting deeply into the hard-crusted slope of snow. At eleven o'clock they passed the point at which Parker and Browne had been turned back by the blizzard. At one they stepped up upon the horse-shoe ridge that forms the summit of the peak. And a few moments later—

"—there still stretched ahead of us," wrote Stuck, "and perhaps one hundred feet above us, another small ridge with a north and south pair of little haycock summits. This is the real top.—With keen excitement we pushed on. Walter Harper, who had been in the lead all day, was the first to scramble up; a native Alaskan, he is the first human being to set foot on the top of Alaska's great mountain, and he had well earned the lifelong distinction. Karstens and Tatum were hard upon his heels, but the last man on the rope had almost to be hauled up the last few feet, and fell unconscious for a moment upon the floor of the little snow basin that occupies the top of the mountain."

Four men stood at last on the summit of North America.

Their first act was to thank God for permitting them to achieve their goal. "This prime duty done," to quote the reverent arch-deacon, they set up the instruments that they had carried with them and took thermometer and barometer readings. Then, and not until then, did they let their eyes sweep out over the stupendous panorama that no man had ever seen before—more than 50,000 square miles of Alaska, peaks and ranges, glaciers and valleys, rivers and plains, from the ice-locked arctic interior to the sea.

But it is not alone for the sake of a "view" that men struggle up to the high places of the earth. Let us allow the conqueror of Mc-Kinley to describe the mountaineer's reward, for no man has ever described it better:

"Only those who have for long years cherished a great and almost inordinate desire, and have had that desire gratified to the limit of their expectation, can enter into the deep thankfulness and content that filled the heart upon the descent of this mountain. There was no pride of conquest, no trace of that exultation of victory some enjoy upon the first ascent of a lofty peak, no gloating over good fortune that had hoisted us a few hundred feet higher than others who had struggled and been discomfited. Rather was the feeling that a privileged communion with the high places of the earth had been granted; that not only had we been permitted to lift up eager eyes to these summits, secret and solitary since the world began, but to enter boldly upon them, to take place, as it were, domestically in their hitherto sealed chambers, to inhabit them, and to cast our eyes down from them, seeing all things as they spread out from the windows of heaven itself."

They constructed a rough cross of birch staves which they had carried with them, thrust it deep into the snow, and, gathering around it, spoke the solemn, joyful words of the Te Deum. Then they started down, the tiredest and happiest of men.

For nineteen years after its conquest no one approached Mc-Kinley. Then, in the spring of 1932, two separate expeditions converged upon it at the same time. One was completely successful in every respect. The other culminated tragically in the only deaths that have occurred in the battle for the mountain.

The successful party was composed of Erling Strom, a well-known Norwegian-American skier, Alfred Lindley, a Minneapolis attorney, Harry Liek, superintendent of McKinley National Park, and Grant Pearson, a park ranger. They reached the upper basin

by substantially the same route as the earlier parties—the ridge
now named for Harry Karstens—and successfully scaled both
north and south peaks, thus becoming the first party to reach both
summits of McKinley.

The unusual feature of this expedition was that it was the first
to make extensive use of skis in the ascent of a large mountain.
This enabled the climbers to save a vast amount of time on reconnaissance trips and in the back-and-forth transportation of supplies, particularly on the Muldrow Glacier and the lower reaches
of the ridge. Strom said of one particular stretch that "each ascent
took us fully half an hour, but we could return to camp in one
minute." In addition, the skis greatly decreased the danger of
falling through the innumerable snow-hidden crevasses.

High on Karstens Ridge the Strom-Lindley party discovered a
thermometer left by Stuck. It had been the archdeacon's belief
that McKinley, in winter, was the coldest place in the world, and
on his descent of the mountain he had cached a minimum thermometer at a point where he hoped the next party would find it.
The climbers of 1932 proved that he had been right. The indi-
cator of the instrument had dropped past the end of the scale,
which was 95° below zero, and was stuck in the bulb, where it
could go no farther. It appeared obvious, therefore, that at one
time or another during the winters of the intervening years, the
temperature had sunk to at least 100° below zero—the greatest
natural cold ever recorded anywhere on earth. After this, the dis-
coverers reported, the mere 20° and 25° below temperatures
encountered on the heights seemed to them almost balmy!

The second 1932 expedition to McKinley did not arrive on the
scene until the first was already high on the mountain. This was
the so-called "Cosmic Ray" expedition, which planned to undertake extensive scientific observations at great altitudes and was
led by Allan Carpé, one of the most accomplished young American
mountaineers. These climbers also brought modern methods to the
technique of mountaineering, but, unlike their rivals, their innova-
tion was not skis, but an airplane. On the same day they found
Stuck's thermometer on Karstens Ridge, Strom and his companions
stared down the face of a precipice to see a plane landing supplies

at the head of the Muldrow Glacier, 4000 feet below. This was the first time in climbing history such a feat had been attempted, much less accomplished.

During the next week, while the first party successfully scaled both the north and south peaks, they saw nothing more of Carpé and his expedition. When at last they descended to the head of the Muldrow, the plane was gone, but two tents were standing near the former site of one of their own camps. And the tents were deserted.

"Immediately," Strom had said, "we felt that something had gone wrong. Inside one tent we found two open sleeping bags and a pot half full of frozen mulligan stew. From the other tent, containing cosmic ray apparatus, we could hear a little mechanism slowly ticking."

From a diary found in one of the sleeping bags they learned that the only occupants of the tents had been Carpé and one companion, Theodore Koven. There being no sign of either man, they pushed on down the glacier, following an almost obliterated track; and it was not long before their worst fears were confirmed. A mile and a half below the camp they spied a tiny dark object against the white immensity of snow. It was Koven's body. One leg had been injured and also the side of his head. He had obviously fallen into a crevasse, but had managed to climb out again, only to collapse and die from exposure.

Carpé's body has never been found.

Thus the story of McKinley, to date, ends in both triumph and tragedy. In 1936 an expedition of the National Geographic and Pan American Societies surveyed the peak from the air, but during the past nine years there has been no further attempt to climb it.

"The Great One" today is not the almost inaccessible mountain it was in the days of the sourdoughs, and of Parker, Browne and Stuck. For the past twenty-three years the country surrounding it has been a National Park. The Alaska Railroad runs within a hundred miles of its summit, and the trail from McKinley Park station is dotted with rangers' cabins nearly to the foot of the Muldrow Glacier. An expedition that formerly required months might be accomplished now in two or three weeks.

Will McKinley be climbed again? To be sure it will. But mountaineers are a strange and hardy breed, and it will be not because of these helping facilities, but in spite of them, that they will come again. And, whatever use they make of trains and planes, of sleds and skis and even tractors, in approaching the mountain, all the marvels of modern science and invention combined will not get them to the top. There is only one key, now as in the past, to the summit of our continent—the endurance and skill and courage of those who seek it.

\* \* \*

Grant H. Pearson, a Mount McKinley Park ranger and later superintendent of Mount McKinley National Park, took part in one of the ascents. In 1962 he wrote with Philip Newill *My Life of High Adventure*. In its appendix he lists all the climbs, attempted as well as successful, that had been made up to that time. They number thirty-three. Of these, twenty took place after the successful Lindley-Liek expedition of 1932, of which he was a member. The following passage deals with one of the most stirring of the ascents of Mount McKinley.

From · · ·

*My Life of High Adventure,* by Grant H. Pearson with Philip Newill

"THE DEFEAT OF DENALI"

*1961.* This was the year that marked Denali's [1] most unexpected defeat. Ever since men had first looked speculatively at McKinley's various soaring, forbidding slopes, when they saw the sheer wall of the south face they turned away with a shrug or a shudder. It included a 6,000-foot cliff of gray granite and bluewhite, shining ice. No place for any human.

On the nineteenth of July, 1961, this defeatist view was put to a decisive end. A team of six men from the Italian Alpine Club

[1] The Indians' name for Mount McKinley (ed.).

scaled that cliff with ropes and pitons and painfully frostbitten feet, finally heaved themselves up over the top ledge and stood up on the South Peak. (I had looked over the top of that cliff when I was up there in '32; my first instinct was to jump back.)

Bradford Washburn, notified of the ascent by telegram, called it "the greatest achievement in American mountaineering history."

The men who accomplished the feat were Riccardo Cassin, 53-year-old leader of the expedition; Gian Canali, Romano Perego, Luigi Alippi, Annibale Zucchi and Luigi Arraldi.

Denali didn't let the six off unscathed. All were lashed by winds and sub-zero temperatures; frostbite stabbed Gian Canali's feet so sharp and deep that after the climb back down the south face cliff his companions had to carry him the rest of the way to their base camp on the glacier. They had one piece of good luck. They had made previous arrangements to have bush pilot Don Sheldon fly in and meet them on a certain date—which date happened to be the very next day. Sheldon landed his ski plane on the glacier on schedule, and was surprised to see the team of climbers sledding a man down the glacier to his plane. Sheldon flew Canali out to safety as he had done with Mrs. Helga Bading the year before.

Earlier in the year three parties had scaled the peak via the now well-explored West Buttress route.

. . . . . . . . . . . . . . .

But it was the six Italians, climbing McKinley's last unconquered south face, who achieved the final taming of Denali. They brought to 116 the number of toiling, mountain-fascinated men who had set foot on the summit of McKinley since Bishop Stuck and Harry Karstens led the first expedition to the top in 1913.

# 24

# *HUNTING FOR GAME*

THE variety of game and fish to be found in the Alaskan
Arctic is effectively described by one who has been a big-game
guide in northern Alaska for the last twenty years, Harmon R.
(Bud) Helmericks. Here are excerpts from an article that appeared in the *Alaska Sportsman* in 1965.

From · · ·

   *The Last New Land,* by Harmon R. Helmericks

     . . . The game of our Arctic, going from north to south, is first
polar bear, white fox, hair seals, walrus and whales. These are all
sea game and technically speaking they are "international game"
as they inhabit the high seas, but Alaska regulates the hunting of
them by people hunting from or returning to Alaska.

   The polar bear is considered by most to be the greatest furred
trophy of the world, and is of course the largest bear in the world.
It is also the only strictly carnivorous bear for it lives entirely
upon meat and mostly the blubber of hair seals. The total number
of polar bears in the arctic ice north of Alaska is perhaps a little
under two thousand. Sound game management would allow a
harvest of about the average take over the years and the polar bear
population has remained stable.

   There has been much controversy in recent years over the use of airplanes in hunting, particularly for hunting polar bear. The main complaints come when two airplanes are used and the game driven, or still shot, from the air. This surely reduces the sport to butchery with a rating of zero.

On the other hand hunting polar bear from an airplane can be one of the most sporting and fascinating of all hunts. As in all sports it isn't the means of travel but the sportsmanship of the participants that counts. The airplane just enables a mediocre-poor sportsman to be a very poor sportsman faster and easier, showing him up for all to see.

A second and more dangerous factor from a conservation standpoint is that when conditions are right polar bears are very easily killed by use of airplanes. It is then that people who aren't particularly interested in the sport jump in to kill a bear because it is easy, and unscrupulous pilots see an easy buck while they pile up fantastic kills of polar bears for a single pair of airplanes. In the near future a strictly regulated permit system of polar bear hunting will be set up.

The use of an airplane in hunting the entire Arctic is the best method, the most practical, and when used by true sportsmen the most sporting. From a conservation standpoint using an airplane is the most desirable as it spreads hunting pressure over the entire area, it leaves the land area unchanged and the original habitat intact. The advances in transportation both in the air and on the ground are forcing us to one of two decisions. The first is to become sportsmen and properly harvest our game. The second is to continue as we have in the past and end up with no game at all.

The Arctic is a land where we have a chance to practice true game management. There is no competition for the range from ranchers or farmers, for indeed, this land will never be so used. Our fish and game are our *ONLY* renewable natural resources and wise game management is of utmost importance to us all.

Polar bear are best hunted in March, April or May. The current season is from October 15 until April 20. It isn't practical for a sportsman to hunt during the dark days of midwinter unless he wants to camp on the ice and make a regular expedition of his hunt. In addition to the regular $10 non-resident hunting license a $150 polar bear tag is required and all polar bear skins must be sealed.

In all Arctic hunting during the winter rifles have to be washed in kerosene and left to dry so they will fire. The best rifle for polar bear, I believe, is the 300 Weatherby loaded with 180 grain bullets. A polar bear is easily killed with any rifle, but the shots can be long, and on the ice judging range is very hard. In more than twenty years of hunting polar bears I have never seen one offer to attack a person no matter what the provocation. In choosing your rifle a telescope sight is real handy and any bolt action rifle from the 270 Winchester on up will do, but rifles larger than the 300 magnums are not desirable except for walrus.

A polar bear hunt may also include hair seals, ugrugs (bearded seals), wolf, wolverine, caribou and ptarmigan, and a well-planned Arctic hunt is most pleasant.

Stalking the hair seal upon the ice is a fascinating and exacting sport. These seals' pelts make beautiful coats, parkas or rugs and all of my hunters prize them highly. Ugrugs are the large bearded seals and range up to eight hundred pounds. They are rare north of Alaska but fairly common off the southern Arctic coast.

Caribou aren't suitable for trophies in the spring because the big bulls have all dropped their antlers although cows and small bulls still have theirs. The long winter hair is worn around the head from pawing and feeding and it breaks off easily, too. Caribou are fun to hunt on the flat prairie and they are good for food. There is no season on them and a nonresident requires a $25 tag.

Wolverines are one of our most fascinating game animals. They are found only in the real wilderness; being easily trapped, man has exterminated them in all settled areas. About 99 per cent of the stories told about wolverines are misinformation repeated again or pure lies. You need a special permit to hunt for them, or a trapping license during trapping season. There is no charge for the permit and your guide will secure one for you. The wolverine is a rare animal and the sportsman who secures one is mighty lucky. They make a lovely life-sized mount.

Wolves are our daily Arctic plains game that you may—with a

special permit—shoot from an airplane. A 12 gauge shotgun and buckshot is best. I like number 0 buckshot although many use number 4s. A rifle can be used, too, either from the air or after landing near the wolf. The big arctic wolves are the largest there are and make a trophy anyone will be proud of.

The bounty system has been a blot upon Alaska's records all too long, in spite of all the game department's efforts to remove it. In the light of sound game management, since the wolf plays such an important role, a closed season and a one wolf limit is needed. The wolf is an absolutely essential part of our caribou economy and to lose the wolf is to lose the caribou herds also.

Shooting a wolf from an airplane is a new kind of hunting. It can be done easily by anyone who can shoot a shotgun. Few people will want more than one wolf though, for a wolf has absolutely no chance of escaping from an airplane upon the open prairie.

In the springtime the ptarmigan are pure white aside from their black tail feathers that are visible only in flight. Large willow ptarmigan are found on the prairie and few hunters can hit them regularly on the wing for they are extremely fast and blend with the white background. The season extends from August 20 until April 30, with a bag limit of twenty birds. You can include ptarmigan on a polar bear hunt along with the other land game.

An Arctic hunt is best planned at least eight months in advance and preferably a year ahead. There are only a handful of guides qualified to hunt the Arctic and they are usually booked up well in advance. You can expect to pay from $2500 to $3500 for a two-week spring hunt using an airplane, with everything except your license furnished. There are a few "cheapies" in the business, of course, and the sportsman who hunts them out gets what he pays for, but in no other area of the world can you pay such a high price for simple mistakes.

The second phase of Arctic sea-ice hunting is in late July and August, as well as early September, for walrus, ugrug, seals and whales.

Hunting walrus at sea carries the same thrill as hunting elephants in Africa, which is the search for big ivory and the challenge of massive bulls that can be dangerous, plus the beauty and power of big herds. They are hunted from a boat so the main problem in walrus hunting is waiting for ice conditions and weather to be right. This can take days or may not even happen during an entire season in some areas. When conditions are right you will find it a grand adventure drifting amid the ice floes. Incidentally, there are no icebergs in the Alaskan Arctic, only the floe ice.

The pitiful thing about walrus hunting is the crippling of animals and dreadful waste. A walrus is big and hard to kill except with a brain shot. Once in the water a dead walrus sinks. In a walrus hunt many are killed and wounded and few recovered unless extreme care is taken, and even then a live walrus may push a dead companion off the ice. A shoulder-type harpoon gun that carries a line should be along on any walrus hunt. By careful use of such a gun the loss is nearly eliminated for a line can be made fast at a range of up to forty yards.

Seals, ugrugs and at times whales are encountered on a walrus hunt. A nonresident needs a $100 walrus tag in addition to the regular hunting license. This tag also enables hunters to take the ivory out of Alaska. Walrus ivory cannot be transported without this permit. You may hunt the ugrug and hair seals (fur seals aren't Arctic animals) with your regular hunting license and the pelts are good for trophies or clothing. Whales are interesting animals, big and quite harmless if left alone. The killer whale is a beautiful animal that is often encountered. They are active animals that at times leap clear of the water. Contrary to popular belief there is no known case of a person being killed by one. A special international license is required to hunt all whales and they are best left alone unless your party is licensed and equipped to hunt them. A well-organized walrus hunt will cost from $1000 to $2000 and will take about ten days if all goes well.

A hunt for the rare and beautiful barren ground grizzly bear is best made in the spring if you want to take the most beautifully furred of all our bears at its best. Few people know of this bear's existence and not more than a dozen sportsmen have ever taken one. The present season is from May 15 until June 15, and from September 1 until December 31. In hunting all of Alaska's bears, aside from the black bear, only adults unaccompanied by cubs may be taken. The barren ground bear lives upon the prairie and there are very few of them. Hunting of these bears must be very carefully regulated. The finest pelts are taken in mid-May or late September. A special hunt for them costs about $2000.

Fall hunting starts with Dall Sheep on August first. The Brooks Mountain Range covers the southern Alaska Arctic from east to west and divides the timbered lands of interior Alaska from the vast Arctic prairie to the north. The southern drainage of the Brooks Range is timbered with spruce, bush, willow, alder and cottonwood. The northern drainage is open prairie-covered mountains. It is a beautiful mountain range to hunt and especially pleasant in the fall. There are a few sheep in the range although not numerous. They also run a little smaller than those of southern Alaska, both in body and horns. They are pure white though, and very similar to the purest strain as well as the most northern of the Dall Sheep. There isn't a single dark hair on them and their horns grow symmetrically and are rarely broomed or broken. The weather is delightful during the early part of the season and there is continuous daylight!

The Arctic prairie is the true home of the caribou. Here are found the vast herds that can number into the tens of thousands. Caribou provide the finest plains hunting in America today. The caribou live in the Arctic the year around and do not migrate south as is often imagined. There is very little snowfall on the Arctic prairie and the caribou find easy grazing the winter through.

Caribou is a mobile species and they are going somewhere most of the time. Thus, they require a tremendous range to survive in.

The old bulls grow massive sets of antlers, in fact, the largest for the animals' size of any of our deer family. A mature bull makes a beautiful trophy and many people feel the caribou is our prettiest big-game animal. All sexes and ages, from calf on, have antlers that develop and are shed at varying times of the year. The big bulls lose the velvet in early September and it is best to hunt them then. In early October the rut starts, and the bulls are unfit for food from that time until early December, when they lose their antlers.

People who are uninformed often believe that animals such as moose and caribou fatten up for the winter because the bulls are quite fat in the fall. This is completely untrue. The animals fatten up for the rut (mating season). They are at their fattest when the rut starts and their thinnest when it is over just a few weeks later. Thus, they enter the winter at their thinnest, and slowly fatten up during the winter and spring with a fantastic fattening growth in early fall until the rut starts again.

The caribou is an extremely valuable animal to us Arctic people for food and clothing, and it is always such a thrill to see the big herds of them. Caribou are generally found in small bands of a half dozen to thirty animals until some mass movement, the mating season or mosquitoes drive them together into a large herd.

Arctic wolves and caribou depend upon each other for their survival. The wolf must have the sick, stragglers, cripples and die-offs for its food supply while the caribou must have the wolf to eliminate the diseased, to keep the herds scattered to prevent over-grazing and clean up the die-offs, thus again preventing the spread of parasites and disease. Caribou can't possibly survive in a healthy state in vast numbers without the wolf's presence.

Moose inhabit the entire Arctic area wherever willows grow, right to the Arctic Ocean where willow thickets extend along the big rivers. They graze upon the short ground willows and in prairie ponds all over the Arctic in summer, but again concentrate along the willow-bordered streams in winter. Willows are our moose's chief food supply. The moose population and willow browse seems to be in an exact state of balance. Prairie dwelling moose do not grow as large a set of antlers as do the southern moose but their bodies run as large or larger. A large bull will stand seven feet at the shoulder. Moose hunting upon the prairie is easier than in the timber. On the south slopes of the Brooks Range moose are found everywhere, and their antlers run as large as any. Moose shed the velvet from their antlers in early September and the rut starts in late September. Like caribou bulls, moose meat isn't suitable for food once the rut starts and they shouldn't be hunted then. When you call a moose it isn't suitable for food, is a good rule to follow. Moose season starts August 20 in the

north, and a $50 tag is required of nonresidents (tags aren't re-
quired of residents), and a harvest ticket is required of all hunters
for both sheep and moose. There is no charge for the harvest ticket
but a report must be filled in and mailed to the game department.

Black bears are found in all of the spruce-timbered Arctic. They
aren't nearly as numerous as in southern Alaska, but you will find
them filling their stomachs with blueberries on the red hillsides
each fall. They are wary fellows and not easily stalked.

A ten dollar tag is required of nonresidents and their pelts, like
those of the grizzly, are prime by late September.

The willow ptarmigan furnishes the best upland shooting found
in Alaska, or perhaps in America today, during their high cycles.
Cleve La Fleur is an avid bird shooter and has hunted birds around
the world for many years. He told me that of all the upland birds
he felt willow ptarmigan shooting was the finest he has known.
The generous bag limit of twenty gives a hunter plenty of shooting.
There are a few of the smaller rock ptarmigan in the Arctic but
they are scarce and often too tame to be considered a sporting bird.

The spruce grouse season opens August 20 also, and they are
found in all the timbered Arctic. They are most fun when hunted
along a lake or stream early in the morning when they come down
to pick gravel. They haven't acquired the fear of man that their
cousin the ruffed grouse has, and when alarmed they will often
just fly up in a tree and look at you.

There are a few of the big Arctic hares in the western Arctic
and the snowshoe hare is found in all the timbered Arctic. These
animals, like the grouse and ptarmigan, go in cycles and are
plentiful some seasons, and all but nonexistent during others. They
can be shot but are most often caught in snares for sport and food.

Other Arctic game is usually trapped. Included are the five
varieties of fox—white, blue, red, cross and silver; the marten—
sable and ermine; otter, muskrat, beaver, mink, lynx and wolf or
wolverine. No one in the Arctic makes a living trapping anymore,
but a few do trap for sport and a little extra income. Running a
trap line gives you a wonderful insight into the lives of the animals
and is a great deal of fun. A nonresident trapping license costs
$100. Special arrangements can be made with some guides to

spend a winter trapping and it is an experience any sportsman will enjoy.

Arctic waters offer grayling, Arctic char, lake trout, pike and shee fish to fishermen, plus whitefish of several varieties and ling cod to net fishermen. Salmon run up most big rivers. The streams and lakes are free of ice by late June and freeze over again in September.

Shee fish run only up the rivers of the southwestern Arctic and are usually caught on a spoon. They are a searun fish like salmon and their size makes them fun to catch. The salmon won't bite in fresh water and are caught in nets.

Grayling are the chief dry fly takers. They find a plentiful supply of food in insects and will even eat cranberries and blueberries that fall into the stream. They are sporting fellows that rarely exceed 16 or 18 inches, and often leap when hooked. I have seen them hit a dry fly in the air and they seem to take an insect or lure on the way down from a leap. They will follow up the smallest streams and live in the pools all summer but when the first bright leaves of fall arrive they head back to the larger rivers and lakes.

The main fish of the lakes are Arctic char and lake trout. In these cold waters fish growth is very slow and the carrying capacities of the lakes very low. Thus no Arctic lake can stand any but the very lightest fishing pressure, and a few careless fishermen can completely ruin a lake in one season. I know of one large lake that was completely fished out by one man in five years' time to where even nets couldn't produce a single fish! The trout and char live chiefly upon fresh water snails.

Pike are found all across the Arctic but as rare visitors. While they grow to good size—the record is 48 inches and 29 pounds— they are too scattered to be considered. Their scarcity is likely due to a shortage of small forage fish.

The Arctic Ocean is still a vast unknown area as far as sport fishing is concerned. I have caught char up to fourteen pounds there, but I have only fished in a few areas. There is always so much to see and do in our newest land that there isn't time to check out all the spots. When I first came to the Arctic most of the lakes and streams were unfished and unknown. You will find there

is a wonderful charm to unfished waters that I'm sure all fishermen will understand.

The Arctic is the nesting ground of many of our waterfowl. They
arrive before the ice has left the lakes, raise their broods in the
steady daylight and depart when the sun starts setting in the fall.
We see their family life and they depart before they have fattened
up for fall. So, while there are millions of ducks and geese in the
Arctic, we don't do much waterfowl shooting. It is wonderful to
see them and to understand their ways of living. We do have all
the eider ducks along the coast and quite a few are shot at places
such as Barrow. They are a large, heavy-bodied duck and the
males are beautifully decorated.

In the southern states the original game is gone, its habitat completely altered and the balance of the wilderness ruined forever.
In our Arctic we have been given a second chance. This land
stands today as the Creator left it. This isn't a land to farm or
build large cities on. This is a land for the wild creatures. Wildlife
is the Arctic's only annual crop. Its careful harvest is the Arctic's
only major industry.

In order to hunt the Arctic and understand it you will need a
guide. A complete listing of Master Guides and Registered Guides
can be obtained by writing the Alaska Department of Fish and
Game, Subport Building, Juneau, Alaska. Your guide will take
care of all arrangements and you may rest assured that you will
have a grand adventure as well as a successful hunt.

For those who wish to travel the land and take part in its way
of living Wien Alaska Airlines offers regular tours to all the towns
and villages of the Arctic. These guided tours give you a firsthand taste of Arctic living.

Whether you are a fisherman, traveler or hunter; whether you
come by canoe and dog team, as I once did, or by jet airliner
and float airplane, you will never forget the vastness, freedom,
beauty and peace of our last new land.

*   *   *

Hunting is a great sport, but not without risk. Every year in
Alaska several hunters—and some nonhunters—are mauled and
even on occasion killed by bears.

Here is a vivid account of such an episode in which, fortunately, the author and victim, Forest H. Young, Jr., survived. It first appeared in *Outdoor Life* in 1957.

## *Day of Terror,* by Forest H. Young, Jr.

Marty Cordes and I spent the last half of September, 1955, hunting moose in the Chilkat River valley north of Haines, Alaska, where we live and work as construction men. We had no luck the first 10 days.

I wounded a bull the second day, in a heavy rain, and followed the blood trail until it washed out. For a week after that we didn't lay eyes on a moose with horns, so finally we loaded our gear in the canoe and outboarded to a vacant cabin 10 miles farther up the Chilkat in moose country that had never failed me. We'd have gone there sooner, but figured it might be too crowded with hunters to suit us.

But there was no cause for complaint on that score. We had things to ourselves, and saw enough moose sign the first day to convince us we'd come to the right place. An hour after we started out next morning, in a patch of willow-grown muskeg about two miles from camp, we ran onto two bulls and several cows feeding. The breeding season for this group either had ended or not yet begun, for mature bull moose aren't often found together during the rut. Anyway, the bulls were good ones and we dropped both of them.

We spent the rest of the day dressing them and packing part of the meat to camp. The remainder of the meat and the two hides we cached in trees, making sure everything was out of reach of bears. Browns and grizzlies are plentiful in the area, and we knew that any meat left where they could get at it would be almost sure to disappear overnight.

The following morning, September 30, we loaded the canoe with meat. Then Marty cranked the outboard and took off for Haines and my freezer. I made more trips for meat that afternoon and the next forenoon, and by the time Marty got back on Saturday, October 1, I had everything in camp except his moose hide. That was still stretched in a good-size birch, 10 or 12 feet off the ground, at the spot where he'd made the kill.

Sunday morning Marty wanted to pick up a mess of grouse for a stew, so I agreed to bring in the hide. We both planned to be back at the cabin about an hour before noon, ready to break camp and head home.

When I arrived at the kill I found that bears had finally taken over. The ground looked as if someone had gone over it with a garden rake, and two neat mounds of grass and moss showed where they'd covered the uneaten entrails of both moose. That should have warned me, but it didn't.

Marty's hide was still in the birch, unmolested. I walked over to the tree and threw my packboard down, and as I glanced up I saw movement in the brush about 300 feet away. I took another look and made out the backs and heads of two bears some 30 feet apart.

They didn't scare me, though I was sure from their color and shape that they were grizzlies. All the bears I'd ever met lit out as soon as they discovered me, and I saw no reason to expect trouble with this pair. But almost instantly they went out of sight, and next thing I knew one was coming headlong at me through the thicket. I couldn't see him, but the brush moved as he smashed through, so I could trace his course by the commotion he made.

I still wasn't scared. I jumped up and down and waved my arms, yelling to frighten him off. Then it dawned on me that this bear wasn't going to bluff out. He was still coming hell-bent.

I wasn't carrying a rifle, or even a hunting knife. I'd gone light, my only purpose being to pack the 80-pound green moose hide into camp. There was only one thing to do. I jumped for a low branch of the birch and started up hand over hand. But before I'd climbed my own height the grizzly broke out of the brush and came swarming at me.

He didn't fool around. He sank his teeth into the back of my right leg just above the knee and pulled me down with one savage yank. I landed on my back, and we tussled for a few seconds. I wound up in a sitting position, with the bear's left front leg across both of mine, pinning me to the ground. With his teeth, he grabbed me by the inside of the thigh just below the crotch, and in one deep, deliberate bite tore away a strip of flesh. Blood spurted, and I braced myself with my left arm and pummeled him in the face with my fist, but he paid no more attention than to a fly buzzing around his head.

That first minute was about as bad as any part of the whole ordeal. The bear's face and mine weren't a foot apart. He had a big, burly head, with long, stiff, gray guard hairs standing out all over his face. His eyes were red and flashing with hate, his muzzle was screwed up in a sullen mask, and he was slobbering as he chewed at my legs. He went on ripping flesh, skin, and clothes to shreds, and every second I expected him to grab me by the throat and finish the job with one shake.

I was wearing wool trousers and heavy wool underwear, but they gave me no protection. I could feel him grind the cloth into the flesh with each bite, and I realized he could tear my legs off and I'd have to sit there and let him do it. I punched him in the face until I broke my hand, but it did no good.

Somewhere I've read that a merciful numbness comes over a man being mauled by a big animal. Maybe that happens in some cases, but it certainly didn't in mine. I was anything but numb. I could feel every bite he took, and it hurt like hell.

I don't know how long it went on. Maybe a minute, maybe only a few seconds, but it seemed like an eternity. Suddenly it flashed through my mind that my only hope for survival was to play dead. I flopped over on my back and side, and made myself go limp.

Instantly, the bear stopped chewing. He stood over me, keeping me pinned down with one leg. I even tried not to breathe. But in spite of my will power and the knowledge that my life hung in the balance, I couldn't hold back a low groan.

He grabbed me as a cat grabs an escaping mouse, and again I felt his teeth sink deep. He slashed through my side and ripped loose a flap of skin and muscle that exposed my bladder. The pain was agonizing, but I lay still and let him tear. He took another bite or two, then dropped me.

I don't know whether I moved that time or whether he just wanted to make sure of finishing me. Anyway, he nailed me once

more, this time by the back below my right shoulder. He bit
through, ripped three ribs loose from the spine, and tore a hole
all the way into my chest cavity. If he'd chomped a little lower,
in the kidney area, that bite would have killed me.

I didn't fight back, move, or groan. I knew now it was a case
of play dead or be dead. He dropped me and walked away. I
couldn't see him without turning my head and I didn't dare risk
that, so I lay motionless and hoped he wouldn't come back.

But suddenly I felt the muskeg shake under me and heard his
heavy feet pounding in. He came with a queer sort of panting
noise, not bawling or growling. I braced myself for another maul-
ing, but he didn't touch me. I could see his feet and lower legs,
a yard from my face. He stood and looked me over for maybe a
minute. Then he turned and slowly walked away.

Perhaps five minutes later he repeated the performance, coming
for me at a panting run, standing over me without molesting me,
then walking off. My possum act must have been pretty good.

For a long time I neither saw nor heard him. It was becoming
hard for me to breathe because of the hole in my back, and I
realized that unless I turned over on my face and let my nose and
mouth drain I would strangle. I waited as long as I could, finally
decided the bear had left for keeps, and slowly and painfully
managed to roll over. Nothing happened, and I began to think
the worst was over.

Long after that I thought I heard faint sounds at the moose
leavings, 100 feet away, but when I held my breath to listen the
noise stopped. That happened three or four times. Then I felt
the muskeg quake under me once more and heard that queer
panting. No noise out of the pit of hell itself could have sounded
worse to me.

The bear must have sensed from my position that I'd moved. He
let out a murderous roar and tore into me again, grabbing me
by the buttocks. He spanned my whole rear with his jaws, bit
through to the bone, then took a deeper bite as if he meant to cut
me in two.

Next he picked me off the ground and shook me until I thought
my back would break or my head snap off. I've seen bears kill

salmon that way, shattering the spine with one flick of their jaws, and I was sure the same thing was going to happen to me. But he dropped me as abruptly as he'd seized me, then lumbered off. I heard his heavy footfalls fade away.

He'd dropped me face down, so I was in no danger of choking. But cold water from the muskeg was seeping through my clothing, chilling me to the bone, and I was in pain beyond description. The bear had torn the flesh away from the bones on the inside of my legs, ripped both buttocks, mangled my right hand, torn one rib entirely out and left two others protruding through the skin, punched a big hole through to my lung cavity, and chewed me from head to knees.

What I did next sounds crazy and impossible, and maybe you won't even believe it. But I'll take an oath that it happened, and before you pass judgment try to imagine my torture.

I was convinced I was going to die. I couldn't see a chance of getting out alive, lying there in the muskeg by myself, not knowing when or if Cordes would find me. Suddenly I decided I couldn't stand the pain any longer. I might as well get it over with. Other men badly mauled by bears had killed themselves, and now I knew why.

I worked a hand down into my pocket and managed to get out a small jackknife I carried. It must have taken me half an hour. Then I moved my arms up in front of my head, opened the knife, and slashed my left wrist deeply, trying for the big artery. No blood came, and I hardly felt the pain over the flashes of agony that were stabbing through my body. I slashed again. At the third slash I exposed my wrist tendons, but still no blood came.

It didn't occur to me that I'd simply missed the artery. I thought I'd lost so much blood there was none left to flow. That meant I couldn't bleed myself to death through the wrist, and if I cut the tendons and then by some miracle survived I'd have a crippled hand for life. I was willing to kill myself, but I wasn't willing to chance that. So I gave up.

The next idea that came to me, born of pain and desperation, was even more horrible. If I could find my jugular vein with my knife, I'd be sure of a quick and merciful death. Something warned

me I mustn't fumble or I'd sever my windpipe instead and strangle
in my own blood. I laid the fingers of my good hand against my
throat, feeling for the pulse that would mark the location of a big
vein, but couldn't find it. The effort was almost too much for me.
I slumped and rested, and started exploring again. Then, off in
the brush, I heard Marty hail!

He was beside himself with horror when he saw me. His first
thought was to try packing me the two miles back to camp. But
when he started to lift me I screamed, and we gave that up. The
pain was more than I could bear. That meant Marty would have
to go for help, all the way to Haines, and I'd have to take my
chances while he was gone. It wasn't a pleasant prospect, but we
agreed there was no choice.

First he made a fast trip to camp and brought back a sleeping
bag and air mattress, shotgun and shells, cigarettes, water bottle,
food, matches, and a gas lantern. He somehow got me into the bag,
hung most of his outer clothing on the bushes over my head to
keep off the cold drizzle that was now falling, laid the loaded
shotgun beside me, lighted the gas lantern, and set it within reach.

"I'll make the fastest trip any man ever made to Haines," he
promised.

"I'll be here when you get back," I told him, but I was far
from sure.

It was now midafternoon. The bear had jumped me about
10:15 A.M. I was sure of the time, since I'd looked at my watch
just before I came in sight of the moose hide in the tree. I couldn't
expect Marty before midnight. He had two miles to get to camp,
a round trip of 30 miles by outboard and 60 by truck, and it would
take him a while to round up a rescue party. Then too, the Chilkat
is a glacial river running through steep country, quick to flood
and also quick to drop. It was at low stage now, and I knew Marty
would have trouble finding enough water for a fast run, especially
coming back upstream in the dark with passengers. At best I
had eight or nine hours to wait for help, maybe more. I doubted
I'd be able to hang on that long. There was also the grizzly to
worry about. I had a feeling he was still around.

An hour or so after Marty left I started to feel better. The pain lessened and I began to warm up, and I decided that maybe I was going to make it after all. The afternoon light faded; dusk was coming. Everything had been quiet and peaceful for hours. I almost stopped worrying about the bear, but I fought off the impulse to doze. Then suddenly the muskeg shook under me and I heard that queer, snuffling, panting noise once more.

My arms were inside the sleeping bag and my face was covered with the top of it. I didn't move. I didn't even breathe. He stopped a few feet away, let out a blood-chilling roar, and then I heard him turn and run off. I suppose the gas lantern, the bag and Marty's clothes draped over the brush were too much for him.

Lord in heaven, what a relief it was when he went away! But I still lay tense with dread for maybe half an hour, and then I heard a new noise over on my right. Something was rustling in the brush.

I had my arms out now, my face uncovered, and my hand on the gun. I twisted my head to look that way, and in the gathering twilight, not more than 15 feet away, stood a small bear cub.

Whether the bear that had attacked me was a sow rather than a male, and whether the cub belonged to her, I'll never know. I don't think it was a sow, for I was mauled by a grizzly, while the cub looked like a young black.

In any case, I was sure his old lady wasn't far off and I didn't want him to bring her down on me. He took a few steps toward me, looking with lively curiosity, and I didn't quite know what to do. If I scared him and he squalled, I'd be in for more trouble. Finally I tried a loud, sharp hiss. That did it. He swapped ends and ran without a sound. Five minutes later I heard more rustling at the edge of the brush. There was the cub again, back with a twin! I hissed at the two of them and they scrammed, but they were too curious to stay away. They came back, like two black imps, and for half an hour kept me on pins and needles, taking turns circling me and pussyfooting in for a look, but never coming closer than about 15 feet. I lay there, not knowing how to drive them off for keeps and dreading the minute when ma would come ambling along to investigate what they'd found. At last they scurried off, and everything grew quiet again.

It was close to full dark when the gas lantern burned down and went out. By itself that was a small happening, but in my situation it was big and terrifying. I felt I had no protection against the oncoming night, and fear that the grizzly might return began to mount in me, bordering on panic. Then he came, just as I knew he would.

I heard the strange panting off in the brush, but he didn't rush me this time. He came slowly, at my head where I couldn't see him, stalking me, probably made cautious by his earlier encounter with the lantern. I figured he'd jump me, once he satisfied himself the light was gone.

I raised the shot gun, aimed it in the direction of the noise, elevated the barrel so no pellets would strike him, and pulled the trigger. A red stab of flame shot from the muzzle, a kick jolted me from head to foot, and a blast ripped the night apart. It must have scared the bear half out of his wits. He let go a strangled roar, and I heard brush crack as he pounded off. Then all was silent.

Soon after that I heard bears at the moose remains, growling and gnawing. It was a horrid noise that went on three or four hours, but nothing came near me. My fear gradually subsided. Given any kind of break now, Marty and the rescue party would find me alive.

But I wasn't quite through with the killer. About an hour before midnight I heard that horrible panting once more. He was coming from my left, walking in cautiously. I brought the shotgun into position with the barrels laid across my body, and got set to nail him.

I knew the risk involved if the shot only wounded him, but anything was better than lying there and letting him get at me. I couldn't take another going over. I'd let him come within 10 feet. If he approached that close he meant business. I'd be able to make him out then and I'd give him both barrels together, square in the face. It might drive him off even if it didn't kill him.

When he was about 25 feet away he stopped. I heard him panting and snuffling, like a giant trying to clear his throat, and then he circled me, prowling in from the other side. I trained the gun that way and waited, but he came no nearer. Apparently the set-up was too strange for him to tackle. He nosed around for five or 10 minutes, then moved off. My bear troubles were over at last.

Around midnight I heard the far-off thrum of Marty's outboard. I doubt I'll ever hear another sound as welcome. It grew louder and nearer, then stopped abrubtly. I figured the rescue party was at the cabin, heading for me on foot.

Afraid they'd have trouble finding me in the darkness, I'd taken half a dozen matches out of my pocket, ready for striking as soon as I heard anyone approaching. I hung onto them for what seemed like hours but actually was only about 30 minutes. While I waited I heard the sound of an outboard once more, miles and hours away downriver, and my hopes sank. I was too far gone to figure out that it was a second boat, feeling its way up the Chilkat behind Marty, but still a long way off.

I listened, trying not to worry, and at last I heard voices. I struck the matches all at once, and somebody said "There he is! There's a light!" I have no words to tell you how I felt right then.

Flashlights winked through the darkness, and half a minute later Marty and two other friends from Haines were standing over me. The tension left me, and I took the first easy breath I'd drawn since the bear grabbed me. I asked what time it was and somebody said 12:45. It had been $14\frac{1}{2}$ hours since my ordeal began. That's a long, long time to wait for death or salvation.

The two friends Marty had brought were Carl Heinmiller and Walt Dueman. Carl is a retired army major, minus three fingers and an eye as a result of a ruckus on a South Sea island in World War II, and the top first-aid authority around Haines. He did what he could do for me, giving me an injection of penicillin and another of morphine, and then they eased me onto a stretcher they'd brought.

They lost the trail in the darkness, and it took them $3\frac{1}{2}$ hours to carry me to the cabin. The pain and jolting weren't as bad as I'd expected, for the morphine was biting in by that time, and I'm sure the trip was just as tough for Walt, Carl, and Marty as for me.

Apparently the bear didn't like giving me up, for twice on the way to camp my friends heard him bawling in the distance. They believed he trailed us about halfway in, sullen and quarrelsome but unwilling to jump a party that size.

A second rescue party of three men was waiting at the cabin.

Their boat was the one I'd heard away off down the Chilkat. They got into camp just before we arrived.

Shortly after 8 o'clock next morning, Dr. Robert Schuler of Juneau reached the cabin. He'd been in Haines the night before when Marty brought in the word about me, and had left at daylight with John Fox in Fox's airboat. They hadn't dared to tackle the river with the fast airboat in the dark, but made it in 45 minutes once they started. It had taken Marty four hours, and the other boat party almost eight. The Chilkat is a toughie to run at night.

By that time the full-scale rescue machinery of both Alaska and Canada was in motion in my behalf. At 10 A.M. a big helicopter from the R.C.A.F. base at Whitehorse, 100 miles away, landed on the little clearing in front of the cabin. The machine had been torn down for overhaul the day before, but when word of my plight reached the base, late in the evening, the repair crew worked all night to put it back together and in shape to undertake the rescue.

The huge whirly-bird carried a five-man crew, including a doctor and nurse, plasma, and drugs, but they didn't waste much time treating me in camp. I was a critical case by that time. They bundled me aboard and got me to Haines in short order, dripping plasma into me on the way. A Coast Guard plane was waiting there, and a little after noon an ambulance unloaded me at St. Anne's Hospital in Juneau.

Just 27 hours after the bear nabbed me I was on the operating table, and a Juneau surgeon, Dr. Cass Carter, an enthusiastic big-game hunter, started in on me.

I didn't get there any too soon. In all, there were more than 100 tooth marks on me, from my shoulders to my knees, plus countless cuts and gashes in my back and side. Several ribs were broken, one was torn out, and part of two had to be removed. The end of one had passed in against a lung, but luckily hadn't punctured it.

The doctor cut, sewed, and patched for three hours, bolstering me with blood transfusions, and he told me later he wouldn't have given two bits for the chances of any man with my injuries unless medical help had got to him within six hours. I had waited a lot longer than that.

My life hung by a thread for days after Dr. Carter was through. After that, though I wouldn't have won any beauty prizes, I was in better shape than I'd any right to expect.

I came out of it pretty well. I was in the hospital from October 3 to December 10 and went home 30 pounds underweight, but I've gained it back. I'm permanently short three ribs, and have some pretty tough-looking scars. My right hand is banged up, the third finger half an inch shorter than it used to be, but I can make out with it. My right side still pains at times, but I'm back at work and getting along all right.

Marty, Dr. Cass, and I built a cabin in that same area last summer, and hunted there last fall. Doc and I both took moose. I nailed mine only about 400 yards from where the bear attacked me. All the time I was out I was looking for a grizzly with stiff gray whiskers. I didn't run into him, but we had proof he or others like him were still around. Cass killed his moose just before dark, and we had time only to dress it out and cover it with a tarp that night. We'd been told that if we built a fence of sticks a couple of feet high around the kill it would keep bears off, so we tried it.

Next morning we found the fence knocked down, the moose head dragged off to one side, and the tarp pulled aside. We even came across a round depression in a patch of sand, made by that fat rump of a bear as he sat to size things up. But the noise of our airboat or our approach must have spooked him, for he left without feeding. We saw no more of him, and packed the meat to the cabin without delay.

You can be sure of one thing, too. We kept a rifle handy while we were doing it. No bear or any other dangerous animal will ever again catch me with my guard down.

One detail is left. We never got that moose hide of Marty's back to camp. It's still in the birch tree, so far as I know, and it can stay there forever for all of me.

*     *     *

More than forty years ago, when Harold McCracken was collecting Alaskan game animals, it was not possible to charter an amphibian plane at Anchorage to put the hunter down where

the game was in abundance. It was then, as he described it in
*Field and Stream*, "a terribly wild Garden of Eden."

## *The Alaskan Grizzly*, by Harold McCracken

The great Alaskan grizzly—the Kodiak brown bear (*Ursus
middendorffi*) and its even larger Alaska Peninsula brother (*Ursus
gyas*)—is probably as far famed as either the African lion or the
Bengal tiger. And yet, probably less is known of its life history
than of any of the other larger mammals. He is, nevertheless, a
sort of fictitious byword at the hearts of all those hunter-sportsmen
who enjoy the savor of genuine hazard in their quest for sport and
trophies. A beast whom most prefer to "talk" about hunting, rather
than face in mortal combat. And his one thousand to two thousand
pounds of brawn and power is unquestionably the embodiment
of all that even the most adventurous care to seek. He is supreme
in size, in brute power, as well as in physical dexterity, sagacity,
and pernicious damnableness in the animal kingdom. And this,
not in the mere belief of a casual observer, but weighed and tried
on the scales of science. To go into details regarding the life history, the "whys" and "whens" and "hows" of his life career,
would entail a goodly volume, which, though immensely interesting in every detail, would be far too cumbersome in such a place
as this.

His home is that long, slightly curved arm that reaches out from
the southwestern corner of Alaska, separating the North Pacific
Ocean from the Bering Sea, and dabbling off in the spattered
Aleutian Islands. The Alaska Peninsula is today one of the most
wild, least visited and less known of all the districts on this
continent.

But in reality, the Alaska Peninsula is, for the most part, a
terribly wild Garden of Eden. Its waterways boast more fine fish
than any other similar sized section of the globe; on its rounded
undulating hills and tundra lands are great herds of caribou, the
finest of edible flesh; it is carpeted with berry bushes; there are
fine furred animals in abundance; millions of wildfowl, duck,
geese, eiders, seals, sea lions; big bears—everything necessary for

the welfare and happiness of primitive man. It is a truly primitive land.

While the great Alaska Peninsula bear is a carnivore, or flesh-eater—and what applies to this bear also applies in many respects to his brothers, the sub- and sub-sub-species of other districts of Alaska—yet he has frequently and correctly been called "the great grass-eating bear" and also "the great fish-eating bear." All animals subsist in the manner and on the foods that demand the least effort, hazard and inconvenience to their life and comfort. Thus the bears of the Alaskan Peninsula have chosen fish and grass and berries as their main diet of food, varied with an occasional caribou, a seal or meal from the carcass of a dead whale or walrus washed up on the beach. During most of the months of the year, the streams are choked with salmon, affording him an inexhaustible supply until well into the middle of the winter. And as hibernation is for the most part only an alternative for existing under winter conditions, when it is hard or sometimes impossible to get food, and as the Alaska Peninsula is in winter moderated by the warming Japan Current, making it quite mild and livable for old Gyas, he is forced to spend but a relatively short period in the "long sleep." This increased activity, together with the abundance of fine food, accounts for the unusual size to which the bears of that district grow.

And he is very much aware of his size and strength; and the fact that he has had no outside natural enemy through the line of his ancestors has made him aggressive, haughty and overbearing, fearing nothing and crushing all that impedes his way.

Thus the Alaska Peninsula grizzly is to be found a most unscrupulous fighter, and his acquaintance with man and his high-powered rifles is as yet too short and limited to have impressed upon his brute mind that here is a most powerful mortal enemy. He usually charges when wounded, more than frequently when a female with very young cubs is suddenly surprised or attacked, and occasionally when watching a fresh "kill" or "cache" and surprised. And if old Gyas decides to fight, woe betide our bold Nimrod unless he is a good shot and non-excitable, or accompanied by someone who possesses these valuable faculties. For a

wounded grizzly will not stop for one to reload his gun, nor pause
to be shot at until the vital spot is struck. He means blood! Fifty
bullets that are not placed in the proper place will not stop him;
and you can't back out once he accepts your challenge. Not that
one is certain of being charged by every Alaskan grizzly that he
fells; I have had even females retreat until knocked down. But
these cases are really the exception, and the experiences of practically all the old bear hunters of that district—I have known most
of them—will bear me out in the statement that these Alaskan
grizzlies almost invariably charge under the three circumstances
I have cited.

The natives of Alaska do not often go to look for these big
bears. They have a great deal of respect for them—as all others
have who know them.

We are at King Cove, a native village near the site of the once
famous village of Belkovski, center of the sea otter hunting grounds
of old. We are about six hundred miles southwest of Kodiak, the
nearest town of over fifteen white inhabitants, and very near the
extreme western end of the Alaska Peninsula, and almost due north
of Honolulu by location. And here, where the traveler is almost
never seen, we will start out to hunt for the biggest of carnivora
—start it by incidentally being shipwrecked, almost drowned and
getting a foot severely frozen.

It was on the morning of Wednesday, November 1, 1916, that
I left King Cove in a twenty-eight-foot covered-over powerboat
with Captain Charlie Madsen. We headed for the Isanotski Straits,
at the end of the peninsula, and the Bering Sea country, where I
intended hunting Grant's Barren Ground caribou and the big
grizzlies at several desirable localities near the end of the peninsula.

It was cloudy; looked like another snowstorm; but the wind
being from the north, rave it might and the low hills of the mainland would protect us until we reached the end of the peninsula,
where we could hunt bear and wait for more favorable winds. But
the winds of the North are most fickle!

It was a most magnetic sight as we plied out toward the cape
at the entrance of the bay, sending flock after flock of salt-water

ducks flopping off over the swelling surface of the blue-green sea. An occasional seal could be seen plunging headlong into the water from the jut of a reef or an outcrop of the rocky shoreline. The hills were gray, dappled with the first settling snows of winter, and the clouds were heavy and leaden-looking.

As we rounded the cape the swells became more pronounced, carrying a deep, rolling, green-sided trough. But our boat plied steadily on, plunging its nose fearlessly into the rising waves.

Breasting some five miles of rocky coastline, we rounded the second cape at the entrance to Cold (Morofski) Bay, which protrudes some twenty-five miles back into the peninsula, almost making what is to the west an island and what is to the east the end of the peninsula. As we had expected, the wind was raging out of the bay to seaward. But heading the boat's nose toward Thin Point, about ten miles distant, we started fighting our way to the protection of the opposite cape.

Madsen had been watching the sky with misgiving and shortly announced that the wind was changing to the southwest.

I naturally inquired what would be the best course to pursue, knowing that it undoubtedly meant more storm and that we would soon be in the thick of it.

"Cap" decided we would take a chance on reaching Thin Point before the wind had swung to the southwest and thrown the storm in our faces. Once behind the cape we would be safe.

But we were not halfway across when the wind, swinging out past the protection of the peninsula and clashing against the tide, was soon lashing the sea into a stormy havoc. Diving into one great swell, the wind toppled its crest over the boat, washing overboard the hatch-cover and pouring a volume of water into the hold upon our supplies and outfit. I got on deck and endeavored to get a piece of canvas nailed over the open hatchway before another big one should pour its volume into the boat, at the same time clinging as best I could to the pitching vessel.

In the midst of all this, and as if to impress more forcibly upon us our insignificance in this big affair, our engine stopped. Gas engines are hellish things anyhow, and always buck in just the wrong place. But one must act quickly in a case such as this, and almost before I knew it the boat's sail was up and we were racing back before the wind, toward the entrance to the bay we had not long left.

I took the rope and wheel, while Madsen endeavored to get the engine running again, though vainly. But the wind was now coming in such gusts that each one nigh turned our boat onto its nose. It was also snowing and sleeting, almost hiding the outline of the coast.

A gust hit our sail, turning the boat clear on its side, taking water over the rail, and we narrowly escaped finding ourselves in the arms of Neptune himself. Madsen left the engine and decided we would run before the wind and tack into King Cove Bay.

We crossed the entrance to the bay, driven at top speed toward the opposite cape and the line of rocky reefs.

Going as close to as safe, the sail was drawn in with an endeavor to throw it to the opposite side, thus turning the boat. But the wind was too strong and the sea too rough, and try as we might, we would only be driven helplessly on toward the reef where the waves were dashing their foam and spray high in the air. Then a big wave took the flopping sail, pulling the boat over onto its side until the canvas was torn from end to end. As a last resort, the anchor was thrown out; this failed to catch sufficiently to hold us and was regained at great difficulty when we saw that hitting the reef was inevitable.

The first rock of the reef that the boat hit jammed its head through the bottom of the hull and we clambered out into the big dory we were towing and started for shore through the narrow, raging channels in the reef. But this being an open boat, it soon swamped in the breakers and we were forced to take to the water and make shore as best we could. Swimming was impossible, but keeping our heads above the water as best we could, and riding the waves, we were soon washed up on the rocky shore, like half-drowned rats.

To build a fire was impossible for lack of material; we must wait until the boat washed over the reef and was driven ashore. So, wet and cold, and facing a biting snow and sleet and rain-pelleted wind, we walked back and forth over the rocks and waited.

Through all this, while we had been battling with the elements, for our very lives, I had noticed with no small interest how very little the storming and havoc had inconvenienced the little creatures that made their homes in or about the sea. The ducks swam about, quacking, and apparently thoroughly enjoying their buoyant existence. So even storms at sea, it seemed, were a mere matter of relativity and part of the everyday life of those that made their home thereon.

Eventually the boat came ashore—it was fortunately high tide—and getting aboard we got out block and tackle, sunk our anchor as a deadman, and pulled the boat up as best we could. Supplies and everything were drenched and several planks in the hull were smashed.

When we had done all that we could we started for the village—a hard hike. It was well after dark when we reached the squatty barrabaras, or native dirt huts, of King Cove, and we were wet and tired and miserable—ready for a meal and the blankets.

As I began to thaw out, however, I found that part of my right foot had frozen—the leather boots I had been wearing having shrunk and stopped the circulation of blood, causing the freezing. I was laid up for over a week with my foot, though it took Madsen, with the assistance of several natives, somewhat longer to get the boat repaired and back to the village.

Such are but a bit of the "pleasures" that often come with hunting big bear at the western end of the Alaskan Peninsula.

I was especially fortunate in making a one-day bag of four of these Alaska Peninsula bears, a big female and her three yearling cubs, the latter being as large as quite mature Southern brown bears I have gotten.

Deciding to spend a day alone in the hills after caribou, I took the .30-.40 Winchester—in consideration of the bear—and followed the beach of a lagoon or bay to its head about two and half miles from the village. From the head of the lagoon a valley rose at an easy pitch for about two miles to a low divide on the opposite side of which was a large valley extending out onto the Pacific. This was a very good place for caribou.

At the head of the lagoon I stopped to shoot some salt-water

ducks with a .22 Colt revolver, but had fired but a few shots when
I was attracted by the bawling of a bear. Glancing in the direction
of the sound, I saw a brown bear making a speedy, somewhat noisy,
getaway up through the alders from where he had been no doubt
eating salmon in the creek a few hundred yards upvalley from me.
He was then a good five hundred yards distant and in the alders. I
fired, hoping at least to turn him back down the hillside, but he
made the top of the ridge and went over it out of sight. I started a
speedy climb up through the alders toward the top, not far from
where he went over. By the time I reached this, Mr. Ursus had
gone down the other side and was making a "hiyu clattewa" along
the opposite side of the valley. I started up the ridge toward an
open space in the alders with the intent of hurrying down to the
creek and descending it with hopes of heading the bear off or getting a shot at him while crossing a wide rock slide a few hundred
yards below. But I had not gone a dozen steps when I saw three
other bears coming along at a good pace on quite the same course
that Number One had taken. This was somewhat more of a "bear
party" than I had really anticipated inviting myself to!

I felt quite certain that they would cross a small saddle through
which the previous one had passed, and I decided to wait until
they had come out of this and were somewhat below me before
chancing a shot. I was alone, I remembered.

Squatting down in the alders, I waited with gun ready and, I
must say, nerves tense. The first one to come through the saddle
was the old female, a big, high-shouldered brute that strode in a
manner indicating it was looking for me every bit as much as I was
waiting for it. She was followed by her other two yearlings—big
fellows almost as tall and as broad as they were long. Being alone,
and feeling that the female would undoubtedly fight, I deemed
it most wise to play doubly safe. Conditions were fortunately in my
favor. The wind was from seaward, and the alders were heavy
enough to conceal me from her none-too-good eyesight, and it
would be difficult for her to determine from just which direction
the report of my rifle came. The dispatching of the old one was of
course my first move. The rest would be comparatively easy. I did
not have an opportunity of a good shot, however, until the three

had reached the creek bed and crossed and started up along the other side. I slipped into a heavy clump of alders and waited. She was not then, I was quite sure, aware of my whereabouts at least. She lumbered slowly along, yet ever watchful, I could see. Coming out in a little open space she stopped and made an apparent survey of the surrounding vicinity. I took a coarse bead and let drive at her shoulder. I could fairly hear the bullet slap into her. With a nasal bellow she wheeled and made a vicious swipe at the nearest yearling. I fired again, at which she wheeled and charged madly along the hillside opposite me. She went into a small ravine and in a moment came up into sight on one side and stopped, snout swaying high in the air to catch a scent of danger. I steadied my aim, and at the report she went down in a heap and rolled out of sight. "A bullseye!" I thought, and breathed a sigh of relief.

The two cubs had made off in the opposite direction, stopping occasionally to look about. I knocked down one of these at the second shot, breaking his back, though he raised on his forelegs and bawled for all he was worth. I was about to let him have another, when out of the ravine came Mrs. Ursus, mad and apparently as much alive as ever, although dragging her right foreleg. She scrambled through the alders straight for the bawling cub. Greatly surprised and a little uneasy, I again let drive at her. She threw her head to one side, at the same time letting forth another nasal cry. At my next shot she wheeled completely around and charged along the mountainside for a short distance with head held high and every nerve strained to its utmost to locate the cause of her molestation——snarling and bawling in a manner that made me perspire uncomfortably. She was desperate and no doubt calling upon the souls of all her past ancestors to assist her in locating the peculiar new enemy. Then she charged back to the cub. Finally she made a dash almost straight in my direction.

One does not fully appreciate the thrills of real bear hunting until he has experienced just such circumstances as this. To be alone in such a case is a quite different matter from being in company—poor though it may be.

She at last came to a standstill, standing half sidelong to me, and I clamped the gold bead square on her neck and let drive. She went down, got up and, tearing a few alders up by the roots, un-willingly sank in a heap. She had finished her career as a big brown bear on the Alaska Peninsula.

The rest was quite easy and uneventful.

With the assistance of three natives I skinned the four, took the necessary measurements for mounting, and brought the pelts in by boat. The natives, however, made a second trip, bringing in every bit of the meat of all four, salting it down for winter use. The pelts were in fine condition and beautiful specimens, the large one measuring a full ten feet. They are now in the Ohio State Museum.

It was on Sunday, November 19, 1916, that I bagged the original "bearcat"—one of the largest bears ever killed on the continent.

We were hunting around the eastern side of Frosty Peak, a high volcanic mountain towering between Morzhovi and Morofski Bays and about ten miles from the Pacific. This is about twenty miles from King Cove, near the end of the peninsula, and a very good place for big bears. It was a *big* one that I wanted now; and though numerous tracks and one medium-sized bear were seen, none were bothered until the original "bearcat" was found. That took two days under Old Frosty.

I had previously been hunting Grant's Barren Ground caribou on the Bering Sea side of the peninsula and before we landed at the foot of Frosty Peak on our return there was a good twelve inches of snow on the ground. In places it had already drifted to a depth of five feet. Bear hunting was quite an easy matter—though a little unpleasant on account of the snow and cold—as it was a small matter to track the animals. The streams were still open and full of salmon, but a small percentage of the bruins had sought their winter quarters, the pads of their big clawed feet having beaten paths along the iced shores of the stream where they came peri-odically to gorge themselves.

It was late afternoon of the second day under Frosty Peak that we found the fresh trail of our longed-for quarry. We had been investigating the broad alder-patched table of one of the valleys that cut up toward the pinnacle of Old Frosty. There were nu-merous tracks along the creek where the brownies had been feast-

ing on the silver salmon, though no fresh ones of a really large
bear. But as we came well up to the head of the valley we saw the
well-distinguished trail of an unquestionably large bear where it
had made its way up through the snow on the mountainside into
a heavy growth of alders. This was at the very foot of the peak
and in the highest growth of alders. Upon reaching the tracks we
were well satisfied that they could have been made only by the
paw and claw of just the bear that we were seeking. Although it
was evident that he had been in no special hurry in making the
climb, yet it was all that a six-foot man could possibly do to step
from one track to the next.

To the left of the alder patch was a comparatively open track of
rocky ground, with only a spare patch of brush here and there. It
was certain that he could not, if still in the thicket, escape in that
direction without being noticed. But on the right there was a low
ridge, the opposite side of which dipped down into a deep wide
ravine. The alders extended to within a few yards of this ridge,
and to see the other side it was necessary to mount to the top of it.
Also, it was quite probable that the bear had already gone over
this ridge and might then be high up in the canyon near to its
hibernation quarters.

Being unable to locate the bear with my glasses, I decided to
make a complete detour around the patch, to be assured whether
or not he was still in there.

So leaving Charlie on the flat below, I took the two natives and
started up through the alders on the trail of old Ursus. As soon as
possible, we mounted the ridge at the right and went along the
extent of it to assure ourselves that the bear had not crossed. This
he had not. But to make doubly sure that he was still in the alder
patch, we went above and around it to complete the circle about
the place. He was without question lying somewhere in that thicket.

Upon reaching the flat, and as a last resource, we fired several
volleys up through the alders. Then one of the natives spotted
him standing in a thick growth of the alders, where he had gotten
up and was looking inquiringly down at us. We moved down
opposite to him and I fired from the shoulder. He started off along
the mountainside, like an animal that has just broken from its

cage. Then I fired again. Mounting a little knoll in the open, he peered dubiously down at us—in unmistakable defiance. I held on him full in the chest for my next shot, at which he let out a bellow and came for us.

My shots had hit, though he had not so much as bit or clawed at the wound on either occasion—merely jumped slightly. He was then about 200 yards distant, though I was well aware of the short time that it would take him to cover that distance. And he was a big fellow—looked more like a load of hay than a bear, coming down the mountainside.

I had previously told the others not to shoot until I called for help, as I was anxious to fell this big brute singlehanded. But on he came, and though try as I might, I could not stop him. My shots seemed to be taking no effect whatever. And then, when he had come about half the distance, I yelled "Shoot!" And I'd have liked to have done so long before. The four guns spoke simultaneously, but old Gyas kept coming.

I squatted down in the snow, and resting my elbows on my knees, decided to take the long chance—a shot for the head. I was confident that Madsen could stop him before he reached us, and determined to take a chance shot of dropping him in a heap. The two natives, however, were not so confident and began to move backward, shooting as they went.

He turned an angle to cross a small ravine, and while he was mounting the opposite side at a decreased pace I held just forward of the snout. The first shot missed, as I saw a small flit of snow where it hit just in front of him. But at the second shot he dropped in a heap, falling on his belly with his nose run into the snow. After waiting for some moments to make certain he was beyond the trouble point, we climbed up through the alders to where he lay. The others stood by with guns ready while I went up and poked him with the end of my own gun. He was dead.

This had all taken but a few moments, though relatively it seemed a great deal longer.

He was indeed a big fellow—a genuine bearcat. We gutted him, and as it was then getting late, hit for camp. The next morning we went back to skin the animal—and no small task it was!

He had been hit twelve times, we found. Nine of the shots had entered the neck and shoulder and two in the head and one in the abdomen. One bullet had hit him squarely in the mouth, shattering the tops of his lower teeth on one side, piercing the tongue and lodging in the back of his throat. Four of the .30 caliber leads were retrieved from the shoulder, where they had not so much as reached the bone. The shot that stopped him struck well up on the brain box, but squarely enough to break the casing of the bone and penetrate the skull, though only a part of the lead entered the brain, the most of it spattering off in the fleshy part of the head. It was a lucky shot on an even more lucky day!

We estimated his live weight at from 1,600 to 1,800 pounds, and the skin at twelve feet in length. The actual measurements of the tanned skin, however, as made by Chas. A. Ziege, noted taxidermist of Spokane, Wash., are: eleven feet four inches maximum length, by ten feet six inches spread of forelegs. The skull measured, one year after killing, eighteen and one-quarter inches, or one-half inch under the world record, according to Washington, D.C., authorities.

*   *   *

In his memorable book, *Look to the Wilderness,* W. Douglas Burden describes the scene when he and Henry Lucas, one of Alaska's best-known guides, went after the giant Kenai moose.

From • • •

*Look to the Wilderness,* by W. Douglas Burden

THE BATTLE OF THE GIANTS

The Siwashing expedition had come to an end and Henry Lucas and I had made ourselves gloriously comfortable in Bill Kaiser's log cabin at the edge of Skilak Lake.

Bill—big, smiling, easygoing—seemed bursting with happiness to have company. He was talkative. On the other hand, I was hungry for reading material and was soon absorbed in some old

*Saturday Evening Posts*. Since this was not to Bill's liking, he disappeared down a trap door and emerged with some potent rhubarb wine. As a result, we soon found ourselves engaged in an enthusiastic shooting competition. Naturally, we were all proud of our prowess and at the outset were quite evenly matched, but by the simple expedient of drinking one drink for their two I soon gained an advantage and finally won.

The shooting led to stories of the great bear and particularly of the giant Kenai moose we were about to pursue. The Kenai moose is the largest of his tribe, far larger than his Canadian cousin. His horns not infrequently weigh a hundred pounds and on rare occasions have a spread of six feet. A moose is a very easy animal to shoot, particularly during the rutting season when he seems to be devoid of fear. Thus the prospect of hunting them offered little challenge. However, when Bill began to bet that we could not get a six-foot head I promptly took him on and told Henry I would not pull the trigger on any animal with a spread of less than seventy-two inches. The situation had suddenly changed. Bill had put an entirely different complexion on our hunt, for we had now set a mark for ourselves that would be far from easy to fill.

For the remainder of the day we made preparations for a trip which we planned on a thoroughly luxurious level. In contrast to our mountain adventures, we would have the very best of wilderness homes, an Indian tepee and, in addition, ample food and bedding.

That night I sat up late reading and at dawn we were off again, rowing down a wave-tossed lake toward the great moose flats.

These so-called moose flats are a broad alluvial plain that slopes off gently northwestward from the base of the Kenai Mountains to Cook Inlet. Rivers from the melting snows meander across this incline which, with its potholes and ponds and swamps and eskers, glacial boulders and curving sand hills, bears all the characteristics of a true glacial morain. Except for Bill Kaiser's cabin, there was no human habitation in the vast stretch of land between Kenai Lake and the tiny Indian village of Kenai where the Kenai River empties into Cook Inlet.

At noon we landed on a sandy beach. The country had been

burned over years before and presented a bleak and dismal aspect. However, the great burn brought into being a young and succulent growth of willow and quaking aspen that produced the largest moose in the world.

We had heavy loads to pack over the ten-mile portage to the Funny River, where we planned to camp. The trail was blazed with bleached moose horns which over the years had been hung on the dead trees to mark the way. Underfoot it was firm from long years of travel by man and beast.

Now that we had left the mountains, I was back in my woods clothes. For comfort in the bush, nothing is more important than proper footgear, and I had the very best—knee-high Eskimo seal-skin boots and smoke-tanned moccasins lashed tight around the ankles. Over my underwear I wore flannel pajamas, the legs of which emerged under the trousers and hung loose and tattered over the skin boots so as to drain off the water from the wet grass on the outside. A sloppy sight, perhaps, but a perfect combination.

While we were packing in, a swollen-necked young bull disputed our passage, giving evidence the rut was on. He walked to within thirty feet of us, the hair on his spine standing on end. We yelled at him again and again and in abusive language ordered him out of there. We even threw stones, all to no avail. Finally we made a big detour and left him where he was.[1]

In the late afternoon, a white moose horn emerging from a pile of debris caught my eye. A brown bear had killed a big moose, as they often do during rutting when an old bull is sleeping against a tree. The bear had eaten his fill and then tried to cache the carcass. Sticks, stones, moss and grass had been scratched up and heaped over the remains—all but one horn.

It was a dismal place, this kill lair of the brown bear. As I thought of the tremendous strength and size of these giant moose, I tried to imagine how even a great bear could lay him low—what power to break a neck so swollen for battle! Henry told me he had once seen a brownie in pursuit, a thundering onslaught at a running moose. They had disappeared behind some spruce, so he did

[1] The behavior of this animal was quite different from that of the tame moose so often seen near Alaskan towns.

not see the kill, but when he arrived the bull was dead—his neck broken.

For a week Henry and I hunted hard. We had breakfast at daybreak and started immediately afterwards, with a bit of the inevitable sourdough bannock to munch on at noon. Every day we saw moose that were too many to count, some with large heads, but each day we returned empty-handed, exhausted by the soft muskeg and endless stretches of spruce that lay in littered confusion all over the land like piles of jackstraws. Nothing we saw even remotely approached horns with a six-foot spread.

The black flies were bad whenever the wind dropped and for these demons we were well prepared with Stockholm tar spiced with citronella. What a joy it was to smear on this revolting mess! It made Henry darker than a Cree and I was not far behind.

Henry was a man dedicated to his task. He spoke little; even under cross-questioning his answers were brief and to the point. Rarely did he permit himself an anecdote.

Only once do I remember a question of abstract curiosity. Our tepee was pitched in a thick sheltering grove of young spruce at the edge of Funny River. I had gone out to cut some more wood, for there is nothing more pleasant than a bright fire on a frosty autumn night. As I returned with an armful and saw the tepee glowing with warm flame, it seemed that no other shelter in the world makes such an inviting home on a cold wilderness night. It is nest and safety and comfort and warmth all combined. Outside is hostile darkness and perhaps storm and wind, rain or snow. Inside is peace and security—brightly lit and toasting, with an endless draft of pure air that comes in the bottom and carries the smoke out the top but which, because of the inside flap, never touches the occupants.

I had dumped my load just inside the entrance and was seated on a raised bedding of logs and boughs while Henry cooked more of his execrable bannocks. After he was through cooking, I added some wood to the flame, building the fire up Indian style so that we would have plenty of light while eating. In the ever-moving flames playing on his strong features, Henry's keen, mobile face was a study; sensitive but with repose and nobility, a face that somehow seemed to belong to this stupendous land. A tin plate was on my knees and I was spreading a thick layer of jam to soften some hard-fried bannock when Henry suddenly turned to me and said, "Douglas, what is fire?" I was surprised and flattered that he should have turned to me with a question that primitive man, forever struggling against darkness and cold, must have asked himself for countless eons. For a long time I gazed into the flames, not knowing how to answer. Finally I murmured, "Henry, fire is energy in the process of being released." This was a tough one, but I added, "Energy is latent in all things—even a piece of rock." I knew he would not understand the word "latent" but I went ahead anyway. "When you set fire to wood, the energy in that piece of wood is released in the form of heat and light." I didn't know what more to add. I felt inadequate to the occasion and failed completely to bridge the gap in our backgrounds. Henry lapsed into silence and disappointment. I wished somehow that I could have answered adequately a question that this lone trapper must have pondered many times.

The following day we were up and off as usual, striding over strewn jackstraws, sinking deep in the soggy lowland moss, and scouting endlessly from every high ridge with the telescope. We worked westward into lower country and at about two o'clock we suddenly saw our moose, his white horns looming large against the brown bracken on which he was lying. Two cows stood guard nearby. He was about three quarters of a mile away on an open ridge facing our way. There was no chance of getting any closer unseen, for between us was a broad expanse of swamp grass. Henry and I were stretched on our stomachs among the prone spruce poles. For a full five minutes Henry studied him through my thirty-power hunting scope. Then he said, "Maybe seventy-two inches— too far be sure." He had a measuring tape in his pocket and, still lying low, he marked out seventy-two inches on a dead spruce log with his hunting knife so as to fix the width in his mind.

We lay there from 2:30 to 4:15 and during all that time the great bull never moved. Henry looked at him through the scope. I looked at him, then Henry looked again. He was in love with my scope and hated to yield it to me even for a few minutes. Finally

he said, "I think him seventy-two inches. We try get him." The
sun came out for a while. The wind dropped and the black flies
were at us. With the cows still standing guard, we could not move,
but now that Henry had given his verdict we were filled with
excitement.

At 4:15 we heard some grunting beyond the ridge. Evidently
a challenge, for the bull got to his feet and strode away from us
over the ridge. That was our chance.

As soon as he and his two cows were out of sight, we jumped up
and sprinted across the intervening marshy ground. Long before
we reached the ridge where he had been lying I was panting hard,
but Henry gave me no respite. We pushed on to the top of the
ridge, where we found ourselves confronted with a rare spectacle.
The terrain before us was like a stadium closed in by ridges slop-
ing down to the level ground in the center. The bronze-brackened
ridges were covered here and there with stands of golden aspen
shimmering in the late evening light. Moose were everywhere—
young and old, cows and bulls, some alone, some in groups. We
started to count them but soon gave up and concluded later there
were at least three hundred in sight.

We looked for our big bull with his light-colored flat-lying horns,
but he was nowhere to be seen. Then we noticed to our right, at the
upper end of the amphitheater, another giant moose. He was standing alone with ears erect, looking out over the floor of the arena.
Except for size and magnificence of appearance, he was totally
different from the animal we were after; his horns were dark with
enormous upturned palms and a forest of brow tines as big as a
man's forearm.

He stood, motionless and alone, king of the herd. His very aspect
carried such defiance we instinctively felt this was a young animal
at the peak of his power. Then he grunted a deep-throated challenge again and again, all the time looking fixedly toward the open
end of the low encircling hills at something we could not see.
Finally came the answer and a moment later our white-horned
giant strode magnificently into view and stood there, head high,
accepting the challenge. Immediately Henry said, "Shoot! Shoot!"
I was still panting from hard running and, though utterly gal-

vanized by the entire situation, I fired and, happily, missed. The
roar of the 9.5 mm. Mannlicher reverberated through the amphitheater but even against the silence the explosion had no more effect on that gathering than the buzz of a mosquito. Not one animal
moved away, they did not so much as look in our direction.

Instead, they seemed to be watching the two giants on the floor
of the arena as though knowing something important was about to
take place. Again Henry said, "Shoot!" "No," I said, "let's
watch." Henry could stand it no longer. "Come," he whispered,
and started to move down the slope.

The two bulls were a hundred yards apart but they had marked
each other as leaders and were slowly advancing for battle. Moose
were on all sides as we sped down the slope. One cow was so close
I could see the erect hair on her spine and thought she was certain
to charge.

At the bottom of the slope was a log where we rested. We were
now not more than fifty yards from the center of the arena. On
the far ridge and to the right were several dark congregations of
animals and I noticed some of the younger bulls were taking advantage of the preoccupation of their seniors.

I had the feeling we had invaded the privacy of the most primitive and prehistoric of all the deer family—nothing was to be
allowed to disturb it. We might as well have been on Mars, so
little did our presence influence the behavior of this primeval
gathering.

The two bulls were closing the gap between them. But there was
no haste, no sudden rush. Their strides were slow and measured
and dignified. Heads down, their necks were arched and bulging.
They moved with great deliberation, sweeping their heavily
pronged antlers ponderously from side to side with each forward
step. I knew their eyes were bloodshot with angry fire.

These animals were no alien species. The attack was not to de-
vour. Yet the will of each to destroy the other was deep in their
blood. It was an urge as basic as sex itself—a part of the aggressive
drive to dominate.

The two great bulls were now within a few yards of each other.
Theirs had been a noble advance. Neither animal had in the slight-

est degree hastened the majestic rhythm of his forward march. Their great heads and enormously swollen necks were still swinging heavily when I became aware of an almost stifling stillness that fell abruptly on that wild assembly. It was like the final moment of quiet before the storm. I glanced at the surrounding hills. Not a single moose was moving. All stood stock-still, gazing down on the arena. We were witnessing something out of the dim and distant past—something not many civilized men would ever witness.

And then it happened: the resounding clash of antlers backed with nearly fifteen hundred pounds of taut sinew and bursting muscle. The mighty forward surge of two great beasts came to a dead stop. For seconds the contenders were so equal the battle seemed motionless—nothing but straining muscles thrusting forward against equal thrust. Forelegs were tucked under the belly, hindlegs braced far back.

At that moment I noticed for the first time the fighting advantage any moose has if his eyes and forehead are well protected with a fine array of brow tines. The younger bull had that protection. The older bull did not have it and soon blood was dripping from his head. For a moment he drew back slightly and then plunged forward again with all his might. The younger animal reeled backward a few paces and I could see how careful he was not to expose his flank to battering horns whose prongs could have driven into his lungs or pierced his intestines.

When moose fight it is often to the death and woe betide any animal that falls, for then the victor uses his sharp hoofs to cut his adversary to shreds. Now the bulls broke apart and as they did so the old one reared and slashed out with his foreleg, striking the young bull's chest.

It was a lightning play that I had seen once before when a spike-horn moose struck at a wolf. The old fellow drew blood but immediately the young bull closed again and there was a great straining back and forth; the soft earth became chewed and muddy as they circled and slashed, seeking some momentary advantage.

Yet in all the maneuvering and hard fighting, there was something about the old bull's behavior that was never completely convincing. Perhaps, I thought, he sensed his age and limitations.

Perhaps he counted on his faithful cows to stand by him even in defeat, but whatever it was, I could not help feeling that here was a gladiator—fighting, defending, but without the determination to kill. Several times he broke off the engagement as if to say "enough is enough," and each time the younger bull came at him again harder than ever.

It is rare, I imagine, that animals so committed quit the field of battle. Yet sometimes an old veteran may decide to do just that. But how was it to be done? With horns thrusting against him, how could he escape? How turn aside without exposing his flank to impalement? But his was a beautiful maneuver, executed with consummate skill. The old bull broke loose the grip of horns, reared high like a stallion about to strike, and then with smooth, almost unbelievable agility, turned in the air and fell back to earth in full retreat, exposing only his rear end for a brief moment. The very instant he landed, he trotted off with head still high. Meantime, the victor stood his ground, not deigning to pursue. The hot breath was streaming from his nostrils. He called several times but no answer came. Among all the moose in that amphitheater there was no movement. I, too, felt immobilized. Now Henry came to his senses as if pulled out of a dream. "Come," he said. It was difficult to rise but when I did, I looked once more over that arena. The victor still stood like a statue even though some of the moose on the surrounding hills were beginning to move again. "Come," repeated Henry. We took off across the field of battle right under the nose of the victor, ran as hard as we could up the ridge, out of the stadium, and onto a broad open area of aspen and spruce. For more than half a mile we ran—when Henry suddenly stopped and pointed. There directly ahead, about a hundred and fifty yards away, was our bull. He was facing away from us, an impossible shot. The two cows, still with him, had seen us, for their ears were up and both had swung around toward us.

When you have been pursuing an animal for a long time and finally catch up with him in a situation where you are certain of a kill, the thought often comes over you to let him go and sometimes you do, for killing then seems wrong. But now, I had no qualms; I wanted that spread more than I had ever wanted anything before. The whole situation had built up to a final climax. The hunt had gotten into our blood. Henry had never secured a seventy-two-inch head. This might be his record as well as mine.

I was still panting hard when I dropped on one knee and moved the safety catch with my thumb. At that moment the old bull swung his head to see what the cows were looking at. In doing so, he exposed his vulnerable neck. I have missed many easy shots in my day. But though this one was far from easy and by all odds the most important shot of my early years, the bullet went home and the big bull fell and never moved again. When we reached him, he was dead. What a magnificent animal! For a moment I knew remorse at destroying a creature so fine. Yet the bull was past his prime, was on the decline, and I consoled myself with the thought that he probably had not had too long to live. Now he was down, his fine white horns shone against the bracken, and there was Henry dancing around him. He pulled the measuring tape from his pocket, fluttered it in the breeze, then jigged about as if daring himself to take the measurement.

Finally Henry sidled up to the wide-spread antlers, placed the end of the tape on the widest prong and asked me to hold it there. Then he ran it out across the total spread and held it for a while without daring to look. He had his thumb at the exact measurement and when at last he took courage and glanced at it, the reading was exactly seventy-two inches. With that my silent Henry burst into cheers and fairly jumped for joy.

We had won our bet and attained our goal and eventually these horns were duly recorded in *Records of Big Game.*

It was a tough trip home in the dark but by ten the next morning we were back with our bull. It was warm and the raw skin, meat, and horns attracted clouds of flies. But I was so proud of my animal I decided to portage the horns myself, no matter what they weighed or how bad the flies, and this I did with packboard and tumpline all the way to camp and then another ten miles to Skilak Lake.

Then came a trip down the foaming rapids to the little Indian village of Kenai. Shooting rapids is always exciting and this wild ride made a glorious end to our adventures. Henry and I had gotten along beautifully. Never had there been the slightest misunderstanding between us. He was a lone-wolf type and I had enough of those feelings myself to have a wonderful sense of kinship with him. Endless days of tough terrain, bad food, and often extreme physical exhaustion measure a man as few things do, and Henry had been grand. It was hard to imagine that we would not meet again.

I wanted to express my appreciation with something other than cash. As we clambered together down the loam cliff from Kenai village and mingled with the Indians boarding a launch for the run up Cook Inlet to Anchorage, I had a sudden inspiration. Digging into my packsack, I pulled out my beautiful telescope and said, "Henry, this is yours. I want you to have it. I will enjoy thinking of you using it." His answering smile was marvelous to see, and when he took the telescope I sensed a certain mistiness in his eyes that told me his heart was happy. He tried to speak, "Douglas . . ." and then he turned and walked away without another word. At the top of the bank he stopped. A moment later, the deep throbbing of a heavy-duty engine shattered the quiet and I was off in an unseaworthy launch overloaded with Indians, waving good-by to a wonderful guide by the name of Henry Lucas.[2]

\*  \*  \*

In addition to being an associate justice of the Supreme Court of the United States, William O. Douglas is a great outdoorsman whose travels have ranged far and wide in all parts of the world. In *My Wilderness* he has set down his impressions of some of the remaining unspoiled and primitive areas of America. The following passages deal with the flora and fauna of the Brooks Range in northern Alaska.

[2] According to the late J. Watson Webb, Henry Lucas later became known as one of the two best guides in Alaska. While with Mr. Webb, Henry suffered a ruptured appendix in a camp and, though it was three days before he reached a hospital in Anchorage, he survived a desperate attack of peritonitis which would certainly have killed a lesser man.

*Note:* Oil has recently been struck on the moose flats of the Kenai. Another magnificent wilderness will thus succumb to the advance of civilization.

From  · · ·

*My Wilderness: The Pacific West,* by William O. Douglas

### BROOKS RANGE

The Arctic has strange stillness that no other wilderness knows. It has loneliness too—a feeling of isolation and remoteness born of vast spaces, the rolling tundra, and the barren domes of limestone mountains. This is a loneliness that is joyous and exhilarating. All the noises of civilization have been left behind; now the music of the wilderness can be heard. The Arctic shows beauty in this bareness and in the shadows cast by clouds over empty land. The beauty is in part the glory of seeing moose, caribou, and wolves living in a natural habitat, untouched by civilization. It is the thrill of seeing birds come thousands of miles to nest and raise their young. The beauty is also in slopes painted cerise by a low-bush rhododendron, in strange mosses and lichens that grow everywhere, and (to one who gets on his hands and knees) in the glories of delicate saxifrage, arctic poppies, and fairy forget-me-nots. The Arctic has a call that is compelling. The distant mountains make one want to go on and on over the next ridge and over the one beyond. The call is that of a wilderness known only to a few. It is a call to adventure. This is not a place to possess like the plateaus of Wyoming or the valleys of Arizona; it is one to behold with wonderment. It is a domain for any restless soul who yearns to discover the startling beauties of creation in a place of quiet and solitude where life exists without molestation by man.

I was sitting under a white spruce on the upper reaches of the Sheenjek River in the Brooks Range of Alaska. Our camp was at 68° 36′ N., 143° 45′ W. Glaciers estimated to be 1400 feet thick once moved over this country. Only a few remnants of them are left and they are at the very head of the Sheenjek. But their work is evident on every hand. The mountain ridges are rounded and polished; the valley is U-shaped; morainal deposits cover the valley floor; potholes dot the area.

We were camped on one pothole filled with dark blue water and over 200 acres in size. It lies at an elevation of about 2000 feet. It is the last one up the Sheenjek Valley large enough for a seaplane to negotiate. And therefore Olaus J. Murie, biologist and conservationist, and his wife Mardy, who were heading a scientific expedition into these mountains, appropriately called it Last Lake.

I sat for an hour or more under my spruce tree. The first friend to approach was an arctic ground squirrel. He was a quiet body, not chattering or scolding like our western species. He had a quiet call, "sik sik"; and that is his Eskimo name. He was curious about my presence but not unduly alarmed. After inspecting me he went to work with a great burst of energy collecting roots and plants for his den under the hummock where I sat. This arctic ground squirrel is a true hibernator, and his winters are long. In June, when the Muries first arrived, the valley of the Sheenjek was still brown. Summer came in a great rush, July being the month when the bloom of the flowers was at the peak. By mid-August summer was gone and fall had set in. Even the first part of August showed fresh snow on the mountains. The arctic ground squirrel had his job cut out for him if he was to finish all his household tasks before freezing weather set in.

This busy animal that ran to and fro at my feet is important in the ecology of the Brooks Range. The grizzly bear digs into hummocks looking for him. The red fox, the lynx, and the wolverine are heavily dependent on him. The golden eagles, whose nest I saw on a cliff some miles east of camp, also hunt the arctic ground squirrel. Gyrfalcons and hawks join the chase. The arctic ground squirrel is essential in the food chain of the Sheenjek.

The next friend to appear was the willow ptarmigan. This bird, which mates in May and nests by the first of June, was quite silent in July and August. The white body feathers had been molted and the birds now wore the brown plumage of summer. This color blends perfectly with the willow, dwarf birch, and spruce boughs where the nests are cleverly hidden. The eggs have the same brown-splotched appearance; and the downies are so perfectly camouflaged they are almost impossible to see. The bird that approached me this morning was a male. He kept at a respectable distance, feeding on bearberries. Once he was startled and fled. It was a short, swift flight with a low trajectory; and though I saw where he landed I could not, for the life of me, see him.

The ptarmigan, like the ground squirrel, is important in the Sheenjek's food chain. Man, of course, finds this bird a delicious dish. The red fox hunts its eggs and its young. So do the ground squirrels. The golden eagle, marsh hawks, short-eared owls, and goshawks pursue the ptarmigan. So do the wolf and the wolverine. Every predator seems to rely on this bird for a part of its diet. And its feathers are important too. They are used by many birds, particularly the tree sparrows and white-crowned sparrows, to line their nests.

Last Lake, which was below me, suddenly seemed to come alive with birds. Cliff swallows hurried by; Brewer's blackbirds set up a chatter; some gray-cheeked thrushes were calling. An old squaw duck came gliding in. A pin-tailed duck with a young brood cruised a marshy point looking for food. Two Pacific loons—whose calls we were to hear infrequently—came out of some reeds, heading quickly for the middle of the lake. A number of lesser yellowlegs and numerous sandpipers—common shore birds in this region— combed the shores of Last Lake, looking for food. But the most frenzied activity was by the short-billed gulls. Two of them had a nest somewhere in the marsh by the lake. We were to see one large young one before we left. This day it was not in view. One of the gulls sat on the high stub of an ancient spruce, guarding the lake. I decided to walk over and inspect the site. I had no sooner started along the shore of the lake then several lesser yellowlegs flew from spruce to spruce, sounding the alarm with their ear-splitting cry—"whew, whew, whew, whew." But the short-billed gull needed no notice of my coming. I was still fifty yards from its perch when it dived on me. I kept going, and it dived again and again. I held my hands over my face as I splashed through the marshy stand of sedges and willows. Once more the gull dived, this time hitting my hat. I ignominiously retreated, taking as my excuse the antics of a female mallard, who feverishly scattered her young ones into the

marshes and scuttled toward the middle of the lake showing a
"broken wing."

I resumed my seat under the white spruce and noted that I was
not the only intruder whom the short-billed gull resented. Out of
the deep stillness of the Sheenjek came the clear, metallic croak
of the raven—a friendly sound in the Arctic, where most voices
are muted. I looked up to see two circling. The short-billed gull
left like a fighter plane after bombers, chasing the ravens and
diving on them from above. The gull resumed its vigil. The loons,
which had been cruising Last Lake, got close to the shore where
the nest of the gulls was located. Down came the gull over their
heads, screaming and scolding. Again and again during our stay
at Last Lake the short-billed gull stayed on guard, driving off any
of our party that ventured close and chasing golden eagles and
goshawks with a vengeance I had never seen.

I love fishing in the Arctic. There were many tributaries of the
Sheenjek below camp—streams that drained Last Lake and the
marshy ponds that lay below it. Some of these were deep sluices
showing black bottoms from the sphagnum moss that flourishes in
this valley. These fresh-water streams ended in a rather extensive
piece of overflow ice that occupied perhaps ten acres or more.
This overflow ice is formed by the pressure of water against the
ice that forms in the stream bed. When the pressure is great, the
water breaks through the ice and flows over it. It in turn is frozen.
The process is repeated until many layers are formed, creating
a body of ice six feet or more deep and many acres in size that
lasts all summer.

Above the overflow ice were large holes in the deep, still water
where I fished with flies. An old friend, the robin, hopped furtively
in a stand of spruce. It was no longer the gay, spirited bird I had
known farther south. But when I turned my back it burst forth
with its old, familiar song. An Alaska jay flew up and scouted me,
filled with curiosity. But in this arctic domain they are not the
"camp robbers" I had expected them to be. They, too, seemed shy
and furtive.

I was whipping my line preparatory to the first cast upstream when a muskrat came up from some pocket on the side of the stream and, seeing me, dived with a splash. These animals that are very much in evidence when the ice goes out and the mating season is on are inconspicuous as July advances. Their secretiveness must be rewarded, for they are sought after by all the birds of prey; and the wolf and the fox find them a delicacy.

I whipped the first piece of open water above the overflow ice without reward. My first cast in the next pool produced a slight swirl that would have gone unnoticed had not my eyes been glued on the spot. I set the hook and brought to net a fourteen-inch grayling. It did not show the fight our rainbow trout give. There was no standing on its tail, no shaking of its head. It went down like a pike and tried to stay there. I was to be rewarded over and again with grayling, striking a wet fly. Bob Krear, a member of the Murie party, knew these fish well and was adept at catching them. He explained that one of their mainstays was the beetle larvae. These waters hatch great quantities of caddis flies; and the pools I saw were rich with nymphs that I was not able to catalogue.

These grayling, which run up to three pounds or more, are not prepossessing. Their small heads and broad-beamed bodies make them seem a bit awkward compared with our streamlined rainbow. But whatever they lack in grace they make up in food. Their flesh is white and their thick steaks cook up into a sweeter and more delicious dish than any trout I have sampled. Bob Krear and I cleaned the grayling by Last Lake, throwing the offal into the shallow water. The short-billed gulls that had attacked me so relentlessly quickly appeared to enjoy the feast. They brought with them their lone offspring, who still was awkward and clumsy; and it was gray, not white like its parents. But it had its parents' aggressive instincts. A pin-tailed duck flew in to examine the shore line and was immediately attacked by the youngster.

It is said there are other fish in the Sheenjek—a word meaning "dog salmon" in the Kutchin Indian language. But I saw no salmon, nor did I see any lake trout, pickerel, or whitefish that have been reputed there. My only reward were the grayling, and they were enough to satisfy any fisherman.

We discovered on one of our exploratory hikes some pools that lie on one of the low knolls that dot this area. The pools, which drain to the river only when the rains come, are deep in the shade of white spruce, which generally forms an open forest but here had grown into a thick stand. Willow—a browse that caribou and moose enjoy in winter—was mixed with the spruce; and there were some stands of dwarf birch. Some of the spruce was hung with beardlike lichens, giving them almost a patriarchal appearance. Others were decorated with crustose lichens that grew like scales on the limbs—some red, some yellow, some gray. The ground around the pools was spongy and soft and covered with a thick mat of mosses. The mountain avens was in bloom, adding streaks of creamy white to the dark green. A dark blue saxifrage was mostly hidden. A tall lousewort—bright blue—showed its tiny heads. A small black berry, known as the crowberry, made a carpet. The arctic poppies were brilliant. Bush cinquefoil added a touch of gaiety. White, yellow, and gray lichens gave life and zest to the leaf litter; and the lovely, delicate, tiny bluebell flower was almost hidden from view. But what caught my eye was a moss I had never seen before, one which George Schaller, also in the Murie party, assured me was scarce. George gave me its technical name, *Splachnum luteum*. It has stems almost eight inches high, topped by small yellow umbrellas or hats. This moss has become so specialized that it can survive only on the dung of moose, an article in abundance around these pools.

It was difficult to express my feelings as I stood beside these dark quiet pools, shaded by spruce. They were so beautiful, so exquisite, that they were unreal. They seemed withdrawn from this earth, though a glorious part of it. The day had been cloudy; now the sun came out, brightening the dark waters. The black of their bottoms showed various tints of green. The delicate colors along the shore added life and zest. Here were pools never touched by man—unspoiled, uncontaminated except perhaps by the awful fall-out from the atomic bombs that is slowly poisoning the whole earth. Here was life in perfect ecological balance. A moose had stopped here to drink. Some water beetles skimmed the surface. Nothing else had seemed to invade this sanctuary.

It was indeed a temple in the glades. Never, I believe, had God worked more wondrously than in the creation of this beautiful, delicate alcove in the remoteness of the Sheenjek Valley.

These white-spruce forests are interesting to explore. They never grow above 3000 feet and their northernmost limit is just short of 69° N. In moist places they sometimes form thick stands. But they usually appear as long fingers, stretching northward up the Sheenjek Valley. They are a small tree with branches that cover the trunk. The branches are short, giving the tree a slim appearance, and the tip is peaked. Their average height is fifteen or twenty feet; and a foot or so from the ground they are usually not more than seven inches in diameter. There are some, however, that are nearly eighteen inches through. The Murie expedition found that it takes over thirty years for a white spruce in the Brooks Range to reach five feet and 100 years to reach twenty feet. The oldest white spruce they found was nearly 300 years old.

These white spruce are slowly reclaiming the Arctic. Their scarcity is due, it is thought, not to unfavorable environment but to the fact that they could take hold only after the ice sheets had receded. Since then the migration of the white spruce northward has never ceased.

But except for the soil hummocks where the white spruce grows most of this Sheenjek Valley country is tundra. In lowland meadows are small islands a foot or so high. The land they enclose is called a polygon, a wet area where mosses, sedges, rushes, and prostrate willow grow. A horsetail—perennial aquatic—flourishes there, as does the wild cranberry. This swampy land surrounds Last Lake. One sloshes through it as he does in any marsh. The more typical tundra is a few feet higher. It is marked by tussocks formed from a variety of vegetation. Most conspicuous is a cotton grass, sometimes known as hare's-tail. In June this cotton grass is in bloom, showing hundreds of acres with a bluish-gray cast. Mosses and lichens grow thick on these tussocks. A bog rosemary with lovely pink blossoms adorns them. Bog bilberries (smaller than blueberries and not good for eating) flourish there. Bearberries with white flowers make a mat. A dwarf and prostrate rhododendron decorates many tussocks. A dwarf trailing willow possesses much of this high ground in the bogs. A vigorous species of the grass of parnassus grows here, mixed with a purple louse-wort, violet butterwort, violet-purple milk vetch, a low, greenish bunchflower, a white false asphodel.

The tussocks are from a few inches to a foot or two broad. They are like tall mushrooms with grassy heads. They are not steady underfoot, sinking and sometimes swaying. Mardy Murie said that one who walked them had to be limp like a rag doll. A hike through the tussock meadows is more strenuous than climbing. One is continuously on edge to keep his balance, for a misstep sends him down into deep slush. The result is that a hiker tends to put on speed, barely touching one tussock and practically jumping to the next. A day of walking a tussock meadow is exhausting. Horses would flounder hopelessly. In the summer this is country only for men with packs. I had seen this tundra on an earlier trip stretching from the north side of the Brooks Range to the Arctic Ocean. That tundra, though differing in botanical detail from the tundra of the Sheenjek, has the same general appearance. It is in the main a dwarf-shrub heath marked by tussocks, and it runs for miles and miles. There is a dreary monotony in its northern expanse. But here on the Sheenjek it is a colorful community broken by knolls where willow, alder, and birch form thickets, by the long fingers of spruce reaching north, and by the backdrop of rounded mountains covered with a soft nap of lichen and moss heath.

One day we hiked far up the Sheenjek, resting frequently on the dry hummocks where the white spruce grow. Usually the Sheenjek is crystal-clear; but the day of our hike was after a storm. So the river was muddy from drainage. Above Last Lake the Sheenjek breaks up into many small streams. The riffles were shallow; the gravel beds highly polished. Small sand bars had built up from favorable currents, and the islands between the fingers of the river were thick with willow. These stands of willow along the river are a favorite habitat of moose. There were many fresh tracks, but we saw none of the animals. Wolves travel this river bed in their hunt for game. The wolf signs—especially the scat—were fresh and numerous this day. Olaus found one track where a front paw measured 6 inches by 5.1 inches. I was to see wolves later, but we saw none on this hike. Red fox also follow the river bed, and while we found their tracks we did not see them. But I heard one barking far off to the west in some willow. We looked at every mud bar for signs of the grizzly bear, but found none. One of our great rewards this day was the low, lush blueberries that grow in splendor on the east bank. Hundreds of acres were in full fruit. The berries were ripe, and they were the sweetest we have known. We picked several pints and ate many for lunch. Then we lay on our backs in these stands of blueberries and took a nap to the soft music of the purling Sheenjek.

The day was bright. The storm that brought us rain left six inches or so of snow on the mountains. These 8000-foot ridges glistened with their white mantles and seemed cool and inviting. No tree broke the soft flow of their lines, and cloud shadows changed their moods and our fantasies.

A turbulent tributary that comes into the Sheenjek about three miles north has white spruce growing thick along it. A few stray cottonwoods are to be found, and poplars flourish there. Beaver frequent the Sheenjek Valley, and some of them had been fresh at work cutting these poplars. These woods were thickly carpeted with moss—rich in color, springy underfoot. Some of it reminded me of the star moss that grows high in the Cascades and Wallowas. One type was a bright green. When we came to higher ground, we found a bright-yellow moss that made a deep carpet on the wilderness floor. And choicest of all was a gray lichen (endemic in Alaska) that Mercedes, my wife, and Mardy collected for its decorative effect on women's hats.

Not far up this tributary we found two large spruce poles standing upright in the ground, spanned by a third one. This was a cache for food made by prospectors, who designed it years ago to keep their supplies safe from animals.

This was ancient land of the Athabaskan Indians, composed of eight tribes making up the Kutchin nation. Their domain extended over the Brooks Range to the Arctic Ocean. Occasionally they fought the Eskimos. But they were essentially hunters and fisher-

men who settled on the Yukon and the larger rivers that feed it.
Probably only a few frequented the Sheenjek, at least in its upper
reaches. Things changed when the gold rush started. Prospectors
came into the Sheenjek Valley. Before then, in 1847, the Hudson's
Bay Company established a post at Fort Yukon and the fur trade
began. The Indians accommodated the fur traders; even Eskimos
crossed the Brooks Range and came down the Sheenjek, bringing
furs to the trading post. Some of the Eskimos stayed, establishing
villages. But since the 1920s little hunting or trapping has been
done here. A few Indians still make excursions into the Brooks
Range from the Yukon flats, looking mainly for wolves, on which
there has been a $50 bounty; but not many of them make the effort.
They are mostly congregated at Fort Yukon, 150 miles to the south
and in Arctic Village, nearly 50 miles to the southwest of our
camp. Some white men have come into the Sheenjek, but they have
been few and far between. The Sheenjek since the 1920s has known
only its primeval quiet and stillness. Life has gone on undisturbed
by men. No food chains have been broken by the introduction of
civilization. There is no more thrilling place to observe life in
complete ecological balance than in this valley on the south slopes
of the Brooks Range.

The spread of the tree line far into the Brooks Range has some
relation to the temperature range. This relationship has been put
by some students into a formula which suggests that if the mean
temperature for the coldest month of the year is $-14°F.$, the mean
for the warmest month must be $50°F.$ If the mean for the coldest
month is $-40°F.$, the mean for the warmest month must reach
$55.4°F.$ The requirements of this formula can be satisfied on the
southern slopes of the Brooks Range.

The summers on the Sheenjek are mostly sunny and warm, the
July daytime average being about $61°F.$ At night the temperature
drops to $40°F.$ and sometimes lower. While the summer days are
in the main bright, clouds often drift in by midday. And July and
August are the months of the year when there is the heaviest
precipitation. We knew several all-rain days, the storms coming
mostly from the south and southeast. But the precipitation on these

south slopes of the Brooks Range is so slight that but for the arctic conditions this would be semidesert. The total precipitation over the period of a quarter century averages slightly under seven inches a year, which is only a bit more than half of that of Wyoming's high plateau. The yearly snowfall is less than four feet on the average. But the winters are long and cold, the average January temperature being −21°F. Summers are short in the Arctic. Early June flowerings produce seeds by July first. Early in August most arctic plants have completed the cycle and entered the seed phase. Even while the seeds are maturing, new leaf and flower buds develop near the surface of the soil, ready for next season's growth. Most of the seeds of these arctic plants are light and specially adapted for transportation by wind. A high percentage of plants depend, indeed, on the high velocity of arctic winds for their spread and migration. This early flowering that comes with such a rush is aided by the fact that the microclimate at which the plants live is warmer than ordinary temperature readings would reveal. For the temperature just under the soil surface may be as much as 40°F. higher than the air temperature. So there may be enough warmth for photosynthesis to take place in the earth, though the air temperature indicates freezing.

But under the soil is permafrost, which conditions much of the life of the Arctic. It lies about fourteen inches beneath the surface in the Sheenjek Valley. This permafrost acts as an impervious layer which prevents normal drainage. Rainfall that would be absorbed by the earth under normal conditions, producing no runoff, has startling effects in the Sheenjek. A half inch of rain or less will raise the level of Last Lake a foot or more, since the water runs off permafrost as it would off concrete. One morning after an all-night rain we found a new creek running by our camp.

These arctic soils are quite acid, due to poor drainage and poor aeration; and they are deficient in nitrogen, because organic decay by bacterial action is very slow.

The thin soil and short growing period emphasize how perishable the arctic wilderness is. Overgrazing would cause great tragedy here. Lichens, on which caribou depend so heavily, would

take a century to restore. This arctic wilderness is truly fragile.
Never can it survive the full impact of civilization.

The Eskimos have graphic names for these summer months:

> May—month-of-fawning
> June—egg-month
> July—mosquito-month
> August—berry-month

July ran true to the Eskimo experience.

I had heard horrible stories of the mosquitoes of Alaska and
went prepared with head nets. But I never used them. There are
mosquitoes—many of them. Even after a frost—one of which we
experienced—new crops of mosquitoes are born. They swarm up
out of the marshland and tundra. They are not too bothersome
when the wind blows. Once it dies down they rise from the
ground on every step; and they are always present where the
stands of spruce or poplar are thick. But the use of modern
mosquito "dope" keeps them off the skin and hands. They still
envelop the head and shoulders like a cloud, following one everywhere. But one gets accustomed to this—except when he eats.
Then he must be in a tent to avoid getting a mouthful of mosquitoes.
A tent with a floor and zipper flap can be made mosquitoproof with
the help of a spray. At night the greater worry for one raised in
a temperate zone is not the mosquito but the light. In July the
sun sets over the Sheenjek Valley about midnight and rises an
hour or two later. This means it sinks below the limestone peaks
to the west, travels only a short arc, and rises. We are accustomed
to darkness for deep sleep and the unraveling of cares. The newcomer misses night in the Arctic. But there are special rewards.
Cloud effects, sunsets, the long afterglow, and the sunrise produce
a riot of colors that even Arizona does not know.

There are lemmings and voles in this arctic region. These
rodents—along with snowshoe hares and arctic ground squirrels
—support an aristocracy of clever predators that include the fox,
the lynx, and the arctic weasel. They are most active in the

summer, collecting and storing roots and grass for their winter needs. Olaus and George were busy trapping them by day and preparing the specimens by night. I followed them as they ran their trap lines, learning much about these animals that a casual visitor to the northland would never know. These tiny mouselike animals live at various elevations in the Brooks Range. Some of them possess networks of runways extending from tussock to tussock in the wet land around Last Lake. There are ponds, higher in the mountains, where they are also found. Some types of voles are found several thousand feet above the Sheenjek with their runways built through carpets of moss and through bare rocky outcrops. They seem never to be found on high, dry slopes. Their preference is for damp edges of lakes and swamps. And when the waters rise and their runways are flooded, they merely retreat temporarily to higher, drier ground.

The lemmings and voles travel cycles of life with periods when the population reaches crash proportions and times when it is at low ebb. The low point for lemmings had been reached this summer, for they were not much in evidence. Lowell Sumner and John Christian have shown that once these animals build to a high population level and then come into a period of food scarcity, they are subject to tremendous emotional stress. This stress leads to an exhaustion of the adreno-pituitary system. The effect on voles and lemmings is similar to the effect of stress on man. These rodents develop inflammation or ulceration of the digestive tract and a permanent metabolic derangement that directly or indirectly causes death. In lemmings this tension becomes so great that it leads to mass migration. This migration is not an orderly, methodical one, like settlers looking for new homes. It is a panicky outburst which amounts to mass suicide. The lemmings go on and on, stopped not even by rivers, lakes, or the ocean where they are destroyed.

There are Dall sheep in the Brooks Range; but they come down into the Sheenjek only in winter. George Schaller scouted the high slopes and found them in alpine meadows protected both above and below by talus slopes.

There are grizzly bear in these mountains, and their tracks and scat were evident on every trip. I also saw many places where they had dug for roots or for squirrels, and some where they had bedded down. But I never came across one, nor did I even see one from a distance. One charged to within thirty feet of George Schaller; another got even closer to Bob Krear on a charge that came to a sudden, grinding stop when Bob thought the end was near. These grizzlies—inherently shy—have very poor eyesight. Even at a hundred feet a man probably looks much like a caribou. The grizzly may have to come much closer to pick up the scent. When he does, he usually will run unless cornered or hurt. The scent of man is the signal of danger. The grizzly gets this message intuitively, for the sight or even the odor of a man is an experience that would come to a grizzly in the Sheenjek only once in a lifetime.

There are many caribou in the Sheenjek, the total number in the herd perhaps reaching 40,000. The caribou are the only members of the deer family where both sexes have antlers. Their summer coat is dark; their winter fur is a light tan. In the early summer they move west. By August first they move east. These migrations are on a broad front of forty or fifty miles, not many caribou being in one group. I had seen small groups feeding around Last Lake. But they seldom stood still; they were a restless, nervous lot, seeming always to be on the move. One night an estimated 2000 caribou crossed the Sheenjek not far above our camp. Their feet pounding in the gravel sounded, as Mardy put it, like "a freight train roaring through the valley."

One day I hiked to a pass that marks the divide between the Sheenjek and the Coleen drainage. At the pass I climbed the southern slopes, looking for flowers. As I rested on a limestone outcropping, a herd of forty caribou crossed below me. They were headed east. Up ahead was a bull with head bowed under the great weight of his antlers. Lesser bulls followed. Then came the cows and the calves. Yearlings raced alongside. But every other animal followed in line, stepping in practically the same tracks as the one ahead of him. Their brown summer hair was prominent, though some had dark only along their backs. By fall a light brown would take the place of the dark color, for the whole

herd and the older bulls would have strikingly white necks. This
day the caribou were traveling so fast that the calves had difficulty
keeping up.

These restless animals depend on lichens, grasses, and sedges
in the winter; on willow and birch, grasses and sedges in the
summer. This day they were driven by some great force that
made this migration an integrated community effort.

This country to the east of Last Lake was good hiking terrain.
Above the tundra were the knolls, thick with stands of dwarf
willow and birch, which by late August turn red and yellow. The
moss makes thick, moist carpets in these thickets. The crowberry
and bog bilberry flourish there. Here I found the Labrador tea
in bloom—a species similar to that I once found along the northern slopes that face the Arctic Ocean. On the open slopes of
these knolls mountain avens and cassiope left streaks of creamy
white. Alpine hedysarum added touches of violet; lousewort
and arnica showed yellow; knotweed was bright pink; the arctic
lupine added bright blue; and the arctic poppy showed gold.
A mosslike silene, known as cushion pink, showed pink and rose
flowers growing on almost stemless stocks. A minute larch-leaf
sandwort also flourished here. But what caught the eye on these
knolls and the slopes above them was the rhododendron. Some call
this plant an azalea, but its name is *Rhododendron lapponicum.*
It virtually blankets the lower hillsides of the Sheenjek Valley,
turning them cerise, and the air is saturated with the fragrance of
its delicate blossoms. To one who has seen the south slopes of the
Brooks Range in July, the sight and smell of the rhododendron
are never forgotten.

The slopes above these knolls are drier. But they too are green
with a nap of sedges, low shrubs, and lichens. White heather is
everywhere. Anemones grow here in white patches. Yellow cinquefoil nod gracefully in the wind. A purple locoweed is found here,
and occasionally a yellow saxifrage. The low evergreen shrub—
kinnikinnick—hugs the ground. So does a dwarf, rose-pink phlox.
The fairy forget-me-not, almost destitute of stems, shows cerulean
blue. Camass lilies grow in clumps.

All life on these slopes is prostrate. I came across prostrate willow and birch that were using the south face of upturned rocks as a trellis where they got added heat from the sun. I stopped to examine their roots and found them running at length horizontally under the surface to avoid the permafrost. In a ravine fed by springs or on a low spot where drainage is poor, meadow conditions exist even high in the Brooks Range. Then the mosses and lichens are on brilliant display. Shooting stars brighten wet spots. Purple monkshood and purple gentians grow against rich green banks. Here, too, are dainty alpine buttercups and the familiar Jacob's ladder, two feet higher and showing dark-blue flowers.

The higher one goes, the scarcer the vegetation. When the talus slopes are reached, the lichens are the only plants that flourish; they spot the rocks red and black and cover the ground in white or yellow patches. An occasional prostrate willow has taken hold in the rocks. Mats of the rosaceae cling stubbornly to thin soil, kept company by the dwarf evergreen cassiope that John Muir loved so much.

One day, while hiking the ridge to the east of camp, I had left the last fingers of white spruce and came to an open, exposed promontory. I heard a deep-throated roar underground. Some great subterranean creek was rushing through the porous limestone that forms these mountains. The wind blew a gale. It was cold and piercing and brought squalls of rain. This was only the third of August, but fall had arrived. Not many days distant Keith Harrington from Fort Yukon would drop through low clouds in his Cessna plane to take us out.

Today the two short-billed gulls with their grayish youngster had taken off, heading for the south. Their departure made the camp seem lonely. Now that I was high above Last Lake, the feeling of loneliness and isolation mounted. As I turned to view the valley at my feet, it seemed that I was remote from our civilization, looking down on this earth from an aperture in the sky. There was not a movement in the vast expanse below me. Suddenly a lone caribou came out of a stand of spruce and willow, moving hurriedly toward a pass that led eastward and nibbling at low shrubs as it went. Far below on the flats, where the river runs, a moose and a calf browsed peacefully. Below the caribou but still high above camp a wolf loped leisurely along. He, too, was headed for the pass. There are black wolves in these mountains, but this was a gray one. It was a magnificent specimen. I had seen wolves before both in this country and in Afghanistan and Persia. Wherever they roam they are considered dangerous. They are fast being removed from our national scene. The Brooks Range is probably their last refuge. But even here they are hunted, a $50 bounty being on them. Why should this be? Why should man be committed to destroy this magnificent animal? These were my thoughts as I watched the great, gray wolf lope gracefully across the slopes below me.

We have some things to learn from the wolf. When wolves circle each other, threatening and growling, the less aggressive one often turns his cheek. This is not a signal to the other one to move in for the kill. The wolf who turns his cheek asks for a truce, and though the snarling continues, the truce is always granted. Turning the other cheek, the wolf teaches us, is not abject surrender but an honorable way to prevent a fight and save the species. As Lorenz wrote in *King Solomon's Ring,* "A wolf has enlightened me: not so that your enemy may strike you again do you turn the other cheek toward him, but to make him unable to do it."

The wolf is a predator. Olaus Murie studied wolf scats collected in the Sheenjek and discovered that of forty-one samples there were thirty-eight that contained caribou. We found several kills around Last Lake. But how many wolves they fed we did not know. How many other predators, such as the red fox and the lynx, are maintained on caribou carrion left by wolves is also not known. But we have reason to think that the wolf is important to their survival.

The wolf, though fast and powerful, cannot outrun a healthy caribou. Apart from those he catches by surprise, he is dependent on cripples and on calves. Sheep also can elude him; and moose usually stand him off. The wolf does not decimate herds; he merely helps control their size, and in that way acts as a curb on the destructive overuse of the national range.

It may be necessary to control the wolf in the environment of ranges where cattle roam. But here in the Sheenjek the wolf is as much a part of the environment as the arctic ground squirrel, the ptarmigan, and the short-billed gulls. This is—and must forever remain—a roadless, primitive area where all food chains are unbroken, where the ancient ecological balance provided by nature is maintained. The wolf helps in that regard. He has, moreover, a charm that is wild and exciting. In this, our last great sanctuary, there should be a place for him. His very being puts life in new dimensions. The sight of a wolf loping across a hillside is as moving as a symphony.

The vast, open spaces of the Arctic are special risks to grizzlies, moose, caribou, and wolves. Men with field glasses and high-powered rifles, hunting from planes, can well-nigh wipe them out. In this land of tundra, big game has few places to hide. That is another reason why this last American living wilderness must remain sacrosanct. This is the place for man turned scientist and explorer, poet and artist. Here he can experience a new reverence for life that is outside his own and yet a vital and joyous part of it.

# 25

# *CLIMYTHOLOGY*

SENATOR Ernest Gruening's address on June 27, 1962, to the two hundred and third national meeting of the American Meteorological Society, convened at the University of Alaska, dealt with the myths about Alaska's climate, for which he coined the word "climythology."

Ernest Gruening's *Address to the American Meteorological Society*

Mr. Emerson, members of the American Meteorological Society, and guests, in extending the invitation, some six months ago, to address this meeting, your toastmaster, who is the regional administrative officer of the United States Weather Bureau for Alaska, wrote me:

"As a longtime Alaskan dedicated to the growth and development of Alaska, you have a comprehensive understanding of the role that meteorology and climatology play in the scheme of things."

I was and am flattered by that, I fear, undeserved assumption of my comprehensive understanding of so vast, spacious, and expanding a pair of related sciences. However, I am delighted to take advantage of this encomium to discuss the influence that these twin disciplines have had, have, and may have on the past, present, and future of the State of the Union in which we are now assembled.

It is an interesting phenomenon that as the field of human knowledge expands, not only are new sciences and subsciences born, but by becoming correlated and interrelated, established sciences give birth to new ones. Thus, physics and geology are the happy progenitors of geophysics—already a lusty adolescent pretty well on its own. Physics and astronomy gave birth to astrophysics. I need not prolong the listing of such offspring of scientific matings. As science expands, new hyphenated sciences are generated.

Geopolitics, a relatively new science created incidental to Pan-Germanic aspirations for domination of the earth by Hitler's presumed master race, may soon, as men land on the moon, become selenopolitics. This will be succeeded, no doubt, by astropolitics or cosmopolitics as the invasion by earthians of our planetary neighbors becomes imminent.

I venture to suggest that a hitherto undesignated child of meteorology and climatology—illegitimate, I regret to state in this respectable company—has played an important part in the history of Alaska, has seriously affected its past and present, and is still to be reckoned with in the future. I could call this offspring meteoromythology or mythometeorology, or climythology. I should probably leave the determination of nomenclature to the philologists, with historians and meteorologists as consultants.

For the time being, as its proponent, I shall call it climythology. Meteoromythology has a good alliterative and onomatopoeic sound, but climythology is simpler and easier to enunciate. This science, or pseudoscience, which perhaps should be classed with alchemy, astrology, phrenology, or palmistry, has nevertheless had, and still has, its numerous followers, and has had a marked effect in shaping, or misshaping Alaska's destiny. I will now trace briefly its origin and effects.

Climythology, as far as Alaska is concerned, came into existence sometime between March 30, 1867, when William Henry Seward consummated the purchase of Alaska, and 1868, when the Congress was called upon to pay the bill.

That bill, for $7,200,000, or approximately two cents an acre, loosed a storm in the House of Representatives. I shall not attempt to say whether it was a hurricane or a tornado, but it was accompanied by a lot of wind, a great flood—a flood of oratory—and some verbal thunder. The sum and substance of it was that while Seward had taken Alaska, he and the United States had been "taken," in the contemporary colloquial sense.

Alaska was pictured on the floor of the House of Representatives and in a substantial section of the press as a frozen waste with a savage climate, where little or nothing could grow, and where few could or would live.

Typical of the statements of climythologists was that of Representative Benjamin F. Loan, of St. Louis, who declared: ". . . the acquisition of this inhospitable and barren waste will never add a dollar to the wealth of our country or furnish any homes to our people. It is utterly worthless. . . . To suppose that anyone would leave the United States . . . to seek a home . . . in the regions of perpetual snow is simply to suppose such a person insane."

Another climythologist was Representative Orange Ferris, of Glens Falls, N.Y., who asserted that Alaska "is a barren, unproductive region covered with ice and snow" and "will never be populated by an enterprising people."

Another Representative from New York, Dennis McCarthy, of Syracuse, cited "reports that every foot of the soil of Alaska is frozen from five to six feet in depth" and ventured that his colleagues would soon hear that Greenland was on the market.

And the minority report of the House Committee on Foreign Relations, in a scathing denunciation, declared that Alaska "had no capacity as an agricultural country . . . no value as a mineral country . . . its timber generally of poor quality and growing upon inaccessible mountains . . . its fur trade . . . of insignificant value, and will speedily come to an end . . . the fisheries of doubtful value . . . in a climate unfit for the habitation of civilized men."

I hope I will not be misunderstood when I point out that these climythologists were all Members of the House of Representatives, and not of the Senate. However, lest I seem to be imputing a greater wisdom and prescience to the Senate membership of that day than that of what is referred to in the Senate as "the other body," I must, in deference to historical accuracy, point out that except for Senator Charles Sumner's address to the Senate urging the purchase, there is no record of what questions his senatorial colleagues asked him and what comments they made, since the treaty was voted on in an executive session, which, but for the result, is not reported. That even Sumner's eloquence barely sufficed to achieve ratification of the Treaty of Cession is shown by the fact that there was just one vote more than the two-thirds majority required by the Constitution.

And so a lot of denigrating epithets were fastened on Alaska, such as Icebergia, Polaria, Walrussia, Seward's Polar Bear Garden, Seward's Icebox, and the one coined by the press, which has endured the longest, Seward's Folly.

It is a well-known axiom of social psychology that error accented as verity can be as potent as truth.

The consequences of this Alaskan climythology were soon evident. Having established and propagated the concept of Alaska as a worthless waste with a savage climate, Congress proceeded to act accordingly. It immediately forgot its new acquisition. In the next seventeen years, it provided no government for what was not even dignified as other American areas had been with the title of Territory. Alaska was merely the District of Alaska.

During those seventeen years, Congress enacted just two laws relating to Alaska. One applied to Alaska our navigation laws, and created Alaska a customs district, which merely meant that imported foreign goods, of which there would be virtually none, would pay the same duties as elsewhere in the Union; and, two, a law turning over the fur seal fisheries of the Pribilof Islands to the Secretary of the Treasury, who promptly leased them as a monopoly to a firm in San Francisco, the Alaska Commercial Co.

Seventeen years may not seem like a long time in the pageant of history, but it is four Presidential administrations plus one year. More pertinent, it is $8\frac{1}{2}$ Congresses. In those days, each Congress usually assembled for three sessions instead of two, as nowadays. To be sure, some twenty-five bills providing civil government for Alaska were introduced. Yet, in the first twenty-four sessions of Congress after the purchase, not one of these bills ever got out of committee and never was vouchsafed a comment on the floor of either house. The prevailing climythology prevented that.

During that unique period, no pioneer who had come hopefully to Alaska could acquire title to the log cabin he had hewn from the forest wilderness nor to the land on which he had settled. No prospector could stake a mining claim with security for his enterprise and toil. Property could not be deeded or transferred. No will was valid. No injured party could secure redress for grievances except through his own acts. Crime could not be punished. Finally, marriage could not be celebrated—a cruel and unusual circumstance—though somehow life went on.

So, for seventeen years the climythology which proclaimed Alaska a frozen waste with a savage climate had in fact frozen the Congress into immobility and placed Alaska in a political and economic deep freeze.

During these years, such authority as there was was exercised de facto and without any legal authority by the commanding general stationed at Sitka. And when, in 1877— ten years after the cession—he and his troops were called back to the States to put down an uprising of Nez Perce Indians, there was not even that semblance of government.

The fear of an Indian uprising was contagious. It haunted all the area west of the Mississippi through that decade. Reverberations of the massacre of General Custer by Sitting Bull and his braves a year earlier traveled far and wide.

The settlers in Alaska shared this alarm and requested their distant government to send some war vessels, a gunboat, perhaps, to overawe any possible uprisers and to help preserve peace, law, and order. This request, repeated with growing urgency and trepidation, was totally ignored. This was before the days of cable and telegraph. Finally, in great alarm, the whites who had settled in Sitka appealed to their neighbors, the Canadians, who promptly responded, and one of Her Majesty's ships performed the service that one of Uncle Sam's naval vessels should have.

When a U.S. sloop of war finally arrived in 1879, the captain of that vessel stationed at Sitka and his successors were, for five years, without legal authority but de facto the rulers of Alaska.

During all this time a stream of complaints flowed from the settlers to Washington. They were ignored. In 1881, representatives elected from various Alaska communities including Sitka, Juneau, and Wrangell, met in convention in Juneau and drafted a memorial to the President and Congress requesting the creation of the Office of Delegate in the House of Representatives. Every territory had been granted this voteless representation. A contest at the convention for that post simmered down to a race between the highest Federal officials stationed in Alaska, the collector of customs and his predecessor. The winner, Collector Mottram D. Ball, carried his plea to Washington, asking that he be seated. He was not, and Alaska had to wait twenty-five more years before the enormous concession of a voteless delegate was granted.

Climythology was unabated.

Finally, in 1884, in response to the proddings of three Presidents, Congress gave Alaska its first body of law, the Organic Act of that year. However, it proved unworkable and worthless. It provided a presidentially appointed Governor, but forbade the establishment of a legislature and of a delegate in Congress. It forbade the application of the general land laws. It made impossible a legal jury system.

For the next fourteen years, the messages and communications of five successive Governors to the President, the Secretary of the Interior, and the Congress were urgent pleas to pay some attention to Alaska, to give it some workable body of law. No heed was paid to any of these requests. Congress was still obsessed with the Alaska climythology of the late 1860's.

When, however, in the late 1890's, gold was discovered in the Klondike and some sixty-thousand gold seekers rushed to Alaska and found their legitimate desires unattainable for lack of suitable laws, Congress was slightly moved by the caustic communications of these constituents and, at the turn of the century, enacted some legislation. But, being drafted by men thousands of miles from the scene and totally unfamiliar with it, this legislation was again inappropriate and unworkable. So the cry for someone who could speak officially for Alaskans—a voteless delegate such as every Territory had had from the very beginning—gathered new force. However, even this slight concession was not granted until 1906. By then, the Alaskans had raised their sights and demanded a legislature, such as every Territory had had. Finally, in 1912, this was conceded. It had taken forty-five years—from 1867 to

1912—to give Alaskans that minimum of self-government to which all Americans feel themselves entitled.

Climythology played an important part in that forty-five-year delay, as it would continue to delay and frustrate the aspirations of Alaskans.

It played its part in making the Organic Act of 1912, though an improvement over its unworkable predecessor, the most restrictive act imposed by the United States on one of its outlying areas. It was notable chiefly for the things it forbade Alaskans to do.

They were still not permitted to make any basic land laws—a vital omission in an area virtually 100 percent public domain and crying for settlement.

They were not permitted to manage their natural resources—their fish and wildlife—as had other territories.

They were not allowed to have their own judiciary.

There were many other restrictions.

So, when the first legislature convened in 1913, after passing what legislation it could, it memorialized Congress to do for the Territory what its legislators were forbidden to do.

These requests, all reasonable and scarcely controversial, were totally ignored by the Congress for forty years, one result of which was the steady depletion, almost to extinction, of Alaska's greatest natural resource, the salmon fishery.

In addition to neglect, downright discrimination followed. Congress excluded Alaska from the provisions of Federal highway aid, although Alaska was paying all Federal taxes—victims of the "taxation without representation" which our forefathers had declared to be tyranny in the eighteenth century.

Congress further placed Alaska in the straitjacket of a steamship monopoly, with the resulting burden of ever-increasing astronomical freight rates.

Climythology had never ceased to function against the aspirations of the people of Alaska. As a matter of fact, climythology has manifested itself like a hardy perennial in virtually every major congressional debate on Alaska.

It appeared during the struggle to give Alaska its limited Territorial government in 1912.

It emerged during the debate on the building of the Alaska Railroad in 1913. Said Representative Martin Dies of Texas (father of another Martin Dies), in opposing the bill:

"We have owned this colossal chunk of frozen earth for more than fifty years and with great labor and expense have succeeded in thawing out only two thousand or three thousand acres."

Representative Thomas W. Hardwell, of Georgia, likewise an opponent, asked: "Why spend this money at the North Pole?" introducing a touch of mythogeography.

Representative Walter Elder, of Louisiana, stated that in the region to be served by the railroad there was "a killing frost every month of the year."

Representative William J. Fields, of Kentucky, said that "before going to Alaska to break the 'ice trust' by building a railroad through it," Congress could better be spending the money in the continental United States.

The next forty years under the restrictions and discriminations imposed by a distant and uninterested Government and by absentee industry were to lead Alaskans to the conviction that statehood was their only way out.

Indeed, the almost forgotten provision of the Treaty of Cession which had admitted the inhabitants "to the enjoyment of all the rights, advantages and immunities of citizens of the United States," constituted, Alaskans believed, a pledge for statehood.

They had had fine verbal support for their aspirations. In 1912, President Taft, in a message to Congress, declared:

"There is nothing in the history of the United States which affords such just reason for criticism as the failure of the Federal Government to extend the benefit of its fostering care to the Territory of Alaska."

And, five years later, in 1917, Secretary of the Interior Franklin K. Lane asserted:

"The statement that the people of Alaska have borne more handicaps than any other people who have pioneered new, undeveloped territory, at least on the North American continent, has been made so often that it has become trite. Nevertheless it is true."

These were fine words. But nothing was done by the Federal authorities to materialize them. In fact, matters became worse until

Alaskans finally, in the 1940's, moved boldly toward statehood.

Inevitably climythology appeared in the statehood debates. One of its leading opponents—in the Senate this time—declared that statehood offered no solution, since Alaska's difficulties were "due to the extreme climate and hazardous living conditions. Congress cannot change the climate," he continued.

To support his case, this Senator quoted from an article in the *New York Times* written by Hanson W. Baldwin, its military expert, who had been reporting the winter military maneuvers north of the Arctic Circle. "It is," Baldwin had written, "a land ... of relentless winters. . . . Brief exposure can mean death."

No change in laws would relieve Alaska, the Senator continued. Its fate and future were all summed up "in that short sentence . . . 'Brief exposure can mean death.' "

The Senate defeated the statehood bill by one vote—45 to 44. Climythology had done it. This was 1952. The people of Alaska had to wait six more years and to make more vigorous and audacious efforts before statehood became a reality. And they did it.

We now have statehood for Alaska—but the heritage and sequelae of ninety-odd years of climythology and colonialism remain to be liquidated. That legacy is with us and its dispersal is the challenging task and duty of those whom the people of Alaska have elected to public office.

For climythology concerning Alaska is still widespread among our fellow citizens in the lower States.

When I used to go back east to Washington during my years in the governorship, the question most frequently put to me was: "What is the weather in Alaska like?"

When asked by my friends, I could generally detect overtones of solicitude. Although not overtly expressed, I could sense the questioner's sympathy with the hardships the Gruenings must have to endure. Could we stand the cold?

So, I would explain, and after a while it became a routine, that it was no more possible to answer in one sentence what the climate of Alaska was like than it would be to answer in one sentence what the climate of the United States—the older forty-eight—was like; that Alaska was as wide and deep as the United States and had several very different climates in its diverse and far-flung regions.

And when I would compare or contrast the winter and summer temperature in Juneau, where we lived, with temperatures in various parts of the lower forty-eight States, I suspect that only those who really trusted me believed that I was not giving a chamber of commerce version.

This would therefore seem an appropriate time and occasion to set the record straight and replace climythology with comparative climatology, dispelling the climyths of the "hazardous living and savage climate" of Alaska.

For surprising as it may be to some, the truth is that—from a climate standpoint—living is less hazardous in Alaska than in any other state of the Union.

Climate—weather—accounts annually for scores of deaths in the other forty-nine States from causes which do not exist in Alaska.

Consider, first, tornadoes. They occur every year in the other States and only a few of the lower forty-nine are exempt.

In the forty-six years beginning in 1916, since the Weather Bureau began recording the casualties from tornadoes, it has recorded 1,217 deaths, an average of over twenty-six a year. In only four of those forty-six years were no deaths recorded, although bodily injuries and property damage were. In 1953 the death toll from tornadoes reached the tragic figure of 244. The number of injured each year is, of course, far greater than the fatalities, and the property damage over the same period is about a quarter of a billion dollars.

Tornadoes occur in every State of the Union except Alaska. No tornado has ever taken a life in Alaska.

Hurricanes annually take a varying toll of lives in the forty-eight lower continental States, ravaging the Atlantic and Gulf coasts in the process. In 1947 they took fifty-three lives, one in Texas, one in South Carolina, twelve in Louisiana, twenty-two in Mississippi.

Hurricanes took four lives in 1948, three in 1949, nineteen in 1950, none in 1951, three in 1952, two in 1953. In 1954, four hurricanes took the tragic total of 193 lives. Hurricane Carol, in that year, killed sixty in New England, and Hurricane Hazel took ninety-five in the Atlantic States north from South Carolina.

The next year, 1955, was even more disastrous, with Hurricane Connie killing twenty-five in Maryland, New Jersey, New York, and New England, and Hurricane Diane killing 184 in Virginia, Pennsylvania, New York, Connecticut, Massachusetts, and Rhode Island.

In 1956, the hurricane deaths dipped to twenty-one—all in Mississippi, Louisiana, Alabama, and Florida.

But 1957 was the worst on record, with 395 dead, of which Hurricane Audrey took 371 in Louisiana. In 1959, there were twenty-four; in 1960, sixty-five, and in 1961, forty-six.

Despite the fact that Alaska's coastline is longer than the combined Atlantic, Gulf, and Pacific coastlines of the forty-eight lower continental States, no hurricane has ever taken its toll of an Alaskan life. Lightning killed 2,054 persons in the lower forty-eight states in the decade 1948 to 1957, according to the Weather Bureau —an average of 205 a year.

Only one State besides Alaska suffered no death from lightning in that decade. Texas led with 150 deaths from lightning; Alabama was next, with 112; Georgia third, with 110; North Carolina had 101; Mississippi, 98; South Carolina, 95.

Thunderstorms are not common in Alaska. Lightning is seen here rarely and no one was ever killed by lightning in our State.

Even our volcanoes, of which some fifty are active, seem to be uniquely benign. Writing on the explosion of Mount Katmai, which took place on June 6, 1912, just fifty years ago this month, George C. Martin, geologist with the U.S. Geological Survey, rendering the first full account in the February 1913 issue of the National Geographical magazine, declared that the eruption was undoubtedly one of the most violent of historic times, adding: "In the violence of the explosion, in the quantity of material thrown out, and in the distance to which the ejected material and sound waves were carried, this was certainly among the greatest eruptions witnessed by man. It differs, however, from almost all other known great eruptions in that the immediate damage to property was almost nothing, and that, as far as known, it was not the direct and sole cause of the loss of a single human life."

As contrasted with the weather fatalities in the lower States from hurricanes, tornadoes, and lightning, averaging hundreds of deaths annually, Alaska can record from natural disasters, in comparable periods of record, only less than a dozen deaths from the two seismic waves which swept the Scotch Cap lighthouse and its personnel into the sea in 1946, and the similar occurrence in the Yakutat area four years ago, where five perished. Both of these were due to earthquakes beneath the ocean floor off the Alaskan coast.[1]

It is for us the living—the living in Alaska, who have experienced neither tornado nor hurricane, nor been struck by lightning—to oppose long-standing climythology with facts.

They will reveal that while the forty-ninth State has the widest range of temperatures under the flag—from 100° above to 76° below zero at Fort Yukon—life, as far as climatic vicissitudes are concerned, is the least hazardous of any State of the Union.

I could and should, no doubt, rest my case there, but I cannot forbear to add a word about Alaska's spaciousness and its grandeur.

Henry Gannett, for many years the chief geographer of the U.S. Geological Survey, gave this "one word of caution to those intending to visit Alaska. . . . 'If you are old, go by all means; but if you are young, wait. The scenery of Alaska is much grander than anything else of the kind in the world, and it is not well to dull one's capacity for enjoyment by seeing the finest first.' "

What distinguishes life in Alaska from life in other States? For one thing, the unspoiled wilderness, with all its abundance, beauty, and mystery is always nearby.

This entrancing land displays both the celestial fireworks of the aurora borealis and the midnight sun—though I will have to admit that even we cannot exhibit both at the same time.

But perhaps most important, the last frontier is inhabited by the friendliest people. There is neither caste nor class in Alaska. Here are no status seekers.

Being both Americans and Alaskans is status enough.

[1] The Good Friday, March 27, Alaska earthquake of 1946—probably the most intense since the scientific recording of these upheavals, with its toll of 115 dead or missing—requires a retroactive revision of this paragraph; but earthquakes, while a natural disaster, cannot be classed as climatic phenomena. (Ed.)

# 26

# THE STRUGGLE FOR STATEHOOD

O N August 12, 1869, Secretary of State William Henry
Seward delivered a historic address in Sitka, Alaska's capital.
After describing Alaska's resources and hailing its citizens as
pioneers, he extolled Alaska's climate and scenery and referred
to its great needs: military protection and territorial civil government. The first of these, he said, Congress had already supplied
"adequately and effectively." The second, he doubted not, Congress would supply "during the coming winter."

Seward proved too optimistic. Military protection ceased eight
years later when the troops stationed at Sitka were withdrawn
to put down an uprising of the Nez Perce Indians in the Northwest.
When the distant Federal authorities failed to heed the increasingly
frantic pleas of the settlers to provide protection from a threatening Indian uprising, it was neighboring Canada that responded
first by sending one of Her Majesty's ships, which furnished protection for several weeks until an American sloop of war arrived.
As for territorial civil government, fifteen "coming winters" passed
without any, and such civil government as was established by the
Act of 1884 proved so limited and unworkable that the pleas of
seven successive territorial governors, whose office it had established, plus the efforts of Alaska's delegates in Congress—which
office was created in 1906—were required to bring about territorial
civil government in 1912.

Seward also forecast statehood, though his timetable was like-

wise overoptimistic. Alaskan statehood was to wait ninety years—
but that was not Seward's fault. Deserved appreciation of his great
achievement is reflected in the Seward place-names in Alaska.
A mighty peninsula, thrust appropriately toward Russia in Asia, a
seaport city, a mountain range, a passage in the Alexander Archipelago, and a creek all bear his name. Likewise, March 30, the
day the Treaty of Cession was signed, is called Seward's Day
and is a holiday in Alaska.

The concluding part of his Sitka address follows.


From · · ·

### William Henry Seward's *Address at Sitka*

. . . You will ask me, however, for guarantees that the hopes
I encourage will not be postponed. I give them.

Within the period of my own recollection, I have seen twenty
new States added to the eighteen which before that time constituted
the American Union; and I now see, besides Alaska, ten Territories
in a forward condition of preparation for entering into the same
great political family. I have seen in my own time not only the
first electric telegraph, but even the first railroad and the first
steamboat invented by man. And even on this present voyage of
mine I have fallen in with the first steamboat, still afloat, that
thirty-five years ago lighted her fires on the Pacific Ocean. These,
citizens of Sitka, are the guarantees, not only that Alaska has a
future, but that that future has already begun. I know that you
want two things just now, when European monopoly is broken
down and United States free trade is being introduced within the
Territory: these are military protection while your number is so
inferior to that of the Indians around you, and you need also a
territorial civil government. Congress has already supplied the
first of these wants adequately and effectually. I doubt not that it
will supply the other want during the coming winter. It must do
this because our political system rejects alike anarchy and executive absolutism. Nor do I doubt that the political society to be
constituted here, first as a Territory, and ultimately as a State or

many States, will prove a worthy constituency of the Republic. To doubt that it will be intelligent, virtuous, prosperous, and enterprising is to doubt the experience of Scotland, Denmark, Sweden, Holland, and Belgium, and New England and New York. Nor do I doubt that it will be forever true in its republican instincts and loyal to the American Union, for the inhabitants will be both mountaineers and seafaring men. I am not among those who apprehend infidelity to liberty and the Union in any quarter hereafter; but I am sure that, if constancy and loyalty are to fail anywhere, the failure will not be in the States which approach nearest to the North Pole.

Fellow citizens, accept once more my thanks, from the heart of my heart, for kindness which can never be forgotten, and suffer me to leave you with a sincere and earnest farewell.

* * *

Harry S. Truman was the first President of the United States to endorse statehood for Alaska. Not only did he urge the granting of statehood to both Alaska and Hawaii in his first State of the Union message in January 1946, but he wrote a unique chapter in American history by subsequently sending a special message to the Congress devoted wholly to Alaska.

In this message in May 1948 President Truman revealed the fullness of his understanding of Alaska's needs and of the value he attached to its admission to statehood, not merely for Alaska's benefit but in the interest of the entire nation.

No similar document exists in our national annals, although there were previous examples of Presidential support for the admission of a particular state, as, for instance, Abraham Lincoln's efforts to bring Nevada into the Union. Needless to say, President Truman's vigorous espousal was an important factor in securing favorable action by a Democratic Congress in 1958.

After the opening passages here given, President Truman discussed Alaska's problems and needs in great detail, with recommendations for appropriate action. This part of the message has been omitted because of lack of space.

From · · ·

### President Harry S. Truman's *Message on Statehood for Alaska*

*To the Congress of the United States:*

Alaska is our last great frontier area, and has the capacity to provide new opportunities for many thousands of our citizens. It contains known resources of food, timber, and minerals of great value to the national economy, and may have much greater resources as yet undiscovered.

It is in the Nation's interest, therefore, for the Government to assist the balanced development of Alaskan resources and to help open economic opportunities on a sound long-term basis. I am recommending in this message a number of actions which will contribute to these purposes.

Since Alaska became part of the United States 80 years ago, a certain amount of development has taken place. A number of industries, principally fisheries and mining, have been established, although unfortunately they have followed too largely the pattern of absentee ownership and exploitation. During the recent war, when the strategic importance of Alaska became obvious, a number of extensive military installations were built or started there.

### 1. Statehood for Alaska

Some 94,000 people now reside in the Territory, and the population is growing. Alaska residents deeply desire statehood. A large proportion of them are from the States and share our long tradition of self-government. Alaska has a larger population and a stronger economic base than did many of our present States when they were admitted to the Union. It has had Territorial government for more than 35 years, surely a sufficient period of preparation for its admission as a State.

I believe, therefore, that we should admit Alaska to statehood at the earliest possible date, and I urge the Congress to enact the necessary legislation. I am pleased to note that the Committee on

Public Lands of the House of Representatives has unanimously recommended such legislation.

It is important to remember that after the Congress acts, it will still be necessary to hold a constitutional convention, draft a constitution, and submit it to the voters for approval before statehood is achieved. Since these steps will require at least a year, they should be started as soon as possible.

Statehood will bring many advantages to the people of Alaska. Most important, it will give them a much greater opportunity to manage their own affairs; they will have the benefits of local freedom and initiative inherent in our system of democratic government. They will be able to put into effect much more fully their own concept of the unified development of all the resources of their vast territory.

In addition, when Alaska is a State, its people will be able to do much for themselves which they now find difficult or impossible. For example through their State government a sound, modern tax structure can be established to replace the present obsolete and inadequate system prescribed 35 years and more ago by the Federal Government. Alaskans will also be able to provide more adequately for education and health, problems which are especially difficult under frontier conditions.

Moreover, statehood will permit Alaskans to take a greater part in the affairs of the Nation. Through voting representation in the Congress and participation in national elections, they will have a direct voice in national decisions. At the same time, as a State Alaska will participate fully in many national programs, such as the Federal-aid highway program, which are now withheld unless special legislation is passed.

While statehood is a wise and necessary step, certain other immediate actions should also be taken, if Alaskans are to achieve steady and balanced industrial, agricultural, and community growth.

. . . . . . . . . . . . . . . .

In the long view, the most important action the Government can take to assure this end is to permit Alaska to become a State. With the additional measures I have recommended, there is every reason to foresee a strong and expanding population of permanent residents, and to expect that the State of Alaska will be a strong partner in our great Union of States.

HARRY S. TRUMAN.

THE WHITE HOUSE, *May 21, 1948.*

The 1945 Territorial Legislature provided for a referendum to be held at the next general election in October 1946 to determine Alaskans' sentiment on statehood. At it Alaskans voted that they desired statehood, and a campaign to achieve that objective was launched. Hearings were held by both Senate and House committees in Washington and Alaska. These committees invariably reported pending statehood bills favorably, but for the next twelve years it proved impossible to get a statehood bill enacted by both houses in the same Congress.

Becoming impatient, the Alaska territorial legislators in 1955 provided for a constitutional convention which would draft a constitution for the hoped-for state. Statewide elections of delegates to the convention followed. They assembled on the campus of the University of Alaska on November 8, 1955. The next day Ernest Gruening, who had been Governor of Alaska from 1939 to 1953, delivered the keynote address.

## Ernest Gruening's *Keynote Address to the Alaska Constitutional Convention*

### LET US END AMERICAN COLONIALISM!

We meet to validate the most basic of American principles, the principle of "government by consent of the governed." We take this historic step because the people of Alaska who elected you have come to see that their long standing and unceasing protests against the restrictions, discriminations, and exclusions to which we are subject have been unheeded by the colonialism that has ruled Alaska for eighty-eight years. The people of Alaska have never ceased to object to these impositions even though they may not have realized that such were part and parcel of their colonial status. Indeed the full realization that Alaska is a colony may not yet have come to many Alaskans, nor may it be even faintly appreciated by those in power who perpetuate our colonial servitude.

Half a century ago, a governor of Alaska, John Green Brady, contemplating the vain efforts of Alaskans for nearly forty years to secure even a modicum of workable self-government, declared: "We are graduates of the school of patience."

Since that time Alaskans have continued to take postgraduate courses. Today, in 1955, sorely tried through eighty-eight years of stepchildhood, and matured to stepadulthood, Alaskans have come to the time when patience has ceased to be a virtue. But our faith in American institutions, our reverence for American traditions, are not only undimmed but intensified by our continuing depriva-tion of them. Our cause is not merely Alaskans'; it is the cause of all Americans. So, we are gathered here, following action by our elected representatives who provided this Constitutional Conven-tion, to do *our* part to "show the world that America practices what it preaches." [1]

These words are not original with me. But they remain as valued and as valid as when they were uttered five years ago. They remain no less valid even if their noble purpose is as yet unfulfilled. We are here to do what lies within our power to hasten their fulfillment.

We meet in a time singularly appropriate. Not that there is ever a greater or lesser timeliness for the application by Americans of American principles. Those principles are as enduring and as eternally timely as the Golden Rule. Indeed democracy is noth-ing less than the application of the Golden Rule to the Great Society. I mean, of course, democracy of deeds, not of lip service; democracy that is faithful to its professions; democracy that matches its pledges with its performance. But there is, neverthe-less, a peculiar timeliness to this Alaskans' enterprise to keep our nation's democracy true to its ideals. For right now that the United States has assumed world leadership, it has shown through the expressions of its leaders its distaste for colonialism. And this

---

[1] In a public address at Denver, September 16, 1950, General Dwight D. Eisen-hower declared: "Quick admission of Alaska and Hawaii to statehood will show the world that America practices what it preaches."

antipathy to colonialism—wherever such colonialism may be found—reflects a deep-seated sentiment among Americans.

For our nation was born of revolt against colonialism. Our charters of liberty—the Declaration of Independence and the Constitution—embody America's opposition to colonialism and to colonialism's inevitable abuses. It is therefore natural and proper that American leadership should set its face against the absenteeism, the discriminations, and the oppressions of colonialism. It is natural and proper that American leadership should lend such aid and comfort as it may to other peoples striving for self-determination and for that universally applicable tenet of American faith—government by consent of the governed. Indeed, as we shall see, we are pledged to do this by recent treaty commitments.

What more ironical, then, what more paradoxical, than that that very same leadership maintains Alaska as a colony?

What could be more destructive of American purpose in the world? And what could be more helpful to that mission of our nation than to rid America of its last blot of colonialism by admitting our only two incorporated territories—Alaska and Hawaii —to the equality they seek, the equality provided by the long-established and only possible formula, namely, statehood?

America does not, alas, practice what it preaches, as long as it retains Alaska in colonial vassalage.

Is there any doubt that Alaska is a colony? Is there any question that in its maintenance of Alaska as a territory against the expressed will of its inhabitants, and subject to the accompanying political and economic disadvantages, the United States has been and is guilty of colonialism?

Lest there be such doubt, lest there be those who would deny this indictment, let the facts be submitted to a candid world.

You will note that this last sentence is borrowed from that immortal document, the Declaration of Independence. It is wholly appropriate to do this. For, in relation to their time, viewed in the light of mankind's progress in the 180 years since the revolt of the thirteen original American colonies, the "abuses and usurpations"—to use again the language of the Declaration—against which we protest today, are as great, if not greater, than those our revolutionary forbears suffered and against which they revolted.

Let us recall the first item of grievance in the Declaration of Independence: "He has refused his assent to laws, the most wholesome and necessary for the public good."

"He," of course, was King George III. Put in his place, in place of the "he," his contemporary equivalent, *our* ruler, the federal government.

Has it, or has it not, "refused assent to laws, the most wholesome and necessary for the public good"?

We Alaskans know that the answer is emphatically "Yes, it has."

*He*, or for the purpose of 1955, *it*, the federal government, has "refused assent," although requested to do so for some forty years, to the following "most wholesome and necessary" laws:

First. A law transferring the control and management of Alaska's greatest natural resource, the fisheries, to the Territory of Alaska, as it transferred the corresponding resources to all other Territories in the past.

Second. It has "refused assent" to a law repealing the thirty-five-year-old discrimination in the Maritime Law of 1920, the "Jones Act," a discrimination uniquely against Alaska.

Third. It has "refused assent" to a reform of our obsolete and unworkable land laws, which would assist and speed population growth, settlement, and development of Alaska. It alone is responsible for over 99 percent of Alaska being still public domain.

Fourth. It has "refused assent" to a law including Alaska in federal aid highway legislation.

Fifth. It has "refused assent" to a law abolishing the barbarous commitment procedure of Alaska's insane which treats them like criminals and confines them in a distant institution in the states.

Sixth. It has "refused assent" to placing our federal lower court judges, the United States commissioners, on salary, and paying them a living wage.

One could cite other examples of such refusal of assent to "laws, the most wholesome and necessary for the public good."

But let us instead pass on to the second item of complaint, which is similar to the first, in the Declaration of Independence: "He has forbidden his Governors to pass Laws of immediate and growing importance. . . ."

Substitute for the "He," then the British royal executive, the present American federal executive, and substitute for "his Governors," his party leaders in Congress, and recall their vote in the House of Representatives last May 10, killing a law "of immediate and growing importance"—the statehood bill.

Let us go still further down the list of our revolutionary forefathers' expressed grievances, again quoting the Declaration of Independence: "He has obstructed the Administration of Justice, by refusing his Assent to Laws establishing Judiciary powers."

"He" is today the whole federal government. It has for a decade "obstructed the Administration of Justice" in Alaska by refusing assent to establishing additional judiciary powers, where they were needed, namely, in the Third Judicial Division, while repeatedly increasing the number of judges in the "mother country," the forty-eight states. And although the population of Alaska has more than tripled in the last forty-six years, the number of federal judges established in Alaska in 1909 remains unchanged. And federal judges are the only judges this colony is permitted to have.

Let us look still further in the Declaration of Independence: "He has affected to render the Military Independent of and superior to the Civil power."

Is there much difference between this and the recent presidential declaration that the defense of Alaska, that is to say, the rule of the military here, could be better carried out if Alaska remains a Territory?

One could go on at length drawing the deadly parallels which caused our revolutionary forefathers to raise the standard of freedom, although, clearly, some of the other abuses complained of in that distant day no longer exist.

But Alaska is no less a colony than were those thirteen colonies along the Atlantic seaboard in 1775. The colonialism which the United States imposes on us, and which we have suffered for eighty-eight years, is no less burdensome, no less unjust, than that against which they poured out their blood and treasure. And while most Alaskans know that full well, we repeat: "To prove this let the facts be submitted to a candid world."

To begin at the beginning, the Treaty of Cession by which Alaska was annexed, contained a solemn and specific commitment:

"The inhabitants of the ceded territory ... shall be admitted to the enjoyment of all the rights, advantages and immunities of citizens of the United States. ..."

That was the pledge. The United States has not kept that pledge. Yet a treaty is the highest law of the land. And it is made in the clear view of all mankind.

The United States has broken that pledge for eighty-eight years. It has not admitted the inhabitants of Alaska to "the enjoyment of all the rights, advantages and immunities of citizens of the United States."

"All the rights, advantages and immunities of citizens of the United States" would entitle us to vote for President and Vice President, to representation in the Congress by two senators and a representative with a vote, and would free us from the restrictions imposed by the Organic Act of 1912, and the Act of Congress of July 30, 1886. Obviously we have neither the vote, nor the representation, nor the freedom from restrictions.

We suffer taxation without representation, which is no less "tyranny" in 1955 than it was in 1775. Actually it is much worse in 1955 than in 1775 because the idea that it was "tyranny" was then new. Since the Revolutionaries abolished it for the states a century and three quarters ago, it has become a national synonym for something repulsive and intolerable.

We are subject to military service for the nation—a privilege and obligation we accept gladly—yet have no voice in the making and ending of the wars into which our young men are drafted.

In this respect we are worse off than our colonial forefathers. King George III did not impose conscription upon them. They were not drafted to fight for the mother country. Therefore there was no revolutionary slogan "no conscription without representation." But it is a valid slogan for Alaskans today.

The treaty obligation of 1867 is an obligation to grant us the full equality of statehood, for which Alaskans did not press in the first eighty years of their subordination, but which now, over-due, they demand as their right.

But that is only a small part of the evidence of our colonialism under the American flag. Let us submit more facts to a candid world.

First, let us ask, what is a colony? And let us answer that question.

A colony has been defined in a standard college textbook by a Columbia University professor as "a geographic area held for political, strategic and economic advantage."

That, as the facts will show, is precisely what the Territory of Alaska is—"a geographic area held for political, strategic and economic advantage."

The maintenance and exploitation of those political, strategic and economic advantages by the holding power is colonialism.

The United States is that holding power.

Inherent in colonialism is an inferior political status.

Inherent in colonialism is an inferior economic status.

The inferior economic status is a consequence of the inferior political status.

The inferior economic status results from discriminatory laws and practices imposed upon the colonials through the superior po-litical strength of the colonial power in the interest of its own noncolonial citizens.

The economic disadvantages of Alaskans which in consequence of such laws and practices redound to the advantage of others living in the states who prosper at the expense of Alaskans—these are the hallmarks of colonialism.

Let us take a look at these hallmarks of colonialism deeply en-graved on the policies of the United States in Alaska in the field of transportation. Transportation is the key to almost all development. None have demonstrated this better than have the Americans within the noncolonial areas of their forty-eight states where transporta-tion of every kind—railways, highways, airways—have linked, built and developed a dynamic domain of continental dimensions.

First, let us scrutinize sea-borne transportation. It was, for seventy-three years, until 1940, the only form of transportation between Alaska and the states. Alaska suffers a unique discrimination in maritime law.

Thirty-five years ago the Congress passed a merchant marine act which is known officially as the Maritime Act of 1920. In Alaska it is referred to as the "Jones Act," after its sponsor, the late Senator Wesley L. Jones of the State of Washington. The act embodied a substantial modification of existing maritime law. It provided that goods shipped across the United States, destined either for the coastal ports of the Atlantic or Pacific or for shipment across those oceans to Europe or to Asia, could use either American or foreign carriers. The foreign carriers principally involved were Canadian.

For example, a shipper from the Atlantic seaboard or from the industrial cities of the Middle West of products destined for points to the west could ship these across the country wholly on American railroads or on Canadian railroads, or partly on either.

And when these goods arrived at their Coast destination, he could send them across the Pacific in either American or foreign vessels, or southward in either. But at that point in the legislation creating this new beneficial arrangement, two words had been inserted in Article 27 of the act. Those two words were, "excluding Alaska."

Now what did those two words signify? They signified that Alaska, alone among the nations, or possessions of nations, on earth, was denied the advantages afforded all other areas. The same discrimination, obviously, applies to products shipped *from* Alaska.

What was the purpose of this discrimination? Its purpose was to subject Alaska to steamship service owned in the city of Seattle. Senator Jones no doubt assumed, and correctly, that this would be most helpful to some of his constituents there, as indeed it proved to be, but at the expense, the heavy expense, from that time on, of our voteless citizens of Alaska.

This was in 1920. Under the limited self-government which Congress had granted Alaska through the Organic Act of 1912, more limited than had been granted any other territory, Alaska was still a youngster. Nevertheless, the fifth Territorial legislature meeting the next year, 1921, protested strenuously against this specific and flagrant discrimination, and ordered the Territorial Attorney-General to take the matter to court. The Territorial legislators believed, and so expressed themselves, that this new legislation, enacted by Congress at the behest of Senator Jones of Seattle, was in violation of the commerce clause of the Constitution, which forbids discrimination against any port of the United States.

The case came to the Supreme Court of the United States on an appeal from a decree of the United States District Court dismissing the suit brought by the Territory and by an Alaskan shipper, the Juneau Hardware Company, which sought to restrain the Collector of Customs in Alaska from confiscating merchandise ordered by the hardware company and others in Alaska from points in the United States, shipped over Canadian railroads, through Canadian ports and thence to Alaska by Canadian vessels, or merchandise to be shipped from Alaska to the United States in like manner.

In pleading the cause of the Territory, Alaska's Attorney-General John Rustgard argued that both the Treaty provisions and the specific extension of the Constitution to Alaska by the Organic Act of 1912 rendered the discriminatory clause unconstitutional. It looked like a clear case.

The Government—our government—which was defending this discriminatory maritime act, was represented by the Solicitor-General of the United States, the Honorable James M. Beck of Pennsylvania.

Let the candid world note well the language of his argument:

"The immunity from discrimination is a reserved right on the part of the constituent states. . . . The clear distinction of governmental power between states and territories must be constantly borne in mind. . . . If the fathers had anticipated the control of the United States over the far-distant Philippine Islands, would they, whose concern was the reserved rights of the states, have considered for a moment a project that any special privilege which the interests of the United States might require for the ports of entry of the several states should by compulsion be extended to the ports of entry of the colonial dependencies . . . ?"

Let the candid world note that the case for the United States was presented on the basis that discrimination against a colonial dependency was proper and legitimate and that "any special privilege" required in the United States would supersede any obligation to a colonial dependency. The colonial dependency involved was and is Alaska.

Mr. Justice McReynolds, in rendering the decision of the court, declared:

"The Act does give preference to the ports of the States over those of the Territories," but he added, the Court could "find nothing in the Constitution itself or its history which compels the conclusion that it was intended to deprive Congress of the power so to Act."

So it was definitively established by the highest court of the land that Congress had discriminated against Alaska, but that, since Alaska was a colonial dependency, such discrimination was permissible and legal.

Every plea of our Alaska legislatures over a period of thirty-five years to rectify this grave and unjust discrimination has been ignored by successive Congresses. They have "refused assent" to every attempt by Alaska's delegates to secure remedial legislation.

Now the question naturally arises whether this discrimination imposed by the legislative branch of the federal government, approved by the executive branch, and sanctified by the judicial branch, was to prove to be more than a mere statement of the legality of such discrimination. Was it more than a mere affirmation of the subordinate and inferior status of Alaska's colonials as compared with the dominating and superior status of the American citizens of the states? Did this discrimination also carry with it economic disadvantages? Indeed it did.

Several private enterprises in Alaska were immediately put out of business by the action of Congress in 1920 even before the Supreme Court upheld the legality of that Congressional action.

A resident of Juneau had established a mill to process Sitka spruce. He was paying the required fees to the Forest Service and had developed a market for his product in the Middle West where it was used in airplane manufacture. He was shipping it through Vancouver, where it cost him five dollars a thousand to ship by rail to his customers.

The "Jones Act" automatically compelled him to ship his spruce boards by way of Seattle. Here he was charged eleven dollars a thousand, as against the five dollars he had been paying, plus some additional charges, which totaled more than his profit. In consequence his mill was shut down and a promising infant industry, utilizing an abundant but little used Alaskan resource, was extinguished. Not only did the "Jones Act" destroy this and other enterprises, but prevented still others from starting and has prevented them ever since. If anyone doubts that political control of the Territory through remote forces and absentee interests does not cause economic damage to the people of Alaska he need but look at the workings of the maritime legislation directed against Alaska and Alaska only.

Its immediate effects were to more than triple the cost of handling Alaska freight in Seattle on purchases made in Seattle, as compared with Seattle-bought cargoes destined for the Orient. Alaska's delegate, at that time the late Dan Sutherland, testified that the Seattle terminal charges on shipments to Hawaii or Asia were only thirty cents a ton, and all handling charges were absorbed by the steamship lines, the result of competition between Canadian and American railways and steamship lines. But for Alaska, where Congressional legislation had eliminated competition, the Seattle terminal charges on local shipments, that is to say, on goods bought in Seattle destined for Alaska, were 100 percent higher, or sixty cents a ton against thirty cents a ton, plus fifty cents a ton wharfage. So Alaskans paid $1.10 a ton for what cost Hawaiians and Asiatics thirty cents a ton—nearly four times as much.

This was by no means all. On shipments anywhere in the United States through Seattle, and destined for points in the Pacific *other* than Alaska, the total handling charges were only thirty cents a ton wharfage, and all other costs were absorbed by railroad and steamship lines. But for identical shipments consigned to Alaska, an unloading charge of sixty-five cents a ton was imposed, plus a wharfage charge of fifty cents a ton, plus a handling charge from wharf to ship of sixty cents a ton. These charges aggregated over five times the cost to a shipper to other points in the Pacific, and had to be paid by the Alaska consignee or shipper, and of course ultimately by the Alaska consumer.

These damaging figures were presented by Delegate Sutherland at a public Congressional committee hearing and made part of the

official printed record. No attempt was made by the representatives of the benefiting stateside interests, either then or later, to
explain, to justify, to palliate, to challenge, to refute or to deny
his facts.

If there is a clearer and cruder example of colonialism anywhere let it be produced! Here is a clear case where the Government
of the United States—through its legislative branch, which enacted
the legislation, the executive branch, through the President, who
signed it, and the judicial branch, which through its courts, upheld
it—imposed a heavy financial burden on Alaskans exclusively,
for the advantage of private business interests in the "mother
country."

Nor is even this by any means all on the subject of railroad and
steamship discrimination against Alaska, and Alaska alone. In
addition to all the above extortions against Alaska's shippers,
suppliers and consumers—the direct result of discriminatory legislation—all the railroads of the United States charge a higher rate,
sometimes as much as 100 percent higher, for shipping goods
across the continent, if these goods are destined for Alaska.

There is a so-called rail export tariff and a rail import tariff,
which apply to a defined geographic area with exceptions made
for other areas, which penalizes Alaska and Alaska alone.

Please note that the service rendered by those railroads, for the
same articles transported, and for the same distance, is exactly
the same, whether the article to be shipped goes ultimately to
Alaska or elsewhere in the Pacific or whether it stays on the mainland of the United States. But the charges for Alaska, and Alaska
only, on that identical article, for identical mileage, and identical
service, are specifically higher, sometimes up to 100 percent higher.

This abuse, as well as the others dating from the "Jones Act,"
have been the subject of unceasing protest from Alaskans. Alaska's
legislatures have repeatedly memorialized the Congress and the
federal executive agencies asking for equal treatment. Again and
again have Alaska's delegates sought to have the discriminatory
clause in the maritime law repealed. But each time the lobbies of
the benefiting stateside interests have been successful in preventing
any relief action.

How powerful these lobbies are and how successful they have

been in maintaining these burdensome manifestations of colonialism may be judged from the unsuccessful efforts of the late Senator Hugh Butler of Nebraska to get the discriminatory words: "excluding Alaska," stricken from the act. He introduced a bill for that purpose.

In a speech on the Senate floor on December 4, 1947, he denounced "the discrimination against the territory in the present law," that is the Maritime Act of 1920, and urged that there was "need for the prompt removal of that discrimination if we are to demonstrate that we are in earnest in our determination to promote the development of Alaska."

In a subsequent communication to Senator Homer Capehart, who was then chairman of a subcommittee on Alaska matters of the Committee on Interstate and Foreign Commerce to which Senator Butler's bill was referred, Senator Butler specified the character and extent of the abuse which Alaska was suffering, saying:

"To-day after 27 years of operation under the Jones Act of 1920, the carriers have failed to establish satisfactory service. . . . The Territory is still without adequate transportation to meet its needs. . . . Most Alaskan coastal towns are not connected with the continental United States, or with each other, by highway or rail. Accordingly they have been at the mercy of a steamship monopoly of long duration. There could be no competition from rail or bus lines which would compel better services or lower rates. American steamship lines have not been able or willing to meet Alaska's transportation requirements. The service has been infrequent and the rates exorbitant."

This caustic language was Senator Butler's. And his testimony and vigorous denunciation are highly significant, not merely because he was very conservative, but because for the first fourteen years of his Senatorial service he was a bitter opponent of statehood for Alaska, a stand which made him the beau ideal of the anti-statehood elements within and without the Territory. He professed conversion to statehood for Alaska in 1954 only a few months before his death. He was still an unqualified opponent of Alaskan statehood when he issued this devastating indictment of the maritime transportation in 1947 and 1948.

After going into further detail on the injurious effects on Alaska of the "Jones Act," and the fact that most of the "merchandise . . . food products . . . and other commodities" shipped to Alaska were "an exclusive Seattle prerogative," Senator Butler continued:

"The passage of this amendment to the 'Jones Act' could well mean the difference between the slow, continued strangulation of Alaska's economy, and the full development of the Territory's vast potentialities."

Senator Butler then spoke of the discriminatory rates in favor of canned salmon, which industry, he pointed out, likewise centered in and around Seattle, saying:

"The people of Alaska have long been subject to higher rates than has the salmon industry, for general cargo. These higher rates are, in fact, a decree penalizing the resident Alaskan for living in Alaska; the lower rates are, in effect, a decree requiring the Alaska resident to make up for whatever deficits accrue from the costs of shipping canned salmon and salmon-cannery needs. . . . The strangling provisions of the present laws would be eliminated by the enactment of S. 1834."

S. 1834 was Senator Butler's bill to remove this manifestation of colonialism.

And Senator Butler concluded: "The development of Alaska would be accelerated, and justice would be done to those permanent residents of our northwestern frontier, who have, for so many years, struggled valiantly against discouraging circumstances to develop the area."

Despite Senator Butler's powerful position as the Chairman of the Committee on Interior and Insular Affairs when his party controlled the Congress, this legislation failed. It did not even come out of committee. Eight more years have passed since that time; the tragic situation as far as Alaska is concerned in its key transportation, has further deteriorated. Steamship freight rates have continued to go up and up, far above the levels that Senator Butler termed "exorbitant."

Invariably, whenever the operators announced another rate increase, the Alaska territorial authorities used to request the maritime regulatory agency to secure an audit of the company's books in order to demonstrate that the increases requested were justified.

But almost invariably the increases were granted without such audit and often without question. It may well be asked whether, if Alaska were not a colony, but a state, its two Senators might not be reasonably effective in at least securing a demonstration from the carrier that its financial situation justified the rate increases demanded and promptly acceded to by the Federal Maritime Bureau.

But actually, if Alaska were a state, the whole discrimination in the "Jones Act" would go out the porthole. Alaska would then get the same treatment in the transportation of freight that is accorded to every other area under the flag and to foreign countries. But as a colony it gets no consideration in this matter either from the legislative branch, the Congress, or from the executive branch, in this instance the Federal Maritime Board, successor to other agencies similarly subservient to the vested interests within the colonial power.

The net result of those cumulative charges—50 to 100 percent higher railroad freight rates to Seattle, higher unloading and transfer charges in Seattle, higher wharfage and higher longshoring charges, and finally higher maritime freight rates to Alaska ports —all higher than anywhere else for any but Alaskans, has been and is greatly to increase the cost of living in Alaska. This in itself has been and continues to be a great hindrance to settlement and permanent residence in Alaska, a heavy burden on private enterprise in Alaska, a forecloser of new enterprise, and obviously a great obstacle to development.

How absurd in the light of these facts—and others similar to be submitted to our candid world—is the allegation of the small minority of Alaskans and of others "outside" that we are not ready for statehood. How shall we get readier with these handicaps? How can we cope with what conservative Senator Butler described as "the slow, continued strangulation of Alaska's economy," if the throttling grip of colonialism is not loosened?

To complete the maritime picture, beginning last year all passenger travel on American boats has ceased. The Alaska Steamship Line has eliminated it. This is a blow to an infant and potentially great industry in Alaska, the tourist industry, which four years ago the Alaska 1951 legislature sought to develop by establishing the Alaska Visitors' Association, financed jointly by territorially appropriated and publicly subscribed funds.

One postscript remains on the subject of maritime transportation before we pass on to other of Alaska's colonial disadvantages. Though it is invariably pointed out by Congressional opponents of statehood that Alaska is a noncontiguous area, separated from the main body of the 48 states by some 700 miles of foreign territory, or 700 miles of either international or foreign coastal waters, the United States persists in maintaining the coastwise shipping laws against Alaska. Their removal would make a steamship line eligible for the subsidies which American flagships in the European, African or Asiatic trade receive. That might, were Congress sufficiently interested, induce some competition in the Alaska steamship trade from other American carriers. That the imposition of the coastwise shipping laws is not a necessary corollary to being a colony is proved by the fact that the United States has suspended the coastwise shipping laws for the Virgin Islands. But it has declined to do so for Alaska.

Let us now turn to a third form of transportation: highways. These catchwords of colonialism, "excluding Alaska," likewise apply to our highway transportation. For Alaska is denied inclusion in the Federal Aid Highway Act. From this beneficent legislation enacted in 1916 and repeatedly amended and amplified, Alaska, alone among the states and incorporated territories, is excluded. Even Puerto Rico, which pays no federal taxes whatever, is included. Yet Alaskans pay all taxes, including the federal gas tax.

The Congressionally wrought substitute—annual appropriation —is a witness to colonialism expressed in cold figures. The results are visible in the lack of an adequate Alaskan highway system. After eighty-eight years of colonialism and forty years after the enactment by Congress of the joint federal aid and state highway program, Alaska has only some 3,500 miles of highway. This is a negligible amount for an area one fifth as large as the forty-eight states and with only one railroad.

For the first thirty-eight years after the cession of Alaska no roads were built by any government agency. With Alaska almost totally public domain, highway construction was clearly a federal responsibility. In the next thirty-six years beginning with the first federal construction in 1905 and the outbreak of World War II in 1941, the federal government appropriated about $19\frac{1}{2}$ million dollars, an average of a trifle over half a million dollars a year—a pittance. During that same period Alaska contributed some 9 million dollars. Thus the federal contribution was 68.4 percent of the total of $28\frac{1}{2}$ million dollars, and Alaska's was 31.6 percent, a far greater proportion than Alaska with its virtual totality of public domain would have had to pay under the Federal Aid Highway Act. It is fair to say, however, that under the Highway Act, federal funds go for construction and not for maintenance.

After road construction had been transferred from the War Department to the Department of the Interior in 1930, for the next decade or more throughout the 1930's, when the federal government and the states were jointly expanding the national highway network, Alaska was given no new highway construction. Maintenance only was granted. Military requirements brought the Alaska Highway and the Glenn Highway, and in the later 1940's a highway program to satisfy defense needs was begun and carried out for five years. But even that has been brought to a virtual halt. For the past three years the federal program has contained no new highway project. This year a token appropriation was included for the desirable Fairbanks-Nenana road, but at the price of halting construction of the important Copper River Highway. In fact the present greatly reduced program spells little more than slow completion and paving of the military highways begun eight years ago. The federal government seems to be heading us back to mere maintenance.

In contrast, the federal aid program in the mother country is being handsomely increased, reaching the largest sums in its history in the current biennial appropriation enacted in the second session of the 83rd Congress.

If Alaska were a state it would be automatically included in the expanding highway program. But as a colony it continues to be discriminated against, and that discrimination instead of lessening is being aggravated.

By the same token Alaska has been excluded from the administration's one-hundred-one-billion-dollar federal highway program. One of the principal justifications, perhaps the principal justification, for this lavish, yet important and valuable proposal, is that it is in part a civilian defense measure to aid evacuation and dispersal in the event of a shooting war with atomic weapons. Yet the same administration that excludes Alaska from this defense measure wishes to keep Alaska in colonial bondage because of alleged national defense reasons.

The enactment of this multibillion-dollar program was deferred in the last session of Congress because of differences of opinion on how to finance it. But in one respect there was no difference of opinion: Alaska would be taxed for the program even if not included in it. The Eisenhower program, presented by General Lucius Clay, called for long term bonding to be repaid out of general funds. Congressional substitutes, on a more nearly "pay-as-you-go" basis, called for increased taxes on gasoline, tires, and other automobile accessories. Efforts to include Alaska in both programs failed, as did subsequent efforts to exclude Alaska from the tax provisions. So Alaskans will be taxed for benefits accruing solely to the residents of the mother country. What else is this but colonialism, crude, stark, undisguised and unashamed?

When both the Presidential and Congressional drafts failed of passage, President Eisenhower declared he was "deeply disappointed" and added:

"The nation badly needs good roads. The good of our people, of our economy, and of our defense requires that the construction of these highways be undertaken at once."

As colonials we can merely note that Alaskans are, in the consideration of our President, apparently not part of "our people, our economy and our defense."

There is yet more of humiliating disregard. The federal administration, while patently uninterested in developing Alaska through its highways, is strongly in favor of completing the Inter-American Highway.

On March 31 last, President Eisenhower in a letter to Vice President Nixon requested an increase in the current appropriation for the Central American portion from five million to seventy-five million dollars, a more than thirteenfold increase. The President gave several reasons for this massive amplification. Three of them emphasized the important economic contribution to the countries through which this highway passes, and a fourth stressed the security aspects of the road.

We may applaud the purpose to complete the Inter-American Highway, with its economic benefits to Guatemala, Honduras, Salvador, Costa Rica, Nicaragua and Panama. We may even enjoy our participation in this philanthropy to these good neighbors, remembering that it is more blessed to give than to receive, and that every Alaskan is paying his share of that 75 million dollars. Still, some of us may wonder why similar consideration is not vouchsafed to Alaska, whose highway and economic needs are great, whose trade is almost exclusively with the United States, and whose relation to national security is certainly much closer than that of the Central American republics. This wonder on our part would be particularly natural since President Eisenhower seems to exhibit concern about Alaska's defense in connection with statehood.

We have now viewed three flagrant examples of colonialism in three of the major means of transportation, shipping, railways and highways. Let us now look at the fourth—airways.

It is superfluous to signalize our air-mindedness to any group of Alaskans. But the candid world should know that Alaskans fly thirty to forty times more than other Americans, and, starting with our bush pilots, early developed a fine system of intra-Alaskan aviation. It was almost wholly an Alaskan enterprise—flown and financed by Alaskans—though for a time without airports, aids to navigation and other assistance provided in the mother country. The Air Commerce Act of 1926—a sort of federal aid act for air —did not supply any of these aids to Alaska, although Alaska was included in the legislation. Nevertheless Alaska again suffered the penalty of being a colony, this time at the hands of the federal executive agency trusted with administration of the act. This time it was the bureaucrats who "excluded" Alaska. But the Alaskan bush pilots flew anyhow and what we have in the way of airways in Alaska is largely due to their courageous and skillful pioneering.

However, air service between Alaska and the States, which required the approval of federal bureaus and investment of outside capital, lagged far behind. The first commercial service connecting

Alaska with the mother country did not take place till 1940, long after American commercial air carriers had spanned the rest of the hemisphere and had established regular service across the Pacific.

Meanwhile the newly created bureaucracies of the Civil Aeronautics Board and the Civil Aeronautics Administration moved into Alaska. They began restricting local enterprise. In the late 1940's, over the widespread protests of Alaskans, the C.A.B. began cracking down on nonscheduled operation, and finally eliminated the "nonscheds" completely. It did not do so in the forty-eight states. Alaska was again the victim of its colonial status. We had no Senators or voting representatives to fend for us.

The successive certification, cases which for over a decade have dealt with transportation between the states and Alaska, have been desperate, and not wholly successful, struggles by Alaskans to overcome the inadequate understanding of the Civil Aeronautics Board that air transportation is relatively much more important in Alaska than in the states with their well-established alternative forms of transportation by railways and highways. Five years ago interior Alaska was saved from insufficient service only by President Truman's overruling the board and granting certification to one of the two Alaskan carriers which the board had denied.

For the last two years our two Alaskan carriers, in the face of steadily mounting traffic, have managed by heroic, all-out effort at least to retain what they had. But it is noteworthy that while the two international carriers serving Alaska, both "mother country" enterprises, have been granted permanent certificates, the certificates for our two Alaskan carriers are only temporary—a handicap to their financing and to their ability to expand.

Alaska's statehood case could rest here. Yet no account of its eighty-eight years of territorialism would be complete without some notice of the salmon fishery. It comes, this year, pretty close to being an obituary notice.

Here *was* Alaska's greatest natural resource.

Here *was* the nation's greatest fishery resource.

For nearly half a century, the federal government has totally ignored, has "refused assent" to the petitions, pleas, prayers, memorials, of legislatures, delegates, governors and of the whole

Alaskan people for measures that would conserve that resource.

The result is written in figures that spell tragedy for Alaska's fishermen and for many others in Alaska's coastal communities whose economy has long depended on the fisheries. The tragedy has deepened year after year. So grave has become the plight that the administration found it necessary to proclaim the fishing villages to be disaster areas. It is a disaster caused by colonialism, and the federal government may charge the costs of disaster relief and loss of federal tax income to its own policies.

From over eight million cases twenty years ago the salmon pack has fallen year by year until in 1955 it has reached the incredible low of 2,382,131 cases, the lowest in forty-six years.

Nowhere, as in the Alaska fisheries fiasco, is the lesson clearer of the superiority, in purely material terms, of self-government to colonialism. In neighboring British Columbia and Washington State, where the fisheries are under home rule, and where fish traps have been abolished, the identical resource has not only been conserved but augmented.

It is colonialism that has both disregarded the interest of the Alaskan people and caused the failure of the prescribed federal conservation function. Colonialism has preferred to conserve the power and perquisites of a distant bureaucracy and the control and special privileges—the fish traps—of a politically potent absentee industry. Alaska has been the victim, but the entire nation has also lost heavily.

Let us by way of a footnote make crystal clear how and why this is colonialism—because some defenders of the *status quo* may deny it is, and we don't want the candid world to be confused.

The people of Alaska have repeatedly and unchangingly manifested their overwhelming opposition to fish traps. It isn't necessary to rehearse all their reasons—the results have amply justified the Alaskans' position. But fish trap beneficiaries, residents of the mother country, want to retain their Alaska traps. So the traps are retained. And it is the power and authority of the federal government which retains them. In a clear-cut issue between the few, profiting, noncolonial Americans and the many, seriously damaged, colonial Alaskans, the stateside interest wins hands down. And it wins because the government, which is also supposed to be *our* government, throws its full weight on their side and against us. *That* is colonialism.

It would be impossible in any one address, even one that assumed the length of a Senate filibuster, to list all the wrongs, disadvantages, and lack of immunities that Alaska has endured in its eighty-eight years as a Territory. They constitute an incredible story. Even for those who know it, it is hard to believe. It is hard for us as Americans who long ago established our faith in American intelligence, competence, good sense, and above all in American fair play, to contemplate the story of American colonialism in Alaska. It has been part of our faith, an abiding faith, that to right deep-seated wrongs in America, one had but to make them sufficiently widely known. And our best hope, does lie, I am convinced, in making the facts known widely—and especially the overshadowing fact of our colonialism—to our fellow Americans and to the rest of the candid world. They should know that what progress has been made in Alaska, and it has been substantial and praiseworthy, has been made in spite of these colonial impositions, and largely because of the character and fiber of the colonials themselves. Coming here from the forty-eight states, following the most cherished American trend, the westward march in search of greater freedom and greater opportunity, they brought to the last frontier and to its friendly native population, the very qualities that have made America. Only distantly man-made problems, the problems created by a remote, often unseen officialdom and its beneficiaries in the mother country, have remained unresolved.

Alaskans have striven consistently to resolve them. Let it be recorded that for 43 years, since the first legislature, and before that by individuals and groups, they have pleaded for relief from the abuses a part of which have been detailed.

Yet after two generations not a single one of these pleas, all of them fair and reasonable, has been granted.

How applicable to Alaska's plight the words of the Declaration of Independence: "In every stage of these Oppressions We have petitioned for Redress in the most humble terms. Our repeated Petitions have been answered only by repeated injury."

Lest these frequent citations from the Declaration of Independence lead anyone to the conclusion that there are any among us who now desire our independence, let such a totally erroneous assumption be promptly corrected. We desire and demand an end to our colonialism. But we seek it through a reaffirmation in deeds for Alaska of the principles which launched the American experiment, and reapplication of the practice that has been followed in thirty-five states.

We Alaskans believe—passionately—that American citizenship is the most precious possession in the world. Hence we want it in full measure; full citizenship instead of half-citizenship; first-class instead of second-class citizenship. We demand equality with all other Americans, and the liberties, long denied us, that go with it. To adapt Daniel Webster's famous phrase uttered as a peroration against impending separatism, we Alaskans want "Liberty *and* Union, now and forever, one and inseparable."

But the keepers of Alaska's colonial status should be reminded that the eighteenth-century colonials for long years sought merely to obtain relief from abuses, for which they—like us—vainly pleaded, before finally resolving that only independence would secure for them the "Life, Liberty and the pursuit of Happiness," which they felt was their natural right.

We trust that the United States will not by similar blindness to our rights and deafness to our pleas drive Alaskans from patient hope to desperation.

We have been challenged in the course of Congressional debates to show as a prerequisite that admission of Alaska to statehood would be beneficial to the nation. That test was never applied to earlier territories seeking and securing statehood. But we gladly accept that challenge and willingly subscribe to it as a condition.

The development of Alaska, the fulfillment of its great destiny, cannot be achieved under colonialism. The whole nation will profit by an Alaska that is populous, prosperous, strong, self-reliant—a great northern and western citadel of the American idea. Statehood would automatically bring us far along that high road.

Nothing could more pathetically reveal the lack of understanding regarding Alaska, and the poor advice concerning Alaska that is given and accepted in the highest places, than the presidential pronouncement in the last State of the Union message:

"As the complex problems of Alaska are resolved that Territory should expect to achieve statehood."

Bless us! The complex problems of Alaska are inherent in its territorial status; they are derived from its colonial status; they will be largely resolved by statehood and only by statehood.

As was promptly called to President Eisenhower's attention this was like the old story of telling a youngster he must learn to swim before going into the water!

So we return to the proposition that America can scarcely afford to perpetuate its colonialism. Our nation is attempting to lead the world into the pathway of peace. No goal could be more worthy. But to lead effectively, it must not only practice what it preaches. It must carry out its solemn commitments. It can scarcely be critical of nations that break their pledges and break its own. It must first cast the beam out of its own eye before attempting to pull the motes of its neighbors' eyes.

For the United States has pledged its good name and good faith in treaties and agreements far more recent than the Treaty of Cession of 1867. Not that our nation's responsibility for not carrying out those original pledges in regard to Alaska is diminished by the passage of time. But there are recent and even contemporary commitments which demand fulfillment.

Article 73 of the United Nations Charter, dealing with non-self-governing territories—and that includes Alaska, which must make annual reports to the U.N.—pledges the signatories:

"To the principle that the interests of the inhabitants of these territories is paramount," and further pledges them:

"To insure . . . their political, economic, social, and educational advancement, their just treatment, and their protection against abuses," and, finally, and this is most pertinent, it pledges them:

"To develop self-government, to take due account of the political aspirations of the peoples and to assist them in the progressive development of their free political institutions. . . ."

The United States pledged itself to that ten years ago. If the English language has not lost its meaning and the United States its integrity, it should some time ago have, and should now, in any event, "take due account of the political aspirations" of Alaskans and enable them to develop the self-government which they seek.

There is an even more recent commitment—the Pacific charter —signed a year ago, in which the signatory nations, including the United States, pledged themselves "to uphold the principle of equal rights and self-determination of peoples," and to reinforce that principle the signatories further pledged that they were "prepared to continue taking effective practical measures to insure conditions favorable to orderly achievement of the foregoing purposes," namely, to self-government.

We are agreed that there is only one form of self-government that is possible for Alaska. And so we are drawing up the constitution for the state that we fervently hope will soon come to be. That hope, it is encouraging to note, is shared by the great majority of Americans. If our eighty-eight-year experience inevitably leads to strictures of the colonialism that has ruled us, let us remember that it is a course not sanctioned by American public opinion. The Gallup polls, which last recorded an 82 percent support of Alaskan statehood, the endorsement of virtually every important national organization, demonstrate clearly that the forces in and out of government which would deny Alaska statehood—in fact the government itself—do not represent prevailing American sentiment.

But while we may derive satisfaction and hope therefrom, let us not delude ourselves that victory is at hand. It ought to be. But too many solemn pledges to Alaska have been honored in the breach to assure that what ought to be will be.

It may be regrettable—or not—but every generation must fight to preserve its freedoms. We have twice in a lifetime participated in our nation's fight to preserve them. In Alaska we still have to *win* them.

This Constitutional Convention is an important mobilization. But the battle still lies ahead, and it will require all our fortitude, audacity, resoluteness—and maybe something more—to achieve victory. When the need for that something more comes, if we have the courage—the guts—to do whatever is necessary, we shall not fail. That the victory will be the nation's as well as Alaska's— and the world's— should deepen our determination to end American colonialism.

# 27

# *HOMESTEADING*
# *THE ALASKA RANGE*

Alaska remains virtually the only American area where homesteading, made possible by the Homestead Act of 1862, still plays a considerable part in the life of its people. Overcoming the difficulties presents a saga of frontiersmen's courage, hardship, adventure, success, and failure. The homesteader's greatest frustrations—apart from the basic unsuitability of Federal legislation, designed for the West, to Alaskan conditions—do not lie in the climatic conditions or the ruggedness of the terrain, although these are a challenge to the pioneering spirit of Alaskans, but in the manmade obstacles erected by a distant Federal bureaucracy— earlier known as the General Land Office, later renamed the Bureau of Land Management, both agencies of the Department of the Interior. Conflicting claims and struggles with the agency or between individual homesteaders have long been and still continue to be among the handicaps faced by Alaska homesteaders. The following story, recounting some of those hardships, was written by Charles J. Keim, dean of the College of Arts and Letters at the University of Alaska, and appeared in the *Alaska Review* in 1964.

*Change*, by Charles J. Keim

The late spring sun already had been hard at work for several hours on the face of the glacier across the river valley when Arne

Olson threw the heavy comforter from his slight body and swung his feet to the cabin floor. The clock above the fireplace ticked away noisily, telling Arne what he already knew. It was 6 A.M. and time for breakfast.

When the spruce wood was crackling in the stove, he walked outside and held a wash pan and the coffee pot under a pipe that tapped off the creek to spill water into a stone basin he used during the summer to keep his food cool. Come freezeup, he'd use the well that he and his partner, Ross Ferrin, had dug alongside the cabin 60 years earlier and which still provided as good water as existed in the entire Alaska Range of mountains.

Water. That as much as gold had prompted him and Ross to stake the two adjoining claims. Maybe they could have scrabbled a better life out of richer gravels elsewhere, but water and the beauty of the place had anchored them there. Ross was gone now. He'd slipped out peacefully seven years earlier while lifting a shovel of gravel into the sluicebox. That's about the way he'd wanted it.

Arne had written a note to the Commissioner at Delta Junction, and then had buried Ross at the far edge of the large meadow below the cabin. In the winter the soft snow blanketed the land and the northern lights played their silent symphony across the sky. Spring and summer there always would be the song of the twin creeks, one clear, the other silty from a glacier and the mining higher up the mountainside. In all seasons moose and caribou would shamble out of the heavy spruce stands which bordered the meadow on both sides as did Silt Creek at the left and Clear Creek at the right below the cabin. And there always would be the view of the river and the mountains and the glacier beyond the open end of the meadow. Arne would rest near Ross, and the old man had mentioned this in the note to the Commissioner.

The note said other things—actually amounted to a will of sorts, something a person always figures to work around to doing, but puts off, what with one thing or another seeming to be more important. Arne had homesteaded the land around the claim and they had figured that Ross would homestead the meadow below, but with living in the cabin which was close for working the claim, it seemed easier to put off the other homesteading venture. Besides, Ross would have had to build and, for a time, live in another cabin, and the one they had put up together was plenty large for two, even more.

Arne's note said that when he was gone the authorities should sell his homestead to a person who would take care of it, keep up the mining and agree to tend the place where Ross and he would be resting. Seemed like he had figured things out right, even to specifying that the money from the sale of the place should go to the Pioneers Home down in Sitka to sort of help out the thinning ranks of their old friends there. There was contentment in that, too.

Arne pondered these things often, even talked to himself about them, like now while he pulled the coffee pot to the cool side of the stove, warmed up the blueberry syrup and fried a stack of six sourdough hotcakes and some bacon, meanwhile watching the sunlight creep from the base of the mountain, then cross the river and start moving toward the meadow. Soon the warmth would be on his doorstep, then climb the mountain to work on a glacier on that side, too. Silt Creek would rise then, for it had its beginnings at the glacier, shallowing in the mountain cold of the short spring and summer nights to just enough water to work the sluice and rising in a few hours of warmth until it raged down the mountain by midday, even rumbling giant rocks along its murky depth to discharge them at last on the river bed far below.

Arne reluctantly retrieved his ill-fitting teeth from a glass near the table, adjusted them, then forked four of the hotcakes from the stack. The other two would go to the squirrels that already were scratching around the house and adding their impatient chattering to the growing number of sounds from the awakening forest. Occasionally there was a discordant note as the sounds of the heavier traffic on the Richardson Highway four miles away would penetrate the valley. When he wished, Arne could tune out these sounds. They had grown over the years as the Fairbanks-Valdez Trail had metamorphosed into the Richardson Highway onto which funneled the commerce between Fairbanks, Anchorage, Valdez, the Yukon Territory border and other points.

Arne would watch the traffic for a while each Wednesday when he would walk over the well-worn ridge trail to the large mailbox set at the edge of the pavement. Then he would hasten back, grateful that the forest gradually would absorb the noise. He disdainfully would reject all proffers of rides during his rare, night-long walks into Delta Junction, but lately he grudgingly would admit to himself that he was finding it harder to turn them down.

Arne looked at the clock. Three minutes to seven. He poured a cup of coffee then reached across the table to switch on his radio. He would hear what was going on in Alaska, wash the dishes, shave, then impale the two hotcakes on a tree limb and head up to the diggings.

As his hand touched the switch, his eye caught the movement of a massive bull moose hurriedly lumbering up to the meadow below the cabin. The animal splashed through Clear Creek, crossed the meadow, then Silt Creek and disappeared into the forest. Arne half rose from his chair, hesitated for a moment as the radio announcer's voice began extolling the merits of aspirin, then the sourdough decisively switched off the set. He could hear the sound that had spooked the moose. Too slow for a plane.

More like a "cat" tractor, the old man thought. Maybe it's another tank.

Once the Army Arctic Indoctrination School at Fort Greely had sent a tank down the trail during maneuvers. It had parked near the Clear Creek edge of the meadow to get a commanding view of the braided river bed. Arne had talked to the tank fellows, told them how the tank could start erosion on the trail. Over coffee, one at a time in his cabin, the men figured they could cover the river just as well a little closer to the highway. Maybe they had forgotten, or new men were running the tank. Well, he would see.

Arne ate his breakfast, missing the news as he listened to the engine coming closer. A flock of ptarmigan flew part way across the meadow then flashed toward the river and out of sight. A curious raven flew about the meadow, waiting to see what was making the noise.

It was a cat, not a tank. The vehicle hesitated uncertainly before it approached Clear Creek. Arne let his fork and bacon drop from his hand when he saw that the cat was pulling a wanigan. Behind this small, house-like structure was tied an old truck, its bed piled high with gear.

The cat halted. Its pulsating roar echoed up and down the mountains as the skinner clambered down then walked toward the wanigan. The door opened and Arne, standing in his own cabin doorway now, watched the man carefully help down a woman. Then they slowly walked hand in hand to Clear Creek.

Arne was half way down the meadow by the time the man again had climbed aboard the cat and pulled the wanigan and truck to the level, tree shaded spot where the woman was standing. This was the best view of the valley, the peaks in front and behind, and Clear Creek flowed past the door. Ross had planned to put his cabin there.

Arne knew that it was useless to try to shout above the racketing of the diesel, but when the driver shut it off, the sourdough's "hold it there, hold it there" brought the couple around to face him. A little girl standing in the wanigan doorway rubbing her eyes as the sunlight touched her curly, yellow hair ran to the woman upon hearing the angry tone in the old man's voice.

Arne hadn't meant to shout, but hs heart had begun pounding harder than ever when he had noticed that the wanigan was mounted upon freshly hewn sledges instead of wheels. These were no curious passersby. Young fellow was dressed in denims, and the crew cut head and neck were perched on broad shoulders and chest above a waist as slim as one of the birches. By now the little girl was clutching her mother's leg, tightening the woman's dress and accentuating the fact that the youngster soon would have a playmate.

With difficulty Arne restrained his heavy breathing and nodded to the trio.

"Morning. Kind of off the track, aren't you?"

The man, standing somewhat defiantly in front of the woman and girl, relaxed his face into an easy grin. Holding out his hand, he walked toward Arne.

"Hello. You're Arne Olson. They told me about you in Delta Junction. You were mining up on the mountainside the two times I came in to look over the land and get some soil for testing.

We're going to be neighbors. We're homesteading 160 acres here."

Arne knew that he had flinched, so to cover up he stepped forward and used the same face he had used on Ross in winter poker games. He shook the firm hand then put both of his own back into his pockets. He knew that they were trembling and he wanted to shake them in the face of this fellow who said he was Don Ward and introduced the woman as his wife, Laura, and the girl as their daughter, Jan.

"Tough homesteading anyplace in Alaska," Arne said. "You need lots of money or another job."

"We know that. We've dragged our first home in with us to prove up on the homestead. We can clear our meadow with the cat, and get in some of our garden this season. I can get a moose this fall. It will be hard work, but our meadow is going to save us a lot of expensive clearing. We haven't got much money left, but we'll make out. I can cut logs for our home, and I might have a few tourist parties come in for fishing. Lots of grayling in the side-streams feeding the river, but then you know about that far better than I do."

Don looked expectantly at Arne, waiting for an answer. Then he picked up Jan.

"You're still sleepy," he said. "Kind of tough sleeping during that bumpy ride over the trail, but you'll do better tonight, sweetheart. We're home."

Arne and Ross had dealt with crises about the land before. But those had concerned claim jumpers and there hadn't been any women or youngsters involved. And after a few years there had been the law to fall back upon. Maybe if Ross had been there, Arne would have kept quiet now, thought it over a day or so and then talked to the intruders, but those final words "We're home," spoken to a youngster and a pregnant woman this young fellow had brought onto his land did it for Arne.

"What do you mean 'home,' 'our meadow,' cutting down trees, fishing parties and all that? Go somewhere else, closer to Delta Junction with all your ideas. This is my land." Arne pointed to the open end of the meadow. "Ross and I settled here before your dad was born. Now get out!"

Jan again clung to her mother's leg.

"Mr. Olson, we want to be friends. If I'd had more time I'd have climbed up to your diggings to explain the first time I came here. Why don't we have a cup of coffee and talk this over?"

Don stepped forward as though to guide Arne toward the wanigan.

"We'll respect the grave. The land was open to homesteading. I've filed for it and we're going to treat it right. The law is on our side, but we want you to understand."

Arne, fearfully remembering how he and Ross had won out when the law had been on their side, stepped toward the trio.

"I'm telling you to leave, and now." He shook his fist at the intruders, then turned and headed for his cabin.

He watched the cat nudge the wanigan into a better position, and Don unload the truck and cover the gear with a tarp. The squirrels chattered unceasingly for their hotcakes that day and Silt Creek rose and fell unnoticed for several more as Arne fretfully observed the hated activity in the meadow below.

He kept his peace until the morning when the sounds of chopping came from the Silt Creek edge of the meadow opposite the wanigan, and one of the isolated spruce trees that had grown larger than those in the groves fell in a long arc to the ground. Another fell before Arne could reach the axeman.

"What do you mean, cutting down the trees?" Arne demanded. "There's plenty of deadfall for firewood."

"That's what we've been using. But I figured that I'd better cut down the trees for the house logs now and drag them over near the wanigan before I clear the land and put in a garden. That way I can get them curing. We'll build next spring. Got time for a cup of coffee?"

"I've got time for nothing with you."

Don's hands tightened on the axe handle as he placed the Alaskan interpretation on the refusal which left little room for reconciliation. Then he shrugged and began limbing the tree. Arne watched for a moment, then looked about. He saw the piled slash from the other tree, firewood stacked neatly near the wanigan, the tarp-covered pole frame under which the Wards had stored

their belongings, a hose tapping off Clear Creek to provide a steady
trickle of water near the wanigan's door.

Overalls, large and small dresses and other clothing hung on
lines which extended from a corner of the wanigan to a small
spruce near the edge of the meadow. The woman was seated in
the wanigan doorway showing magazine pictures to the girl while
more washing water heated on a gasoline stove.

Then the solution to Arne's problem flitted through his mind
infinitely faster than his sweeping look at the intruders and their
activities. Just as quickly Arne dismissed it and angrily turned
around and strode back to his cabin. That day he worked at the
sluicebox, but there was small satisfaction in that, even when the
cleanup yielded several ounces of gold. The trees continued to
fall, and Arne felt himself shake as each new crash signalled
another change in the meadow below.

Numerous long scars criss-crossed the more open part of the
meadow like deeply worn game trails when Arne returned from
his diggings one day. Don had dragged the logs alongside the
wanigan where he could peel them in company with his family
and add the bark to the fuel pile. That evening and for several
others Arne could hear the steady chink, chink, chink of the pole-
axe stripping the fallen trees as he fell into troubled sleep.

Rain awakened Arne early one morning. For a time it drummed
steadily on the corrugated metal roof, and when the wind blew
up the meadow to the cabin and the peaks behind, it played an
unfamiliar tune while moving through the thinned ranks of the
trees, seemingly complaining at the times of its greatest force
that some of its harp strings were missing.

Arne pondered all this at breakfast, his hand cradled around
the familiar coffee cup, but deriving little satisfaction from the
warmth, aroma and taste. He gripped the cup more firmly when
the racketing of the diesel suddenly broke the silence. Soon the
cat crossed Clear Creek, lumbered into the wet meadow and
stopped amid the logging ruts. The cat blade lowered, then
scraped a long trail across the meadow toward Silt Creek. Don
nudged the accumulated jumble of brush, rocks and rotted logs
into the creek which by noon would be high enough to transport

the mass into the already silty and debris-filled river far below.

Arne's anger, like the debris in front of the cat, mounted higher and higher as the scar lengthened. He crashed the cup to the floor and hastened to intercept Don before he would begin a second cut across the land.

Don cut the diesel when the old man planted himself in the cat's path and peremptorily signalled Don to come to him.

"Good morning, Arne."

Don's politeness, his seeming lack of contrition for what he was doing, intensified Arne's fury.

"Good morning, hell!" Arne shouted. He moved closer to Don. "Do you know what you're doing?"

"Clearing my land."

"Clearing *my* land, you mean. Get out of here now before you cut it all to hell. I've seen your kind before. A lot of you come to Alaska all fired up to be pioneers. You cut down trees, clear some of the land, then get tired of your little game and clear out."

"Not all of them, Arne."

"Lots of them."

"I plan to stick."

"Yeah? Then find some land of your own. All the room in Alaska, and you have to park on what's rightfully my land, and start cutting it all up."

"Arne, let's get something straight. You've been using the land one way every time you've shovelled some gravel into your sluice. And that's all right. You and your kind opened the country. But it can't stay the same. We're building where you left off. If I wouldn't homestead here, somebody else would. There has to be change."

"Don't lecture me. Clear out, or you'll wish that you had."

Don shrugged. Then he restarted the diesel and, when Arne remained standing in its path, carefully steered around him, isolating the old man on a tiny island between the two clearing swaths.

That afternoon on the edge of his own property Arne carefully diverted a part of Silt Creek into Clear Creek. At noon when Don dipped a pail into Clear Creek he brought up a silty mixture unfit for drinking or other uses before long settling.

The channel widened and dumped more silt into Clear Creek. The Wards endured the silty water until the day before wash day, then Don closed the channel with the cat. When Arne returned from his digging and saw what Don had done, his emotions at first balanced between anger and stubborn determination to cut another channel. The balance began shifting when he noticed with a twinge of regret that the washing flapping on the line below his property was gray and dingy and that the woman was carrying another pail of the as yet somewhat silty water to the tubs beneath the tree. But Don had trespassed to close the channel, and in the sourdough's absence had cleared a great expanse of the meadow and now was working the cat near Ross's grave. Well, he'd clear Ward out of there!

Arne seized his old Model '95 Winchester from the caribou rack above the fireplace and hastened toward the tractor. He was drawing deep gasps of air when he had almost reached the grave site and he drew an even deeper one when he noticed that Don carefully had constructed a neat, white birch pole enclosure around the grave and skirted the plot a wide margin while clearing with the cat.

Arne looked toward the tractor which Don was working in his direction approximately 75 yards away. Then the old man's attention came back to the grave when his eyes caught a slight movement in the untended meadow grass near the wooden marker. Seated there was the little girl, watching him wide-eyed like a caribou calf. She was leaning on one arm; the other was moving into position to enable her to scramble to her feet.

She sat upright as Arne's eyes caught hers then switched from her solemn little face to the shiny object near the marker. It was a glass jar with aluminum foil crimped around it and holding an assortment of tawny colored Coltsfoot flowers, red-purplish Dwarf Fireweed, and Pink Plumes.

"What are you doing there?" Arne asked gruffly and really louder than he had intended because by now the noise of the approaching tractor was intensifying, arousing earlier emotions.

The girl sprang to her feet and, as she dodged under the birch poles, Arne seized her arm to get an answer to his question—to settle his puzzlement. Then he felt a strong grip on his own arm, the one that still held the rifle. Surprised, he relaxed his grip on the struggling girl who ran to the edge of Clear Creek.

"You deal with me, Olson, instead of punishing my wife and child!" Don sharply snapped down Arne's arm and the Winchester fell to the ground.

Arne did not struggle, but poured his strength into the bitterness of his words.

"Tried to soften me up with that fence and putting your girl to pick a few flowers." The old man glared at Don then looked downward briefly as the younger man's grip on his arm intensified at the words. Arne's eyes traveled in an instant from Don's hand to the neatly patched pant leg then to Don's foot encased in an ancient paratrooper's boot which he had planted on the barrel of the rifle.

"The fence and flowers were my wife's idea. Now get this straight. We're homesteading here. We're going to stay." Don levered the cartridges from the gun and handed it to Arne. "We haven't the money or the time now to take this to court. You can divert all of Silt Creek into Clear Creek and we'll still stay, even if I have to haul water from another creek and melt snow in winter. Now get off my land!"

The girl was standing by Clear Creek as Arne slowly walked toward his cabin. She clenched her little hands and stared at the old man, and when their eyes caught he could read the anger and fright in her face which was besmudged on each cheek where she had wiped away her tears.

Arne still could see those eyes as he dug another small channel from Silt Creek to Clear Creek, this time higher up on rockier ground where the digging was harder, but there was less danger of erosion and where the cat would have to contend with boulders if Don again would try to undo his work. As he worked Arne had ample time to ponder the scene which had occurred at the grave. When the milky water began racing into Clear Creek, Arne even test panned some of the gravel he'd dug, and he found a bit of color.

Arne heard the cat at work early in the morning after he had

linked the two creeks. His first impulse was to hasten down the
slope with his rifle, but his anger, memory of the girl's face, Don's
snapping the rifle from his hand, the dingy wash all coupled with
the warmth of the bed dissolved his resolution. For a long time he
lay there, tracing and retracing the corrugated pattern of the
ceiling and pondering the events of the past few days. But dammit,
he was protecting his land as Don claimed he was doing with the
meadow. Then Arne heard the squeal of the cat blade as it began
working among the boulders. An unusually loud noise brought him
from his bed. From the window he could see Don examining the
cat blade and its lifts. Arne saw the small figure suddenly throw
his hands despairingly into the air then drop from shoulders that
sagged now like one side of the damaged blade as Don backed
the machine protestingly down to the meadow. One end of the
blade dragged like the broken wing of a ptarmigan.

The sunlight had just begun crossing the river when Arne heard
Don's old truck cough into life and move to the cat. Don worked
for a time on the blade and its lift, then Arne saw him hoist a large
piece of the machinery into the truck bed, wave goodbye to his
wife and daughter and head toward the ridge trail, evidently to
Delta Junction and a welding shop.

"Good," the old man grunted aloud, but remembering meantime Don's badly worn boots, the patched denims and his remark
about no money. Arne pulled on his hip boots, shouldered his
shovel and hastened toward the creek. He'd dig out a very shallow
part of the channel Don had filled before he'd broken the tractor.
Silt Creek would rise when the sun would reach the glacier behind
his cabin and even the smallest rivulet soon would wash away the
loose dirt and rock and scour out the old channel.

Arne discovered that Don, naturally enough, had filled in the
channel next to Silt Creek first. Good, Arne thought. I'll leave the
plug there while I dig the rest. Soon he was working approximately
10 feet from an as yet shallow Silt Creek and moving toward
turbulent Clear Creek. As he neared that stream, Arne found the
boulder that had broken the cat. At first glance the rock looked
small enough, and from the seat of the cat must have looked
smaller yet. Arne could tell from its slope that, just like an Arctic

Ocean iceberg, the major portion was out of sight. The Silt Creek water pouring through the new channel had swirled around this obstruction, widened the channel considerably and deposited a bed of oozy silt before it continued racing at a sharper angle to Clear Creek.

Arne stooped to pick up a small piece of metal evidently broken from the cat and lying at the edge of the bank that dipped sharply into the ooze filled bowl. As he raised the metal to study its fracture, his right foot slipped in the rubble of the slope and he was forced to drop the metal and his shovel and run heavily down the incline to maintain balance.

Arne's momentum slowed as he splashed through the ooze, and he stopped when he had moved approximately eight feet into the cloying mess. Winded, he stood there for a moment, then experience told him to move out fast as his feet began to sink even deeper. Here was a quicksand of sorts built up from the silt deposited by the channel water which also had turned the clayey bottom into a heavy, tenacious gumbo that successfully had defied the strength of the stream.

Unruffled, but still tired from his jolting run in his heavy boots, Arne put an arm around each side of his leg then locked his fingers together behind the knee. As he pulled upward he carefully worked the leg back and forth.

Arne's foot moved upward in the boot. He locked his fingers more tightly. Then the movement of the boot widened its muddy prison a bit and lifted slightly. Arne continued working the leg and pulling upward. As he did so he sensed more than he really felt that his other leg was sinking more deeply into the muck. He locked his fingers behind the knee of that leg and began pulling upward. The leg he partially had freed again sank into the muck, not quite as deeply as before. Back and forth, right leg, left leg, unlock, lock, up a bit, sink a bit the old man worked, but he was tiring now. The perspiration rolled down his as yet unshaven face and he took a hurried swipe at it, leaving a muddy, dripping smudge across his lips and chin.

He straightened up for a moment to ease his back. As he did so he noticed a tiny, harmless looking thread of water moving across the mucky surface toward him. Before the thread reached him, it spread into tiny hairs as it followed the depressions on the surface of the muck. Then it was gone. Arne watched, and as he watched his legs sank deeper. Another thread of water, a wider thread, moved toward him. It, too, broke up in small webs and disappeared. But the next one was larger and began cutting a tiny channel toward Arne then disappeared around his boots. Silt Creek was building up. Each new surge of water was working at the plug between the creeks, wearing it down.

Arne pulled again and this time he heard the sucking noise of the water that had raced across the mud and disappeared beneath him.

Well, he'd been stuck before. He'd have to pull his legs from the boots and belly crawl and roll across the muck to safety. He'd lose the boots, but they were old ones anyway.

Too old. He unclenched his fingers to permit his right leg to pull free from the boot, and as he pulled the boot tore at the knee, the ripping sound of the fabric coming clearly to Arne's ears for a moment before the ooze rushing into the boot swallowed the sound.

For the first time, then, Arne felt fear. It gripped him for a moment like the cold ooze that filled around his leg. Then the fear left as his body heat killed the chill.

He carefully pulled his left leg free from its boot and deliberately fell with a splash onto the now watery surface of the muck. His fall pushed a tiny wall of water upstream, but the water coming downstream soon countered the movement and pushed its force against and then around Arne.

He wiped at the muck on his face and pulled on the imprisoned leg, but the movement merely forced the water from the broken boot and compacted the silt more firmly around the foot and calf. He placed his fingers in the rip and pulled. The boot tore neatly around his leg, separated, and left his leg imprisoned in what now was a tall overshoe.

Arne splashed over on his back into the deepening water and reached into his muddy pocket for his knife. It was gone. He splashed back to a belly position and tried to crawl, the effort driving both arms deep into the ooze. He rested for a moment, turtlelike, his neck and head raised above the level of his body. He moved his head back and forth, desperately looking for a branch, a log, anything to put under his body. The shovel was there, out of reach. He saw something else downstream on the opposite bank of a now muddying Clear Creek. It was the little girl, watching Arne as solemnly as she had earlier near Ross's grave.

"Get help," he wanted to shout, then the absurdity of the desire stopped him. Very soon the channel would be too badly eroded to block off with a shovel. Who could pull him out, a pregnant woman surely too far along even to cross Clear Creek?

Arne struggled again and momentarily freed his hands and arms. He turned his body as far as he could to face the girl and at the same time enable him to fall back on unchurned mud. Both legs were sinking more deeply. He reared his muddy body upward and splashed back into the rising water. When his eyes cleared, the girl was gone. Frightened at the sight of me, Arne thought, then coughed. He had opened his mouth, but he hadn't shouted, and he'd swallowed mud and water.

The water was fluttering his shirt now, ballooning it. Again he raised his body and tore the garment from him. It grounded for a moment, then the waves created by his splash downward pushed it reluctantly toward Clear Creek. Arne watched the shirt accelerate as it neared Clear Creek then whisk from his sight as another object, then two, entered it. The girl and her mother were stumbling over the rocky bank of Clear Creek, the girl leading, the mother following and trailing a piece of clothesline to which three tiny stockings still were securely pinned.

Again Arne raised his body, not so high this time because there was no unchurned mud on which to place his arms, and the water was higher and he was tired. The mother placed the girl on a large rock, waved an admonitory finger and said something Arne couldn't hear above the gurgling of the channel water and the singing of Clear Creek. Then the woman moved upstream, above the confluence of the channel and the creek and almost from Arne's sight.

She'll never make it across Clear Creek, Arne thought. Then

the action he witnessed in the next few tortuous minutes came in broken, muddy yet related sequences as he fought the water and the mud and his growing inclination to just let things happen.

The woman picked up a stout stick, tied the rope around her body, then held the loose gathers in her hands. She threw the rope around a large boulder and as she entered the creek and pushed and probed and leaned with the stick she slowly paid out the gathers. Arne saw her fall once and he groaned aloud; she had no business risking two lives for that of an old man.

"Stay there," he shouted as she rose from the water, the stick gone and her dress plastered to her round body, still holding onto the taut rope. When Arne had floundered twice more, she was across, resting for a moment, then letting go of the remaining gathers of rope and its loose end and pulling it from around the boulder on the opposite side of the creek and toward her.

When she reached the edge of the bank above Arne, he splashed around in the sharpening current to face her. She hurriedly picked her way down the incline as the water again swung his body to face downstream. Then she was just a few feet away and throwing him the loop she had knotted at the end of the rope. The other end still was knotted above her distended waist. Arne fought to place the loop over his head and under his arms. She moved downstream until the rope tautened between them and across her back. She sat down and braced her feet against a boulder. Arne stood. As his legs sank deeper into the mud and water his eyes traveled the length of the taut rope, up to the woman's face, her eyes. The water gurgled around Arne's buttocks and he heard that sound and the blessed caw-caw of a raven and the breeze in the spruce and still their eyes held. Then he could see that she was breathing hard, almost gasping, and she flicked her eyes downward for a second to look at her belly and then again at the old man. And Arne lowered his eyes for an instant to look at his body sinking deeper, deeper into the mud and water.

"Tie it around a stone," he cried. "I'll pull myself out." His body would be anchored by the rope so he could rest beside Ross, and Arne was almost ready to rest now.

He felt the rope bite into his shoulders and back and he saw that the woman still was sitting down and bracing against another stone.

He grasped the rope with both hands for balance and strained to free the unbooted leg. When that reluctantly came loose he dug the freed foot alongside the imprisoned one to widen the hole around the boot. Then he again strained to pull out the bootless foot. The woman braced against another stone to take up the bit of slack. Then Arne deliberately fell into the water that was deep enough now to flow over his back. Its chill would sap his strength further, but help to push his straining body downstream toward the woman and shock him into action for a time at least.

Arne fought then with the last of his strength to save his life and to help that woman on the bank. He clawed into the mud and water and pushed with his free leg as the water rose higher and higher—killing him, yet its force helping him, too.

Then he was free, not gradually, but all at once as his leg pulled from the boot and his frantic clawing and the steady pull of the rope brought him up the channel bank.

Arne grasped the dry stones, retched, dragged himself higher, then lay still in the almost stupefying combination of warm sun and earth and exhaustion.

He felt a slight tug on the rope, another more insistent one, and he wanted to ignore them both, but coupled with a third tug was a moan that was louder than the gurgling, steadily rising water in the channel. Arne had heard that moan before—once in the cabin of an Indian friend in the Copper River Valley and a second time at the Black Rapids Roadhouse.

He raised his head. The woman was sitting near a large boulder. Her need reached out to Arne and brought him slowly to his feet. When he was certain of his equilibrium, he looked again. The woman had tugged the rope from her body and thrown back her head while her fingers dug into the unyielding gravel.

Arne lurched drunkenly toward Clear Creek, pulling the loop from his body while his filthy trousers restricted his movement. He looked for a moment at the cold water, then at the girl who was standing on the stone where her mother had placed her.

He lowered himself deliberately into the stream shallows above the confluence, and the cold waters shocked and cleansed his body.

"Tell your daddy the rest of his family is at my cabin," he croaked to the girl. He returned to the woman and helped her there.

# 28

# *CONTEMPORARY ALASKAN POETRY*

THE Poetry Society of Alaska, Inc., located in Juneau, is a statewide society whose purposes are "to promote the recognition and appreciation of the art of poetry and to encourage the writing of poetry by Alaskans."

Three anthologies of contemporary poetry have appeared in Alaska, and a fourth is in prospect. They owe their publication largely to Margaret G. Mielke, who lives at Peter's Creek, Chugiak, and works in Anchorage. She herself is a poet; in 1963 the Alaska legislature adopted a resolution naming her the Poet Laureate of Alaska.

The *Alaska Review*, an excellent quarterly published by Alaska Methodist University at Anchorage, the first four numbers of which were edited by Robert O. Bowen, devoted its Winter, 1965 issue almost wholly to contemporary poetry. In his editorial foreword, Mr. Bowen wrote:

> The most interesting aspect of poetry in Alaska is not ... the variety of form and content but the fact that so many Alaskans read and write poetry. ... While we note ... certain primitive qualities in Alaskan life, we insist that most Alaskans are in general more sophisticated and more intellectual than most Outsiders. In the first place, the Alaskan usually came to Alaska from some other place and so tends to have a broader view. ...

In the *Review*'s second issue (Spring, 1964) Hans Autor, a poet who has lived long in Alaska, in a thoughtful article entitled

"Alaskan Poetry" wrote: ". . . being amateur, Alaskan poetic expressions are the emotional outburst in response to the primitive grandeurs of the land [and are] true to the spirit of the nonconformist, which characterizes the Alaskan."

So, although there may be a difference of opinion about the quality of some Alaskan verse, it reflects living experience and is characterized by deep sincerity, and it is therefore welcome in this *Reader*. (The poems are printed here with the permission of the authors, who reserve all rights for further use.)

The first poem, "The Moose Kill," is by Poet Laureate Margaret Mielke. Next is "The Enchanted Mountains" by the late Caryl I. Hancock of Rabbit Creek.

Two poems express distaste for the litterbug and plead for an end to the practice which has concerned President and Mrs. Lyndon B. Johnson and the Congress: "The Everlasting Blossoms" by Louise Juhnke of Anchorage and "Accolade to the Bard of the Beer Can Saga" by Margy R. Call of Chugiak.

"Alaska—Source of Deep, Undying Pride" is by A. B. (Toby) See, the author of "Ballad of Windy Bill," which is considered an Alaskan classic. Next comes "My Day" by Olive Van Dine, an autobiographical account of a café operator's daily grind.

"The Nome Creek Ghost" by Darrell R. Kniffen reflects an important economic and social change in Alaska. The discovery of gold led to the founding of Juneau in 1880 and, in the 1890's, when strikes were made in the Klondike, Tanana Valley, and Nome, to the rediscovery of Alaska. At first the pioneers did their panning by primitive methods, with rocker, cradle, and pan, but soon these were replaced by modern machinery as gold mining became big business. The new machine was the dredge, a mammoth affair used in placer operations. When the Franklin D. Roosevelt administration raised the price of gold from $20.70 to $35 an ounce in 1934, the declining industry took on new life. But subsequent Federal administrations, disregarding steadily increasing operational costs, imposed a unique handicap on gold mining: gold had to be sold only to the Federal Government and at the price established in 1934. As a consequence, Alaskan gold mining declined almost to the vanishing point in the middle 1960's. One by one the great dredges in the Fairbanks and Nome areas suspended operations; the huge machines, tangible symbols of a vanishing era, stood abandoned and silent. So Darrell Kniffen has composed a dirge for a dredge.

"Totem Trance" is by Carol Beery Davis, a teacher of piano and organ and a longtime resident of Juneau. She has published a volume of verse called *Alaska Driftwood*.

Richard Peter is represented by "Untamed." A resident of Juneau, he is by profession a newscaster and radio and television commentator; he has also been an Alaska State Senator.

Dr. David T. Hoopes, author of "Adak Crabber," is a biologist and a graduate of the University of Alaska. He is in charge of king crab research at the fisheries laboratory of the U.S. Fish and Wildlife Service at Auke Bay, near Juneau.

E. Myrtle Terry, a resident of Skagway, deals in "The Antlers" with the tangible vestiges of a great struggle in the Alaskan wilds between rival bull moose. Such relics are greatly prized by museums.

Phyllis Lesher, who celebrates Alaska's centenary in "1967," was the first white child born in the Indian village of Kake on Kupreanof Island in southeastern Alaska.

### *The Moose Kill*, by Margaret G. Mielke

This is something I would have the boys remember:
The moose kill in Alaska each September.
The annual trip by dory to horizon land
Across the water, where the pastel mountains stand;
Leaves of copper scaled and shiny
On the sponge-moss ground.
The padded oars, the queer excitement of no sound.
The spotting of the animal against a distant space,
Our beating temples, and the moose's homely face,
The long, long aim and quick, quick shot, releasing blood,
The work of men and knives and axe that turn it into food.
The heavy quarters that with pride we load
With provider's knowledge that the meat is good.

This knowing that when snow is crowding white
There will be roasts and steaks and stews at night.
The journey home, the beaching on home shore,
The lifting of the quartered meat again, the chore.
The pride and climax of getting what we went for;
The wife's one look, knowing whom it's meant for.
Then the hunting stories, the telling and the swapping;
Sawing steaks and cutting roasts, and then the wrapping.
The final storing in the locker that is cold;
The neat and packaged moose now looks like gold.
There is not a chance the boys will not remember—
No one could forget moose season in Alaska in September.


## *The Enchanted Mountains*, by Caryl I. Hancock

Veiled in gossamer mist they will slowly appear
Seeming far, far away, or again very near
Ethereal as moon glow, shimmering white
The *Alaska Range is a fairy sight.*
Like phantom sentinels with heads reared high
The stretch to the west where the sea meets the sky.

I see magic cities immersed in soft lights
Resembling a picture from "The Arabian Nights."
Each castle, spire and rampart bold
Is transformed by the sun into rose and gold.
Enchanted mountains they are to me
Wrapped in iridescent beauty and eternal mystery.


## *The Everlasting Blossoms*, by Louise Juhnke

Here is Alaska, the beer cans are blooming.
They bud with the thaw and grow every day.
There's Schlitz, Lucky Lager, Budweiser and Regal.
You'll find every brand along the highway.

The papers and trash are beginning to come now,
All colors and sizes they'll be by this fall.
You can't see real flowers because of this makeshift,
The eyesore that's with us till snow covers all.

Citizens all, let us rise up with horror
And destroy these as we do garden weeds.
Have pride in Alaska; keep true beauty blooming
Instead of these flowers from litterbug seeds.


## *Accolade to the Bard of the Beer Can Saga,* by Margy R. Call

Twinkle, twinkle little star,
How I wonder what you are
Up the road beside that boulder—
Shining brightly beyond the shoulder!

Could it be a Mouse—or Moose?
Rabbit shy—or Fox?
Lynx cat, Bear or Caribou—
Any one of these would do!

But, as our headlights stab the night,
It's only Beer cans shining bright—
And in our disappointment sad
This makes us mighty awful mad!

We're robbed of a thrill again, it seems,
For always and ever, it's beer-can gleams
That greet our roving, questing eyes,
As hope for glimpse of wildlife dies.

Sister Bard—your words I cherish!
The crusading pen must never perish!
Though the words may fall on empty air,
Perchance they'll be heard *someday—somewhere!*

## *Alaska—Source of Deep, Undying Pride,*
## by A. B. (Toby) See

Beneath the tall and stately spruce
The black bear wends his waddly way,
The home of caribou and moose
That browse at break of day.

Up on the crags the Dall sheep roam
And mountain goats feed on the plain.
The marmot leaves his rocky home
To rule in high domain.

In nearby pond the beaver mends
His home of mud and trees,
While on the bank the iris bends
In graceful homage to the breeze.

The grayling waves its flowing fins
And rises to a drowning fly.
The mighty eagle wheels and spins
In faultless circles in the sky.

The ptarmigan sits on her nest
And blends with moss and stone.
The pied grebe lifts its snowy crest,
A wolf gnaws on a bone.

The brown bear breasts the rushing stream,
Flings salmon to the shore.
The sportsman likes to sit and dream
These gifts forevermore.

Where else in this great world of ours
Can all these things be found—
The birds, the bees, the game, the flowers
And gold still in the ground?

Alaskans take these in their stride.
Cheechakos love them, too.
A source of deep, undying pride
For me and you—and you.

## *Autumn in Alaska,* by Jim Nail

### (With Signs of Winter)

The bears are going back to den;
The salmon, most, have all come in;
The ducks and geese are flying out,
Their necks, outstretched, like searching snout.

The moose are on their annual run,
To keep away from hunter's gun;
The fireweeds, all, are shedding plumes,
The trees are gay in bright costumes.

The days grow shorter, one by one—
Not long, from morn till setting sun;
The air is finely fresh and cool;
The children, going back to school.

By all these signs it must be fall
That holds this world in pageant-thrall;
I see the squirrels, darting to and fro—
Don't let me see just where they go.

For me, I've donned my warmer suits—
I've darned wool socks—and shined snow boots;
That's just in case should come the need
When winter's cold returns, indeed.

I find my last year's red ones, long,
Almost, have sung their last warm song;
At least, they're chanting tired refrain,
To send me shopping, once again.

Unless I find a refuge, like the bear—
Or else, I had his fur to wear—
I'll have to purchase some things, new,
To keep the cold from biting through.

Too much of cooling zero freeze,
To old-man *me*, might give a wheeze;
Or worse, "pumony," on my chest—
A-coughing so, I'd bust my vest.

I'll take a lesson, then, to heart,
And practice some of Nature's art,
By getting ready, days ahead—
Like squirrel, fixing up his bed.

(Dedicated to my fine young friend, Miss **Trudy Mielke**)

## *My Day*, by Olive Van Dine

The alarm clock rings at quarter past four.
I make a mad dash for the bathroom door.
I brush my teeth and other duties—
That time of the morning we gals ain't cuties.
Back to the bedroom and into my duds—
A nice white uniform fresh from the suds.
I pull on my coat and grab my purse
Thinking this working is surely a curse,
Rush out the door and snap the lock
With a quick over-shoulder glance at the clock.
I crawl into the car and I'm on the way
With an on-time start for another day.
Downtown I rush to the parking lot,
Arriving at four forty-five—on the dot.
Into the cafe in a second or two,
Hang up my coat, put the coffee to brew,
Out to the kitchen, put the bread to rise,
Then turn my attention to making the pies.

I make some double crust and open face
Putting each one in its proper place.
The dough has risen—I give it a punch
And think about the matter of lunch.
First I make some soup and a kettle of stew.
The doughnuts are ready so I fry a few.
Now the place is open, the door swings wide,
A man wants a short stack—ham on the side.
Each one wants his eggs a different way.
The joint is jumping—we're in full sway.
The gal's out of cups and saucers, too,
So I turn on the machine and wash a few.
The dough's up again and ready to go,
So I knock out some rolls—four dozen or so.
I make some salad—cook off a roast.
While thus occupied, I burn the toast,
Ham and bacon and graveyard stew.
Then comes an order for that ol' poach two.
Bread man, butcher, milk man, too,
Will you please sign here so I'll get what's due.
The telephone rings—"What's the Bill of Fare?"
Lunch ain't ready and I don't care.
I dash around and swear and sweat.
Twelve o'clock—no relief cook yet.
Oh! Here she comes—right on the dot!
The crowd wants everything we haven't got.
Ah! Time marches on—the clock says one.
Another day's work is finally done.
I drag my footsteps out the door
And head on home—to my bed once more—
Perhaps you've guessed—I run a cafe,
And this, my friends is a typical day.

## *The Nome Creek Ghost,* by Darrell R. Kniffen

There was a dredge on a far North shore,
A golden boat in Alaskan lore;
And year after year when breakups came,
She dug more gold to add to her fame.

The "Ship of Gold" they called her then,
For her course was set by mining men;
And claim by claim from Thirty Above,
She reaped the rocks in work of love.

Men sang of the times her buckets struck,
And she took pure nuggets from the muck;
And told how her whistle blasting steam,
Defied the eagle's most mighty scream.

Her riffles gleamed by day or night,
She was proud and new with cables tight;
And her engines split the air with groans,
As she tore the riches from the stones.

She rent the bedrock in her rages,
Her shoremen cut the crop of ages;
And cord by cord to feed her sluices,
Her bolsters ate the hillside spruces.

She piled tailings in jagged rows,
She gouged from breakup till the snows;
And mined the creek from strand to strand,
And filled the waters full of sand.

She flooded the darkness full of light,
She scared the bull moose out of sight;
And grayling fled from the muddied rills,
While wild things scampered to the hills.

So digging true to the shining streak,
The monster dredger gleaned the creek;
And wrote the pages of her story
In one long blaze of golden glory.

\* \* \*

Then Winter came and in pond of ice,
She proudly moored all snug and nice;
And the "Ship of Gold" fresh out of pay,
Awaited Spring and the water's play.

There is a dredge on a far North shore,
Her buckets burrow for gold no more;
And those who manned her in her day,
Have left her in search of better pay.

The "Nome Creek Ghost" who was once so proud
Wears the cloak of winter for her shroud;
And her hulk lies grounded on Ten Below,
Where wild things leave their tracks in the snow.

She rests there in the bend of the creek,
Mute testament to the lost pay streak;
And her rusty engines do not whine,
For there is no paydirt left to mine.

Her stacker has fallen to the tails,
Soundly she sleeps as the lone wolf wails,
And while she dreams of her bygone day,
The hills look down in their ageless way.

Never again will her winches sing,
She harkens not to the Song of Spring;
And though the breakups batter her stern,
The rush of waters is no concern.

The rust and the weather take their toll,
Numbly she waits as the seasons roll;
And graying she grows more like a ghost,
Riches she dug a forgotten toast.

New spruces grow on earth once spoiled,
Clear again run the waters roiled;
And she slowly sinks beneath the moss,
Where there was gold there's now but dross.

The eagle screams in the summer sky,
An old bull moose saunters by;
And the beavers build out from the bank,
And flood the bar where the gold-boat sank.

\* \* \*

Now grayling leap in the sparkling stream,
Autumn's leaves are the golden gleam;
And the "Nome Creek Ghost" cannot dig gold,
So Nature reigns as she did of old.

## *Totem Trance*, by Carol Beery Davis

See the slender, leaning totems—
Silhouettes against the moon!
How they haunt with strange insistence,
Wreathed in mist from the lagoon.
Wonderment and fascination
Stir with ancient dramas here,
Where dumb history is written
Of a vanished tribal year.

Do you tell weird myth or legend,
Or the tale of family crest?
Were you carved for your tribe's chieftain—
His memorial, "At Rest"?

Did he step upon a feather
Of the powerful Thunderbird?
Do you hold his earthly ashes
Close within you, as we've heard?

Whether Frog, Shark, Whale or Beaver,
Whether Raven, Wolf or Bear,—
Starlight, mist and flood-tide odors,
Quicken symbols that you wear.
Colors made from hemlock fungus—
Yellow, red or black; or those
Mixed of spruce sap, juice of berries—
Are the arts lost years enclose.

Here the salt breeze hints of campfires
Smoldering in the Klingit past.
*"Yas ka na na"* echoes linger
From feast dances, wild and fast.
*"Gau a yar tah, gau a ya tah,"*
Chant the tom-tom drums once more—
"We are made of spider-crab shells—
Shells that were retrieved from shore."

When the moonlight frames your symbols,
Or the sunlight cuts your shade,
Or your form is traced in starlight,
Epochs gone, well up and fade.
Monument to all of living—
Feastings, burial and birth,
Woodcuts of an age departed—
Totems—weirdest shrines on earth!

## *Untamed,* by Richard Peter

The great bear tastes his wounds and waits the chance
    To take revenge upon the wolves when they
Return. The snarling pack's last bold advance
    Has weakened his defense. But not yet prey
To their fierce hunger, he will fight again
    As he has maimed the guides who sought with nets
To take him prisoner. But even then
    Had he been caged with other giant pets
He would have plagued his keepers night and day,
    Disdaining food and favors in his pride,
And nursing vengeance as he stalked his way
    Around the cruel cell with hobbled stride.

Alaska is not tamed. And never will
    It cease attacking men who try to hold
Its savagery at bay. They'll get their fill
    Of frostbite from the anesthetic cold.
Snow, rain and fog, aloft and low, will blind
    The rash intruders. And their very path
With avalanche and earthquake will be mined.
    In bay and stream their boats will face the wrath
Of tide and winds. The crippling roots and bogs
    Will slow their steps, and crazed beasts take their toll.
The trees will kill—alive, or vengeful logs—
    All these are poised to keep man from his goal.

Like fire, it has a beauty masking hate.
    Stone mountains cup the eucharistic sun,
But their sharp fingers subtly lie in wait
    To claw men from the sky before they've won
The day, or brush them from the heights they try
    To scale. The wilderness will never yield
In this its last retreat. It will not die
    Though humankind in millions takes the field,

Because fierce nature here is queen and will
  Not rest again upon her rocky throne
Till there are no more strangers left to kill,
  And she can truly call this land her own.


## *Adak Crabber,* by David T. Hoopes

　　Above deck, the sea,
　　Implacable and relentless,
　　Dirty green, dirty gray-green.
　　Surging waves of the Bering Sea,
　　With their white and streaming guidons
　　Of flung spray and trailing spume.

　　Below deck, yellow incandescence,
　　Wild shadows and dim corners.
　　Slip, slide, slam,
　　Down the ladder from the bridge,
　　Aft to the galley's warmth and
　　Thick, scarred mugs of searing coffee.

　　Above deck, the swells
　　Advance in disorderly phalanx
　　Against the black-wet bastions of the Chain,
　　Or roll sou'east through ragged breaches
　　At Unimak, Akutan, Umnak and Amchitka
　　On into the gale-swept Pacific.

　　Below deck, wet wool's
　　Musty smell mixes with
　　The aroma of a hot beef roast.
　　Slabs of juicy meat
　　Roll backward from the knife
　　To windrow on the heavy china platter.

Above deck, sleet and snow
Combine with the driven scud
To slap an icy frosting
On the cake-shaped crab pots aft,
Or slant with an icy sizzle
Into the black and heaving night.

Below deck, pitch, roll,
Rubber boots squeek while oilskins
Glisten yellow, black, sway and drip
To diesel-thudding rhythm from below.
All thought, all sound, time itself
Smears together in ceaseless motion.

Above deck, the seas
Advance, attack, withdraw.
Marching combers break aboard,
Only to retreat in foamy frenzy
From the scuppers and the decks,
Then fall astern with a dying hiss.

## The Antlers, by E. Myrtle Terry

Within a wild, sequestered glen,
Afar from common haunts of men
Two pairs of antlers once were found,
Well locked together on the ground.

So firmly were they interknit
That neither strength nor cunning wit
Could serve to separate their prongs
Once locked avenging savage wrongs.

The noble elk they once adorned
To yield to rival mind had scorned
And knew no way to win their right
Except by force of savage might.

They doubtless loved the selfsame doe,
Those monarchs of the long ago,
And in their effort to decide
Which one should gain her love, they died.

I seem to see that sylvan scene,
Where those wild kings fought for their queen,
And how their sharp hooves cut the ground
And scattered broken earth around.

How, viciously, they rushed and leaped,
Their hearts in wildest hatred steeped,
And how their red blood stained the moss,
Though each was careless of its loss.

And, standing near, the timid doe
While there they struggled to and fro,
As, half in fear and half in awe,
Their contest for her love she saw.

But all their battling was in vain,
And all their hatred, all their pain,
For, of a sudden, as they fought,
Their branching antlers met and caught.

So hopelessly their prongs were locked
That Death their efforts only mocked
As back and forth within the glen
They struggled to be free again.

At last, their noble strength was spent,
To earth their antlered heads were bent,
And, swaying weakly, there they fell
And died for her they loved so well.

*1967*, by Phyllis Lesher

Epic Century—
a stepchild you no longer
a leader now of men

No Red Star for you
Thank God for men of vision
One hundred years ago

DATE DUE

| MAY 13 1996 | |
| --- | --- |
| | |
| | |
| | |
| | |
| | |
| | |
| | |
| | |
| | |
| | |
| | |
| | |
| | |
| | |

GAYLORD                                    PRINTED IN U.S.A.